Psychosis and Near Psychosis

The goal of psychotherapy as formulated in this revision of a classic text is to improve ego function of severely disturbed patients who are often hospitalized. This book shows why and how. It describes the psychotherapeutic techniques that aid patients to understand the meaning of the psychotic symbols so that they can experience reality and their emotions as separate entities. Medication effects and the neurobiology of psychotic and near psychotic patients are explained and evaluated in terms of specific ego dysfunction so that psychopharmacology may be targeted. With the first edition, originally a recipient of the prestigious Heinz Hartmann Award, this valuable resource is a go-to guide for clinicians who treat patients suffering from crippling mental disorders.

Eric R. Marcus, MD, is the director of the Columbia University Center for Psychoanalytic Training and Research and professor of clinical psychiatry in the department of psychiatry of the Columbia University College of Physicians and Surgeons.

"In *Psychosis and Near Psychosis*, psychiatry residents will find an ideal vision of how contemporary psychiatry could be, but rarely is, practiced. Eric Marcus integrates general psychiatry and psychoanalytic understanding with cognitive neuroscience and psychopharmacology to describe combined treatment with different patients. This book offers the only chapter in print on the effects of medication on mental structure. The many detailed case examples serve perfectly to show students how to bridge the gap between theoretical complexity and clinical practice."
—Elizabeth L. Auchincloss, MD, Vice-chair, Education, professor of clinical psychiatry, DeWitt Wallace Senior Scholar, Department of Psychiatry, Weill Cornell Medical College

"General psychiatrists interested in understanding the psychological experience of very ill psychiatric patients will find this gem of a book indispensable. We know that significant difficulties persist for most patients with psychotic disorders who are receiving optimal medication management. This book describes in detail how psychodynamic psychotherapy can help such patients build reality testing and self-observation. The illuminating chapter on the impact of medication on mental structure is by itself worth the price of this book!"
—Francine Cournos, MD, professor of clinical psychiatry (in Epidemiology), Columbia University

Psychosis and Near Psychosis

Ego Function, Symbol Structure, Treatment

Third Edition

Eric R. Marcus

NEW YORK AND LONDON

Third edition published 2017
by Routledge
711 Third Avenue, New York, NY 10017

and by Routledge
2 Park Square, Milton Park, Abingdon, Oxon, OX14 4RN

Routledge is an imprint of the Taylor & Francis Group, an informa business

© 2017 Taylor & Francis

The right of Eric R. Marcus to be identified as author of this work has been asserted by him in accordance with sections 77 and 78 of the Copyright, Designs and Patents Act 1988.

All rights reserved. No part of this book may be reprinted or reproduced or utilised in any form or by any electronic, mechanical, or other means, now known or hereafter invented, including photocopying and recording, or in any information storage or retrieval system, without permission in writing from the publishers.

Trademark notice: Product or corporate names may be trademarks or registered trademarks, and are used only for identification and explanation without intent to infringe.

First edition published by Springer, 1992

Second edition published by International Universities Press, 2003

Library of Congress Cataloging-in-Publication Data
Names: Marcus, Eric R. (Eric Robert), 1944– author.
Title: Psychosis and near psychosis : ego function, symbol
    structure, treatment / by Eric R. Marcus.
Description: Third editon. | New York, NY : Routledge, 2017. |
    Includes bibliographical references and index.
Identifiers: LCCN 2016053795 | ISBN 9781138925977 (hbk :
    alk. paper) | ISBN 9781138925991 (pbk : alk. paper) |
    ISBN 9781315675855 (ebk)Subjects: LCSH: Psychoses. |
    Psychoses—Treatment.
Classification: LCC RC512 .M36 2017 DDC 616.89/5—dc23
LC record available at https://lccn.loc.gov/2016053795

ISBN: 978-1-138-92597-7 (hbk)
ISBN: 978-1-138-92599-1 (pbk)
ISBN: 978-1-315-67585-5 (ebk)

Typeset in Sabon
by Apex CoVantage, LLC

To my late Mother, Pearl Marcus and
my late Father, Victor Marcus

Nodding his head politely, the stranger walked noiselessly to the bench and sat down, and Kovrin recognized the Black Monk. For a minute they looked at one another, Kovrin with astonishment but the Monk kindly and, as before, with a sly expression on his face.

"But you are a mirage," said Kovrin. "Why are you here, and why do you sit in one place? That is not in accordance with the legend." "It is all the same," replied the Monk softly, turning his face toward Kovrin. "The legend, the mirage, I—all are products of your own excited imagination. I am a phantom." "That is to say, you don't exist?" asked Kovrin.

"Think us you like," replied the Monk, smiling faintly. "I exist in your imagination, and as your imagination is a part of nature, I must exist also in nature."

—Anton Chekhov ("The Black Monk"), 1894

Contents

	Acknowledgments	x
	Introduction	xiii
1	Ego Functions	1
2	Psychotic Structure	44
3	Near Psychotic Structure	74
4	Mental Status Examination	110
5	Psychiatric Illnesses and Mental Structure	135
6	Medication and Mental Structure	179
7	Psychoanalytic Psychotherapy and Psychoanalysis of Psychosis	209
8	Psychoanalytic Psychotherapy and Psychoanalysis of Near Psychosis	244
9	Hospital Treatment	270
	References	286
	Name Index	302
	Subject Index	306

Acknowledgments

My wife, Dr. Eslee Samberg, read parts of this book and offered helpful advice based on her high standards of psychiatric and psychoanalytic work and also on her appreciation of language and syntax.

I have been fortunate in seeing much good therapy, which serves as a continuing model. I am especially grateful to the late Drs. Daniel Shapiro, Winslow Hunt, and Drs. Will Fey, also David Moltz, Frank Ferrelly, Arthur Schwartz, and the late Dr. Carl A. Whitaker.

Dr. Stuart Yudofsky, retired chair of psychiatry at Baylor University College of Medicine, directed the Acute Neuropsychiatric Diagnosis and Treatment Unit at Columbia University Medical Center when I was co-director and later, director. He built a unit that inspired us all, with its integration of biological and psychological treatment.

Dr. Jeffrey Lieberman—Chair, Department of Psychiatry, Columbia University and Director, The New York State Psychiatric Institute, and of psychiatry at New York Presbyterian Hospital at Columbia University Medical Center—has encouraged and protected education and scholarship as well as research and clinical care in both psychiatry and psychoanalysis.

Dr. Herbert Pardes—formerly president, chief executive officer, New York-Presbyterian Hospital, and formerly Vice President for Health Sciences at Columbia University and Dean of the Columbia University College of Physicians and Surgeons—has supported education, general psychiatry, and psychoanalysis, catalyzing the growth of all three.

Dr. John Oldham—formerly Director of the New York State Psychiatric Institute and interim chair, Department of Psychiatry, Columbia University, presently Interim Chair, Department of Psychiatry, Baylor University—knows how to keep the peace during turbulent times.

All scholarly work done at The New York State Psychiatric Institute is indebted to David Lane, the former librarian and safe-keeper of one of the finest general psychiatry libraries.

Dr. Thomas Q. Morris—past President of Presbyterian Hospital of Columbia-Presbyterian Medical Center and former Interim Dean of the

College of Physicians and Surgeons, Columbia University—and the late Dr. Sidney Malitz—past Acting Director of the New York State Psychiatric Institute, and past interim chair, Department of Psychiatry, Columbia University—were mentors whose clinical values form the basis of my work with patients.

Sarah Bradley, M.S.W., taught me a great deal as we discussed many of my ideas as applied to daily care of hospitalized patients and their families. I learned milieu organization of hospital units from Lois Marin Mahonchak, R.N. I learned behavioral limit setting from Mental Health Technicians Mrs. Pauline Wade, Mr. David Whitaker, and Mr. Otis Lee Barnes. I learned about diagnosis with patient drawings from Mrs. Phyllis Ward Reichbach.

The late Dr. Rita Rudel and especially her colleague the late Dr. Rita Haggerty taught me about the neuropsychology of ego dysfunction, ideas so crucial to my work and to the care of patients.

One of the most helpful educational experiences in clinical work is personal supervision. I have been most fortunate in having as supervisors Drs. Otto Kernberg, Roger MacKinnon, Leonard Diamond, the late Donald Meyers, and the late Robert Liebert. I was also helpfully supervised by Dr. Michael Stone, the late Dr. Harry Albert, Dr. Jerry Finkel, Dr. Joel Hoffman, and Dr. Mark Mankoff.

Dr. Ira Feirstein has been my professional compatriot since internship. This book is in some sense the result of his example, and he has understood and encouraged it since its very first scribbling. My good friend Dr. Richard Weiss first introduced me to an ego psychological approach to the psychoses by pointing out the work of Thomas Freeman. The late Professor Richard Kuhns and his wife, Dr. Margaret Kuhns, read an early manuscript of the book and offered many helpful suggestions. Professor Kuhns and I jointly taught a graduate seminar in the Department of Philosophy at Columbia University from which my interest in symbolic processes was greatly enriched. Dr. Richard C. Friedman went over an early draft of this book and offered many challenging suggestions along with encouragement to truly speak my mind.

Routledge and George Zimmar have the knowledge and courage to like a book such as mine. To these and many others, my thanks and my gratitude.

Introduction

Welcome to this third edition of *Psychosis and Near Psychosis*. This book is written for those clinicians who wish to help very ill psychiatric patients by listening to them and talking to them. In the years since the first and second editions, it has been found that some medications (which are crucial and necessary) may also have limitations if this is the only form of treatment. Both medications and psychotherapy help the patient handle the illness and its symptoms. A more complete recovery therefore may involve both medication and psychotherapy: combination treatments are more powerful than either alone.

The purpose of this book is to describe the structure of psychotic and near psychotic mental states. This description is used as the basis of an approach to treatment which integrates the phenomenology of psychosis or near psychosis, the symptoms and organizations of some specific psychiatric illnesses, the mental effect of psychotropic medication, the technique of psychoanalytic psychotherapy and psychoanalysis, and relevant aspects of clinical theory.

This can be done because daily work with psychotic and near psychotic patients over the last 40 years convinces me that these illnesses have a specific mental structure.

Mental structure means mental experience that is stable over time, both in content and in relationship of elements: both forms and processes, including dynamic intensity relationships. For a review of the concept of structure in psychoanalytic theory see T. Shapiro (1988). For a different view of psychoanalytic structure, see Slap and Slap-Shelton (1991). Many mental experiences are organized in stable, dynamic forms of relationships; psychotic and near psychotic ones, perhaps especially so.

Psychiatry has classified psychopathology into disease categories according to conscious symptoms and behavior. Psychoanalysis has described unconscious emotional life and its stable organizations. Psychoanalysis properly calls these unconscious emotional organizations structures because they also are registered, stored, stable, mental experiences. Therefore, I use the concept of structure to include both conscious and unconscious elements. Because I believe conscious elements are linked to unconscious elements in characteristic ways in psychotic and near psychotic patients, psychoanalysis could profitably consider both conscious and unconscious aspects without worrying that the focus will shift away from important emotional experience.

Psychoanalysis has used clusters of unconscious mental experience with thematic, dynamic, emotional content as psychoanalytic illness categories. These illnesses are called the neuroses. The content and organizations of these unconscious, dynamic, emotional structures, particularly in defenses, describe the different neurotic illnesses for psychoanalysis. General psychiatry has not needed to look at the unconscious for its illness categories, since conscious experience and easily observable behavior are usually so extreme in psychotic illnesses. But if conscious psychotic experiences and behaviors are characteristically linked to the unconscious, emotional life of psychotic and near psychotic patients, then the unconscious experience of psychosis is congruent with and elaborates those psychiatric illness categories. The unconscious and the conscious in the psychotic and near psychotic illnesses are affected by the illness process in specific ways. Therefore, the continuum of intensities and plastically organized contents of the unconscious fits into the more rigidly bordered categories of general psychiatry. The use of psychoanalytic observations about the dynamic unconscious for description of the stable, psychodynamic experience of illness makes the general psychiatric categories of illness richer and more understandable to the treating physician. It makes treatment decisions clearer. It makes accurate, empathic, psychotherapeutic contact easier.

The conscious and unconscious structures are influenced by reality, illness transformation processes, the phase of mental development in which the illness occurs, the evolving developmental processes that may be interrupted or altered, and the innate symbolic content and processes of man's symbolizing function. Whether psychosis is stable and unchanging or unstable and rapidly changing, it is describable in structural terms as characteristic stabilities or characteristic losses of stabilities. The concept of stable mental experience structures is even more crucial for psychosis than for neurosis because when mental illness seems chaotic, guidelines for treatment are lost unless one sees the structure of the change and deviations from normal structure that are occurring. Actually, much psychotic illness is not chaotic but rigidly fixed. Again, the concept of structure is so helpful because the content and processes have a structure that, once described clearly, can guide treatment.

I will argue that psychotic and near psychotic structure results from specific changes in ego function. I will describe the resulting universal features of all psychotic and near psychotic structure as well as what specific psychiatric illnesses do to that structure.

Process structure is a concept inherent in the psychoanalytic use of the term structure, which tries to capture structure both as stable in content and as changing in intensities and in relationship of intensities. I also feel there is a relationship between change in intensity and change in content. The interaction between changing, emotional aspects of mental functioning, and fixed, relatively unchanging aspects, such as ideas or attitudes, or seemingly fixed aspects of ego function, such as intelligence, is a dynamic process that can also be stable if its rules of organization never change. For example, elements and the relationship of elements can remain stable while the intensities or expressions of these elements fluctuate. Many, perhaps all, of the ego's regulating processes play a role in psychic structure. This dynamic process structure combination is what is meant by mental structure as it is actually observed in the clinical setting, especially in psychotic and near psychotic states. These observed process structures are one of the bases of descriptive clinical theory.

Descriptive clinical theory is an early phase of scientific research in which observation leads to a hypothesis, an observational hypothesis. These observational hypotheses describe elements and hypothesize how they relate to each other. Observational hypotheses can be misconstrued to imply etiology in addition to phenomenology. Clinical work is heavily and rightfully dependent on these observational hypotheses, because therapeutics often must precede an understanding of etiology and may be effective before the reason for the effectiveness is known. This is true for all branches of medicine and surgery. Observational hypotheses of clinical work are therefore crucial to treatment; they can also be heuristic, but they are not yet etiologic.

What do psychoanalysts think about etiology in the psychoses (see Frosch, 1983)? From Sigmund Freud on, psychoanalysis has been theoretically rooted in biological influences on mental life. Freud described the growth and development of biologically determined libidinal stages and their effect on emotions, especially conflicted emotional states. Freud believed the conscious mind might be helped to gain more control over the mental effects of these biological processes. Psychoanalysis since Freud has also been interested in the interplay between emotions, with their innate disposition patterns of libidinal stages, and reality experience. Since it was not known, and scientific technology did not exist to discover the relationship between brain biology, emotional conflict, and reality events, the issue became a suspended question (Freud, 1917b). But psychoanalytic investigations continued to look at mental experience and the interplay between emotions, experience, and illness. This led gradually to nonbiological etiologic implications or to outright etiologic statements. These etiologic implications have been most problematic, I believe, in psychotic and near psychotic states. They have implied that emotional conflict and/or emotional experiences from reality cause psychosis or near psychosis.

Those who believe emotional conflict causes psychosis focus on the quality of the conflict, its content and phase of emotional life, or the intensity of that conflict, or both. This statement unites otherwise diverse authors such as Freud, Arlow and Brenner (1964), Kernberg (1975), Klein (1975), and Pao (1979). Some look specifically to developmental deficits resulting from childhood experience, a perspective uniting otherwise divergent authors such as Anna Freud (1936), Mahler (1968), Pao (1979), Blanck and Blanck (1979, 1986), Frosch (1983), and Freeman (1988; Freeman, Cameron, and McGhie, 1958). More recently, child observation has tried to understand prospective development of mental structure: psychotic (Mahler, 1968), normal (Mahler, Pine, and Bergman, 1975; Stern, 1985), and neurotic (A. Freud, 1936).

A few believe a central problem is brain pathology in the adult, an approach that unites modern biological psychiatry and Freud (1917a).

Psychoanalysis has thus looked to emotional dynamics, inborn energies, instinctual developmental lines, and retrospective emotional psychogenetics of historical, external, and internal object relations in its search for etiology. It has based this focus on the content of dynamic fantasies elicited in the psychoanalytic setting and on necessities of psychoanalytic theory sometimes imposed on clinical data.

The evidence for the biological—neuromental etiology of psychosis and near psychosis includes the following:

1 Impairment in reality organizing mental processes that are part of neurological function as well as the mental function;
2 Neuropsychological testing of neuromental functions in psychosis and near psychosis;
3 Neurophysiological and neuroanatomical testing of brain function;
4 Inheritance of psychotic illness predispositions;
5 Medication effects on the mind via their effects on the brain;
6 Clinical observation of emotional dynamic similarities between neurosis, psychosis, and near psychosis therefore dynamics can't solely be causal.

On the other hand, the following evidence is against the theory of biological—neuromental etiology and in favor of emotional etiology:

1 Clinical observation of emotional dynamic similarities between psychosis and neurosis therefore dynamics are involved in all mental illness;
2 Observations about triggering events and relationships and the correlation of this material in pathological symbolic representations and object relations;
3 The observation that psychoanalytic interpretation of dynamics may help ego dysfunction.

The leading research lines follow trails of observation of brain function via neurochemical abnormalities, often seen indirectly via clues from drug effects. Psychiatric epidemiologists look at inheritance patterns. Psychogeneticists look at the genes and chromosomes. Psychoneuroendocrinologists use possible endocrine abnormalities and their neuropathways to try to indirectly chart brain pathology. Neuroscientists look at changes in anatomic and physiological mechanisms within and between cells. New imaging techniques allow direct observation of this neurochemistry and neuroanatomical physiology in living psychotic patients (for a recent review in regard to schizophrenia see Willick, 1991b; McGlashen and Hoffman, 2000).

Biological research makes one thing clear: there are biological factors in the psychoses. It is not yet known (1) what are the biological factors, (2) what causes these abnormalities; (3) where these abnormalities operate; or (4) how the mind and its emotional experiences interact with the brain in the etiology of psychotic illness. We have found no virus that attacks the brain in psychosis or near psychosis. But we have not yet found the universal schizophrenogenic mother nor the always applicable dynamic formulation. We are therefore thrown back to descriptive theory with which much science begins until biological research catches up to us.

I believe there is an interaction between biology and psychology varying from case to case, always with major inborn constitutional factors affecting autonomous ego capacities and temperament. This may be magnified or ameliorated by experience. Experience may lead to specific psychological trigger points. However, it also seems to me clear that unknown neurobiological factors operate directly on autonomous ego apparatuses in the adult, because there are some patients who become psychotic and do not seem to have typical prodromata or psychogenetics in their childhood histories (for a recent review see Willick, 1991a).

In spite of my belief in a major biological component to these illnesses, it is my hope that this book will encourage psychoanalysts to consider once again their role in treating these patients. Freud (1924a, b) and Abraham (1911) discussed the treatment of psychotic and near psychotic patients, but since the 1960s analysts have shown less interest. Neuroleptic and later antidepressant medication has played a growing role in this loss of interest because of their marked efficacy in treating certain aspects of these illnesses. However, as I will show, they do not treat other aspects. In addition, the Menninger study, most recently described by Wallerstein (1986), looked at analyses of neurotic, near psychotic, and psychotic patients. It found that all so-called heroic psychoanalyses with psychotic patients failed. However, because of advances in medication, neuropsychology as it applies to neuromental functioning, the psychoanalytic understanding of autonomous ego functions (Hartmann, 1939, 1964), and descriptions of autonomous ego effects in psychotic and near psychotic illnesses (Bellak, Hurvich, and Gediman, 1973), it seems an ideal time to try again to discuss these illnesses and their treatment within a now broadened psychoanalytic descriptive theory (see also Karush, 1966; Bellak and Goldsmith, 1984). Also very helpful are recent advances in psychiatry that clarify psychiatric illness categories. The DSM system, now DSM 5, has major advances in categories, despite excesses and limitations especially for psychotic illnesses. But it has helped dispel the belief of psychiatrists, and unfortunately some psychoanalysts, that all psychoses are the same regardless of the psychiatric illness involved, or that all psychoses are schizophrenia. This misunderstanding was based on the lack of specific criteria to distinguish the psychoses and near psychoses in general psychiatry. It was also based on psychoanalytic inability to specifically describe ego function as Hartmann (1939, 1964), Freeman (1969), and Bellak et al. (1973) have done. Because of this lack of knowledge, emotional dynamics were described and given etiologic importance. Hence, all psychosis was one, and all etiology was unconscious dynamics.

I believe a psychoanalytically based approach to an integrated treatment of psychosis and near psychosis can now be achieved; this approach organizes psychotherapy, medication, and hospital and milieu interventions into a powerful therapeutic tool. My own observations are that this integrated combination is dramatically successful (Marcus and Bradley, 1990). This book describes advances in descriptive theory and their integrative use in treatment by describing the structure of psychotic and near psychotic states, the effect of psychiatric illnesses on that structure, the effect of medication on that structure, and the changes in technique of psychoanalytic psychotherapy and psychoanalysis mandated by this new description of the structure. I will focus on the ego and especially on ego functions mediating reality experience.

I try to define most terms that I use, even the elementary ones. One reason is to make the book accessible to newcomers to clinical work in this area and also to others working in related areas. (See especially Auchinclos and Samberg, 2012.)

The second reason is the ambiguity of many of these terms. Psychoanalysts often do not agree on these definitions. I need precisely to define terms pertinent to psychosis and near psychosis to achieve clarity of exposition. Third, I emphasize certain aspects of the definitions of commonly used terms or modify some aspects. This is necessary in order to enlarge existing psychoanalytic theory to include my observations about intrapsychic structural psychopathology and also to better link with general psychiatry's advances in descriptive psychopathology.

As a result of starting with basic descriptive definitions, the book tends to move from the relatively more elementary to the relatively more complex within each section and chapter, and from one chapter to the next.

I hope it will thereby be useful to therapists at all levels of experience. I especially hope that experienced psychoanalysts will read the book and rethink the possibility of a modern, psychoanalytically informed treatment of these states.

This is a clinical and clinical theory book. I discuss the psychoanalytic and psychiatric literature relevant to my views. The most thorough review of the psychoanalytic literature is Frosch (1983). My work is especially indebted to the work of Freud, Hartmann, Winnicott, Rapaport (1951b), Freeman, Schafer (1968b), Arieti (1974, 1976), and Bellak et al. (1973).

For this this third, revised edition, the latest relevant neuroscience findings on psychotic processing are reviewed. The science of these illnesses has rapidly advanced in the area of neuroscience. Imaging of psychotic and pre-psychotic patients lends credence to the ideas in this book about thing presentation experiences. It also is validating the importance of psychotherapy.

Advances continue to be made also in the area of neuropsychology of autonomous ego functions. These become captured by severe mental illnesses. The major psychiatric illnesses leave their characteristic signatures on the organization of symbolic function and its symbol products. The illnesses affect the form as well as the content of symbolic meaning structures. Understanding symbolic structures will help clarify diagnosis.

Modern ego psychology is the branch of psychoanalysis that is most concerned with ego function and its role in representation (Marcus, 1999). Psychotic and near psychotic experiences are symbolic representations of an emotionally meaningful reality that is organized by the ego. Knowing their structure can help in understanding what to say and how to help. The symbolic structures are structures of meaning. Helping the patient understand their meaning can help him or her organize meaning in his or her reality and emotional experience rather than his or her psychotic experience. This is the goal of strengthening ego functions.

Thus, the main reason for talking to patients who have severe psychiatric illness is to make contact with the person experiencing that illness in order to talk to them about the illness. Understanding the symbolic structure elements which constitute alterations of reality can help patients rally intact ego functions to fight their illness and reclaim their reality experience. It is these ego strengths which both medication and psychotherapy help.

Understanding more accurately the patient's experiences will help strengthen the therapeutic alliance. This will help with patients' understanding of their illness and help them construct and cooperate with a treatment plan.

Understanding the structures of symbolic alterations of reality may reveal any precipitating reality events that are helping to trigger the symptoms. Changing the reality experience of ill patients is crucial to their recovery. Knowing what to help them change is key.

Understanding the emotional dynamics organized in symbolic representations will help in understanding the personality dynamics of the patient. These personality dynamics may be contributing to interference in the therapeutic alliance. They may contribute to defenses that enable the maintenance of psychotic and near psychotic symptoms. There may be a vicious cycle in which disturbed personality dynamics are expressed in social behavior causing reality to destructively react. The resulting social failures and destructive reactions may then trigger the illness. Helping patients understand this vicious cycle may help ward off the next episode.

The book is meant to be a contribution to an integrative theory of modern ego psychology demonstrating the clinical utility of such an approach to descriptive clinical theory. The book attempts to show the integrative relationship among all areas of mental function: the dynamic and the cognitive, the psychogenetic and the present adaptive, the psychological and the biological. We are all at the beginning of this effort (c.f. Pine, 1990; Robbins, 1993).

The demands are challenging for patients and their therapists in their journey together. This book is meant to provide a road map.

Chapter 1

Ego Functions

Introduction

The *ego* is the term psychoanalysis uses to categorize and describe mental processes that regulate and mediate between the experience of reality and the experience of emotions. This chapter discusses those mediating and regulating ego functions, experiences, and organizations of experiences that are particularly relevant to understanding psychotic and near psychotic illnesses.

According to Hinsie and Campbell (1963), the ego is "a part of the psychic apparatus which is the mediator between the person and reality; the perception of reality and adaptation to it" (cf. Campbell, 1989).

Laplanche and Pontalis (1967) review the history of the term *ego* in psychoanalysis. They clearly describe the evolution of Freud's use of this term: the ego meaning person or self, the ego meaning a collection of emotional defenses, and the tension between these two uses.

Hartmann (1939, 1964) focused on a third aspect of the ego: mechanisms of regulation between reality and the person, which he called *ego apparatuses*. These processes mature from birth onward according to their own timetable. They are aspects of mental functioning which especially mediate the perception, organization, and use of reality. Examples are vision, memory, and certain kinds of logic. I will later subdivide and add to these.

Because of Hartmann's focus on reality rather than unconscious fantasy, because the apparatuses seem to mature according to a neurological rather than only a psychological timetable, because the apparatuses are said to be relatively free of unconscious emotional conflict, and because apparatuses correlate with conscious and cognitive functioning as well as other aspects of general psychiatry, Hartmann's apparatus concept has been criticized as nonpsychoanalytic, i.e., nondynamic or nonemotional.

But the concept is not easily dismissed. Schafer (1968b), Blanck and Blanck (1979, 1986), and Loewald (1988) all focus in varying ways on the ego as a set of integrative regulations. They especially focus on the superordinate result of the functioning of this apparatus which mediates the integration we know as normal mental life. (For a review of Hartmann's description of ego function as an integrative and regulatory process, see L. Friedman [1989]; also Rapaport [1951a, 1959] and Holt [1965]).

All psychoanalysts agree that the term *ego* is used, in part, to describe the mental interaction with reality. It is this aspect of ego function in particular that this book focuses on, because in psychotic and near psychotic illnesses, alterations in reality ego function are the most dramatic and distinguishing feature.

When specific problems with the ego's interaction with reality are described, one ends up describing specific ego functions that Hartmann called autonomous ego apparatuses and ego functions. This is the clinical fact. A careful description of psychotic and near psychotic ego functioning leads inevitably to some apparatus concept. The exact relationship between these functions and emotional or dynamic material varies, and hence the degree of autonomy varies. But I believe it is a damaged ego apparatus function that gives psychotic and near psychotic organization to dynamic, emotional material and to object relations. This hypothesis grows out of the observation that intercurrent psychotic illness can cause a dramatic reorganization of dynamic elements without necessarily changing the dynamic content.

Hartmann's ego psychology divides ego functions not by reality experience and emotional experience but into *autonomous* ego functions or apparatuses, *primary* or *secondary*, and *defensive* functions. I will be discussing *primary autonomous apparatuses*. Though these apparatuses can also perform defensive functions, primary autonomous apparatuses refer to aspects of reality-oriented cognitive thinking ability and perceptual ego functioning in the area of reality experience. The autonomous ego function apparatuses deal, for the most part, with outside phenomena. They deal with percepts, their recording and organization. Schafer (1968b) discusses autonomous ego functions which include nonperceptual aspects of cognition. Autonomous ego functions are also integration functions. They are reality based and organize reality experience. They also organize certain relationships between reality experience and emotional experience. In healthy people, these functions are relatively free of, and hence not completely distorted by, emotional experience. In this sense, they are autonomous.

How do these ego functions get damaged? No one knows. I believe there are biological factors in the etiology of psychosis which operate especially at the ego apparatus level because we observe that the apparatuses that deal with reality are so altered in psychotic and near psychotic states. These apparatuses have neurological properties (e.g., sometimes known neurological pathways as in sensation and memory) in addition to psychological properties, which are clearly also influenced by learning and emotional state. I hypothesize but am unable to prove that, in psychosis, the apparatuses are a major area where neurobiological factors exert their effect on adult psychology.

Emotional conflict may play a role in triggering apparatus decompensation in some illnesses. The mechanisms of this triggering are unknown, but the effects and treatments are known. Psychological stress, a crucial factor that often plays a describable role, is unique to each individual and is encoded in mental structures along with apparatus function. For some patients, specific psychological stress can trigger biologically determined psychotic or near psychotic reactions. This relationship can be described.

Emotional life is encoded, translated, and experienced differently when ego apparatus functions are damaged. For each patient, one can describe specific ego deficits and conflicts. One can then prescribe a treatment that will address the combination.

I will now describe ego functions relevant to psychotic and near psychotic structure.

The Ego and the Experience of Reality

Reality Experience

I need a term for the mental sensation and organization of outer reality. I will use the simple, descriptive term *reality experience*.[1] I distinguish reality experience from reality per se and also from the perception of that reality.

There probably can be no universal agreement or descriptive definition of the experience of reality. However, the unusual, striking, and descriptively definitional phenomenon of psychosis and near psychosis is the special experience of reality that occurs.

The experience of reality often involves the experience of external stimuli (Kraepelin, 1915). Reality-mediating mental processes form sensory information out of perceptual data. Reality experience is, therefore, often built on sensory information. But reality experience also uses abstract concepts built by conscious, conceptual, logical thinking. Reality experience tends to be organized logically, with inductive and deductive reasoning building links between perceptual information and concepts. Reality experience builds in complexity from the interaction of perception with conceptual thinking.

Reality experiencing capacity is mediated by a complex, partly autonomous, neuropsychological, maturational and developmental ego function apparatus. This is why Piaget (1954) can describe its evolving course throughout childhood (see also White, 1963; Weil, 1970; Sterm, 1985; Greenspan, 1988, 1989; see also Table 1.1). Reality experience depends

4 Ego Functions

Table 1.1 Reality Experience

1 Relies on percept
2 Relies on reality-oriented logic
3 Evaluates inside and outside
4 Uses as information processing strategies: learned patterns, deductive and inductive reasoning
5 Builds abstract concepts; generalizes and applies
6 Recruits emotional experience for validity, motivation, and decision but not for percept or for logic
7 Requires regulating and modulating functions of the ego
8 Often relies on observing ego
9 Makes judgments for action

Table 1.2 Ego Functions Important for Reality Experience

Logic	
	Secondary Process
	Sequential Time
	Cause-Effect
Memory	
	Sequential events
	Spatial
	Coordinated Working Memory
Percept	
	Registration
	Recording
	Accessing
	Manipulation
	Integration
	(forms a "virtual perceptual reality" based on real sensorial events and secondary process logic)
Boundaries	
	Keeping faculties separate and intact in conscious experience
Reality Testing	
Observing Ego	

on many subsidiary, partly autonomous ego functions, the major group of which is called logical or *secondary process* thinking.

One cannot equate ego apparatus function and the ego's reality experience (Table 1.2). Reality experience is an experience and not a function. This experience has qualities, quantities, modalities, and domains. In addition, the ego's apparatus function can be used at times defensively for emotional purposes. Also, aspects of reality stimuli are registered and encoded by the emotions. Nonetheless, reality experience is mediated by, and depends upon, certain autonomous ego functions and integrations of functions. Those integrations of functions are sometimes called superordinate ego function.[2]

Secondary Process

Freud called conscious, reality-oriented logic *secondary process* because he thought this capacity developed later than emotional experience organization, which he called *primary process*. Freud was probably wrong, because the latest research with infants seems to demonstrate secondary process development from birth (Sterm, 1985; see also Piaget and Inhelder, 1958; Piaget, 1977). I will use this traditional psychoanalytic term nonetheless.

Secondary processes are those mostly conscious, reality-oriented, logical thinking processes that gather data via percepts and assemble those percepts into information according to learned schemes and also according to deductive and inductive reasoning. Concepts are built, abstracted, generalized, and applied. Various levels of abstraction are used and related to each other and to real-world tasks. Words and numbers are used to sort and arrange information. Words and numbers are defined and specific, and therefore have relatively finite information contents.

Autonomous apparatuses tend to be organized around these principles of secondary process logical thinking. These logical principles include the ideas that cause is different from effect, the part is separate from the whole, a part is separate from another part, and time is sequential. This type of thinking relies upon clear categories, usually with definable boundaries and finite date contents. Data and categories tend to be digital. Categories group ideas and data logically and describe relationships to larger entities. Relationships are congruent with perceptually based rules following spatial, temporal, and sequential experience. There are distinctions between concept, percept, and affect with concept or percept as the main organizer. These categories mature as cognitive skills mature, and develop as reality experience accumulates.

Secondary process capacities use functions of cognition that should be relatively uninfluenced by emotional conflict. Secondary processes mediate and buttress reality experience but are not the same as reality experience. Reality experience includes more than secondary process. Reality experience is an experience and not just a group of processes.

The Experience of Emotions

Emotional experience is quite different from reality experience. Emotional experience is the experience especially of emotion with its own quality, quantity, organization, and ideational content. It has a different base, follows different rules of organization, and has a different mental locus of experience. The base of emotional experience is feelings, also called *affects*. The rules of their organization are psychological rules called *primary processes*. These processes use different types of categories

6 Ego Functions

and different causal relationships from reality experience. Emotional experience is based on but not limited to primary process.

The mental locus of emotional experience is partly a visceral body and sensation locus that may take pictorial form. The quality is the experience of percept, of physical sensation, and of affect. The pictures are visual transformations of affects and have the quality of percepts. This percept aspect is a normal link to reality experience.

The ego can attach and experience affect in association with events, concepts, percepts, or as "free-floating." Different levels of consciousness, processing systems (primary or secondary process), psychiatric illnesses, phases of illness, and stages of normal development all influence the ego's positioning, organization, and experience of affect.

Affect often provides motivating force and hence positive or negative direction to behavior, ideas, and pictorial forms. Affects vary in *quality* from pleasurable to unpleasurable; they vary in *intensity* from strong to faint; they vary in *content* such as anger and love; they vary in domain from visual to visceral.

Primary process is an information processing system especially for affects. Hence intensities, qualities, and domains form the organizing basis of contents and their categories. Infinite information contents, each within inexact limits based on intensity and quality, form the basis of concepts or, more precisely, contain the concepts.

Emotional experience builds in complexity by mixing intensities, qualities, and domains in complex patterns according to primary process psychological rules.

Primary process, just like secondary process, is a function of sophisticated information processing.[3] I believe primary process function has its own developmental timetable. Some illnesses, like schizophrenia or severe dementia, destroy this function. More commonly, when only the boundary between primary process and secondary process is damaged by psychiatric illness, the primary process is left intact, but an invasion of primary process into secondary process thereby occurs disrupting secondary process.

Primary Process

I will focus on those aspects of primary process important in psychotic and near psychotic organization and experience. Primary process is unconscious, preconscious, and sometimes conscious. Primary process thinking is the organization of our feelings in "thought" which is dominated by the content, organization, and qualities of affect. Aspects of reality experience play only certain limited roles. Categories are not logically based on reality experience but are psychologically based on emotional experience. Emotional experience is determinate.

Primary process thinking often relies upon mental images, as in dreams. Dreams are stories composed of a series of condensed images. The images are called symbols, because each element is composed of and represents many feelings and experiences put together.

Condensation is the ability of the mind to form a complex representation of many related percepts, ideas, and feelings. Condensation is the fundamental principle of the primary process. One characteristic of condensation is that the linkage of various aspects of idea, feeling, and percept is determined by the emotional feelings about the ideas and percepts. Another characteristic is that most of the many thoughts and feelings represented are not conscious except as they are alluded to or collapsed into the available conscious aspects of the condensation. Manifest, conscious elements also condense with each other. The combination of condensations usually involves aspects of reality experience to build the image and express the unconscious emotion. Aspects of reality experience, together with emotional primary processing, determine the representability or form.

Condensations involve data categories that are porously boundaried and overlapping. Data contents within a category may be infinite in number. The sequences of data, categories, and cause–effect relationships may be unidirectional, reverse-directional, bidirectional, multidirectional, or simultaneous. In primary process, there may be a part instead of the whole, or a part greater and more significant than the whole. Time may be of no consequence. Within the condensation, there are transmodal changes between percept, affect, and concept. One may be used to convey, express, experience, and represent the other. Because the main organizer of the process is affect, its themes, qualities, and quantities determine data collection, category sorting, and transmodal processing. It is an analog process. This means that qualities especially, and quantities of those qualities, will determine organization, transmodal processes, linkages, and, to some extent, contents and meaning.

The resulting primary process integration gains its coherence through this analog process. Understanding especially this aspect of quality and quantity allows deciphering of what is otherwise a system of infinite and ambiguous possibilities. The other crucial factor in this regard is the day residue. There is a characteristic structure to these condensations described later in the day residue section.

Displacement is another characteristic of emotional process thinking. The most significant emotional aspect of an idea or the affect itself may be "displaced" to a part of the symbol that is not central according to secondary process rules of logic. There may be displacements from one symbol to another or from one element of one symbol to one element of another. Abstraction is also displaced from concept to details of the concrete thing. Specific patterns of displacements are common. I believe

8 Ego Functions

that what it is displaced *to* is as important as what it is displaced *from*. The reason the specific part was chosen as a displacement target is crucial to meaning and to the emotional experience. Therefore, "displaced to details" also means "expressed in details."

The ways in which condensation occurs and the forms it takes are characteristic of the symbolic milieus in which it is formed. Examples of these discrete symbolic milieus are specific cultures, specific illness states, and specific, individual emotional experiences. Understanding specific condensation–displacement patterns of symbolic milieus is one task of *psychoanalysts*.

The Relationship of Reality Experience to Emotional Experience

Complex mental experiences build from both areas. Ideas are intellectual abstractions that are often built from reality experience, but which may also conceptualize emotional experience. Emotional experience clearly records and expresses both stimuli in reality and the affect experience of these stimuli. It does so in the emotional locus of affect experiences with their typical organization and qualities.

Therefore, one relationship that reality experience and emotional experience may have is a similarity of external stimulus content. Another is the experience of percepts, which may be due to external reality stimuli or to strong internal affect stimuli taking pictorial form in certain states of consciousness.

Reality experience and emotional experience have other characteristic, stable, and describable ways of relating to each other. There are mental phenomena that allow the experience and expression of that relationship. The ego gives organization to this relationship.

Summary

The *ego* is a term used to describe certain receiving, recording, elaborating, and regulating functions of the experience of reality, the experience of emotions, and their relationship to each other. The ego has processes which help keep areas and functions separate. The ego also must be able to integrate different areas and relationships into a relatively coherent, unified, and stable experience. While awake, a person's conscious ego should be unified under the logical control of the experience of reality.

In psychosis and near psychosis, this conscious, reality-based control is disturbed in specific and describable ways so that reality and fantasy, percept and affect, merge. There is no awareness that a merger has occurred. This is almost a descriptive, ego definition of psychosis and near psychosis.

A patient example of the merger of emotional experience with reality experience follows:

> People in the old neighborhood are talking about her. They say she didn't pay taxes after World War II. Why would they say that? She doesn't steal. Once she was accused of stealing money when she first started working but it wasn't true. Now they say she's a shoplifter.

Autonomous Apparatuses

Following is an expanded description of the autonomous apparatuses characteristically disrupted by psychotic and near psychotic illness. These disrupted autonomous apparatuses permit psychotic or near psychotic experience by altering the usual control of the relationship between reality experience and emotional experience.

Boundaries

A mental boundary is the ability to keep experiences separate from each other. There are a number of boundaries. We are not usually aware of a boundary function, but we are aware of the result. Boundary problems are ubiquitous in psychotic and near psychotic illnesses and play a crucial role in their structure.

Federn (1934; see also Hinsie and Campbell, 1963) first defined the ego boundary concept in psychoanalysis. He described the *repression boundary*, an inner boundary between conscious and unconscious. He also described the boundary between the mind and the external world that involves the sense organs. Bellak et al. (1973) review the historical development in the psychoanalytic literature of the ego boundary description as it expanded to include specific boundaries between self and object representations, the boundary of bodily experience, and other ego boundaries. For a modern and experimental view of boundary see E. Hartmann (1991). I further expand the concept to include all boundaries between ego functions, between domains and modalities of ego experiences, and between affects and affect modalities. I do so because damage to these boundaries is seen so dramatically in psychotic and near psychotic illness.

There has been much confusion in the psychoanalytic literature because of the failure to distinguish conscious from unconscious boundary function. The unconscious works according to primary process and is characterized by mergers that cross logical boundaries. In normal people, most of these mergers are unconscious or in conscious emotional experience. The conscious logical mind, however, functions to a great extent by keeping certain experiential categories and capacities separate. Very ill

10 Ego Functions

patients have trouble in their conscious mind separating mental experiences. Boundary problems are crucial to this difficulty.

Inside–Outside

The most important boundary separates mental experiences of inside and outside. The mind should have the conscious ability to perceive the origin of stimuli that occur inside itself and to distinguish them from those that it experiences as originating outside of itself. This is the main ego boundary.

A merger occurs when what should be two distinct experiences are put together and experienced as one. The analytic literature uses two terms for the merger that ensues from the loss of the inside–outside boundary: *fusion* and *condensation*. Psychoanalysts often use these terms interchangeably. They should not do so because both describe types of merger, but the boundary that is usually crossed by each is different, and the mechanisms and results are quite different.

Fusion is a crossing of the inside–outside ego boundary. The contents of stimuli in reality go directly into and fuse with experience of one's own body and mind. The content of the experience is based on the content of stimuli in reality. This fusion is a conscious, cognitive inability, not a fantasy or a worry. It is presumably a neuromental problem because it involves external stimulus registration, not only affect or psychological content, and because proper medication rapidly repairs this boundary. The crucial point is that mental experiences resulting from fusion are based on the content and qualities of stimuli in reality that burst into mental experience from the outside once the screening boundary between inside and outside is lost. The resulting mental experiences are filled with the experience of those stimuli. Which reality stimuli invade mental experience, both reality experience and emotional experience, depends on the degree of loss of the boundary between inside and outside and also on the intensity of the outside stimuli. True fusion does not depend on the content or meaning the outside stimuli have for the person.

In addition, with this boundary disturbance, intense affect may be perceived as coming from outside in the form of percept and reality stimuli. The stronger the affect, the more the experience will "spill over" into percept and contaminate the experience of outer, perceptual reality.

There can be internal fusions where any content of one inside emotional category goes immediately to the content of some other inside logical category if the original is intense enough. This is a special kind of fusion that is seen in certain illnesses; like all fusions, it depends on intensity and not content or meaning.

Condensation, on the other hand, is quite different. First, it is a joining of two inside experiences. Condensation usually involves the inside experience of reality joined with the inside experience of emotion. The second difference is that only certain points merge. The aspects of reality chosen and the precise mechanisms for joining are determined by the emotional meaning of the reality experience. What is merged depends upon the person's feelings and not upon the environment, except as the environment corresponds to and/or evokes certain feelings. Condensation is organized according to primary process rules. The environment is only providing emotionally relevant attachment points for those feelings. This condensation can be conscious, preconscious, or an unconscious fantasy. The location varies from illness to illness and with the level (degree of severity) of illness. Psychosis and near psychosis have condensations in characteristic locations with characteristic effects on mental experience. Relevant aspects of external reality can be chosen because there is already a coherent, organized, and internal experience of reality.

The treatment of condensations is quite different from the treatment of fusions. Because merger points in condensations are emotionally meaningful, they are called symbolic. Fusions are not symbolic in their structure, although they may have secondary symbolic elaborations.

In summary, ego boundary 1 is between inside and outside: between inside experience and outside stimuli in reality. When this boundary function is missing, fusion occurs. Whatever stimuli occur in reality will be fused with the experience of thought and feelings.

Ego boundary 2 separates inner experiences of feelings from the inner experiences of reality. This boundary separates two inside experiences. When this boundary function is gone, it is usually gone only at specific points via the mechanism of condensation. Only emotionally relevant reality experience is merged, and therefore only certain attachment points occur.

It is these emotionally meaningful condensations that form the unique symbolic alterations of psychosis and near psychosis.

Percept Boundaries

Percepts are inner, mental, sensory experiences (see S. Friedman and Fisher, 1960). They are triggered by stimuli in reality. These stimuli are external to the mind and often external to the body. There is no one-to-one relationship between a stimulus and the percept, because the central and peripheral nervous systems have their own recording properties. In addition, percept is affected by learning, inhibition, and emotional state (Piaget, 1953; see also Westlundh and Smith, 1983).

The ego should be able to set a boundary to conscious percept so that it does not contaminate, and is not contaminated by, other mental events such as concept or affect.

12   Ego Functions

Reality experience includes more than percept, but perceptual experience is important to the ego's reality experience (Beres [1960]; on the development of perception, see Banglow and Sadow [1971]; on the relationship of perception to psychic representation, see Karush [1966]).

Concept Boundaries

The ego should be able to set some boundaries in consciousness to conceptual experience so that it can remain an integration mode of abstract thinking, and not be interchangeable with or flooded by affect or percept. Conceptualization might use perceptual and affect information, but should also remain a separate experience. Important to conceptualization are abstraction, generalization, and application. Conceptualization and its subsidiary processes are ego functions that should be relatively autonomous.

Affect Boundaries

Likewise, the conscious ego should be able to boundary affects so that they do not transmodally flood conscious percept, concept, or other affects. There are two different boundary functions concerning affects. One separates different affects, such as anger and sexual desire. The other separates specific affects from other mental functions and experiences. Although the boundaries should be flexible, they should be stable enough to be regulatory. If these regulating boundary capacities are destroyed, affect fuses with affect, affect spreads to mood, and affect invades logical thinking. This causes secondary process disruption by the condensation of secondary process categories with affect organized emotional experience categories. Recruitment of content based on intense affect experience results in many categories of reality experience with associated contents further condensing. In this way, affect spreads to mood. The recruitment is based on recurrent affect themes. These themes cross reality categories. Transcategorical crossing as determined by quality and quantity of feelings is the whole point of primary processing, but this should not take over reality experience.

Creative people are those who have access to transcategorical condensations in their conscious minds, but who are not massively flooded and disrupted. They can control and use such condensation experiences to reassemble new reality categories for real world use and communication. The ability of the ego to use these condensations for secondary process gain is the important ability.

Control of intensity, generalization, and spread of affect is a crucial ego function often dramatically damaged in very ill patients. The ego should be able to regulate the intensity of stimulus perception, the intensity of the affect reaction evoked by the stimulus, and the spread of this evoked reaction throughout conscious reality experience and emotional experience. This means that the ego should be able to modulate and regulate the intensity of affect, how dramatically these evoked feelings and ideas erupt into consciousness, and how dramatically and disruptively they spread across categories of experience, whether the stimulus is outer reality or inner drive. Intensity may challenge modulating capacities, which then challenge boundary functions.

Because uncontrolled affect intensities and resulting condensations are an important determinant of primary process dominance, the affect–intensity boundary is an important determinant of illness in the ego. The form this lack of modulating and regulating capacity takes varies according to type and phase of specific illnesses and will be discussed in Chapter 5. The relationship between this boundary and the other boundaries described varies from illness to illness.

Conscious–Preconscious–Unconscious Boundaries

Another crucial set of boundaries is between those mental experiences that are conscious, those almost conscious mental experiences called preconscious, and those mental experiences that are unconscious. The mind should have the ability to screen from consciousness (1) continuous sensory impressions from the outside; (2) continuous emotional reactions from inside; and (3) conflicted emotions causing distress. The ability to modulate and screen is a crucial boundary function of the ego. Having this boundary means that there will be an ability to separate conscious reality content from unconscious feelings about that content (Federn, 1934). Conscious thinking is usually dominated by logical, reality-organized thinking. Preconscious thinking includes both logical and emotional thinking. Unconscious thinking is mostly emotional process thinking (Freud, 1915b). When boundaries among these three levels are disrupted, aspects of a lower level predominate in the functions of a higher level. Although one definition of mental health is some availability between levels of awareness, very ill patients have severe damage in this function. Distinguishing conscious from unconscious mental functioning is crucial if one is to understand that dynamic psychological material has not only content but place. The flooding and disruption of conscious thinking by intense psychodynamic material is a hallmark of very ill patients. Disrupted ego boundaries mediate this disruption.

Primary Process–Secondary Process Boundary

The boundary between primary process emotional thinking and secondary process logical, reality thinking is not exactly the same as the

14 Ego Functions

conscious–preconscious–unconscious boundaries, because some aspects of primary process normally occur in conscious thinking. However, the ability to distinguish between primary and secondary process thinking should be maintained at the level of consciousness. Very ill patients have a defective boundary between primary and secondary process thinking in their conscious minds, so logical thinking is flooded by emotional thinking. The specific forms of this flooding differ from illness to illness and will be described in Chapter 5.

Reality Testing

The next crucial ego function for understanding very ill psychiatric patients is *reality testing*, which is the mind's ability to test emotional experience against reality experience, to use secondary process logic in the service of this test, and, most importantly, to maintain doubt and to change reality conclusions.[4] It depends upon an ego boundary between reality testing experience and the rest of mental experience.

Notice that I have not said *reality*; I have said *reality experience*. This is because someone can be sane but wrong. Likewise, someone can be correct but insane.

Most commonly, psychotic reality testing problems manifest themselves in one area of mental functioning. If that area is in the realm of idea formation, the phenomenon is called a *delusion*. If the area is in the realm of sensation, the phenomenon is called a *hallucination*. Hallucinations can be in any of the sensory modalities: visual, auditory, or somatic.

In very ill psychotic states, reality testing is lost for all mental areas. This condition is rare; usually, significant areas of reality ego remain, even in very psychotic patients—this is a key to treatment.

Losses of reality testing can be categorized according to the degree of loss. Rigid losses of reality testing that are impervious to exploration, interaction, and even confrontation in a psychiatric interview are *psychotic* losses of reality testing (Kernberg, 1977). *Near psychotic* patients only suspend their reality testing function. If this occurs in the realm of sensation, it is called a *pseudohallucination*. If it occurs in the realm of ideas, I call it a *pseudodelusion*.

There is an intermediate category of phenomena where reality testing is preserved but a strong sensory perception is registered without a reality stimulus. This phenomenon is called *hallucinosis*.

A chart organizing this important material is shown in Chapter 4 (Table 4.1). The important point for now is that reality testing in the psychoses is rigidly absent. Reality testing in near psychotic states is suspended in functioning, but the capacity is potentially present. In neurotic illnesses, there may be intense emotional experiences and/or rigidities of mental content, but the ability to test reality experience is neither lost nor suspended.

It is usually believed that the ability to test reality experience depends on the ability to distinguish internal from external. But there are patients who show fusion of inside and outside experience who can test reality, especially during the period that the therapist is helping them. Some of these patients, however, cannot do so. Conversely, there are patients who cannot test reality even with the therapist's help, but who are quite able to keep inside and outside separate. The point is that reality testing is a separate ego function from the ego function of maintaining a boundary between inside and outside.

Observing Ego

Observing ego is the mind's ability to mentally look at its own experience. The ego should be able to both experience itself, the experiencing ego, and to mentally observe itself, the observing ego. This ability is crucial to call upon when treating the very ill, as will be made clear in Chapter 7. Observing ego is a quite separate ego function from reality testing. A person may be unable to distinguish real from unreal and still be able to observe his or her own mental functioning and experience. By definition, psychotic illness affects reality testing, but it need not affect observing ego capacity. A patient can be delusional and know he or she is delusional. This is readily observed in many psychotic patients and is a crucial step to helping them in their treatment. A delusional patient with observing ego may say, "I know what I believe is part of my illness but I believe it anyway." An exploration of observing ego as distinct from reality testing is a crucial part of the evaluation of any psychotic patient. The careful separation and use of observing ego for the therapeutic alliance and beginning treatment is the crucial first step in psychotherapy with psychotic patients. Interferences with observing ego, even in psychotic patients, are often of a nonpsychotic nature. Commonly, interferences are due to nonpsychotic character defenses. This will be described in Chapters 2 and 3 on psychotic and near psychotic structure, Chapter 7 on the psychotherapy of psychosis, and in the section discussing the relationship of character pathology to psychosis.

Integrating Capacity

Integrating capacity is the ability of the mind to put together emotional experience and reality experience in a regular organization within each of these areas and also between these areas, especially consciously. What one sees, hears, thinks, feels, remembers, and fantasizes should fit together. The way the mind does this varies from person to person, and failures in this function vary from illness to illness. A second definition of very ill patients, psychotic and near psychotic, is severe and characteristic disruption in integrative capacities, especially conscious capacities.

Crucial to secondary process integration is the faculty of conceptualization and the subsidiary capacities to abstract, generalize, and apply. Secondary process attends to affect, but under the auspices of conceptual organization. Primary process has a different integration system, in which affect is the crucial organizer to which logic and concept are subsumed.

Neurotic patients may weigh some aspects more heavily in their integrations, such as ideas (obsessive) or emotions (hysteric), but these cognitive styles (D. Shapiro, 1965) do not interfere severely with real-world functioning because they are not severe disturbances of secondary process reality experience. Very ill patients show extreme disturbances in integrating capacity that affect secondary process and reality experience. Although they are often based in and reflective of severe boundary disturbances, such integration problems can also be in addition to or instead of boundary disturbances. This is a separate capacity or deficit. The distinct and characteristic integrative problems for each of the illnesses are described in Chapter 5. There are various kinds of integration problems which disturb the relationship of content to content, affect to content, affect to affect (splitting), and affect or ideational content of emotional experience to reality experience.

Regulation of the Relationship of Reality Experience to Emotional Experience

The ego functions just described are crucial to the ability to control the relationship of reality experience to emotional experience. The relationship of reality experience to emotional experience involves the regulation of the overlap between the two experiences.

The intermediate or transitional zone between the two areas is a crucial area of human experience (Winnicott, 1953, 1971). Characteristic of normal experience are the availability in the preconscious and conscious intermediate zone of emotional experience for reality view, the availability of reality experience for evoked emotional reaction, and the condensations between the two that result in symbols. There should be dominance, control, and use of this intermediate experience by reality experience and its rules of secondary process logic. The intermediate or transitional zone involves mixtures of primary and secondary processes, called tertiary process by Arieti (1976). Here, reality experience and emotional experience mix. There is preservation of a separate reality experience, as in a daydream (Schafer, 1968b).

In psychosis, this intermediate function moves into reality experience. Psychotic experience does not occur in the intermediate zone. Psychotic experience occurs in the zone of reality experience. Psychotic process occurs when autonomous ego boundaries are broken through and emotional experience invades reality experience, usually at specific

Ego Functions 17

condensation points. The form this takes as the material enters reality experience depends on illness-specific patterns of autonomous ego disruptions. The form will also depend on specific primary process content and mechanisms from the invading emotional processes.

In psychotic and near psychotic patients, the content and process of emotional experience may change, but more importantly, the content and process of reality experience changes. There are changes in the rules of organization of the relationship between reality experience and emotional experience. There is a change in the level of consciousness where this relationship is out of control.

Day Residues

The primary process with its major features of condensation and displacement is most clearly illustrated by dreams, which build their images and stories, in part, around events that occur during the day. These events are often conscious reality events. Freud called them the *day residue*. They are a crucial organizing part of the primary process. They may appear unchanged but used for emotional purposes, or they may be symbolically represented and altered according to primary process rules. They are aspects of reality experience.[5] Often, the day residue in psychosis and near psychosis is a present-day reality repetition of the reality past, displacement from the emotional past, and displacement from the emotional present—all condensed. The condensation preserves some aspects of the reality day residue and symbolically alters other aspects.

The waking mind should have the ability to keep the day residue, if conscious, separate from the emotional reaction and symbolic use or alteration of the day residue. In psychosis, and to an extent in near psychosis, the day residue is experienced condensed with the experience of its symbolic alteration.

Delusions are stories experienced by psychotic patients that are analogous to dreams. (See Freud [1900, 1907, 1917b] for his discussion of the similarities. I have somewhat different views.) Delusions are structured with an organizing center from reality experience akin to the day residue of a dream. This center of reality experience is condensed with feelings from emotional experience and symbolically altered in reality experience. The alteration and the reality are represented and experienced as one. The exact construction is described in Chapter 2.

The day residue in psychosis and near psychosis is an event, usually in reality, usually significant, that evokes feelings. In dreams, often, and in psychotic and near psychotic phenomena sometimes, the day residue may be just a thought. It may be an insignificant reality event that receives its power solely through displacement from another reality experience in the past or from emotional experience in the past condensed with emotional experience in the present.[6] In either case, the day residue originates from reality experience, either factual or imagined, and in psychosis is condensed with its symbolic representation. The condensation retains reality experience qualities.

The day residue is therefore a bridge between reality and fantasy, present and past, secondary process and primary process, abstraction and concrete things, concept and percept. Obviously, any day residue is a crucial point in the structure of both dreams and delusions.

The sequence and context of the day residue are crucial for psychotic and near psychotic states. The day residue is not just an event involving an object, animate or inanimate, but also an event in sequence and context with other reality and emotional events. A day residue is meaningful not just because it happened, but also because of when it happened and what else was happening or not happening. The day residue might, in fact, be something that was wanted but that failed to happen at a certain sequential point.

The structure of psychosis and near psychosis tends to encode sequence and context in the symbolic representation differently from the static day residue event, person, or thing. This is one of the reasons psychotic phenomena seem, at first glance, so inexplicable (see Chapter 2).

Conclusion: there are usually highly specific points where reality and fantasy condense in psychotic and near psychotic phenomena. These points are located at the day residue. This is the point at which the most obvious condensations occur. It is the ego that determines the structure of the condensations in psychosis and near psychosis.

Thing Presentation

Freud used the term *object presentation* to refer to the central nervous system encoding of mental *representation*. He believed the object presentation had two components: a verbal component called *word presentation* and a visual component he called *thing presentation* (Breuer and Freud, 1893–1895; Freud, 1900, 1915b, Appendix C).

Freud meant thing presentation to refer to a neurological encoding. A stimulus is presented to the central nervous system for encoding as percept. I believe that affect, also a central nervous system response, is encoded, in part, along with percept to form a combined affect–percept presentation. I believe the crux of the psychotic and near psychotic experience is a particular mental experience of these rigid, formed, stereotyped, repetitive affect–percepts. These affect–percepts are neuromental phenomena and have no psychoanalytic name. I believe Freud was getting close to describing them with his thing presentation term. This term has the advantage of calling attention to the perceptual encoding, the presentation characteristics of the representation, and the neuromental relationship. This term may also help remind us that the entire perceptual environment, not just people, is encoded with affect and used symbolically (Searles, 1960) (for a more standard view of what Freud meant by word presentation and thing presentation, see Arlow and Brenner [1964, Chapter 10]; for a modern view of the cortical processing of words, see Ojemann and Mateer [1979]; for a recent review of the psychoanalytic implications of word presentations, see Rizzuto [1989, 1990]; for the relationships of Freud's view of aphasia to his view of representation and mental organization, see Grossman [1992]).

Words are capable of rendering concept and abstraction directly. It is crucial for the understanding of psychosis and near psychosis to understand that thing presentations must express concepts through the medium of perceived physical things and the altering of perceived physical things and events. The reality experienced thing is used to express an emotional metaphor (see Freud, 1915b; cf. Arlow, 1989). The metaphor is contained in the picture of the reality thing that is used. An example is an image of the female breast used as a metaphor for the concept of a longing to be taken care of. The thing presentation is therefore the experience of something in reality used to express feelings. An aspect of reality experience, usually perceptual, has been borrowed by emotional experience. The emotional language of the experience of reality things occurs in all primary process phenomena. The things are used as symbols that make up a story. The affect is experienced as a perception experience of the thing as well as or instead of an affect reaction to the thing. The thing presentation is a way of perceiving, thinking, and feeling, at the same time, through the experience of concrete images. Perception is encoding affect, concept, and the conflict of affect concepts in a perceptual primary process synthesis.

Changes in reality things to convey emotional experience I call symbolic alterations of reality experience. Sequence and context can also be altered for purposes of symbolizing. Symbolic alterations of reality experience are emotional alterations of day residues according to primary process rules of conceptual organization. They involve the emotional transformation of the experience of real things for the purpose of symbolizing emotional experience.

Thing presentations are symbolic experiences which combine concept and affect together with percept. Thing presentations are sensory affects or sensory emotions. The affect mobilizes and is experienced as an exteroceptive sensory event. Thing presentations act like central nervous system encodings that, under certain conditions such as dreaming or psychosis, are presented to conscious mental experience. Thing presentation is an involuntary brain–mind event. Thing presentation experience is a mental experience of great emotional power. In psychosis, the thing presentation experience dominates conscious, cognitive, superordinate reality experience. An example is a hallucination.

20 Ego Functions

> **Example:**
>
> The young woman is frightened. The world is coming to an end. God is killing all the people by burning them because of their sins. She is Judas who has betrayed. God's voice says she can fly. If she opens a window and jumps she could save the world and get forgiveness for sins. She heard God tell her to jump. She smelled burning. She told her family, but they did not believe her.

Freud (1915b, Appendix C) describes how thing presentations are "open to a complex of presentations," and how word presentations are linked to thing presentations by sound and image-visual links. Piaget (1981) describes affects that become linked to percepts. Stern (1985) reviews experiments showing the appearance in the 3-week-old infant of the ability to "cross-modally" recognize in one sensory modality an object first perceived in a different sensory modality. He also describes perception-elicited affect as in the viewing of art. I extend all these ideas to describe the basic thing presentation transmodal crossing and condensation of concept and affect into percept. In this way, conflicts and their compromise formations may be synthesized in these condensed percept symbol experiences.

Le Doux (1989) may be describing one neuroanatomical path of this transmodal processing system. He describes amygdala–hippocampal affect encoding areas for fear in animals. These affect-encoding areas are connected to thalamic regions, which have their own sensory input from peripheral sensory organs bypassing the cortex.

But we know that the thalamus also connects to and from the cortex, including sensory cortex, association cortex, and prefrontal integration areas. This suggests a beginning neurology of thing presentations and of symbolic alterations of reality.

Le Doux, Iwata, Cicchetti, and Reis (1998) postulated that through neural interactions between the amygdala and brain areas involved in cognition, "affect can influence cognition and cognition can influence affect." He then proposes that "emotional experience results when stimulus representations, affect representations, and self-representations coincide in working memory" (c.f. Le Doux, 1996). I think that when these are condensed, not just simultaneous, and experienced as sensory, a thing presentation is experienced. Also, there are other relations where thing presentations can be experienced, not just working memory.

Since the first edition of this book (1992), there has been much more PET and other modern neuroimagining research. Morris, Frith, Perrett, Rowland, Young, Calder, and Dolan (1996) confirm the amygdala fear circuit in humans. They point out that, here, primitive amygdala receives substantial inputs from temporal visual association areas and suggest that the amygdala is appropriately placed in relation to sensory and autonomic systems to enable integrated responses to the emotional significance of complex stimuli.

Maquet, Peters, Aerts, Delfione, Degueldre, Luxen, and French (1996) demonstrate similar regional circuitry in dreaming. They conclude that the amygdaloid complexes have reciprocal connections with many cortical areas which enable the amygdala to establish cross-modal sensory-affect association.

But the best evidence for the neuroanatomic validity of thing presentation phenomenology in psychosis comes from neuroimaging hallucinated patients. Silbersweig et al. (1995) demonstrate a hallucination circuit with many of the same regional areas of the thalamus, striatal-limbic-hippocampus, orbitofrontal cortex, and association and secondary sensory cortex. This work provides a neuroanatomic and neurophysiologic validation for my phenomenological description of hallucinatory thing presentations. Silbersweig et al. show them to be real sensorial events in association with affect and conceptual areas of the brain. For a summary of imaging studies in auditory hallucinated states, see David (1999). For clinical elaborations of this idea, see Brockman, 1998.

In recent years, there has been accumulating evidence for brain correlations with thing presentation phenomena. Morris et al. (1996) shows that the amygdala response to fearful faces increases with the intensity of emotion. Kosslyn (2003) summarizes a number of different studies to reach the conclusion that visual mental imagery activates primary visual cortex. Sacco and Sacchetti (2010) ask if emotional memory is stored in the secondary sensory cortex and show that, for sensory stimuli associated with highly charged emotional situations, the sensory takes on affective qualities. They conclude that "although emotional meaning storage is a matter of debate, nonetheless secondary sensory cortices support memory storage retrieval of sensory stimuli that have acquired a behavioral salience with experience." Zatorre and Halpern (2005) show that auditory cortex can be recruited for imaginary music. Raballo and Laroi (2011) describe abnormal sonorization of the inner dialogue and perceptualization of thought found at the beginning of the prodromal phase of psychosis. Colibazzi (2015, 2017) is showing that in the connectome between the temporal lobes and the frontal lobes, and thalamus, of psychotic and pre-psychotic patients, there is decreased neural traffic from word presentation language centers and increased traffic from object assembly areas.

These studies increasingly validate the idea of thing presentations as a sensory emotion by showing their neurophysiology to involve the sensory cortex. This is a neurological validation of their experiential qualities of perceptual reality.

22 Ego Functions

Thing Presentation Quality

Thing presentation means not just the concrete image, but most importantly, a quality of experience. The quality is that of an intense perceptual experience of reality condensed with intense affect. A reality thing is used for emotional metaphor, but the metaphor has the quality of a reality experience. Thing presentation quality refers to the affect-perceptual quality of reality experience. Affect is thus also experienced as part of the reality experience of the thing. Thing presentation quality is a condensation of both affect quality and perceptual quality.

The phenomenon also includes a displacement of the quality of felt reality away from the concept or the emotion and onto the perceptual qualities of the thing itself. Experience of reality, experience of emotion, and experience of the quality of reality are all condensed together but experienced as a property of the thing and not of how one feels about the thing. Emotional validity and veracity have moved out of the realm of emotional experience into a validity and veracity experience of reality. Children sometimes think this way.

Example:

A 6-year-old girl complains to her parents, not about the sleeping arrangements of the family, but about the actual beds. "How come you two get the most comfortable bed in the house?"

In the primary process, then, the quality of felt reality is attached to the thing. In psychosis, this reality quality is consciously experienced and is in the manifest content of thoughts. In delusional illness, if secondary process logic is not disrupted, thing presentation quality may be the only aspect of primary process thinking present to indicate the condensation of reality experience with emotional experience.

Where in consciousness the quality of reality is experienced depends upon the ego. Ego function determines whether the conscious quality of reality is attached to a thing, an affect, or a concept. Reality quality is characteristic of the different levels of illness, depending on how the illness affects the ego.

Psychotic patients often try to describe the perceptual reality experience of an idea in their delusion. They stress the reality, strength, and clarity of it, the conviction it carries, and the peculiar quality it has. They ascribe to the delusional idea all the qualities of the perceptual reality experience except standard visual, auditory, or somatic sensation.

Ego Functions 23

There are thus two aspects of primary process. One aspect is the thing presentation symbol itself, which is a condensation of psychological meaning with details of the physical thing taken from reality experience. The second aspect is the quality of reality that perceptual things have in our experience of them. This perceptual quality dominates the experience of feelings, and therefore of meaning, in the patient's experience of a psychotic or near psychotic condensation.

The concept of thing presentation describes an affective experience of wishes, fears, and their conflicts, together with experiential qualities of perceptual reality, that are rigidly bound and contained within the confines of the concrete symbol. In the primary process, the thing presentation is concrete. However, very ill patients experience the concrete as real. Damage occurs to the ego's translating mechanisms between thing presentations and word presentations, primary process and secondary process, percept and concept, affect and concept, affect and percept, and emotional experience and reality experience. The task of the analytic therapist in psychosis and near psychosis is to diagnose the specific form, causes, and associated illness of the ego damage and to treat it with medication and words. This is in addition to the usual analytic task of understanding the content and origin of mental conflict.

Pictorial symbolic thinking has advantages and disadvantages. It may be that the aphorism "a picture is worth a thousand words" is a description of a certain necessity of emotional experience. For affects and their plastic integrations, thing presentations may well be able to express emotional experience and creative transcategoricals better than words. This is why metaphor is so powerful and so adaptive. It can express and synthesize many different aspects, conflicts, and levels of mental life.

However, a picture is ambiguous. It contains within it many different feelings and conflicts. It expresses many different complexities of relationships among feelings and between feelings and reality. It must be translated for precision and for causality, especially sequential causality in reality experience. The treatment for all thing presentations is to decode them by translating into words the metaphorical image that has invaded reality experience or behavior (Table 1.3). This will allow

Table 1.3 Thing Presentations

A condensation of percepts, affects, and concepts
A perceptual symbolic representation of affect–concepts
A sensory emotional experience
A transmodal condensation of unconscious conflict
Integration Processes
Secondary process: concept related to affect.
Primary process: concept condensed with affect.
Thing presentation: concept and affect condensed with percept.

24   Ego Functions

concept and affect, reality experience and emotional experience, to separate. Translating mechanisms are broken in different ways in psychotic and near psychotic illnesses. To release the emotions contained, translate thing presentations into words and concepts. Affects will then emerge as feelings. Describe them in context with the relevant realities and emotions of present and past (Varese et al. 2016) (see Chapters 7 and 8).

Agency Contents

Psychological content is divided by psychoanalysis into content areas called *agencies*. *Id* is the name given to drive content (Freud, 1923; Schur, 1966). *Superego* is the name given to certain aspects and functions of conscious content. *Ego* is the name given to certain reality mediating functions, experiences of emotions and defenses against emotions, and regulations between the two areas of reality and emotion. All agencies deal in their own way with aspects of reality and emotions; all have aspects that are conscious and major areas that are unconscious. Because of this overlap, the agency labels refer only to psychological content and function.

An understanding of agency content is important, because all symptoms—neurotic, near psychotic, and psychotic—are composed of conflicts within or between agencies, which are symbolically altered. The symptom is the disguised symbol, which is derivative of the agency conflict and constitutes a compromise formation between agencies. In psychosis and near psychosis, as well as in some neurotic symptoms, one of the elements of the compromise symptom is a condensation which involves reality experience. This condensed reality experience takes a particular structural location in psychosis and near psychosis which differentiates it from the neuroses.

Boundary between Psychic Agencies

Although mental functioning is normally an integrative blend of all agencies, this integration requires regulation of the contribution of each. Such integration requires flexible, porous, subtle, but definite boundaries between psychic agencies. These boundaries are special boundaries; they are permeable and permit integration; they always allow a relationship, but they usually prevent flooding of one agency's contents by another.

The mind should be able to repress from consciousness aspects of the agency categories of emotional experience called *id* and *superego* and *defensive ego*. There should be the ability to keep these emotional agency contents separate from reality experience and from perception. Although agency contents are mostly emotionally experienced categories, the boundaries between them should involve some autonomous regulating, modulating, and integrating functions.

Unconscious conflict among these agencies is etiologic in the neuroses. Condensations within and between these agencies and their conflicts, which then dominate conscious or pre-conscious reality experience, are characteristic of psychosis and near psychosis. Any boundary disturbance described between reality and fantasy includes the boundary problem between psychic agencies. The only reason a separate boundary function is listed here is that certain psychotic phenomena are dominated by one of the agency content areas as it floods into conscious or near conscious reality experience. Certain illnesses are characterized by the domination of one agency content area (see Chapter 5).

Defenses

The mind has specific emotional maneuvers to deal with charged and conflicted affects. Because these maneuvers are used as self-protection, they are called defenses.[7] Defensive apparatuses are preconscious, primary process, mental functions that organize emotional experience in an attempt to prevent flooding of the conscious mind with either too much or too painful emotional material. Defenses are primarily concerned with emotional states and intersect with reality experience mainly in terms of the emotion that is evoked by reality experience. Reality experience and secondary process predominate in organization of autonomous apparatuses. In defenses, emotional experience and primary process predominate in the organization. Defenses are emotionally organized and are not autonomous from emotional experience. They are crucial aspects of emotional experience.

The content of the defenses, how they are organized, the specific mechanisms used, and what is being defended against all vary according to individual, type of illness, phase of illness, and severity of illness. Some general statements can be made.

Defenses attempt to compromise mental conflict. Are psychotic and near psychotic defenses different from neurotic defenses? Put another way, are psychotic and near psychotic symbolic alterations composed of defenses or used defensively? When we try to apply the concept of *defense* to psychotic and near psychotic phenomena, a number of problems arise.

Defense has two meanings, depending on what is defended against. Defenses (e.g., repression, a basic defense) operate to screen mental conflict but also to regulate internal stimuli. In psychosis and, to some degree, near psychosis, this internal stimulus barrier function may be damaged. Likewise, the in–out barrier may be damaged. This use of the word *defense* is different from the defense against conflict that psychoanalysis speaks of in neurosis. This stimulus barrier problem, I believe, is in part due to a direct biological attack on an autonomous neuromental boundary. It is not primarily due to conflict formation, and as a result treatment may not involve only conflict resolution. However, defense

26 Ego Functions

against painful emotional conflict, the classic meaning of defense in neurotic illness, is also important in psychosis and near psychosis; but here, too, there are problems.

The problem is whether psychotic and near psychotic defenses are different from neurotic defenses, and if so whether the difference involves defenses against reality in psychosis and near psychosis but not in neurosis. What is usually meant by the concept of defense against reality is a defense against reality *experience*. This does not actually distinguish neurotic from near psychotic from psychotic. The neurotic hysteric who represses the memory of a sexual incident, and the obsessive who "overlooks" a crucial, emotionally laden reality detail are both defending against aspects of reality experience. But in these cases, aspects of reality experience have been repressed into unconscious emotional experience. In psychosis and near psychosis, emotional experience, with its layered defenses, has invaded preconscious and/or conscious reality experience. Instead of, or in addition to, repressing reality experience, psychotic and near psychotic defenses alter reality experience in consciousness or near consciousness. Within the psychotic phenomenon itself, however, there may be layers of defenses that defend against more unconscious aspects of emotional experience: this is true in a delusion or hallucination. The delusion is usually a condensation of conflict. It is not necessarily more in conflict with reality than in a neurotic symptom, but, in psychosis and near psychosis, it is always a conflict erupting through autonomous ego boundaries into conscious or preconscious reality experience. Therefore, only the location of the conflict is different.

In the psychoses and near psychoses, reality experience is overwhelmed. Reality experience is usually overwhelmed in highly specific ways according to the emotional significance of the content of reality experience. This has led psychoanalysts to believe that the overwhelming itself is a defense against conflict. This theory, however, does not explain symptom-level, global psychotic states with fusion experiences determined by reality stimuli, and the action of medication.

Defense as a concept describes neurotic illnesses where a childhood experience, whether factual, emotional, or both, underwent repression from consciousness because of conflict and anxiety. The emotional reaction reappeared in the form of a primary process organized symptom, containing the memory of the original event(s) and their conflicted feelings, highly disguised by the defensive alterations. The symptom does not impinge on conscious, adult, reality experience, even though it may affect behavior. At worst, it impinges on the emotional experience of adult reality, and even then, mostly preconsciously and especially unconsciously.

Although it is true that psychotic and near psychotic phenomena contain psychological conflict in their structures, ego boundary functions that should be independent of emotional conflict lose the ability to contain emotional conflict away from conscious reality experience. This distinguishes psychosis or near psychosis from neurosis or conscious fantasies (see Table 1.4).

It is more parsimonious to say, therefore, that psychosis and near psychosis involve defenses that have erupted through autonomous ego boundaries and functions. This leaves the etiology of the ego dysfunction open, and a search for direct (biological) as well as indirect (psychological) causes can ensue. A brain tumor, a drug, or a metabolic alteration can all cause forms of psychosis and near psychosis. Focusing on the relationship among defenses, conflict, and autonomous ego from the viewpoint of autonomous ego is more congruent with descriptive psycho pathology, physical pathology, neuropsychological studies, medication effects, and necessary psychoanalytic treatment parameters.

The degree to which reality experience alteration is due to conflict and defense against conflict, or the degree to which reality experience alteration is used in the service of defense, in fact, varies according to illness type, severity, and phase. In general, however, there is a direct attack on ego function that is biological and neuromental instead of, or in addition to, psychological conflict and ensuing defensive maneuvers.

However, psychotic and near psychotic process can be used defensively and contains defenses in its structure. And conflict can be part of etiology in terms of vulnerability, just as there is an as yet unclear biological vulnerability.

The exact relationship among stress, temperament, psychological conflict, and psychosis or near psychosis is unknown. My own clinical experience tends to indicate a spectrum of vulnerability (Weil, 1978) from little or no discernable stress or consistent psychological conflict to highly specific stress and conflict. For patients at this latter end of the spectrum, combined psychological and biological treatment or, in some cases, just psychological treatment, is crucial. In all cases, however, otherwise autonomous ego functions are damaged and/or captured.

Table 1.4 Defenses in Psychosis and Near Psychosis

Defense Against	Defense Location in Psychosis	Defense Location in Near Psychosis	Defense Location in Neurosis
Reality experience	Conscious	Preconscious	Unconscious
Deeper layers of emotional experience	Conscious and preconscious	Preconscious and unconscious	Unconscious
Observing ego	Conscious and preconscious	Preconscious	Preconscious
Integration	Conscious and preconscious	Preconscious	Preconscious

28 Ego Functions

Regardless of the etiology of the autonomous ego deficits, emotional conflicts and defenses are phenomenologically very apparent in psychotic and near psychotic states. But the striking thing is always their effect on reality experience. The flooding of reality experiences is due to any or all of the following autonomous ego problems:

1   Boundary disturbances between reality experience and emotional experience;
2   Contamination of perceptual representations by emotional representations and consequent acquisition of reality experience quality by emotional quality;
3   Loss of secondary process integrating and translating ability.

Defenses, being primary process, are usually less disrupted in their organization in psychosis and near psychosis than autonomous functions. One can see this most clearly in a patient's defensive organization and content as the patient recovers and moves from psychotic organization to neurotic organization, without necessarily changing the content of his or her defenses.

Defenses are more important than damaged ego boundaries in psychosis and near psychosis when they defend against the observing ego and against some aspects of the integration of emotional experience. These, however, are particular defenses at particular spots in the psychotic and near psychotic structure. They are usually more important in near psychotic than in psychotic phenomena (see Chapters 2 and 3).

To summarize so far—defenses are for two purposes: one is primary, involves repression, and is merely an inner stimulus barrier for material that is never conscious. The other is a defense against conflict, aspects of which were at one time conscious. The first is an autonomous ego boundary. The second is an emotional, primary process, preconscious experience characteristic of individual neurotic symptoms and personality. Both are usually involved in psychosis and in near psychosis.

In psychosis and near psychosis, autonomous ego boundaries fail to keep the conflict (1) away from reality experience (always); (2) repressed (usually); (3) under dense disguise (usually); and (4) integrated (usually).

In *psychosis*, defenses condense with conscious aspects of reality experience, and reality testing is lost.

In *near psychosis*, defenses condense with aspects of reality experience, but only preconsciously and reality testing is not fully lost.

In *severe psychosis*, the stimulus barrier is damaged, and reality stimuli from without and emotional and perceptual stimuli from within determine reality experience and are called fusions.

A major emphasis of this book is that damaged autonomous apparatuses primarily, and the ego defensive mechanisms only secondarily, determine the organizational structure of experience in the psychoses and near psychoses.

The Primary Process and Conflict

The relationship of agency content, conflict, and defense to the primary process form of symptom formation and symbolism is a topic of psychoanalytic disagreement. For me, the problem is that conflict is a categorical process with feelings and contents from different categories in conflict with each other. The primary process, however, is unitary and transcategorical in its form. Primary process, therefore, is a phenomenon that synthesizes conflict as well as being composed of conflict elements.

Primary process symbolically alters and transcategorizes in its condensations. To *transcategorize* means to categorize across logical category boundaries creating something new and different. Condensations are groups of emotional associations transcategonzing and hence synthesizing categories of emotional conflict, day residue, the present, and the past. The term *compromise formation* (Brenner, 1976) expresses the concept of conflict but takes no particular notice of the synthesis. That is, it takes no particular notice of type, location, or quality of the compromise.[8] Condensation is a specific term for a primary process form of compromise.

In psychosis and near psychosis, synthetic aspects are primary processed condensations, dramatically available and specifically organized, are specifically located, and have certain specific qualities.

The synthesis is in the primary process symbol. The conflict is in the dissociations between the symbol and the rest of emotional and reality experience, and also, in the classical sense, when the symbol content itself is psychoanalyzed into parts that are in conflict. But conflict elements within the symbol are condensed in different types of psychotic and near psychotic synthetic processes that are typical of different types of psychotic and near psychotic illnesses.

Psychotic and near psychotic patients often feel they have special access to new transcategorical syntheses and therefore experience their psychotic and near psychotic phenomena as revelatory. They are not wrong, but it is an emotional revelation which they experience as a reality revelation. The psychoanalyst can help the patient understand the emotional revelation and thereby help the patient separate revelation from reality experience. It helps if the psychoanalyst does not immediately analyze the parts of the conflict within each symbol before understanding the newly revealed synthetic solution in the psychotic and near psychotic phenomenon, and the revelatory quality of that experience.

Object Relations

The mind tends to organize its functions of compromise, defense, agency, symbolic representation, and affect into mental experiences of people and their relationships. Freud used the term *object* to describe the object of the drives. But it was Klein (1940) who described early fantasies of these objects in relationship to self and object representations. Her early defenses were mechanisms that operated on the basis of these fantasies of self and object representations. Jacobson (1964) described the relationship of object relations to the self, psychic structure, and development, an endeavor continued and expanded on by Kernberg (1976b). I will not discuss the exact relationship in the history of psychoanalytic theory of object relations to drive, structure, function, memory, and reality experience (Modell, 1968; Pine, 1990), because I am concentrating on the ego function aspect of descriptive phenomenological theory in psychosis and near psychosis. However, I will discuss the distinctions between fantasy and reality objects, presentation and representation of objects, conscious and unconscious objects, and ego dysfunction and object relations.

The experiences of oneself and other people, combined with memories, fantasies, and feelings about these experiences, are called object relations (see Table 1.5). Descriptions and hypotheses about their reception, recording, organization, and elaboration through development and symbolic transformations are called object relations theory. The term *object relations* includes one's view of others (object representations) and also of oneself (self representations).

An object relationship can be conceptualized as composed of a self representation in an emotional relationship (affect) with an object representation (Fairbairn, 1952; Kernberg, 1976b; Sandler and Sandler, 1978) and contains id, ego-defensive, and superego elements in both the object representation and the self representation (Schafer, 1968b).

Aspects of object relations experience are in the experience of objects in reality and in feelings about objects in our emotional experience.

I will ascribe the experience of object relations to the ego, both reality experience and emotional experience, both conscious and unconscious (Schafer, 1968b). Psychoanalysts do not agree about this. Aspects of content and affect are determined by agencies other than the ego, but whether actual felt experience can occur in other agencies than the ego depends on definitions of id and unconscious that have never been agreed upon. For the more severe illnesses, which disrupt ego function, and for this book, which focuses on ego function in those illnesses, it is most helpful to look at the ego aspects of the experience of object relations. Autonomous ego functioning disturbances result in the most profound and dramatic disturbances in the ego's experience of object relations.

In the ego, there are conscious elements of attributes of the object in reality, conscious aspects of memories, fantasies, and feelings that these

Ego Functions 31

Table 1.5 Object Relations Definitions

I

A Object in reality

1 Behavior and feelings of others as they act in the real world and as they really feel
2 Occurs outside the mind

B Self in reality

1 Our real stimulus properties. How we are in reality, including our behavior in reality
2 Ourselves in the real world; our physical presence

C Thing in reality

1 Stimulus properties of the real world of the inanimate
2 Outside the mind; the actual physical thing

II

A Real object

1 Recording in the mind of outer reality of others
2 The inner experience of others in reality
3 Mostly conscious

B Real self

1 The inner experience of our real selves
2 How we experience ourselves to be in reality
3 Mostly conscious

C Real thing

1 The inner experience of external reality stimuli of inanimate things
2 Mostly conscious

III

A Object representation

1 The inner, emotional experience of another
2 Our hopes, fears, and fantasies of others
3 Mostly unconscious

B Self representation

1 Our inner, emotional experience of ourselves
2 Our hopes, fears, and fantasies of ourselves
3 Mostly unconscious

C Thing representation

1 The emotional experience of inanimate things
2 The representation of inanimate things as determined by the feelings they evoke
3 Mostly unconscious

objects evoke, and large unconscious areas of memories, fantasies, and feelings. I believe attributes of the object in reality are also stored in unconscious object representations. Everything that has been said about object representations holds equally true for self representations.

The crucial point is that distortions that will be described for psychosis and near psychosis occur not only in the unconscious realm of object relations but also, because of autonomous ego dysfunction in very ill patients, in the conscious part of object relations. The illness affects integration, relationships with each other, and most crucially, the relationship between reality experience of objects and the emotional experience of object representations.

We shall see the distortions and characteristic integrations of these object relationships in very ill patients. Typical distortions, typical emotional experiences, typical contents, and typical integrations guide treatment.

In summary, the term *object relations* refers to (1) an external self or object that is (2) represented in the mind and also to (3) an internal, emotional view of oneself and objects. The term usually refers to conscious, preconscious, and unconscious aspects of 2 and 3 but may refer to 1, 2, and 3.

Object Relations: Boundaries

Now we have a problem. The term *object relation* is most unclear in psychoanalysis because it refers both to inside and outside and also to two different kinds of inside experience. These phenomena are condensed in the unconscious of neurotic patients who consciously have the ability to tell the reality experience aspect of object relations from the emotional experience aspect.[9] Psychoanalysis focuses in neurosis on the unconscious, and therefore the ambiguity of the term with regard to reality versus emotion is no disadvantage. In sicker patients, however, we must distinguish, because they consciously do not. I will do so now by using different terms to describe the different ego aspects of the object world experience that are important in understanding psychotic and near psychotic patients.

The *object in reality* will refer to the stimulus properties of the real world. In the realm of people, *objects in reality* will refer to people in reality, to their behaviors in reality, and to their feelings as they feel them. The *object in reality* does not refer to a mental experience of the patient. It refers to stimulus properties of the external world. It includes inanimate things in reality.

The *real object* will refer to the recording of this outer reality in the mind of the patient. This is the inner mental experience of reality.

The *object representation* will refer to emotional experience. The object representation contains fantasies, hopes, and fears.

The same is true for the self in reality, the real self experience, and the experience of the self representations. How we are in reality is not the same as how we experience ourselves to be in reality, nor is it the same as our self representation composed of our hopes, fears, and wishes about ourselves.

Much of the real self or real object experience is usually conscious. Most of the self or object representation is usually unconscious (see Table 1.5).

There are two further confusions. One is the confusion between using "self" to mean self representations but also to mean the total self of all emotional, inner experience, including object representations, self representations, and one's own view of one's self in reality. I will avoid especially using *self* to mean the totality of all mental life in order to avoid confusion when discussing condensations and fusions between elements of total self experience. I will also avoid the use of the term *self* when I mean self representation experience. The second confusion in reading the literature on object relations is that it is usually unspecified whether the phenomenon under discussion is conscious or unconscious. Such specificity is crucial to discussions of psychotic or near psychotic phenomena. In neurosis, usually the author is referring to unconscious phenomena. But in psychosis and near psychosis, these phenomena are conscious, and this fact is crucial in understanding and treating the ego structures that organize psychotic and near psychotic experience.

Because of these confusions, when one reads in the psychoanalytic literature that in psychosis the self is merged with the object, it is impossible to know what is meant. With various authors, various phenomena are meant. I will try to be careful to specify. An example of the confusion that results when specificity is not adhered to is when "self and object fusion" is used to mean "self representation merged with object representation." This is actually relatively healthy on the ego scale of psychotic and near psychotic phenomena. Both self representation and object representation are emotional experiences, not experiences of reality. For reality to be contaminated, there must be a further step into real self or real object.

Disturbances of the boundary between reality experience and emotional experience cause *merger*. Two types of merger have been described: fusion and condensation. In *fusion*, the outside object in reality merges with some inside experience, usually with many inside experiences. The mental result is determined by the stimulus properties of outside. In *condensation*, the two merged experiences are already inside the mental apparatus but more importantly, the merger is determined not by stimuli in reality but by emotional significance. The merger of condensation tends, therefore, to be at specific and limited points of internal experience. These points are symbolic because they express emotional significance in their content and perhaps in their processes.

It is important to realize that in both types of psychotic merger, fusion and condensation, the merger is occurring in the conscious area of the ego experience of reality. This is what makes psychoses so dramatic and so different from neuroses. The relationships of the object in reality to real object to the object representation and the corresponding relationship in the self representation system are mostly unexplored in psychoanalysis. I will provide no systematic description now other than the definitions I just gave. Using these definitions, I will explore for psychosis and near psychosis the relationship of the real object to the object representation, the real self to the self representation, the real self to the object representation, and the self representation to the real object. This is because the most common disturbances, and the psychoanalytically interesting symbolic alterations, are at these loci in psychosis and near psychosis (see Chapters 2 and 3).

In summary, ego boundaries between real object and object representation, real self and self representation are the boundaries between the experience of reality and the experience of emotions in the area of people and relationships. When these boundaries go, psychosis and near psychosis ensue. The crucial conclusion to be drawn from this description is that the ego organizes the forms of object relations.

In the neurotic illnesses, the therapist is dealing only with unconscious aspects of the object representations and self representations and their emotional connections. Reality memory, if condensed in the representation, is unconscious.

The therapist of very ill patients needs to attend to badly distorted conscious elements because of the effect of illness on what should be primary autonomous ego apparatuses and boundaries. In very ill patients, the object representation or self representation overwhelms the part that is real object, or real self. The content of the overwhelming is conscious at the point of the overwhelming. Only the process, the fact of the overwhelming, is unconscious either descriptively or dynamically or both.

I will now summarize the relationship of the real object to emotional feelings in the various illness states, from psychotic to neurotic.

Hierarchy of Organization of Real Object: Psychotic to Neurotic

1 Psychotic: merger occurs; in condensation type of merger, consciously cannot tell the difference between real object and feelings about the object called the object representation, between symbolic transformations of the real object based on feelings, and the reality experience of the object; i.e., between real object and object representation, between real self and self representation, or between real object and self representation.

2 Near psychotic: consciously can tell the factual difference but consciously does not care because the contents of real object and object representation or real self and self representation are condensed just below awareness in preconscious, latent content; this latent condensation is compelling and overwhelming in its emotional effect on conscious reality experience.

3 Very ill neurotic: consciously can tell the difference and does care, but preconsciously wants to change the object in reality as if that would change the inner real object.
4 Healthier neurotics and normals: consciously can tell the difference and no great preconscious push to actualize (to change the real object); effective separation of conscious aspects of real object from unconscious levels of object representation.

In summary, then, the ego's alteration of reality experience in object relating takes place (1) in the psychotic: in manifest content of conscious material; (2) in the near psychotic: in preconscious upper layers of latent material; (3) in the neurotic: in unconscious deeper layers of latent material as seen in free associations, dreams, parapraxes, and highly disguised in daily interpersonal life.

The psychotic and near psychotic are distinguished from neurotic and normal by the part of a person's mental organization in which the experience of the object representation occurs. This distinction involves boundary apparatuses that should be autonomous. Chapters 2 and 3 describe how these distinctions are organized in psychotic, near psychotic, and neurotic structure. Chapters 7 and 8 will describe the implications these differences have for psychoanalytic psychotherapy. Some attention in treatment must be paid to how the real object is handled, because psychodynamics, the way one feels, can be similar in all of these states and yet the manifestations can be so different. Attention to the dynamics of feelings may not deal with the alterations of autonomous boundary and other apparatus dysfunctions that determine psychotic and near psychotic experiences of the object representation.

Symbolism, Symbolic Representation, and Symbolic Alterations of Reality

Symbolism means one element standing for another. The simplest symbol is a signal that stands for something in a one-to-one relationship. Complex signals have many parts used to signal. In addition, they may refer to more than one referent, or to a referent with a number of parts. There is always a specific number of referents with an exact, specifiable, even mathematical relationship to the signal. In both simple and complex signals, the form the signal takes may be related to the form of the referent or it may be arbitrary. In either case, signals are usually chosen from conscious reality experience and always according to some logical rules of secondary process.

The expression to *represent* or *symbolically represent* is used by psychoanalysis instead of the terms to *signal* or *stand for* (cf. Beres and Joseph, 1970). To represent, however, is different from signaling. A symbolic representation stands for many, perhaps unlimited, referents. There

36 Ego Functions

is a relationship of theme and not of number. Representation can also imply that what is stood for is actually pictured or represented, albeit changed. This implies a relationship between manifest and latent contents which psychoanalysis has never clarified. I believe the relationship is specific in psychosis and near psychosis.

Symbolic representation may mean either a reality representation, an emotional representation, or both (Yaholom, 1967). The symbolic representation's form and content are not consciously chosen in psychoanalytic symbols. The organization of the symbol is usually a primary process. The symbol is always experienced emotionally, not just consciously but also unconsciously and preconsciously, where *unconscious* means not just subliminally unconscious (unchanged in form and content) but dynamically unconscious (changed in form and content). The form and content of the experience are different at different levels of consciousness.

The relationship of reality experience to emotional experience is unspecified, but the term *represent* implies one in the other. The representation may be mostly an emotional representation in form and content.[10]

Symbolic representation is a broad term. All self and object representations in usual psychoanalytic usage are symbolic representations because they are composed of mixtures of reality, fantasy, memory, percept, and affect. It is these components, their various integrations and illness caused disintegrations, however, that need to be precisely described in order to understand psychotic and near psychotic phenomena.

The broad term *symbolic representation* includes symbolic processes and nonhuman contents not always implied in the term *object representation*. In addition, the term *symbolic representation* correlates with other fields psychoanalysis ought to interact with such as philosophy (Langer, 1942; Cassirer, 1955; Werner and Kaplan, 1963; Kuhns, 1983), anthropology (Obeyeskere, 1990), and art (Waldheim, 1984). (For an introduction to the literature on symbolism, see Jones [1912]; Symons [1925]; Langer [1942]; Ferenczi [1952]; Cassirer [1955, 1979]; Matte-Blanco [1959]; Panel [1961]; Werner and Kaplan [1963]; Blum [1978]; Segal [1978]; Loewald [1988]; and especially Bucci [1997]; Aragno [1997]; on the development of the symbolic process, see Piaget and Inhelder [1958]; and Sarnoff [1976, 1987]).

If emotional experiences use reality experiences for symbols, then reality experiences are changed in order to convey emotional meaning. Percept, content, and sequence or context of the reality thing or object, or a combination of these features, may be changed. An example of sequence or context change is a group of things collected according to emotional theme rather than logical category: this is the primary process. An example of change in the content of the thing itself is a change in details of form.

I will call symbolic representations that alter reality experience *symbolic alterations of reality*. This has crucial relevance to psychotic and near psychotic phenomena. The ego helps organize symbolic forms. Because the ego is changed by various types and degrees of psychiatric illnesses, the organization of symbolic forms will also be changed. This change will be characteristic of the specific illness and level of illness. The important aspect of symbol formation in psychosis and near psychosis is the use of and alteration of conscious or near conscious reality experience. This is because emotionally determined symbolic alterations invade and dominate reality representations. The symbolic alteration of reality in psychosis and near psychosis has a special locus, a special structure, and a special experience. This varies from illness to illness and will be described in Chapter 5. There are also commonalities that will be described in Chapters 2 and 3 on psychotic and near psychotic structure. For now, I will only describe the result in symbol formation of the ego function disruptions described in this chapter.

The ego organizes symbolic forms and uses. Ego problems of boundary, regulation, and secondary process integration permit a significant area of reality experience to be symbolically altered in the conscious and manifest content of reality experience. This determines the form of psychotic and near psychotic symbols.

The ability to use these primary process symbols varies with ego function. The ego functions especially pertinent are the abilities to abstract, generalize, apply, integrate, reality test, observe, and keep reality experience and fantasy experience separate. Ego functions important in use of symbols as symbols are as follows:

1   Ability to boundary (especially between reality experience and emotional experience, i.e., between percept, concept, and affect).
2   Ability to reality test.
3   Ability to abstract.
4   Ability to generalize.
5   Ability to apply.
6   Ability to observe.

Psychoanalysis has looked at emotional aspects of symbol formation, because neurotic patients can tell reality experience from emotional experience and also because the interesting aspects of neurotic symptoms are the preconscious and unconscious emotional symbols. The manifest, conscious symbolic elements are interesting in neurosis only because they refer to the latent content and condensations of deeper affects and conflicts. In neurosis, referents are unconscious. They are events and associated object relations in the past with associated painful, conflicted affects.

38 Ego Functions

Table 1.6 Comparison of Signals to Psychoanalytic Symbols

	Signal	Symbol
Form/content	From reality experience	From reality experience and/or emotional experience
Referent	Reality experience	Emotional experience
Organization	Secondary process	Primary process—condensations and displacements
Experience locus	Reality experience	Emotional experience and reality experience
Experience level	Conscious or subliminal	Referent always in dynamic unconscious, also usually preconscious, and sometimes conscious
Experience quality	Neutral	Affect-ridden or evoked, emotional qualities, often with thing presentation qualities

An emotional compromise appears highly disguised in the conscious aspects of the emotional experience of the neurotic symbol or symptom.

Psychosis and near psychosis are different because the emotional symbol has invaded and condensed with present and ongoing reality experience. The condensations occur at specific, meaningful points and emotionally alter reality experience at those points. Therefore, what aspects of reality experience are chosen, and what alterations take place, are symbolically meaningful. Understanding this meaning will enable an understanding of the emotional meaning, in the present as well as the past, of the psychotic and near psychotic symbol process and symbol content. This is why the manifest aspects of the symbolic alterations of reality in psychotic and near psychotic symbolic experiences are important. Because reality experience is specifically invaded at conscious condensation points, the symbolic alterations of reality in psychosis and near psychosis can be observed to be linked to the latent, emotional aspects of the symbol. These linkages occur at conscious condensation points of reality and fantasy.

Thing presentation symbols of this condensation have the reality quality originally borrowed from reality, especially sensory, experience, and the affect quality from emotional experience condensed. It is important to realize how much of the pertinent affect experience is encoded in the thing presentation symbol and experienced as a reality thing. This means that affect is experienced along with the perceptual experience of reality things. Therefore, the invasion into reality experience by this symbol has the thing presentation quality of perceptual experience, plus the emotional quality of affect experience, both in conscious reality experience, but the *organization* of primary process emotional experience.

A definition of all psychotic and near psychotic experience is that thing presentations reinvade reality experience by the condensation mechanism, resulting in specific and structured symbolic alterations of reality experienced in consciousness or near consciousness. This happens primarily because of ego boundary disruptions.

Symbolic processes are, in part, biologically determined by cognitive phases of maturation and developmental object relations phases. But object relations are also influenced by objects in reality and reality experience.

Specific illnesses within each of these categories have characteristic mechanisms of symbolic representation, and hence characteristic effects on the organization and content of symbolic alterations of reality experience. In addition, specific illnesses may have specific themes to the content of the reality experience alterations chosen. Therefore, this book is really a discussion of illness-specific symbolic alterations of reality (c.f. Kubie, 1953).

Notes

1 There are problems with subdividing mental experience heuristically into faculties or compartments, especially a compartment called *reality* experience. Mental life is integrative as well as compartmentalized; reality experience and perception are always influenced by emotion. However, the conscious mental experience of reality is often different from that of emotional feelings about reality. But conscious reality experience has its own typical mental organization and qualities. These are dramatically altered in psychosis and near psychosis. Although somewhat artificial, the focus on reality experience allows clinical descriptive accuracy for the purposes of accurate diagnosis and treatment of psychosis and near psychosis. The distinction between reality experience and emotional experience is clear in the conscious mental experience of normal patients and neurotic patients. Psychotic and near psychotic patients have difficulty experiencing a division between these two mental qualities. Psychotic and near psychotic illnesses involve reality experience alterations resulting from condensations of reality experience and emotional experiences that are typical for psychosis and near psychosis and their respective illnesses. In order to describe these particular condensations, it is helpful to describe their categorical components.

The division I describe is actually an old one in the philosophy of knowledge. Plato's categories were the real versus the ideal; Freud's categories were secondary process versus primary process.

The complications involved in this distinction arise not from the definitions, nor from the experience, but from the decision about which phenomena belong where. It is a decision that philosophers of knowledge have discussed for centuries. Psychoanalysts working with very ill patients can avoid this discussion if they wish, because psychotic and near psychotic patients have their own characteristic method of sorting and characteristic type of failure to sort.

40   Ego Functions

One difficulty in sorting phenomena into these two categories is the experience of the body. The body can be experienced as a source of reality stimuli external to the mind or it can be experienced emotionally. Emotions also have their place as "real" occurrences (see the Anton Chekhov quote in the epigraph at the beginning of this book), but they are internal in the experience of the mind.

Again, the careful study of psychopathology can be clarifying because the sorting and categorizing process is characteristic, not of our philosophy, but of patients and their illnesses. This book describes the effects of psychotic and near psychotic illness on mental sorting and categorizing.

2 *Reality experience*, as I use the term, requires superordinate or compound ego functions (see Hartmann, 1939, 1964; Bellak et al., 1973; Blanck and Blanck, 1986). The concept of superordinate ego function is reviewed extensively in Blanck and Blanck. They discuss the similar ego psychology concepts of synthetic function (Nunberg, 1931), executive function (Glover, 1958), and integrative function or organizing function (Hartmann, 1964). Complex ego functions working together are called *superordinate ego functions*.

3 Dr. Gregory Heimarck, faculty, Columbia University Center for Psychoanalytic Training and Research, pointed this out in his section on affects as part of the third-year theory course. He brought my attention to Plutchik and Kellerman (1980), and also Izard (1978). This is part of psychoanalytic general psychology (Klein, 1975; Rosenblatt and Thickstun, 1977).

4 In the *Project for a Scientific Psychology* Freud dealt with the issue of how we "decide if something is real or not" (1895, pp. 325, n2; Strachey's explanation). Laplanche and Pontalis (1967) point out the lack of a systematic description in Freud and the luck of agreement in the later psychoanalytic literature about the descriptive distinction of reality testing. Different authors stress different ego aspects from perception, to memory, to imagination, to quantity, to quality, to the more narrow comparison function (Frosch, 1964).

Laplanche and Pontalis point to two different meanings in Freud's use of the term: (1) a *distinction* between mental representation and perception, and (2) a *comparison* between mental representation and perception.

My own view is to limit reality testing to the comparison function, as is common in general psychiatry, because perception and representation in psychosis can show various alterations (the discrimination function) while the comparison function is always altered. The discrimination function in the psychotic symptom may be altered, but this is not limited to psychosis. There are nonpsychotic alterations of discrimination function in hallucinosis (see chapter 4), near psychosis (see chapter 3), eidetic fantasy, and, indeed, in all thing presentations that enter conscious experience (see chapters 1 and 2). For a review of the recent psychoanalytic literature, see Frosch (1983, 1990; Thoma and Kachele, 1985; see also Hurvich, 1970).

5 Freud (1900, chapter 6, section D) was interested in the variables determining the form of primary process condensation. He called this *representability* and defined it as "the selection and transformation of dream thoughts so as to make them capable of being represented by images" (Laplanche and Pontalis, 1967, p. 389). But psychotic and near psychotic patients select and transform reality so as to make reality capable of representing latent thoughts. How are the aspects of reality incorporated into the delusional systems and hallucinations chosen? Just as important day residue events, people, and things in the life of the psychotic and near psychotic patient are often chosen, reality elements are chosen because they are suited as images, pictorially, physically,

to symbolically express concepts. In this sense, representability means the selection of the day residue reality experience according to realities that are graphically capable of representing latent thoughts (Freud, 1900, 1958).

6 There is a major theoretical difficulty in applying Freud's observations about dreams to psychotic phenomena. Freud believed the day residue might be insignificant in reality experience. Some psychoanalysts restrict the concept to this view. The insignificant reality event then gains its emotional power, not by the present-day evoked emotion of reality, but through its past emotional significance. There are two ways this emotional significance can be achieved. One is that the day residue had an emotional similarity to a significant reality experience in the past. The significance of the day residue was, by association, an emotional displacement from the past event. The other way is that the physical characteristics of the reality event were well suited to represent the past emotional experience. The significance of the day residue is then a displacement from emotion onto physical details of the reality experienced thing or event. In either case, a repressed affect memory is stirred.

However, Freud did not restrict his concept of the day residue to the insignificant in reality experience. Although he said it was often insignificant in reality or even absent in reality experience and only present as a conscious or preconscious thought, day residue could certainty consist of significant reality experiences and evokers of strong emotional reactions in the present. This is amply illustrated in many of Freud's dream examples (1900). The role of present, emotionally provocative, reality experienced day residues is often neglected by psychoanalysts.

Traditional psychoanalytic interpretations of psychosis and near psychosis tend to look at the emotion and/or events of the past in hallucinations and delusions just as psychoanalysts do in neurotic symptoms. But many times, these events have an important echo in a reality, present-day event. This present-day event plays an important role in organizing the emotional structure of the symptom and even in triggering and organizing a psychotic or near psychotic episode. The triggering events can be identified because when they occur they become the day residues in the structures of psychotic and near psychotic phenomena and are characteristically encoded (see chapter 2).

7 For a complete discussion of the history of the concept of defense in psychoanalysis, see A. Freud (1936); Laplanche and Pontalis (1967); Brenner (1976). There are two arguments in the literature, one relevant to us and one not. The irrelevant one is between Anna Freud and Brenner. They disagree as to whether the defenses are limited to specific preconscious primary process maneuvers, or can involve any aspect of mental function. The former is somewhat Anna Freud's view and the latter is Brenner's. The second argument is whether psychotic illness is a defense, and whether the etiology of psychosis is therefore psychological conflict. A more complete discussion of this issue follows in chapter 2. Suffice it to say, as I have before, that autonomous ego usually is damaged independently of defense in the psychotic and near psychotic illnesses, allowing emotional defenses to dominate reality experience. When mental processes are used for defense, regardless of their original organization and function, they become subtly infiltrated with primary process content, organization, or use.

8 There are several terms that, while different, refer to aspects of the same phenomena. Freud (1900) called certain putting together processes of the primary process *condensation*. In this phenomenon, different "associations" or aspects are put together in a new form. Brenner (1976) uses the term

42 Ego Functions

compromise formation to mean putting together aspects of all agencies but not necessarily in or only in primary process condensation form. Waelder's (1936) principle of *multiple function*, from which Brenner's concept is derived, merely states that in analysis of a patient any one mental phenomenon can be shown to serve many purposes, e.g., the purposes of all three agencies.

The point for this book is that in psychosis and near psychosis, certain aspects of autonomous ego are captured; not just averaged like a vector, as in the compromise formation concept, but actually primary processed as in the condensation concept. Nersession (1989) makes a similar point about dreams. The *compromise formation* term takes no particular notice of level of consciousness, symbol elements, or primary process organization. It does not distinguish unconscious emotional experience from conscious reality experience. There can be no way, therefore, to define a psychotic compromise.

It is the ego which is the major organizer of the form of the compromise. In this sense, the ego is not coequal with other agencies. When the ego is damaged, the elements and the organization of the compromise formation will be different from when the ego is not severely ill. Furthermore, the specific illnesses, their type and severity, will have characteristic effects on the elements and organization of the compromise. For instance, primary process organization and thing presentation experience may predominate in psychotic consciousness. Compromise formation as usually described may be organized with secondary process revisions.

In addition, because *compromise formation* is so broad a term, it can easily be used to also imply etiology thereby equating psychotic and near psychotic illnesses with neurotic illnesses. The compromise formation does not cause a capture of reality experience in psychosis; the psychotic illness attacks and destroys the autonomous ego boundary and the resulting capture is the result, not the cause.

In summary, the term *compromise formation* may be reductionist: of etiology, process organization, element qualities, and symbol experience. This is especially so in psychosis and near psychosis, where such symbols are conscious, primary process, thing presentation experiences.

9 Klein (1940), who, after Freud, elaborated the concept of the object world, was actually quite clear about the relationship of objects to drive, representation, symbol, and reality. She understood that there is a difference between the real object, which she called the *actual object*, and the object representation. She elaborated on the object representation because this was the new contribution she had to make, just as Freud (1900) concentrated on primary process rather than secondary process.

Schafer (1968b, p. 142) describes the object representation as including the real object, thereby acknowledging the real object. I say the conscious mind should be able to distinguish a relatively autonomous real object from its emotional representations.

10 The term *symbol* in psychoanalysis has been debated and misunderstood. Freud (1900) first used the term *symbol*, as translated by Strachey, in his dream book to mean *signal*. Symbols were manifest content signals always referring to the same unconscious meaning. The meaning was a bodily experience. His term for what we now call *symbol* was translated as *plastic representation*, meaning condensation symbols with many referents.

Many psychoanalysts have followed Jones, who used the word *symbol* for what Freud called *symbol* but was really a signal (1948). Jones went one step

Ego Functions   43

further. He defined, along with Ferenczi, a psychoanalytic symbol (signal) as affect symbols.

My own view of these matters is that a psychoanalytic symbol is a primary process symbol (plastic representation), not a signal, and that is the only universal descriptive. The role of affect, level of awareness, and relationship to symbolic elements all vary. This is true in psychosis and near psychosis, in dreams, and in all other phenomena that have been used as definitional. In psychosis and near psychosis, the variations occur mainly because of the structure of the ego. I say, therefore, that descriptive aspects of all symbol formation depend on ego functioning. This can be observed in the various illness effects on symbol formation (see chapters 2 and 5). Elements that are conscious, preconscious, or unconscious and affect that is manifest, latent, encoded, or free-floating all vary with illness effect on ego functioning. For instance, in psychosis and near psychosis, affect may be free-floating and all-encompassing. *All-encompassing* means that it is experienced directly and affects all conscious mental contents. The affect may be free-floating and dissociated, experienced directly but separated from conscious contents. The affect may be experienced only as a thing presentation, consciously or preconsciously, but always in reality experience.

There is another problem in the psychoanalytic use of the term *symbol*. Freud meant, in his earliest use of unconscious symbol, the anemic symbol, in which there is a memory hidden and symbolized in the plastic representation of a symptom. That memory contains the unconscious affect. Some psychoanalysts restrict their use of the word *symbol* to this. In psychosis and near psychosis, the present is also symbolically represented. Freud also said the present was always important, even in the outbreak of hysterical neurosis.

Chapter 2

Psychotic Structure

Introduction

This chapter describes the common features of the psychological organization of psychotic phenomena. Although the psychoses are a variety of illnesses that have different mental organizations, they have two structural aspects in common: a loss of reality testing and a condensation of reality with fantasy. This condensation takes place in a particular way and is in a particular relationship to the rest of mental experience. This is why we can describe a category of mental experience called psychotic structure.

A *structure* is a mental organization that is specific and stable. Elements in the structure and relationships among elements are, therefore, reasonably predictable. This fact can guide diagnostic inquiry and treatment.

Neurotic, near psychotic, and psychotic structures differ with respect to what mental processes are involved, what areas of experience are involved, where in consciousness the processes are occurring, and whether certain autonomous ego apparatuses are involved.

Aspects of psychological structure may be conscious, preconscious, or deeply unconscious. Psychoanalysis, in describing structure, is usually describing the preconscious and unconscious structure so important in neurosis. In psychotic structure, however, important elements are in consciousness. Therefore I will describe not just stable mechanisms of psychotic processes but also their location in levels of awareness. I start with ego boundaries because these are crucial aspects in the organization of psychotic structures.

Autonomous Apparatuses

Boundaries

Four boundaries do *not* show universal changes in consciousness in psychosis: in–out, conscious–unconscious, primary process–secondary process, and affect–affect boundaries. Although changes in these four boundaries are common, the presence, degree, and role of the changes vary. Many analytic writers about psychosis consider them universal and pathognomonic, but I do not agree. When present, they are important and readily observed, but because they are not always present, focusing on them will limit the ability to make accurate general statements about psychotic structure. In addition, these four boundaries may be altered in nonpsychotic states.

In–Out Boundary

Acute psychotic states that are rapid in onset or wide in ego effect, some psychoses that are untreated, and some that have deteriorated may show complete loss of the in–out boundary. Outer and inner experiences fuse depending on the intensity of stimuli in the real world and/or the intensity of affect (see Chapter 1). An unstable, rapidly changing, chaotic mental state results. Some illnesses are more likely to produce severe damage to this boundary than others (see Chapter 5).

Although this boundary is not universally damaged in psychoses, the analytic literature says it is. Because fusion and condensation are not clearly distinguished, it is not clear whether the boundary refers to mental—outer world, or internal self—internal other boundaries.

Conscious–Unconscious Boundary

For this boundary also, there is no description universally true of all psychotic states. The degree of porosity of the repression barrier varies enormously, from extreme states with in–out boundary and conscious–unconscious boundary gone, to those tightly organized, logically contained, and rigid psychotic states where only thing presentation quality is contaminating conscious idea or sensation and merging with reality testing and reality experience.

Primary Process–Secondary Process Boundary

Here also, the contamination of logical thinking by primary process varies widely in extent, depending on illness type, severity, duration, and treatment. There is no universal description true of all psychotic structure. Some psychotic states show pure primary process organization with condensations, displacements, affective links, and thematic integrations between ideas. Other psychotic states are logical and tightly organized, operating almost entirely according to secondary process. This boundary problem thus varies according to illness type and severity.

46 Psychotic Structure

Affect–Affect Boundary

Again, damage to this boundary varies. Extreme, chaotic psychotic states may show affect fusions and dissociations, with intense discharges into impulses, like a string of firecrackers going off. Other psychotic states are tightly organized, rigidly repress affect, and show only a monotonal affect generalized to mood as in certain depressions.

Four ego functions that *are* universally affected, but variably so, are conceptualization, abstraction, generalization, and application. Concept moves out of abstraction and abstraction becomes concrete. Generalization and application are lost in the relationship to the psychotic area, and perhaps separated and sequestered in nonpsychotic areas of the ego. Application is affected separately and apart from the psychosis, as an aspect of nonpsychotic illness, or it is damaged secondarily because psychosis has concretely rendered the generalization. These changes are the first sign, and in some cases the only sign, of primary process intrusions in psychosis.

But the preservation of these ego functions in psychotic illness varies depending on the type and severity of the illness and on whether these ego functions ever developed. Because there is so much variation, all that can be said is that these ego functions are always damaged in some way in psychosis, but are not components of the psychotic structure. The next section describes the universal, always present, and invariable ego structure of psychotic experience (see Table 2.1).

Table 2.1 Ego Functions Affected by Psychosis

Universally Affected and Part of Psychotic Condensation

Reality testing
Reality experience, especially percept boundaries
Aspects of emotional experience
Secondary process integrity of day residue (becomes primary process)
Easy flow of fantasy and reality (becomes fixed at point of psychotic condensation)

Distinction between real object and object representation, or real self and self representation, or real self and object representation, or real object and self representation (become condensed)

Word presentation (shift to thing presentation; concept and affect shift to percept)
Symbolic processes (shift away from fantasy to use of reality)

Not Invariably Part of Psychotic Structure but Often Damaged

Secondary process integrity of day residue as to sequence and context (becomes dissociated)
Secondary process superordinate integration principles of the relationship of emotional experience to reality experience (becomes primary processed and/or dissociated)

In–out boundary
Conscious–unconscious boundary
Primary process–secondary process boundary
Affect–affect boundary

Universally Affected but Not Part of Psychotic Condensation

Conceptualization
Abstraction
Generalization
Application
Integration
Observing ego

Relationship of Reality Experience to Emotional Experience in Psychotic Structure

Chapter 1 describes the experience, content, and organization of different areas of mental life. Psychotic experience consists of specific mergers between areas that cross normally uncrossed, autonomous boundaries. This occurs in stable forms with predictable illness organizations, involving typical autonomous boundary problems (hallucinations and delusions are examples). The particular, stable, and predictable boundary problems that emotional experience and reality experience have in all psychoses I call *psychotic structure*.

Percept–Affect–Concept Boundaries

In psychosis, a boundary disruption universally and invariably occurs in the relationship of percept to other mental events. Protection and containment of percept boundaries fail. Affect and concept spread past percept boundaries to fuse transmodally with percepts. In psychotic states, concepts and affects initiate and organize percepts. Psychotic condensations involve percept–concept–affect condensations. Freud (1900, 1923) described this for dreams. These concept–affect–percept condensations I include in Freud's term *thing presentation* (see Chapter 1). They are the experiential form of the primary process. They give psychotic experience and psychotic ideas their powerful sense of validity because it is a sensory validity.

Where and how affect is experienced depends on ego function and structure. In psychosis, crucial affect experiences are transmodally processed and experienced as percept with thing presentation qualities of both reality percept and affect. An example is the psychotic patient who instead of saying he feels bad about himself says that he "smells like shit" and experiences himself as literally covered with feces, which he can actually smell.

48 Psychotic Structure

Condensation of Fantasy with Reality

Normal mental experience is a mixture of reality experience and emotional experience of various degrees, availabilities, and relationships. In psychosis, fantasy and reality are merged and indistinguishable by the patient, even with conscious effort. This merger is organized and structured by mechanisms of condensation around the reality experience of the day residue. This is the crucial aspect of the reality experience merger in psychotic structure.

Unfortunately, *reality* is a variously used term in psychoanalytic writings. It may refer either to the object in reality or to the experience of the real object. Some analysts include fantasy: so-called psychic reality (Arlow, 1985). It may also mean a specific, complex psychic reality experience called the day residue, an emotionally precipitating reality experience of events, their sequences, and contexts. This day residue plays an organizing role in dreams (Freud, 1900, 1917b). Because the day residue is often an event in reality, there is often a kernel of truth in psychotic phenomena (Freud, 1907). The term *reality* can also refer to this kernel. All different aspects of reality experience are differently encoded in psychotic structure.

Psychotic structure tends to locate and process the day residue real object experience quite differently from the day residue sequencing experience. The day residue object is usually in consciousness, undisplaced, but always condensed with fantasy in the manifest content. Day residue sequence and context may be disorganized but are usually only repressed subliminally into preconscious experience where they are often intact. In addition, primary process derivatives of event, sequence, and context are encoded in the psychotic material.

Delusions or hallucinations, like dreams, are stories. The stories relate to reality as well as to the patient's feelings. It can be hard to understand the delusional story because of the organization of the conscious story and because parts of the story are not conscious. Knowing where various parts of the story are and how they are encoded in the structure of delusions can be helpful in understanding delusional experience and communication.

An aspect of reality experience often evokes, or is incorporated into, the emotional experience a hallucination or delusion expresses. The hallucination or delusion expresses this through the particular transformation process of the particular reality experience chosen by emotional experience. The emotional experience and the reality experience are thus condensed. For this reason, we can talk about symbolic transformations of reality and their illness-specific forms. In a hallucination or delusion, there is usually a kernel of accurate reality perception and experience (Freud, 1907). This reality experience may be the precipitating event of a psychotic illness, just as it may be a day residue if a dream is precipitated.

The day residue precipitating event is usually a repetition in reality of an event or a fantasy meaning to an event that happened, in reality or emotionally, earlier in life, evoking the same strong feelings then as it does now. Psychotic patients condense these past and present feelings with reality experience in the present. This is another important example of the particular condensation phenomena of psychotic structure. Psychotic patients use these reality events not just as precipitants of emotional reactions, but also, because of the condensation between emotional experience and reality experience, as condensed symbols in their reality experience. The emotional themes play themselves out and are revealed in the patient's psychotic experience of reality, his or her behavior in reality, and reality's reactive behavior back toward the patient.

Reality, in delusions as in dreams, can be altered symbolically from a little to a lot. Major symbolic changes may be in manifest content as well as in latent content. This varies according to the type and severity of illness. Regardless, the merger of reality and fantasy and the loss of reality testing invade consciousness in psychosis.

Delusions and hallucinations vary in the relative amount of story material that is primary or secondary process, conscious or unconscious, organized or disorganized, changing or unchanging, with or without obvious reality day residues, and manifestly affectively ridden or ideationally ridden. The various illness states tend to produce psychoses that vary along these axes. Hence, the forms of symbolic alterations of reality are illness specific.

Dreams or delusions have three components in their structure. The first is the mental experience of perceived reality. This perceived reality involves both a perception of real people, called real objects (or real self), and of real event occurrences, sequences, contexts, and causalities. The second component is the feelings evoked by the reality experience (Freud, 1915b). These feelings are organized and include memories and emotionally associated ideas, wishes, and fears (Freud, 1900, 1917b). The third component is some psychological phenomenon that expresses the condensation of the first two components. The condensation takes the form of an image or fantasy. The third component is a symbolic alteration because of how the patient feels about reality based on what the perceived experience is, how the patient tends to feel, and what his or her past experiences have been. The third component may be a sequence of symbols dramatized to form a fantasy story, a dream, or a delusion. In psychosis, this third component becomes conscious and enters the experience of the first component.

Dreams or delusions can therefore be used for information about feelings, the unconscious, and the past. They can be used for information about emotionally relevant reality experiences and feelings in the present. They can be about the relationship between past and present.

Dreams contain wishes and conflicts (Freud, 1900); so do hallucinations and delusions. These wishes and conflicts determine psychotic content (Freud, 1915–1916). But to say that wishes and conflicts are therefore the sole cause of hallucinations and delusions is to equate phenomenology with etiology, and psychodynamics with psychopathology (for reviews of psychodynamics in psychotic illnesses, see Frosch [1990] and Gabbard [2014]).

In the normal person, perception of reality can be separated from feelings about reality. The normal person can consciously connect feelings with ideas and with reality perceptions without confusing the categories. Sometimes, in the normal person, condensation occurs so that category reality and category feelings become one and there is no distinction. But this occurs unconsciously, or in the form of a dream while asleep, or a fantasy while awake, with reality experience preserved. Only in dreaming or in waking psychotic experience is reality experience captured by emotional experience without reality testing.

In the neurotic, the condensation is unconscious but reappears in the form of an emotional experience. The symptom may be a fear, a behavioral avoidance, or a behavioral action. The condensation between reality and feelings remains unconscious.

In the psychotic patient, the condensation of reality experience with emotional experience appears in manifest content consciousness, including reality testing, and is dominating and predominant. This is the most important phenomenon of the structure of psychotic experience.

The psychotic experience is the experience of this condensation structure. The experience of *becoming* psychotic is the experience of this structure as it invades conscious reality experience and reality testing. The experience of *being* psychotic is the experience of this structure over time. *In summary, psychotic structure consists of primary process condensations between an aspect of reality experience, an aspect of emotional experience, and reality testing. This condensation is located in conscious reality experience.* The particular primary process mechanism of the condensation varies depending on illness and characteristic individual psychological mechanisms.

Reality Testing

As described in Chapter 1, reality testing is the mind's ability to compare its experience of perception and logic with its experience of feelings and to modify conclusions about the perceived world based on perceptions and logical conclusions rather than feelings. This capacity always is lost in psychosis. Where is this loss located? How is the loss organized? What form does the loss take? All of these factors play a special role in the condensations of psychotic structure.

Reality testing in the neuroses is relatively separate from the emotional structure of symptoms. In psychosis, reality testing is completely captured, in content and process, by an emotional content and process allowing a psychotic content and experience (Freud, 1924a, 1924b). Reality testing is then part of the psychotic structure. Although consciously still experienced as part of reality experience, reality testing in the psychoses has primary process rather than secondary process organization. Furthermore, the content in the reality testing area becomes merged with the emotional content of the psychotic process (see Table 2.2).

Loss of reality testing by merger with the content and specific primary processes of emotional experience is a central feature of the structure of psychotic phenomena: a delusion or hallucination.

Reality testing should be experienced apart from other experience, especially emotional experience but also, to some extent, separate from reality content. Reality testing should use secondary process, not primary process. When the boundary between the separate faculties of reality testing, reality experience, and emotional experience is lost, the combined psychotic experience invades and determines the process and content of conscious reality experience and reality testing.

Psychotic Structures

In psychosis, reality testing, reality experience, and emotional experience are all condensed in the psychotic structure.

Certain acute or severely chronic psychotic states in certain illnesses show fusion among these three elements. In such cases psychosis is only partly or even negligibly mediated by condensation. Such fusion states are not common, but they are extreme, neuromental difficulties. They are dependent for their content on stimuli in reality. Their symbolic processes are secondary or negligible. I will therefore omit them from the psychoanalytic description of psychotic structure.

The experience of psychosis can now be restated. Psychosis is the experience of a specific and organized condensation between a segment of reality experience and a segment of emotional experience, invading and capturing reality testing, content, and process, and experienced *in*

Table 2.2 Reality Testing in Psychoses

Location of loss of reality testing	Always lost in consciousness
Organization of loss of reality testing	Usually organized according to primary process
Form of loss of reality testing	Always a condensation of reality testing content and processes with emotional content

conscious reality. This is my definition of psychotic structure. The linkages are specific primary process condensation mechanisms among the three components: reality experience, emotional experience, and reality testing. These three components together form a psychotic structure when experienced as conscious reality experience.

The Day Residue in Psychotic Structure

We are now ready to further describe the structure of psychotic condensations. We will look again at the day residue because it structurally forms an organizing center in manifest content of those psychotic phenomena that are organized. I will now compare the day residue in a psychotic's delusion with the day residue in a neurotic's dream.

The day residue was first described by Freud (1900) as an important part of the psychological structure of dreams. The day residue is the reality experience that is the nidus around which latent feelings appear in the night's dream story and images. The day residue may be merely a conscious thought of the day, later repressed. Freud (1917b) said that usually the significant precipitating event of the dream was unconscious and appeared in the latent dream content, while a displaced, insignificant day residue appeared in the manifest content. My own observation is that this may or may not be true of dreams, but it depends on the type of dream. In some psychotic illnesses, the day residue is a potent traumatic evocator as well as a unique, individually relevant symbol. In other psychotic states, the day residue is negligible or abstract. In waking psychotic states, a significant day residue often appears undisplaced in the psychotic manifest content but is symbolically altered in the manifest content through a condensation with emotional experience. Freud (1900, 1917b) also said the day residue might be insignificant in reality, but it has strong emotional associations from infantile instinctual wishes that give it its power (see Chapter 1). But he also gives examples of day residues that would be potent evocators for anyone. The particular significance and power of reality for an individual is unique to that individual's associations. This is part of Freud's definition of a day residue.

The day residue concept contains two aspects of reality that are handled separately in psychosis. One is the reality experience of the self or object in reality. The other is the reality experience of the event with its sequences, especially cause and effect, and associated contexts. Sequence and context provide clues to reality meanings which trigger and shape emotional meanings. The reality sequence and context in normal people are processed consciously or subliminally, by the secondary process.

Because sequence and context may be upsetting triggers in psychosis, even more than the real object event occurrence, sequence and context are defended against. A crucial part of the therapeutic process is to reassemble the day residue sequence and context. Interestingly, and most important for psychoanalytic psychotherapy, the sequence and context are often not part of the psychotic structure but are dissociated and/or repressed and defended against by the psychotic structure. The day residue sequence may be captured in deeper areas of the delusion and handled by primary process, which contributes to difficulty with reality testing and to extreme distortions of reality, but is often also intact and unaltered, although dissociated and partially repressed.

In summary: psychotic structures, such as delusions, are like dreams in their structure, except that (1) reality testing is lost in the waking state; (2) the day residue object is usually undisplaced and always condensed with primary process fantasy in the manifest content of consciousness; (3) the day residue sequence and context are dissociated and partially repressed into subliminal experience where they are often preserved separately from the psychotic condensation structure. (In some acute organic psychoses, however, they may be disorganized and/or never registered. In these states, fusion is usually the dominant psychotic mechanism.) I describe sequence and context location so carefully because they are not a priori expected in considering psychotic structure, and because dissociation of sequence and context plays a crucial role in the psychoanalytic psychotherapy of these states. This will be described in Chapter 7. For now, it is only important to realize that psychotic structure may or may not contain sequence or context, but in addition, sequence and context are often preserved separately from psychotic structure (see Table 2.3).

Observing Ego

Although by definition reality testing is lost in the area of delusion formation, observing ego may be present. If observing ego is fully present, then

Table 2.3 Location of the Day Residue in Pathological Structures

	Psychosis	Near Psychosis	Neurosis
Structure	Delusion	Pseudodelusion	Dreams or symptoms
Day residue object	Merged in consciousness with emotional experience	Merged in the preconscious with emotional experience	Merged in the unconscious with emotional experience
Day residue sequence	(a) Disorganized (rare) or (b) dissociated and repressed into unaltered subliminal preconscious	Preconscious and primary processed	Conscious and unaltered or repressed and subliminal

the patient is aware that he or she has an illness and even that the delusional idea is part of the illness. However, the patient still believes in the delusion and will act on that belief. It is important to realize that observing ego may not be fully blocked by the psychotic process. If observing ego is lacking, it may be blocked by nonpsychotic character defenses rather than the psychosis. This means that the analytic therapist can use interpretation of character defenses to make observing ego more available and to attach the therapeutic alliance at that point. This is often the only point of attachment possible. Observing ego is often not captured by psychosis; it is not usually part of psychotic structure. Although it may be seriously overwhelmed, it is often not part of the psychotic condensation, and this contributes to the horror of the psychotic experience.

Object Relations

Object relations, the experience of our feelings in the form of people and stories about people, including ourselves, have both conscious and unconscious aspects in the ego. Clearly, the organization of the ego will affect the organization and experience of object relations. In psychosis, severe object relations disturbances occur. However, the different psychotic illnesses affect the ego differently. What can we say in general about psychotic object relations? In psychosis, reality experience and emotional experience of objects condense in consciousness. The location of this particular condensation in the conscious manifest content is a subdefinition of the usual type of psychotic structure.

Often, the experience of the real object condenses with object representations in the conscious and manifest content of an area of mental life. There are some psychotic illnesses that result in condensations of the experience of the real self with the experience of the self representation. Exactly the same rules hold as when the object is involved, except that the psychological content of the structure is self experience rather than object experience. This is particularly important in the affective illnesses (Chapter 5).

The psychotic condensation may, on occasion, involve the real self and the object representation, or the real object and the self representation. Rarely, there may be a condensation between the real self and the real object experience. Regardless of the exact components, in psychosis, an agent of reality representation is captured by emotional experience.

Much more rarely, the merger in manifest content occurs as a fusion between the object experience and the self experience. In psychosis, this fusion is between the object in reality and the real self experience. This is a different type of psychotic structure. It usually involves fusion, not condensation.

Example:

Doctor scratches own leg.
Patient says, "Why are you scratching my leg?"

All psychotic structure involves some merger, either condensation or fusion or both, in conscious, manifest content of object relations, which includes reality experience of aspects of the self and/or object system.

However, most psychoanalytic literature describes merger of self with object (Jacobson, 1964, 1967; Kernberg, 1986). This is ambiguous. Sometimes merger of self representation with object representation is specified and described as characteristic of psychosis. Under my definitional scheme, both self representation and object representation are emotional experiences. Their merger, whether condensation or fusion, would not be psychotic unless they were also merged with the reality experience of object or self. This can occur as multiple, changing, chaotic fusion states in some types of acute psychosis where the real object fuses with the real self. The more common situation, however, when aspects of self representation merge with aspects of object representation, is a condensation, not a fusion. Furthermore, if the condensation is of self representation and object representation, more commonly it is unconscious, as in neurosis, or preconscious, as in near psychosis. By far the most common mergers of self representation with object representation are, at the worst, near psychotic. The usual invasion occurring at the upper level of consciousness in psychosis involves the condensation of object representation with the real object or self representation with the real self. The different illnesses have different likelihoods of these different mergers (see Chapter 5; Table 2.4).

Table 2.4 Object Relations in Severe Mental Illnesses

Real self fusions with the object in reality and the self in reality	Some schizophrenias, especially acute
	Some organic brain syndromes, especially acute
	Severe mania
Real self condensations with the real object	Some schizophrenias
	Some extreme mania
	Some organic brain syndromes
Self representation condensing with real self	Severe depression
	Mania
	Some schizophrenias

56 Psychotic Structure

Table 2.5 Boundary Alterations in Psychoses

Always:	Increased porosity of boundaries between:
	Real object/object representation
	Real self/self representation
	Real self/real object
	Reality experience/emotional experience/reality testing
	Concept/affect/percept
	Symbolic representation/symbolic alteration of reality
	Dissociation with decreased porosity of boundary between psychotic condensation and intact autonomous ego functioning.

In summary: in the usual psychotic structure, real object condenses in consciousness with object representation or real self condenses with self representation. In chaotic, usually acute psychoses, real self experiences fuse with the stimuli from objects in reality (see Table 2.5).

Vertical Dissociations

Psychotic experience usually does not involve all areas of mental functioning. Reality testing is present in large areas. A patient can, therefore, have two very different conscious experiences of reality. Because the nonpsychotic reality experience does not affect the psychotic reality experience, although both are conscious, the two are said to be dissociated. Psychotic dissociations are constructed of areas of mental content in conscious reality experience that are separated from other areas of conscious mental functioning. In the dissociated psychotic area, reality testing is absent and condensations of reality experience with fantasy occur. The boundaries of the dissociation are often well delineated and stable.

I will use the term *vertical dissociation*[1] (see Fliess [1973] and Kohut [1971]) because the two dissociated areas are not only at the same level of consciousness but also because the psychological content of the psychotic area travels down into the preconscious. It does so in rather sharply defined and organized paths, with theme and affect consistent, rather than integrating horizontally with the rest of mental life at a given level of mental awareness. Vertical dissociation is almost always present in delusional structure and it is the major ego-integrative dysfunction of psychotic and near psychotic structure.

Splitting is a type of vertical dissociation based on separation of oppositely valenced affect, love versus hate, in the preconscious defensive emotional structure of the ego. *Vertical dissociation* is a more inclusive term and refers to an area of psychological content, sometimes with both positive and negative affect merged in each, but each one separated in conscious reality experience from the other conscious reality experiences, which then extends down into the preconscious and upper layer of the unconscious, maintaining the dissociation at those levels also. What we are describing, then, is one aspect of conscious experience unintegrated with other aspects of conscious experience.

In neurotic structure, two mental experiences are cut off from each other because one is not conscious but is behind a repression barrier away from the rest of experience in the conscious. The two experiences of psychological content are at two different levels of consciousness. This can be called a *horizontal dissociation* (Kohut, 1971). The only indication is a mysterious conscious symptom. The symptom may be experienced as "not-me," ego dystonic. Neurotic, ego dystonic symptoms are horizontal dissociations secondarily vertically dissociated only in the conscious, not-me experience. Character symptoms are pure horizontal dissociations and are not experienced as ego dystonic.

There are other failures of integration possible, from affect splitting to fragmentation to subtle discoordinations between levels of abstraction and their application. These usually apply to nonpsychotic areas as well as being distributed throughout the psychotic material and thus are nonspecific, i.e., have no predictable relationship to psychotic structure. Nonetheless, they are crucial to diagnosis, to specific illnesses, to empathic understanding, and to treatment.

Lack of integrative ego function is a crucial aspect of psychosis. Vertical dissociations are part of most psychotic structure, at the edges of the psychotic experience. A vertical dissociation is one type of lack of integration in the ego. In summary: stable psychotic structure is usually vertically dissociated from nonpsychotic structure.

Thing Presentation, Thing Presentation Quality, and Delusional Structure

Reality condensations with fantasy appear as the consciously experienced thing presentations of primary process thinking. The intensity, rigidity, stereotypy, and consuming quality of the delusional or hallucinated experience is due not only to the loss of reality testing and to the condensation of reality with fantasy, but also to the quality of thing presentation experience. The key experiential aspect of thing presentations is the quality of perceptual reality that is organized according to primary process rules and with primary process contents. There is a condensation of intense affects in an experience of a concrete, perceived thing that seems real. It is therefore quite consuming. The compelling quality of these percept experiences may not be apparent to the observer of the manifest content. For example, a patient wanted to kill himself because voices were calling him a bird.

The experience of the thing presentation, its affect, and its perceptual reality quality may be associated with additional dissociated conscious

58 Psychotic Structure

affect, unconscious affect, or disguised, conscious derivative affect. This will depend on the extent to which the psychotic process has infiltrated, disorganized, or spared the rest of the personality organization.

Affect has partly determined symbol choice, so the thing presentation represents affect and has an affect quality experience. In addition, affect plays a role in the aspect of reality experience chosen, and the affect experience therefore has a reality experience with a sensory component. Often, there is an overlap between psychotic experience and things in reality because the psychotic experience has chosen a things-in-reality nidus. The themes in reality objects occur over and over because the patient enacts in reality behavior the same psychological theme over and over because the themes repeat over and over in emotional experience. This leads to an uncanny experience of summation and to further recruitment of reality content and to affect intensification and further blurring of the ability of the autonomous ego to maintain reality testing. This is true of both psychosis and near psychosis. It is a particularly characteristic feature of psychotic structure and is the psychotic equivalent of the neurotic repetition compulsion.

Neurotic symptoms, in contrast, are disguised actions, avoidances, and fears, and are not consciously experienced as living thing presentations. The patient can speak of such symptoms more dispassionately, because the affect and perceptual quality in symbolic things are horizontally dissociated in the repressed unconscious and tend not to be available for conscious experience. There are summation cycles in reality experience, only in derivative form, especially in severe character neuroses.

A core component of psychotic structure, then, is the eruption into reality experience consciousness of a thing presentation. These are eruptions of specific, intense, emotional experiences contained in a concrete and specific symbol taken from reality experience. A thing is representing and providing an emotional experience. It has the reality quality of a percept but the primary process emotional organization of affect. It captures reality testing and is then vertically dissociated from the rest of autonomous ego function thus becoming a psychotic experience.

Therefore, we can again further summarize psychotic experience. It is the experience of a condensation structure composed of a specific segment of reality experience, a part of emotional experience, and reality testing, erupting into consciousness with the percept–affect quality of a thing presentation.

The real object and object representation condensation or the real self and self representation condensation is experienced as a thing presentation involving the perceptual features of the real self and real others.

The condensation is a *process*. The thing presentation is a modality; a specific visual image and also a felt quality.

Example:

A middle-aged homosexual man is hospitalized with the delusion that his face is swollen. The illness occurred after his lover left him for a younger man. Because the patient's self-esteem has always been concentrated in his physical appearance, and because his lover left him for a younger man, the patient experiences himself as no longer beautiful, especially in comparison to the younger man, who he thinks is more beautiful and thinner. Because the lover left, he feels worthless and ugly. Because his worthlessness is experienced as a humiliation, the affect of the experience is a shameful, crying sadness. His face is swollen from age, shame, and crying. In his life history is a mother who left him several times when he was young.

In psychotic phenomena, hallucinations and delusions, thing presentation and thing presentation quality capture a total area of reality experience and reality testing. In the above example, the patient's experience of his real self, his face, was captured in the psychotic condensation. In creativity, if thing presentations are experienced, it is in a third space, pre-consciously and consciously, between reality experience and emotional experience (Winnicott, 1953). It is a type of eidetic experience, usually only partial. Not all creative people experience conscious thing presentation qualities, but when they do, it is in the third space, and autonomous ego can use the experience for creative, esthetic constructions and communication.

Classification of Psychotic Structures Such as Delusions and Hallucinations

Psychopathology has always been classified, as have all diseases, in an attempt to find patterns for diagnoses, prognosis, and consistent, coherent treatment. General psychiatry has categorized delusions usually by manifest content. These categories determine medication treatment. The question for us is whether the structural description of psychosis already given in this book can be usefully further subcategorized so that traditional psychiatric illness categories are included. If so, the categories of psychoanalytic structure and of general psychiatry will be coordinated. This will help lead to coordination of medication treatment and psychoanalytic psychotherapy. The concept of psychotic structure implies stability in organization, and so one should be able to categorize the different psychotic structures.

60 Psychotic Structure

There are various classifications for delusional structure. Delusions typically found in psychotic depression, such as delusions of guilt, or in psychotic mania, such as delusions of grandeur, are classified by content and the relationship of typical manifest content to typical mood states. This is a general psychiatric classification of manifest content according to illness category. However, sometimes to classify delusional structures according to illness nosology, more than the manifest content must be considered when the manifest content themes are not clear. This involves getting the more latent, preconscious layers during the psychoanalytic interview. This is done in two ways. The first way is to listen and ask for the patient's associations to the delusional material. The second is to observe the relationship of the delusional material to the content of the rest of mental functioning, especially personality psychology, and the relationship of both of these to affect, the reality circumstances of the patient, and normal life phase development.

The latent content is hidden in very ill patients, however, not only by lack of conscious availability but also by dissociation. Although it is dissociated to the patient, it may be obvious to the observer that there is a thematic and affect connection between the psychological delusional content, the rest of the patient's personality psychology, and the reality circumstances. Especially helpful in understanding the proper integration of these three are the associations which reveal the deeper layers of latent content and affect and, therefore, a unifying theme or relationship. Access to this latent material may even liberate a helpful missing piece, like the organizing sequence and context of the reality event. Delusions are then more clearly characteristic in their content and organization of the illnesses with which they together appear. In this, I differ from many other psychoanalysts and general psychiatrists who see no connection between the content or organization of psychological material and the descriptive illness nosology used by general psychiatrists. I think a lack of concordance has been found in the past because not enough attention has been paid to the methods of (1) eliciting the latent content and (2) reintegrating the dissociated delusional phenomenon along thematic lines. Both these techniques result in a clearer and more coherent delusional story that is more easily classified.

Classifying the structure of delusions by the psychological themes they contain also enables classification of delusional systems according to the model of traditional ego psychology with the tripartite divisions of superego, ego, and id. Location of thematic content within these agencies is possible because when the latent material is known, a theme from one mental agency may predominate. For instance, in delusional depression, guilt, foreboding, and punishment appear in the story, either manifestly or latently or both, and are important diagnostic aids. In addition, this content is organized within superego structures of the patient's personality, and treatment leads even further into the pathology and distortions of superego functioning in character and in nonpsychotic defenses. One can therefore classify the depressive delusions as superego delusions.

Another method of classification has to do with the organization of the ego. Chapter 1 discussed how varying levels in organization of defenses and autonomous ego are the rule rather than the exception in ego functioning. The description of varying levels of organization becomes crucial in the classification of psychotic pathology, because ego variation within the psychotic individual is, again, the rule rather than the exception. Patients may be seen not only with pure psychotic mental functioning, but with mixtures of psychotic and neurotic, psychotic and near psychotic, or psychotic, near psychotic, and neurotic mental functioning. These mixtures can be classified. The classification is important in treating the very ill patient (Chapters 7 and 8). Each treatment must be specific for each level of ego function.

Variable levels of ego function have important ramifications for the purely psychiatric descriptive phenomenology of psychosis. If variability in the ego caused by illness or by lack of development is not considered, classification will be confused or impossible and treatment will then be confused.

An example of development problems that confound classification is the issue of depressive, guilt-ridden delusions which presuppose a level of psychological development that has reached the stage of organized superego development. We should expect, therefore, in the history of such psychotic patients, to hear that they in fact did develop through oedipal phases into organized superego functioning. In addition, if the illness is not too severe, there will be large areas of nonpsychotic and integrated mental functioning involving conscious material with associated neurotic defenses based on repression. A patient who is borderline, however, and without well-integrated, guilt-infused ideational content from superego functioning, who then becomes psychotically depressed, cannot have neurotic, guilty content in their delusional system. It is said, therefore, that such delusional systems cannot be classified according to general psychiatric nosology, or that the borderline patient is not suffering an additional illness called delusional depression. This crucial aspect is then not treated effectively. However, if the latent content of retributory rage is elicited and the superego is found characteristic in content and organization of borderline patients, and the remainder of ego structure is noted to be borderline, and if the history of the patient demonstrates the stable borderline integration before the psychotic event, one can then understand that the retributory rage, together with early shame and humiliation experiences, classifies this psychotic delusional material as a psychotic depressive reaction in a patient with borderline character and hence early superego organization.

62 Psychotic Structure

Structurally, then, patients can be categorized according to levels of ego organization including levels of nonpsychotic defenses and other mental agency organization. There are, in fact, neurotic, borderline, and psychotic patients with psychosis.

Neurotic patients with psychosis have intact areas of autonomous ego functioning, defenses based on repression, and integrated superego function, with an area of eruptive psychological material about which reality testing is lost. In these patients, within the delusional material itself, repression may be the dominant defensive mechanism.

Borderline patients with psychosis have the autonomous ego weaknesses characteristic of borderline patients, with impulse control dysfunction, affect dissociative integrative problems, affect-blocked observing ego problems, and defenses riddled with primitive projective mechanisms and primitive denial. Within this, there is an eruption into idea formation and behavior of psychological material about which reality testing is lost. Therefore, they are, in addition, psychotic. Of note may be the presence of splitting mechanisms within the area of lost reality testing as well as within the defensive structures of the rest of the personality.

Psychotic patients with psychosis have a global loss of reality testing in every area, and also an organized delusional system. In addition, there are patients who have an ever-present delusional potential because their character attitudes are psychotic in regard to theme, but are not stable in regard to specific content. These patients show psychotic character structure. They do not have stable delusional systems, but for every intense affect state they enter, reality testing may be lost. I call them, ironically, psychotics without psychosis, i.e., without stable delusions.

In all psychotic patients, the integration features within the psychotic areas themselves tend to vary according to the level of overall ego function attained before the psychotic illness intervened. Neurotic patients who become psychotic tend to have integrated affective valence in their psychotic content. Borderline patients with psychosis show splitting of affect in their psychotic content. Globally psychotic patients have the most disorganized delusions and hallucinations (see Table 2.6).

I have now demonstrated four ways of classifying delusional systems. The first is a correlation of thematic content, especially latent, with psychiatric disease category like depression or mania. The second is a characterization of the dominant thematic material, including latent themes, according to psychoanalytic mental agencies of superego, ego, or id. The third is the mixture of ego organization, autonomous and defensive, i.e., neurotic, borderline, or psychotic, found in the nonpsychotic areas of the patient's character organization. Related to this third way is a fourth: to categorize the integration of the psychotic material itself according to its dominant method of ego defensive organization. These four methods coincide to provide an in-depth diagnosis of psychotic patients that

Psychotic Structure 63

Table 2.6 Psychotic Ego Phenomena According to Mixtures of Ego Organization

Neurotic with Psychosis

Focal area of psychotic, conscious condensation of reality experience with emotional experience

Psychotic area dissociated from remainder of ego function and personality

Remainder of autonomous and defensive ego neurotically integrated

Psychotic area often integrated and layered

Borderline with Psychosis

Focal area of psychotic, conscious condensation of reality experience with emotional experience

Remainder of autonomous and defensive ego with typical borderline weaknesses and failures of integration

Psychotic area organized by splitting of affect

Psychotic with Psychosis, Two Types

1 Global, conscious, psychotic condensations of reality experience with emotional experience

2 Global, psychotic condensations and in addition an area of organized and stable content in a psychotic delusion; usually extensively disorganized

Therefore all aspects of ego function are involved

Psychotic without Psychosis (i.e., without stable delusional system)

Changing area of psychotic condensations of reality experience with emotional experience depending on events, intensity of feelings, and content of ideas

No safe area of mental experience; psychotic ego organization always possible; psychotic attitudes

Psychotic content phenomena, when they coalesce, may be variably organized depending on illness; usually with splitting of affect

---

can guide biologic and psychoanalytic treatment. The dynamic feelings and ideas represented in delusional symbolic representation will organize themselves according to these structures.

Defensive Structures in Psychosis

Crucial to psychoanalytic ego psychological theory and treatment is the concept of defense. As stated in Chapter 1, defenses are preconscious mental experiences that defend against other, more unpleasant mental experiences. A broader view would be that any mental function could be used defensively. However, the process, reason, and content of the use are preconscious and unconscious, and in emotional experience and not in reality experience, for neurotic illness even when autonomous ego is used for defense. This is not so for psychotic illnesses.

In neurotic illnesses, when the defensive nature of the symptoms is understood consciously, the symptom disappears. The emotional material which the symptom represents and against which the symptom defends can be experienced and integrated into the rest of ego functioning. The origin of the particular choice of defense within neurotic illness is not well understood, but the symptomatic use of preconscious defense for unconscious purposes is almost a structural definition of neurosis for psychoanalysis.

This defense concept has difficulties in application to psychotic illness where the distortion of autonomous ego is so crucial. Purely biological illnesses such as brain tumors can use psychosis. Biological interventions can suffice to repair these autonomous ego dysfunctions. I therefore do not believe that the defensive aspects of psychosis are solely etiologic in the illness. However, the psychosis once triggered is used for defensive purposes by the mind, and within the structure of the psychotic event itself are layers, or splits, one of which defends against the other. These defenses capture aspects of reality experience, usually by condensation.

Reality experience capture by defense occurs in many levels of illness, but the capture in psychotic illness occurs in conscious reality experience. This is a characteristic of psychotic structure.

Example:

A late-adolescent male felt access to a sexual partner was blocked by his parents' disapproval. He was afraid to feel angry and take reality steps toward either defying his parents while still remaining with them or moving out of the household. He became depressed and fearful and developed the delusion that the girl he was attracted to was in love with him and was looking for him night and day, unable to find him because he was locked up in the hospital where he was taken after accosting her. The illness served as a defense against anger at his parents which would, in the extreme, have led to his separating from them and moving out of the house. He was terrified of taking this step. He unconsciously felt that he could not live on his own. In this sense, the delusional psychosis was the defense against a deeper neurotic illness, which was a fear of growing up and separating from his family. His psychosis was used as a defense against a real life problem and the associated feelings which constituted his chronic neurotic psychological conflict. The defense of projection of love and seeking in the delusion captured his reality experience of his wish for the girl.

If one observes which aspects of reality are captured by which aspects of the defensive processes in delusional systems, one sees that there are typical captures in the structure. Personality conflicts and defenses can provoke or experience reality in stressful ways that may trigger a psychotic event.

Defenses against reality in psychosis are defenses against the reality experience of fact. The psychotic symptoms function to defend against logical and evidential confrontation of the delusional system with secondary process and reality. The delusional phenomena also protect against deeper layers of idea and affect. The delusion selects or changes reality experience to correspond more closely to the unconscious view of the object world, or it changes reality experience to correspond more closely to the dissociated but conscious view of the object world for psychological reasons that are unconscious.

Neurotics avoid reality experience which is at odds with their unconscious fantasies and/or try to alter reality experience unconsciously. The borderline patient takes action to alter preconscious reality experience. The near psychotic (see Chapter 3) takes action to alter preconscious reality experience not in behavior but in preconscious ideas. The psychotic patient alters reality experience by incorporation of emotional experience into the conscious manifest experience of reality (for a somewhat different view, see Jacobson [1967]).

The significance of personality defense to psychosis is thus not just the content of the defensive fantasy but the location of that defense structurally. Defenses that cross into reality experience enter into the psychotic structure, crossing autonomous ego boundaries to reality experience. Psychotic defenses are aspects of psychotic condensations. Psychotic defenses are those defenses that condense with conscious reality experience and reality testing in the psychotic structure.

There are, in addition, two nonpsychotic defenses important in psychotic states: mediating defenses against integration of the vertical dissociation of the psychotic structure, and defenses against observing ego. (For a general discussion of the relationships of ego function to defense in psychosis, see Arlow and Brenner [1964]. For a critique I agree with, see Frosch [1983].)

Mediating Defenses

What kinds of mental experiences are at the boundary of vertically dissociated psychotic experience? Around most delusions is an area of pseudodelusion; around every area of psychosis is an area of near psychosis. These areas reveal emotional processes that are basic to the patient's character. Defenses around a delusional system, not in the delusional system, are not psychotic. They are open to reality testing and hence open to interpretation. They enable the continued existence of a delusional system as much as the lack of autonomous ego integration, loss of boundaries, and loss of reality testing do. I call them, therefore, *mediating* or *enabling* defenses. Mediating defenses are preconscious emotional experience and are not part of conscious reality experience.

Psychotic structure, thus, may have a crucial nonpsychotic aspect consisting of the character defenses that surround and enable the vertical dissociation of psychotic phenomena. These defenses defend the psychotic area against nonpsychotic ego function.

The defenses are said to *surround* the psychotic phenomena because when you talk to such a patient about a delusional system, no matter what angle or approach you take, you are blocked from full access, exploration, consideration, and integration of the psychotic area by these defense mechanisms.

Enabling or mediating defenses are defenses against integration of a vertical dissociation. As such, they defend the psychotic structure against the secondary process and reality-perceptual evidence of the nonpsychotic ego.

There are also nonpsychotic mediating character defenses against dissociated observing ego and other autonomous ego functions (Holmes, 1996).

Definitions of Levels of Illness

We are now ready to define sicker patients according to the descriptions of structure just elaborated.

Sicker patients have damage to what should be autonomous ego function. The sicker patient's structure shows less and less reality testing. The sicker patient's structure shows less and less integration of one aspect of conscious mental life with other aspects of conscious mental life. The patient also shows less integration of behavior with the reality of his or her environment. The sicker patient's structures are more and more rigid in his or her defenses. These defenses capture conscious reality experience. All of this leads to less and less facility at adapting to reality experience, with less adaptive means of satisfying emotional needs. Notice that observing ego is not on this axis because, in my observation, observing ego can be gone in neurotic, borderline, or psychotic conditions and also because the interference with observing ego usually has to do with nonpsychotic character defenses.

It is said that, in sicker patients, psychological theme and content is conscious that is more unconscious in neurotic patients. This is not always so. In some very sick patients, aside from the loss of reality testing, the material that erupts in a delusional system is quite integrated and layered with neurotic defenses structuring the delusion. Even in borderline organized patients with an intercurrent psychosis, the material that is revealed, though more primitive, has defensive functions against unconscious material, just as in the neurotic. However, in these very ill patients, the manifest is congruent with latent layers of thematic material. This is because the very ill ego phenomenon is a vertical dissociation in which one or several related strands of psychological life erupt and become separated from the rest of emotional organization, both conscious and preconscious.

The neurotic symptom has an integration and disguise. This is because the neurotic ego can repress, integrate, and disguise conflicting themes and affects in the symptomatic area.

Another measure along the sickness-to-health axis is the degree of "primitive material" that is apparent in the manifest content. *Primitive* may mean that aspects of drive, instead of being defended against, erupt, infiltrate, and are expressed, relatively undisguised, in the manifest content of the material (Reich, 1933b; Kernberg, 1975). At the same time, primitive means that the associated fears are likewise erupting and expressed simultaneously either in the delusional system or in behavior. Even here, however, there is still a latent content of subtleties, elaborations, and links to associated contents. The latent in each content area tends to be congruent with the manifest content area.

Primitive usually refers to contents; *primary process* refers to organization. If *primitive* is used to refer to process, then all primary process is primitive. I, however, use *primitive* to mean that aspects of autonomous secondary process reality experience are captured by feelings (for a somewhat similar view, see Willick [1983]). This is what makes certain mental processes primitive. Since I believe the primary process develops, there is complex, sophisticated primary process and simple primary process. In this sense, primary process may be more primitive or not.

But the most difficult-to-treat marker of very ill structure is the rigidity with which a psychological phenomenon is encoded and dissociated. In fact, rigidities of structure and defense are more difficult to treat than absences of reality testing or eruptions of primitive content or of primary processing. In that sense, a very rigid neurotic patient can be sicker than a more plastically organized borderline patient. *Rigid* in this sense means very resistant to change. *Sicker* in this last sense clearly means harder to do psychotherapy with or to structurally change. The rigidity may manifest itself in either one of two other ways: one is the rigidity of the repression brought to bear against psychological material; the other is the rigidity of the dissociation of the psychological material.

Therefore, not just the content, organization, and autonomous ego deficits, but especially the rigidities of psychological structure will determine the ease of treatment and therefore the prognosis. Psychoanalysts should remember this when making prognostic evaluations of very sick patients.

Character and Psychosis

The psychodynamic relationship between psychological themes in character structure and themes in psychotic symptoms is the same as the relationship in the neurotic between neurotic symptom and character structure, except for the loss of reality testing and the condensations with reality experience in the psychotic. Dynamic themes in personality may be congruent with symptoms, whether neurotic or psychotic. Personality conflicts affect attitudes which color reality experience with emotional meaning and may help reality stressors trigger symptoms, whether neurotic or psychotic.

No one knows why psychological conflict may trigger or form the nidus of a psychotic symptom rather than a neurotic symptom. I and others presume that biological–neurological factors are involved.

Character defenses are emotional defenses characteristic of an individual and characteristic of a diagnostic category and not perceived by the person as a symptom, but as part of his or her personality. In psychoses, these defenses:

1   Are potential stress points in psychological functioning; they block emotional and reality confrontation and adaptation;
2   Contribute their themes and conflicts to the content of the psychotic material and to the condensation with reality experience;
3   Defend against integration of psychotic dissociation, as in mediating defenses;
4   Block the observing ego and hence the therapeutic alliance.

Character themes are both inside and outside the psychotic structure. Character defenses, the processes, are probably best reserved in description for nonpsychotic defensive processes of character outside psychotic structure. When they enter the psychotic structure *itself*, as they often do, it is probably best to refer to them as psychotic defenses, since they are so different from usual character defenses in that they:

1   Are condensed with reality experience, reality testing, and the rest of the psychotic structure;
2   Are intense, perhaps more so than *in* the rest of character structure;
3   May involve content that is both conscious and preconscious, although deeply unconscious in the rest of personality.

An example is a man with a neurotic symptom of phobic avoidance of school performance and career, especially the focal-neurotic symptom of panic in test situations. Associations to this symptom revealed one of the meanings of a test to be a competitive situation. It was very difficult to deal with the symptom in treatment, because the character defenses were reaction formations against competitive loss and despair. These defenses were activated in the transference. This meant that the patient constantly competed with me. He interrupted me and would not let me say anything. If I insisted on saying what I had to say, he either said "no" and went on with his story, or "yes" but would promptly change the topic. So we have a layered neurotic symptom with equivalent layering of the same theme in character structure, with the reaction formations against the underlying fear expressed in the transference relationship.

It is the same in the delusional system of a psychotic patient where the background character structure is the same in organization. An example is a female patient who had a problem of a preconscious, controlling, aggressive, and dominating character reaction formations against the unconscious fear of being controlled. But she had a conscious sexual symptom in which orgasm could only be reached by a fantasy of a strong, assertive, and controlling man using his hand to masturbate her. Sexual fantasies often, like dreams or delusions, involve eruptions of otherwise unconscious character dynamics. In reality, she avoided assertive lovers. When she became intercurrently psychotically depressed, the manifest content of her delusional system involved nurses sticking needles into her hands. This was probably associated as punishment, not for adult sex, but for childhood masturbation and associated screen memories of seductions in which she had been masturbated, controlled by the man, but highly aroused and so felt actively complicit. Thus, there are aspects of the same dynamic conflict in character, in sexual fantasy, and in delusions.

The Structure of Symbolic Representation and Symbolic Alterations of Reality in the Structure of Psychosis

The typical structure of symbolic alterations in psychosis is the use of reality day residue experience for symbolic purposes. This reality day residue is symbolically altered by the primary process. Thus, primary processes and contents change the reality day residue in ways that symbolize and express affect responses to the reality day residue. This may be called a symbolic alteration of reality. In psychosis, this symbolic alteration of reality (symbol) is condensed with the original day residue (referent). The condensation has the primary process experience of an intense, perceptual quality, thing presentation. Psychotic symbols are, therefore, thing presentation experiences in which the day residue and its symbolic alteration of reality are condensed together in conscious reality experience. Reality testing is also similarly altered and condensed into the psychotic symbol (see Table 2.7).

70 Psychotic Structure

Table 2.7 Definitions of Symbolic Processes

Symbol

> Manifest *element* standing for something else
> One standing for another
> Especially where one represents another, more abstract

Primary Process

> *Rules* of organization of emotional experience and its symbols
> Condensation of representations according to affect themes
> Refers to complex, condensed, affect referents

Thing Presentation

> Name of an *experience* of affect–percept and concept–percept
> A complex, perceptual quality symbol experience organized according to
> primary process rules

Psychotic Symbol

> The *experience* of a complex, primary process, symbolic condensation
> of a reality day residue together with its symbolic alteration of
> reality. Captures and condenses with reality testing processes. An
> intense, affect–percept and concept–percept thing presentation
> symbol experience which dominates conscious, superordinate reality
> experience

In the normal and in the neurotic, the day residue is conscious or preconscious and unaltered; while altered symbolically it is also separate. The separate symbol experience is not in reality experience but in emotional experience or intermediate experience. There is no conscious thing presentation experience of the symbol. If there is, it occurs in the intermediate experience (Winnicott, 1953) and not in reality experience. Symbolic alterations of reality are those symbols which result from processes that use or alter reality and reality experience to gain or create a discharge target for dynamic conflict (Sarnoff, 1987). Emotional experience and latent layers are condensed into the undisplaced reality experience and the affect usually follows (Freud, 1900; Kubie, 1978; Frosch, 1983).

The symbolic alteration of reality in psychosis is not experienced as symbolic. The symbolic structure has incorporated a piece of conscious reality experience, including associated reality testing processes. It has condensed emotion with it and, in addition, takes on the new symbolic form of a thing presentation, with perceptual thing presentation quality. Psychotic thing presentation quality has its own characteristic intensity, veracity, validity, and esthetic (see Table 2.8). This complex condensation with many areas of reality and perceptual experience has then moved into and captured a major section of superordinate reality experience. The originally incorporated, conscious reality day residue is

Psychotic Structure 71

Table 2.8 Validity and Veracity Experiences

Reality Experience: "I think it is true"

Superordinate
Percept
Secondary process logical organization of concepts and percepts
Deduction/induction
Concept
Abstraction
Generalization
Application
Discrete, boundaried categories

Emotional Experience: "I feel it is true"

Superordinate
Affect
Primary process concepts
Thematic
Infinite content categories
Blurred intermixing of thematic trends
Plastic, only relatively stable, repetitive processes

Thing Presentation: "I see it is true"

Percept/affect
Percept/concept
Primary process organization
Concrete

Psychotic Experience: "It is true!"

Validity and veracity experience from all three, forming a new, psychotic validity and veracity experience. The strongest contribution is from thing presentation.

Table 2.9 Psychotic Structure

Psychotic condensations are condensations of reality experience, emotional experience, and reality testing. The three domains condense in conscious reality experience. This is the structure of psychotic condensations.
When this happens, certain processing mergers and shifts occur:
Object representation may merge with real object
Self representation may merge with real self
Self representation may merge with real object
Real self may merge with real object
Word presentations shift to thing presentations
Secondary process shifts to primary process
Symbolic representations shift to symbolic alterations of reality

then experienced only in the symbolic alteration of reality in psychotic structure. This is another unique feature of psychotic alterations of reality (see Table 2.9).

72 Psychotic Structure

Table 2.10 Psychotic Structure

In summary, then, psychotic structure = delusional structure = hallucinatory structure. This structure is characterized by:

Always:

1 reality experience and emotional experience are condensed in conscious reality experience
2 condensation includes reality testing, contents and processes
3 day residue real object and object representation (or real self and self representation) are condensed in the manifest content of reality, forming part of the psychotic structure
4 thing presentation quality is present in conscious reality experience
5 day residue context and sequence are disorganized or repressed in deeper layers of latent content

Usually:

1 primary process infiltrated
2 vertically dissociated from the rest of reality experience and from the rest of personality experience
3 mediating defenses surround psychotic phenomena and help maintain vertical dissociation; these mediating defenses are near psychotic

The form the psychotic material takes depends on:

1 how the particular type of illness disrupts the ego
2 the cognitive and emotional organizational level of development reached before the psychotic illness

The content depends on:

1 content of past and present emotional and reality experience
2 psychological conflicts in and between the areas of reality experience and emotional experience

Brief summary of results of transformations of autonomous ego in psychosis:

1 fantasy moves into reality experience
2 word presentations move into thing presentations
3 conceptual and affective experience move into perceptual experience

Different illnesses impose different forms on psychotic symbol structure. Some illnesses symbolically alter reality extensively in manifest content. Some merely use the manifest reality without alteration but with thing presentation quality experience, condensed with reality testing and without conscious ability to tell that this is happening. In this case, the content of reality experience will not be altered. The experience of reality will be altered in quality. Psychotic symbolic representation is in the quality of experience and in the loss of reality testing about the veracity that this quality lends to the experience of personal and concrete meaning.

But usually a reality experience is altered extensively, with content and organization characteristic of illnesses, level of prior development, content of emotional conflicts, and content of reality experiences. These are

Psychotic Structure 73

always condensed and usually extensively primary processed. They have characteristic structures, with the day residue or provoking experience forming a nidus, condensed with psychotic elaboration from primary processes, surrounded by pseudopsychotic elaborations in the layered, mediating defenses of character structure.

For summary of elements of psychotic structure see Table 2.10.

Note

1 Freud first used the term *dissociation* to mean the separation of idea, usually a mnemic image or memory filled with affect, from the rest of mental functioning (ego). These were important aspects of what he described as hysterical neuroses (Breuer and Freud, 1893–1895). We now believe many of these original cases to have been sicker, borderline patients where dissociative failure of mental integration is prominent (see chapter 3).

Freud introduced ambiguity into the term by later using *splitting of the ego* to refer to this dissociation phenomenon. Klein used the term, shortened it to *splitting*, but then used it to refer to only one type of dissociation, the unconscious dissociation of object relations fantasies based on positive or negative affects (love or hate). Kernberg follows this usage and has popularized this use within psychoanalysis in America. Rosenfeld and others did the same in Britain.

But what about those patients who dissociate ideas or complex affects/ideas and, furthermore, do so across boundaries of consciousness? This is actually closer to Freud's use of the term.

Kohut (1971) resurrected this use to describe the integrative pathology of a type of sicker patient. He used the term *vertical dissociation* to mean conscious, preconscious, and maybe unconscious separation of ideas and associated complex affect, both positive and negative. I follow his use because it is accurately descriptive of a common, almost universal type of ego pathology in sicker patients where the dissociation is based not on affect, or not only on affect, and not on fantasy–emotional–unconscious experience, but also on conscious reality experience, and not just in defenses but also in autonomous processes. He also used the term *horizontal* dissociation to refer to repression. Fliess (1973) used the terms *longitudinal split* and *transverse split*.

Chapter 3

Near Psychotic Structure

Introduction

Near psychotic states are usually called borderline. In spite of considerable work on these states, ambiguity remains about their definition and descriptive nosology. What elements are to be used as criteria, and whether those elements are to be mental or behavioral or both, are still undecided, because the relationship of the behavioral to the mental in near psychosis has not yet been specifically described.

General psychiatrists tend to describe behavior in borderline patients because it is so dramatic and easily observable. In addition to behavior, psychoanalysts also describe the intrapsychic, but tend to look especially at emotional experience and defensive organization. The two can only meet if behavior has a specific, defensive organization in mental experience. I believe it does in near psychosis, especially when the relationship of autonomous ego function to defensive organization is considered.

The term *borderline* has been used by general psychiatry in two different ways. One use was to delineate a psychiatric illness. *Borderline* therefore sometimes means a partial expression of a psychiatric illness (schizophrenia is an example), and from the beginning, an intermediate form was described (Bleuler, 1950). *Borderline* now refers to a type of personality disorder (see APA, 1980, 1987, 1994). The other use was to delineate a midpoint between two levels of illness, the neurotic and the psychotic. Psychoanalysts tended toward this use, although some psychoanalysts were aware of both the illness use and the level use.

I am interested in both illness and level because both are always part of the diagnosis. But the causative illness may not be, or may not *only* be, a personality disorder. Intermediate forms of manic-depressive illness, of atypical depression, of schizophrenia, or organic brain syndromes may be involved. If the cause is only a personality disorder, then the subtype must be diagnosed. The *borderline* term is therefore best used as a severity term and a syndromal term, not as a specific illness term.

I will describe the mental organization characteristic of this level of illness, concentrating on descriptions of ego function. Knight (1953) also did so, but he concentrated on describing only a few of what Hartmann (1939) called *autonomous ego apparatuses*. He also described, but did not well define, the primitive defenses in these conditions. Klein (1975), Fairbairn (1952), and Jacobson (1964) focused especially on object relations. Kernberg (1975) and Frosch (1988) discussed many aspects of ego function, but especially object relations, in defenses (Kernberg) and in the ego dysfunctions of impulse control and reality relations (Frosch). The earlier discussion is based on the best review of the general psychiatric literature on near psychosis, Michael Stone's *The Borderline Syndromes* (1980).

DSM-III-R and DSM-IV (APA, 1987, 1994) list ego criteria for borderline states that focus on apparatus dysfunction, especially behavioral dysregulation, and are heavily influenced by Kernberg (1975) and Gunderson (1984) criteria.

I will describe all aspects of ego functions: apparatuses, object relations, and defenses. More importantly, I will describe the universal structural ego organization of all these functions in near psychosis. It is this particular organization that I believe defines the near psychotic state.

My own view is that near psychosis is a specific organization of mental experience, with specific ego apparatus dysfunction and typical defensive organization. Behavior dyscontrol is only one aspect and must be diagnosed not on the basis of the manifest behavior but on whether there is near psychotic ego organization of this behavior. The ego apparatus dysfunction shapes the mental organization of all near psychotic phenomena and the near psychotic form of defenses.

Near psychosis, like psychosis, is a mental state in which reality experience is used for purposes of expressing emotional experience. I call it *near psychosis* because the resulting condensation has nearly invaded conscious reality experience. Near psychosis is distinguished from psychosis by two main features: (1) the pathological condensation structure is in preconsciousness and not consciousness, and (2) reality testing processes are not part of the near psychotic condensation.

There are two types of near psychotic states. In one type, the near psychotic condensation expresses itself intrusively in behavior. These are the states that are now called borderline personality. In the other, behavior is not severely affected and the near psychotic condensation is intrusively present only in the area of a circumscribed mental phenomenon, usually an idea. I call this type the *pseudodelusional* type. Different illnesses can cause these two types of psychotic ego organization.

The only crucial autonomous ego difference between the two types of near psychosis is at the behavioral ego boundary, usually the affect–behavior boundary.

Because these two subtypes of near psychosis have not been clearly distinguished, very common near psychotic states which do not affect behavior are often treated in psychotherapy as neurotic problems and therefore may fail to show improvement. Nonbehavioral near psychotic states are extremely common in office practice and may require special psychotherapeutic consideration of their particular structure for improvement. This type of near psychotic condensation may be the major feature of a depression, and if it is overlooked, needed medication or psychotherapeutic focus on reality condensations may be withheld.

The psychological structure of all near psychotic states has characteristic features because specific autonomous ego functions are altered. I will discuss the autonomous ego problems common to all near psychotic states before discussing the characteristic near psychotic condensation. However, it will be difficult to neatly separate the description of near psychosis into a description of the autonomous ego dysfunctions and a description of the near psychotic condensation, because near psychotic condensations involve autonomous ego functions.

Autonomous Apparatuses

The autonomous apparatuses in near psychotic states are not as severely affected as they are in psychosis. However, just as in psychotic states, the apparatuses affected are specific. These disturbances of autonomous ego functions in the near psychoses can result from neurological, biochemical, or psychological causes or from combinations of these three (see Chapter 5).

Boundaries

Most of the autonomous ego apparatuses affected are boundaries. Near psychotic patients are said to have "boundary disturbances." It is extremely important to understand the exact form these boundary disturbances may take. The boundaries are between feelings and behavior, unconscious and preconscious, reality experience and emotional experience, concept and affect, the concrete and the general, the word presentation experience of reality and the thing presentation experience of percept–affect. More importantly, the relationship of preconscious reality experience to emotional experience moves from mostly autonomous secondary process control to mostly emotional primary process control.

Inside–Outside Boundary

In near psychotic states, there is no difficulty in the conscious ability to perceive the difference between stimuli originating inside the mind

Near Psychotic Structure 77

and stimuli originating outside the mind. Therefore fusions across this boundary are neither usual nor characteristic. There is an experience of inside and an experience of outside.

Merger phenomena do occur across the quite separate barrier between the *experience* of inside and the *experience* of outside. The mergers in near psychosis are condensations. In near psychosis, these condensation crossings occur at the preconscious inside–outside experience boundary between emotional and reality experience, especially between affect and idea.

Boundary between Levels of Consciousness

Although the boundaries between levels of consciousness should be somewhat porous in all people, in the near psychotic, there is a typical type of porosity. There is an easy access into the preconscious near psychotic structure from unconscious emotional experience, but very reluctant and rigidly defended entry into the near psychotic structure from the experience of conscious reality. It is this structural aspect that makes the near psychotic so reactive, yet so difficult to treat. The person is reactive to the reality-evoked emotional experience, but not to the characteristics of the conscious reality experience per se.

The Preconscious and Near Psychosis

In the near psychotic states, the preconscious contains the major mechanisms, the major condensations with reality experience, and the major affective states. What are the implications of the preconscious level for near psychotic experience?

The mind experiences differently at different levels of consciousness and according to whether primary or secondary process is most dominant. It is especially in the preconscious, just below full awareness, that these two processes mix (for discussions of the preconscious, see Freud [1900, 1915b, 1917b]; Kris [1950]; Eissler [1962]; Sandler and Holder [1973]).

The specific organization of near psychosis is due to disturbances, particularly in autonomous boundary function, between ideational content categories and emotion, between this aspect of reality experience and that aspect of emotional experience. These boundary problems result in an exaggerated experience of the preconscious, because the boundary between feelings and ideational content is less rigid and the two become condensed. The two become one and express each other and evoke each other interchangeably. What one feels suddenly becomes the idea, or is indistinguishable from the idea.

The enlarged preconscious can come about in either or both of two ways. First, affect intensity may contaminate thinking as primary processing attempts to express and synthesize intense emotional states. The intensity of feelings and imagery strains the boundary between primary and secondary process and between conscious and unconscious. There is a compensatory attempt at repression which only holds the process in the preconscious. Affective illness is an example. Second, the boundary between primary process and secondary process may be damaged independently of affect intensity. Such patients show primary process dominance without intensity of affect. Mild forms of schizophrenia or organic brain syndromes are examples.

The preconscious also contains the near psychotic condensation. This partially repressed, specific condensation, and its porous relationship to the conscious and unconscious, is another reason for the exaggerated preconscious experience in near psychosis.

Because it is held in the preconscious, the near psychotic condensation is unavailable to certain conscious ego functions. The location of the near psychotic condensation of reality experience with emotional experience just out of awareness in preconsciousness protects the near psychotic experience from conscious reality testing, conscious observing ego, and new conscious reality experience.

Primary Process–Secondary Process

Because of the preconscious location and because of the porous boundary disturbance, primary process captures secondary process in the near psychotic pathological area. The primary process functions to express emotional intensities as specific ideational contents. Rules of condensation predominate. Emotional symbols acquire aspects of captured preconscious reality experience with perceptual qualities. The primary process–secondary process condensations of form that occur in near psychotic patients occur just out of awareness and strongly influence conscious reasoning, decision making, and experience.

Affect Boundaries

Affect boundaries regulate (1) the separation and mixture of different affects, (2) their intensity, and (3) their spread. All three functions are usually damaged in near psychotic structure, because of either affect intensity problems or direct damage to affect-regulating boundaries, or both. Manic-depressive illness is an example of the first and schizophrenia or attention deficit disorders are examples of the second. In any case, the result is an affect intensity of flooding proportions. This results in dramatic content, intensity, and perhaps behavior. Discharge of affect intensity becomes a goal. When this discharge is content organized in a stable fantasy, the patient talks about seeking satisfaction. Because this stable fantasy links emotion with ongoing reality experience, the satisfaction is sought consciously in terms of a reality experience even though it is intensity discharge of mostly preconscious emotion that is motivational. It is this pressure of the near psychotic fantasy into reality experience of behavior or ideas that is so characteristic of the near psychotic state.

The affect boundary borders the interchange between affect and affect, affect and concept, affect and percept qualities, affect and mood, affect and logic, affect and behavior, and affect and judgment. This gives the near psychotic condensation its power.

The degree to which an affect experience is organized and stable over time in near psychotic fantasy structure depends on the stability and organization of the ego and superego. This is more true for the pseudodelusional type. In the behavioral type, there may be thematic stabilities of affect that are quite fixed, but the content and details of the plot may never quite condense or may change over time.

Affect Modulating Capacity

The capacity of the near psychotic ego to modulate affective states is severely impaired. Affects are seen in unintegrated form or in fused form. Fusions of affect summate their intensities rather than integrate and neutralize each other. The lack of modulating capacity prevents a regulation of the intensity of affect. Affect, if intense enough, recruits affects from different domains. It is this characteristic of many near psychotic states that shows their frequent links to the affective illnesses. However, the autonomous ego function of modulating capacity can be damaged directly, as in certain types of neurological damage. The exact diagnosis for the lack of modulating capacity is crucial to the treatment of these conditions. Medication or interpretative psychotherapy will be variously effective, alone or in combination, depending on the exact diagnosis and etiology of the particular ego deficits. In any case, the lack of modulating capacity leading to exaggerated intensities of affect experience means that the integrating capacity of the ego is under great strain.

Reality Testing

Reality testing in the near psychotic states is said to be suspended but not totally lost.[1] This means that the behavior of the borderline or the thoughts of the pseudodelusional are not constrained by the secondary process of conscious reality testing nor by the content of conscious reality experience. Instead, reality testing is highly influenced by the near psychotic condensation, especially its affect and quality, but also its content. However, when confronted by an outside, overwhelming reality or by the psychiatric interviewer who seeks to do this in words, some in fact dissociated reality testing processes will be shown to be functional and not totally captured by the near psychotic condensation (Kernberg, 1977). This means that reality testing in the near psychotic has maintained its separate, secondary process, logical reality testing process capacity. This is true even if reality testing content is heavily influenced by the near psychotic condensation. The extent to which reality testing content overlaps or is condensed with the near psychotic structure varies from patient to patient and from etiology to etiology. Traumatic near psychotic states involve considerable overlap, although not true condensations. One thing is always true, however. Although *content* may overlap between the near psychotic condensation and reality testing, reality testing *process* in near psychotic states is never totally part of the near psychotic condensation structure. This means that the capture of reality experience is potentially not as rigidly fixed as in psychosis. The use of reality as a vehicle for emotional conflict and as a resistance to the exploration of inner states can be more easily interpreted, engaging deeper layers of the patient's psychology.

Even though the near psychotic condensation can influence reality testing contents, reality testing processes do not influence the near psychotic condensation until the condensation is made more fully conscious. Then conscious reality testing processes can be brought to bear. Helpful in this respect is the interpretation of any defenses mediating the dissociated reality testing processes.

This reality testing problem broadly affects behavior in the borderline patient and narrowly affects ideational content in the pseudodelusional near psychotic. For pseudodelusional patients, reality testing is suspended in only one specific area of mental functioning: a pseudodelusion or pseudohallucination. This can occur in the absence of a broad infiltration of near psychotic condensation into reality experience. This is particularly true of otherwise neurotically organized patients who enter a time of very severe mental illness. The autonomous ego functions, better developed and integrated, and better organized neurotic ego defenses, serve to better contain the near psychotic illness. The primary process affect eruption can be contained in one affect-laden idea and does not immediately spill into other ideas or action (for a historical review of the reality testing concept in psychoanalysis, see Frosch [1983]).

Observing Ego

The observing ego in near psychotic states is most often only suspended but may be captured. The observing ego may therefore be part of the near psychotic condensation, almost a part of it, or dissociated and blocked from it.

Because the observing ego looks partly toward reality experience, especially reality experience of mental functioning, the potential reinforcement by the observing ego to reality experience is great. Its interference is almost always through primitive defenses that capture its reality view. Analysts often despair about patients who lack an observing ego. Sometimes such patients are said to lack psychological mindedness. But this is not exactly the same thing as the observing ego. The observing ego is neither a necessary nor a sufficient component of psychological mindedness. However, a main trunk of the therapeutic alliance does attach to the ego structure via the observing ego. The observing ego allows the formation of a true, useful, therapeutic alliance. Agreement about the reality experience of the doctor, the patient's symptoms, and the treatment setting permits treatment for change. A first order of business, therefore, is to free the observing ego from its condensations and/or dissociations. A dissociated observing ego is an easier treatment situation than an observing ego that is captured by the near psychotic condensation. In either case, the analyst attempts to help the patient free the observing ego. When blocked, the capture blocks access and insight to the near psychotic area. This is the defensive function of the capture of observing ego.

Reality Experience, Emotional Experience, and Their Relationship

In near psychotic states, the relationship of reality experience to emotional experience is a condensation capture of part of reality experience by part of emotional experience in the preconscious. This condensation is then dissociated vertically and partly repressed (horizontally).

Because reality testing is suspended, because there is a condensation between reality and fantasy, because this fantasy is just out of awareness, and because this condensation affects reality experience, there is a specific mental experience of near psychosis. The experience is akin to the uncanny (Freud, 1919) or dêja vu. Those experiences, while of different structure, also involve momentary conscious uncertainty about reality experience.

The most common near psychotic structure involves specific condensation points of affect content. Only emotionally relevant reality experience is captured. Some very ill near psychotic patients, however, have attitude propensities to near psychotic condensations along broad thematic areas, of which the broadest is mood. In these patients, transient near psychotic condensations may occur whenever reality content evokes and intensifies mood-congruent affect.

Thus, the regulation problem of the relationship between reality experience and emotional experience may be broad or narrow, intermittent or constant.

The relationship between reality experience and emotional experience in near psychosis is the relationship of (1) the captured reality experience to emotional experience, and (2) the resulting dissociated and incompletely repressed condensation to the rest of mental life, especially to the totality of conscious reality experience. Many areas and aspects of conscious autonomous ego function may be intact, more so in the pseudodelusional than in the behavioral (borderline) type. In addition, each patient varies and each illness varies. The near psychotic condensation is specific, fixed, intense, dominating, and has the quality of reality experience. This condensation is usually in a dissociated relationship with the rest of mental life, but the condensation affects conscious reality experience in affect, quality of experience, and nuance of ideas without necessarily totally capturing reality testing.

The point is that the relationship between reality experience and emotional experience is no longer strongly organized by the reality-oriented secondary process. Instead, the relationship is emotionally oriented and primary process organized at specific points of affect-laden ideas or along a broad front of mood.

I will now describe the relationship of reality experience to emotional experience within the near psychotic condensation. Intense affects are preconscious and are condensed with reality experience. What is felt is felt to be almost real. At the same time that what is felt is felt to be almost real, it is also felt as feelings. The near psychotic experience is of both feelings and reality at the same time and of their uncanny similarity. Are they the same or are they different? Are they two or are they one? Are they true or false? The near psychotic experience is that the two, affect and reality experience, are the same, even though the near psychotic patient knows they are not. The major boundary crossing is between preconscious reality experience and preconscious emotional experience. I will now describe other ego problems and how they affect the near psychotic condensation.

Mental Experience and Behavior

This brings us to a boundary between mental experience, especially between affect and behavior, i.e., that separates thoughts and feelings from action. This boundary is strained in all near psychotic states but is severely damaged in the behavioral borderline type. Borderline patients are those with near psychotic behavioral actions. They act out their reality experience–emotional experience condensations directly into the environment in reality. This may involve projection of the near psychotic condensation. They are not, however, projecting onto the object in reality; the inside–outside boundary is intact. They are projecting onto their own preconscious real mental object or real self and then behaving in accordance. Their ability at the same time to perceive an accurate object or self in reality is intact although blurred by their own intense projection.

In the pseudodelusional form of this illness group, there are various projections onto the preconscious experience of the real object or real self, but they are not acted upon. This makes an outpatient treatment more tempting and, potentially, more possible. However, even in the pseudodelusional, behavior boundaries are under strain. Affect responsiveness to reality interventions can be hair-trigger, and the behavior boundary can be breached abruptly and massively, especially in the intense transference. This is why consistent limit setting in the treatment is required. Treating these patients is a most interesting experience requiring the greatest concentration on the details of structure that will determine the technique of therapy (see Chapter 8).

Except for the behavior boundary, the structure, location, and quality of near psychotic experience are the same for both the borderline and the pseudodelusional. The mental experience of near psychotic behavior is specific in its structure. The structure is identical to the structure of near psychotic ideas except for the affect–behavioral and the more general fantasy–behavioral boundary problem.

Integrating Capacity

The ability of the near psychotic patient to integrate mental experience is severely impaired. The exact nature of the integrative disturbance has been variously described. The inability to integrate emotional life has usually been focused on identifications (Stone [1986]; Searles [1986]; object relations based on affect: Kernberg [1975]). But the impairment takes place at the level of autonomous ego functioning, just as it takes place in defensive structures. The impairment involves an inability to integrate near psychotic experience with reality experience but also with emotional experience and with other areas of personality functioning.

The ego should normally be able to synthesize reality experience, emotional experience, conscious experience, preconscious experience, primary process, and secondary process in an even-flowing, integrated, and sublimated mental life.

It is this overall synthetic function that is damaged in near psychosis. The synthetic function (Nunberg, 1931) is a compound ego function (Bellak et al., 1973) or superordinate ego function (Hartmann, 1939; Blanck and Blanck, 1986) and is badly distorted by the ego problems already listed.

The inability to integrate emotional experience or object relations experiences occurs not only in near psychosis, but also in various illnesses and in nonillness states as an ego variation. The specific feature of near psychosis is the autonomous ego integration failures in preconscious reality

84 Near Psychotic Structure

experience and not just the lack of defensive integration in emotional experience. Autonomous ego difficulties are crucially involved. The most severe aspects are the integration problems where emotional experience intersects with reality experience. Near psychotic structure is characterized by the location, composition, and dissociation of this difficulty. The main feature of near psychotic structure is the particular dissociated preconscious condensation experience that results. This condensation lies unintegrated in near consciousness. The characteristic lack of integration is the dissociation of this condensation. The characteristic dissociation is a vertical and horizontal dissociation. The near psychotic horizontal dissociation (repression) is a partial repression into the preconscious of the near psychotic condensation. There is a faulty open channel from the unconscious into this preconscious condensation, but little or no interchange between conscious reality experience and the condensation. Instead, current reality provokers evoke affect and unconscious primary process contents, which then evoke and energize the preconscious condensation, and which then spills over into conscious reality experience. The near psychotic experience is usually vertically dissociated from other aspects of preconscious reality and emotional experience and weakly horizontally dissociated from conscious reality experience. The near psychotic condensation is, therefore, isolated, both vertically and horizontally.

The vertically dissociated near psychotic preconscious experience exists alongside other preconscious and conscious experience, but is not changed by these other experiences. The separation extends along content and affect congruent lines down into upper layers of the unconscious and up into lower layers of consciousness. The extent to which the vertical dissociation extends into consciousness does vary. The dissociation has mediating autonomous ego deficits, just as it has mediating defense mechanisms.

The dissociated area may have affect that has opposite valence, but the lack of integration may involve a content area with layered or even integrated affect. The latter is more true of the pseudodelusional type. In either case, the near psychotic condensation is dissociated with the widest and most rigidly fixed aspects of that dissociation located in the preconscious.

The lack of integration in near psychosis of emotional experience and reality experience takes its special form because of both the condensation and its dissociation. The dissociation is not between reality experience and emotional experience but between the focal preconscious condensed reality experience/emotional experience and everything else.

What ego problems mediate vertical dissociations?

1 Lack of secondary process synthetic integration, alone or in combination with
2 Failures of generalization and application,
3 Failure of word presentations to contain and organize affect,
4 Failures of affect modulation (causing unintegratable intensities),

Near Psychotic Structure   85

5   Failures of primary process–secondary process boundary,
6   Failures of reality experience–emotional experience boundary and integration, and
7   Enabling character defenses.

Object Relations

The pathognomonic feature of near psychotic autonomous ego problems in the area of object relations is the loss of the boundary in the preconscious between the reality experienced real object and the representation of emotional experience in the object representation, or between the real self and self representation, or between the self representation and the real object. Condensations take place between these realms. The two realms are the emotional experience and the reality experience of self or objects. Real self or real object experiences are always involved. The near psychotic ego experience is the mental experience of this preconscious object relations condensation.

Usually, the condensation preconsciously involves real object with object representation or real self with self representation. If the real object/object representation condensation is also suffering a projection from the self representation, it is usually a more deeply unconscious projection. The patient may experience the affect simultaneously in the real object, the object representation, and the real self. Various combinations of these possibilities commonly occur.

Projection of unconscious affect from self representation to object representation without the conscious experience of affect in the real self is the neurotic phenomenon. In near psychotic states, the preconscious projections and condensations always involve the real self or real object experience (Weston, 1990).

Autonomous apparatuses of boundary determine what aspects of object relations are condensed and where and at what level the condensation occurs. All near psychotic object relations condensations involve an aspect of the reality experienced object relation condensed with an aspect of the emotionally experienced object relation in the preconscious.[2]

Other autonomous ego problems often found in near psychotic states, such as decreased repression barriers, decreased affect intensity modulation, decreased affect spread regulation, and increased recruitment of affect associated ideational contents, mean that intense and undiluted affects and contents will appear in preconscious object relations, making them extreme, polarized, whole object relations units with clear story lines. This means that at the preconscious level, one does not have just preconscious mechanisms or processes with contents that are more deeply repressed as in the neurotic, but processes and mechanisms that are linked to content at the same level of consciousness. It was Schafer (1968a) who pointed out that defense mechanisms have an emotional

86 Near Psychotic Structure

content. In near psychosis, defensive mechanisms are linked to clear object relations scenarios in the preconscious. Instead of an emotion being projected, an entire self or object image with affect and content is projected. For this reason, object relations in near psychosis are spoken of as defenses, and defense mechanisms are filled with dramatic object relations. In near psychosis, the two concepts become one because of the changes that occur in the preconscious level of near psychotic mental life, especially boundary function.

American ego psychologists tend to describe defensive functioning of processes in emotional experience, whereas British object relations theorists and their American counterparts tend to describe defensive object relations in emotional experience. Neither describes autonomous ego functions well or extensively except for the American Bellak (Bellak et al., 1973). See Table 3.1 for autonomous ego function in near psychosis.

Table 3.1 Autonomous Ego Function in Near Psychosis (partial list)

I Disrupted:

  A Boundaries

    1 Between inside emotional experience and inside reality experience (merged by condensation at limited points in the preconscious)
    2 Between unconscious and preconscious (increased porosity)
    3 Between conscious reality experience and preconscious near psychotic condensation in near psychotic area (decreased porosity)
    4 Between conscious reality experience and preconscious affect (increased porosity)
    5 Between primary and secondary process in the preconscious (increased porosity, and often this problem extends into consciousness)
    6 Between affects in preconscious (increased porosity)
    7 Between affect and mood (increased porosity)
    8 Between affect and concept (increased porosity)
    9 Between real object and object representation or between real self and self representation (increased porosity)

  B Integrations

    1 Integration failure between reality experience and emotional experience at a particular point in the preconscious
    2 Dissociative lack of integration of the resulting condensation from conscious reality experience
    3 Lack of integration of affects and their associated ideational contents

  C Observing ego
    May be captured by primitive defenses and sometimes condensed with near psychotic structure

II Not Disrupted

  A Reality testing
    (Suspended in consciousness and not part of near psychotic structure)
  B Boundary between inside and outside

Near Psychotic Structure 87

Typical near psychotic defenses such as denial of fact or projective identification are often described in object relations terms when describing very ill patients. However, the ego mechanism for emotional negation or neurotic projection is inadequate to describe the sicker forms where reality experience is captured and object relations content is close to consciousness and to manifest content. The usual object relations description of near psychosis fails to distinguish the crucial role of the capture of real object or real self experience.

Defenses are mechanisms; object relations are contents; both deal with affects. These affects are transformed by defenses, disguised by defenses, and expressed in defenses. The defense mechanism itself has an emotional content and experience. All of these phenomena have object relations contents condensed at the preconscious level in near psychosis.

The point is that as the boundary between conscious and unconscious and also between real and emotional changes, the boundary between object relations elements changes. The key to differential object relations experiences is the autonomous ego boundaries.

For example, real object introjection may describe a phase of normal growth and development. It is abnormal, however, when there is an especially porous boundary resulting in affect flooding, and/or if affect goes back and forth and is poorly localized, and/or if the real self or real object is then captured. Therefore, all object relations experiences and hence descriptions are defined by aspects of apparatus ego function.

Because these apparatuses can be changed by psychotropic medication, we see that they do have a level of autonomy from the dynamic content of object relations even as they are affected by them, and for this reason they are also responsive to psychotherapy. One can see this most dramatically when medication reduces a psychotic projection to a borderline projection and together with the help of psychotherapy reduces that to a neurotic projection without ever changing the content theme of the projection.

Table 3.2 Some Object Relations and Ego Boundary Functions

I Real Self Projections

  A Real self projected to self representation

    1 Normal: role acquisition; no fixed condensation
    2 Neurotic: conflicted projections to and evocations by real self experience; an unconscious projection process
    3 Near psychotic: condensations in the preconscious (severe physical illness in childhood, severe childhood trauma, severe behavioral disturbances which proceed to identification)
    4 Psychotic: conscious fusion states; in—out boundary damage (organic mental syndrome, acute schizophrenia, extreme mania)

(Continued)

Table 3.2 (Continued)

B Real Self Projected to Object Representation

1 Normal: growth and development; evolution of psychic change in life course; alterations of emotional view of others based on self in reality and real self changes

2 Neurotic: unchanging relationship due to growth and development conflicts (oedipal and preoedipal)

3 Near psychotic: condensation in preconscious (may be in defensive relationship to a fixed, unchanging, unconscious object representation as in the ideal object of near psychotic narcissistic disorders)

4 Psychotic: conscious condensations with idealized or debased object representation as in manic grandiosity or psychotic depression

C Real Self Projected to Real Object

1 Normal: reality interchange; no condensation; based on self in reality and object in reality interactions

2 Neurotic: same as above except there are unconscious emotional conflicts about this interchange

3 Near psychotic: preconscious condensed interchanges of affect between real self and real object

4 Psychotic: damaged in—out boundary, with resultant real self and real object fusion, or real self—delusional projections to real object (in dyslexia, there may be conscious or subliminal interchanges, but no fixed condensation and accurate secondary process sorting can occur when attention is focused)

II Real Self Introjections

A Real Self Introjections from the Self Representation

1 Normal: an aspect of normal learning or growth and development; part of role acquisition (trial learning, aspirations, role fantasies)

2 Neurotic: unconscious conflicts and condensations where self representation conflicts with real self (viz., assumption of initiate role in real life)

3 Near psychotic: condensations in the preconscious (condensations in hypomania with ideal self and real self; near psychotic depressions with condensation of debased self representations with real self)

4 Psychotic: conscious condensations (viz., mania: conscious condensations with ideal aspect of self representations and real self or psychotic depressive condensations with debased self representations)

B Real Self Introjections from Object Representation

1 Normal: an aspect of normal role acquisition; a type of identification; no conscious condensation

2 Neurotic: unconscious conflict (viz., conflict over assumption of authority role)

3 Near psychosis: condensation in preconscious (viz., severe sadomasochistic or paranoid characters; near psychotic depressions; an aspect of the second phase of projective identification)

4 Delusional identification: paranoid schizophrenia; some severe chronic manias; conscious aspect of some delusional depressions

C Real Self Introjections from the Real Object

1 Normal: a type of identification as in the representation of role acquisition experiences
2 Neurotic: unconscious, conflicted identifications (viz., narcissistic fantasies of grandiosity or debasement)
3 Near psychotic: condensations in the preconscious as in pseudodelusional narcissistic fantasies of grandiosity or depressive debasement
4 Psychotic: conscious condensations with losses of reality testing as in psychotic depression, fusion states in acute schizophrenia, organic mental syndrome, or mania

III Real Object Projections

A Real Object Projected to Object Representation

1 Normal: social learning
2 Neurotic: unconscious, conflicted, or traumatic experiences
3 Near psychotic: preconscious condensations (viz., severe trauma)
4 Psychotic: an aspect of psychotic fusion states or of grandiose delusions or of psychotic depression after real object has been contaminated with projections

B Real Object Projected to Self Representation

1 Normal: learning; romantic love (a type of identification where the intense focus of experience is the real object)
2 Neurotic: unconscious condensation; intense, conflicted as in hysteria
3 Near psychotic: condensation in preconscious (viz., near psychotic narcissistic condensations of real object, real self, and self representation); see Kernberg (1975)
4 Psychotic: condensations in consciousness (psychotic grandiosity; some schizophrenic delusions)

C Real Object Projected to Real Self

1 Normal: encoding of normal social role interchanges; no condensations; conscious and preconscious
2 Neurotic: unconscious condensation fantasies expressing yearnings and fears for similarities and special relationships
3 Near psychotic: condensations in preconscious (near psychotic depressions with reality disappointment in previously idealized objects) (without condensation and preconscious subliminally in some organic brain syndromes with porous in–out boundary)
4 Psychotic: psychotic condensations and/or fusions (mania, paranoid schizophrenia, acute organic brain syndrome)

IV Real Object Introjections

A Real Object Introjections from the Object Representation

1 Normal: a type of relationship and identification with real objects in social interactions of growth and development; the shaping and changing of the object aspect of identifications. No condensation
2 Neurotic: unconscious condensations expressing strong wishes and fears about the real object

(Continued)

90   Near Psychotic Structure

Table 3.2 (Continued)

3 Near psychotic: condensation in the preconscious (viz., aspect of projective identification in depressions and manias)
4 Psychotic: condensations in consciousness (psychotic depression, psychotic mania, schizophrenia)
B Real Object Introjections from the Self Representation
I Normal: in social role performance
2 Neurotic: unconscious, conflicted emotional contamination of real object
3 Near psychotic: preconscious condensations as in affect captures of manic-depressive illness
4 Psychotic: conscious condensations as in psychotic mania or depression
C Real Object Introjections from the Real Self
I Normal: an aspect of social learning/growth and development
2 Neurotic: unconscious, conflicted condensations
3 Near psychotic: preconscious condensations as in some near psychotic affective illnesses
4 Psychotic: as an aspect of conscious fusion states

Table 3.2 shows that the key to different object relations experiences is the ego boundaries between elements, especially between reality experience and emotional experience and between levels of consciousness. The argument is over whether the boundary disturbances are caused by the object relations or, as I say, the object relations disturbance is also caused by the autonomous ego boundary disturbance in psychotic and many near psychotic illnesses.

Day Residues

Because near psychosis captures reality experience, we are interested in what reality experiences are captured and why. I have been using the term *day residue* as analogous to precipitating event or organizing event: a reality event, with its sequences and contexts, that is meaningful and therefore is a reality evoker of affect and of symbol. Because there are propensities to structure that are developmental and biological, it is not quite accurate to call a reality trigger a cause, necessary and sufficient. But the day residue is a nidus, and while not sufficient, it may be a provoker. Perhaps it is better to say that we need to look at how what happened becomes organized in the psychotic or near psychotic structure. We are interested, then, in the process organizing the day residue into the symbolic transformations of near psychotic structure.

In the near psychotic patient, the day residue object or event is in the same preconscious layer as the symbolic transformations, or just below. It is part of the near psychotic condensation. It may also be intact and dissociated. Sequence and context are also usually captured.

There is a condensation summation experience between the day residue, the symbolically altered day residue, and emotional experience that is intense and overwhelms reality experience in the preconscious. A therapist can find out what in reality is upsetting or triggering such a patient fairly soon after exploring the emotional material, because the point of condensation between reality experience and emotional experience is at the day residue point. This point is almost conscious and often has intense affect which is conscious and marks the available edge of near psychotic ideational content. The condensation is primary process. In this sense, it is like a temper tantrum of a small child who is not making logical sense but who, after being comforted and listened to, can finally calm down enough to tell you what happened.

The day residue in near psychosis, because it is significant in reality as well as emotionally significant, like the day residue in psychosis or the day residue in traumatic dreams, is a reality bridge between fact and fantasy, present and past, primary process and secondary process, and conscious and unconscious. It symbolically represents the emotional conflicts that emerge disguised and expressed in the primary process alterations of reality that occur. In near psychosis, all of this is primary processed at the preconscious level.

The day residue in near psychosis can be an event in reality that seems dramatic or minor, but near psychotic day residues are never minor to the patient. They are events in reality that trigger emotional experience because they are similar to or evoke the same emotional experience as genetic events in the past and may be real traumas and deprivations in the present.

The conscious percept experience in near psychosis tends to be the affect significance of the percept rather than an altered percept. A significant displacement of emotional experience onto reality experience is involved, especially of genetic emotional experience onto present, reality, perceptual day residue experience.

Because the day residue object or event is part of the near psychotic condensation, the contamination of reality experience tends to be quite significant. This is as significant as in psychosis, except that in near psychosis the contamination of the day residue tends to be in the preconscious, is more fluid, and does not fully contaminate conscious reality experience and conscious reality testing.

Thus, we see that there are differences between dreams, psychosis, and near psychosis in the location of the day residue and its symbolic alterations but similarities in the primary processing of reality experiences. The day residue experience in near psychosis is condensed with emotional experience in the preconscious, but in addition, there may be intact day residue dissociated. If this is so, the dissociation is either conscious but disavowed, or preconscious and denied. Many times, however, there is no intact dissociated day residue of secondary process and it must be disentangled by interpretation from the primary process condensation location in which it is trapped.

Sequence and context in the day residue experience, unlike sequence and context in the psychoses, tends to be captured by the condensation in the preconscious. This can be a key to interpretive leverage by disentangling the day residue event or object from the primary process. Also helpful is that the sequence and context are usually less rigidly captured than the day residue event or object.

Thing Presentation

The near psychotic condensation takes thing presentation form. Near perceptual experiences, alterations, significances, are percept-affects organized according to primary processes to convey concepts. In near psychosis, this is in the location of near consciousness. Thus, we have a thing presentation form, content, and experience of emotion fixed and partially repressed in the preconscious, influencing but unavailable to conscious word presentations and secondary processes. Aspects of conscious reality experience will be actively contaminated by intense emotional alterations of reality with perceptual qualities. This experience will be almost available to consciousness and will strongly influence conscious decision making, but it will be unavailable to the secondary process logic of conscious reality experience because of preconscious location and dissociation. The influence of the preconscious thing presentation and its processes will form its own motivating system because it seems almost real, has intense affect and validity, and requires discharge. It will also influence the selection and organization of new reality experience. This accounts for the maladaptation of near psychotic states.

Because of the thing presentation phenomenon, the preconscious near psychotic idea is not a concept but a concrete representation. The near psychotic behavior is not a response that is adaptive to external reality stimuli but is a concrete enactment of, and response to, the affects and the concepts in the thing presentation. The near psychotic attitude or affect is in behavior or encoded idea in these preconscious thing presentations. Psychoanalytic treatment of near psychosis is the understanding and treatment of these thing presentations, whether in behavior, idea, affect, or only in attitude.

All thing presentation phenomena involve affect-determined percepts and primary process organization. All thing presentation phenomena borrow from reality experience and have the perceptual qualities of those reality experiences. Only some thing presentation phenomena, however, occur in reality experience in near consciousness and are vertically dissociated from the rest of mental life. These are near psychotic thing presentations. This is the form of experience the near psychotic condensation takes.

When reality experience–emotional experience condensations are expressed in a thing presentation in near consciousness, emotions will be concrete, almost perceptual, and experienced as almost real. Near psychotic thing presentations protrude their intense reality, perceptual, affect experience qualities into consciousness.

The thing presentation in near psychosis tends to be rigidly fixed, stereotyped, and repetitive in content and affect. It is vertically dissociated in the preconscious and is therefore unchanged by other preconscious experience, unavailable to creative play, and automatically intensified by triggering day residues. Because the thing presentation is preconscious, it may be more influenced, than in psychosis, by affect intensification, mood, and mood-congruent provocative reality events.

The preconscious thing presentation tends to influence consciousness not only because it has perceptual qualities but also because it does not totally contain the affect. This echo of affect in consciousness adds validity to the conscious experience, which then reinforces the preconscious ideas. Also, the conscious translating mechanism between primary and secondary process, thing presentation and word presentation, and affect and concept, is either overwhelmed, damaged, or both. Symbolic thinking is therefore limited in the near delusional idea to preconscious concrete pictorial thing presentation experience.

Rigid, fixed, porous, preconscious thing presentations are the basic mental experience of all near psychotic phenomena. Object relations, for instance, in near psychosis take a concrete thing presentation form of preconscious perceptual reality. Their use as emotional symbols is stereotyped, repetitive, dissociated, with a fixed relationship to day residue triggers.

Thing Presentation Quality

Crucial to psychotic and near psychotic experience is the quality of the experience. This quality is a mixture of emotional and reality experience, with a perceptual quality of reality experience dominating. In near psychosis, this is just out of awareness but pushing into consciousness. This affect–percept quality charges ideas or behavior or attitudes with intensity and a near reality veracity. The near reality quality of the experience is its own motivation to actualize in reality and to gain satisfaction in reality. This occurs without the content or process of the condensation being fully conscious. The condensation in the preconscious is between affect and percept, and only secondarily with the idea.

This causes a shift in the experience of validity. Validity is heavily influenced by the thing presentation experience at the expense of other validating mental experience, because both the quality of perceptual reality and the quality of affect are focused together. This makes the associated idea seem emotionally valid. It is this quality of reality and validity in the preconscious that gives the near psychotic experience its particular and peculiar essence.[3]

When reality quality energizes affect, the motto is, "I feel, therefore my view of reality must be true." When reality quality infiltrates ideas, the motto is "I know it is so, therefore my view of reality must be true." When reality quality infiltrates behavior, the motto is, "I took action, therefore my view of reality must be true."

Near psychosis is not a strong memory or imagination or daydream. Eidetic people have very strong memories and often imagination experiences that may be conscious, perceptual sense experiences. These states are not near psychotic because they do not have near psychotic condensation structure, location, and influence. They occur in an intermediate area between conscious reality experience and emotional experience. They are often reality memory traces uncondensed with present reality experience, although perhaps triggered by present reality day residues and their similar affects.

Experiences that May Seem to be Near Psychosis but do not Have Near Psychotic Structure

1 Eidetic—thing presentation content and quality intensely and fully experienced but in a conscious zone intermediate between reality experience and emotional experience.[4] It is memory or imagination with strong perceptual qualities about which reality testing and observing ego are intact.

2 Imagination—thing presentation content usually not conscious, but if so, reality experience may be borrowed but not captured; thing presentation quality experience, if any, is in superordinate emotional experience or intermediate ego, as in eidetic.

3 Uncanny—reality quality intense due to an overlap of preconscious emotional experience and memory with the conscious situation in reality; takes place in emotional experience; no condensation capture of reality experience; the reality quality is from the conscious experience of the thing in reality, from reality properties of memory of a real event in the past and only secondarily from overlapping emotional experience. There is no preconscious condensed thing presentation.

4 Trauma and "flashbacks"—reality experience triggers a "flashback" of eidetic memory experience of trauma which overlaps with present-day reality experience; no true condensation occurs; intense affect charges the traumatic memory but does not lead to near psychotic condensation, although the experience may strongly resemble near psychotic condensation. Some early traumas or adult traumas that trigger a mood disorder may lead to near psychotic condensations.

Defenses

The unique feature of near psychotic defenses is their capture of preconscious reality experience.[5] The defensive capture is organized according to primary process rules. Defenses in psychosis and near psychosis function to avoid reality experienced evidential and cognitive–logical confrontation. In near psychosis, deeper and/or dissociated layers of emotional conflict experience are protected by certain aspects of captured reality experiences. The defensive capture of reality may occur through intensity that overwhelms, as in chronic childhood trauma or manic-depressive illness, or through direct boundary damage, as in schizophrenia or attention deficit disorders. Near psychotic defenses tend to be quite rigid, inflexible, and maladaptive. One reason is that defenses operate against aspects of reality functioning and therefore must maintain a rigid stance because the potential confrontational input of reality may be fairly constant. The second reason is that the intensity of affect in many of the near psychotic illnesses is great and constantly pressing, so that defenses must be maintained continuously and inflexibly. Third, certain near psychotic defenses, for instance in states of depression, involve intense and angry superego contents and functions condensed with ego defensive operations, and the intensities and rigidities, therefore, summate (Coen, 1988). However, there are some more plastically organized near psychotic patients whose defenses are not rigidly fixed in content or in intensity of affect. But these defenses also operate continuously to change reality experience, especially interpersonal social experience.

Defenses in near psychosis are part of the near psychotic condensation. They involve reality experience, emotional experience, observing ego content, reality testing content but not processes, mediating defenses of vertical dissociations, and horizontal defenses of repression across a broad front of basic personality functioning. These condensations occur preconsciously, and so the integration characteristics of the primary process/secondary process preconscious determine form. The summation of these different areas, with their contents, affects, and autonomous ego captures, makes near psychotic experience seem chaotic. However, this seeming chaos is in no sense random. There are specific and stable autonomous ego problems, specific and stable character attitudes and defenses, and stable themes of object relations conflicts, with limited numbers of condensation points.

The degree to which there is a vertical dissociation, small or large, between this near psychotic condensation and the rest of personality function varies from fluid in the behavioral borderline patient to rigid and fixed in the near delusional. There is always, in both types, a large vertical dissociation from intact conscious and preconscious autonomous ego functions. In the near delusional patient, a near psychotic condensation may involve one interpersonal relationship and content area and be dissociated from the remainder of personality functioning and associated conscious cognitive functioning. There are two separate areas of reality testing content and two separate areas of observing ego function. One relates to the near psychotic condensation and the other relates to the rest of mental functioning. As in the psychotic patient, mediating the vertical dissociation are defense mechanisms that are often basic to the personality attitude structure of the patient. The difference between these mediating defenses of vertical dissociations in near psychotic patients and those of psychotic patients is that the enabling defenses in the near psychotic are part of the near psychotic condensation. This may make initial confrontation and exploration of the near psychotic content more difficult, but once entry into the defensive system has been achieved, progress may be rapid because it allows immediate entry into the near psychotic condensation.

An effort has been made in the analytic literature to describe the peculiar and particular characteristics of near psychotic defenses. Words like *primitive* and *splitting* are often used. There are various definitions of these phenomena. The point, for me, is that all near psychotic defenses capture or alter reality experience in the preconscious and press into the conscious experience of reality. There are various dissociative mechanisms involved in maintaining and organizing this capture. I will use *primitive* to mean capture of reality experience. I will limit *splitting* to mean a particular type of vertical dissociation based on affect valence.[6] Splitting is a lack of integration in emotional experience. In near psychosis, this splitting is only a first step toward a second step which captures an aspect of reality experience. The usual second step is a projection onto the real object or the real self. Not all near psychotic defenses involve splitting. All near psychotic defenses, however, are primitive in that they capture part of reality experience (cf. Willick, 1983). These defenses always function to isolate the near psychotic condensation from the remainder of reality experience, and sometimes from other aspects of personality functioning and defense. Because defenses in near psychosis involve the capture of reality experience, they have a different function and target than in the neuroses. The defenses in near psychoses operate against aspects of reality experience by primary processing aspects of reality experience as part of a condensation structure.

The most common ways reality experience can be defensively affected are through projection or denial. I will describe both for near psychotic states. Before I do so, I need to say something about defense content themes. Defense content themes tend to be more homogeneous in near psychotic states. Even if they are mixtures of themes, there are limited numbers of themes in the mixture. Thus, thematic content is characteristic of each patient and each category of near psychotic character disorder;

Near Psychotic Structure 97

indeed, all character disorders have characteristic themes. These themes express themselves especially in behavior and attitude. For this reason, an archaic term for these disorders is *behavior neurosis*. I prefer the term *attitude neurosis*, because the behavior is an expression of the underlying attitude that forms the premise for the idea of behavioral action, and because there are many patients with near psychotic attitudes who do not go on to enact in behavior (Compton, 1987).

Projective Identification

When projection involves reality experience alterations, it is called *projective identification*. It is based on three autonomous ego problems. One is the problem with reality testing, which is either suspended or dissociated. The second is the lack of ability to repress the intensity and associated content of strong emotions. The third, and the most important, is the projection onto reality experience, usually onto the real object from the object representation, or onto the real self from the self representation. Projective identification describes a level of mental organization which permits a certain type of capture of reality experience by emotion. Neurotic projection involves an unconscious feeling in the self experience projected onto the preconscious emotional experience of self or object representation but not onto the real self or real object. A neurotic statement reflecting this fact is "Are you angry at me? I worry you are angry at me." By contrast, sicker patients project onto the reality experience. These patients are fairly certain that the person is angry at them. In addition, because of repression incompleteness and lack of integration, it is not just a feeling that is projected, but also an entire object relationship. The projection contains not just a feeling but also its associated ideational contents. The patient feels the other person really is angry, and also knows why the person is angry and how the person feels about the patient because of the anger.

This merger onto reality experience in near psychosis occurs preconsciously. The condensation is preconscious. Deeper layers of affect and content are unconscious. The resulting feeling and idea may be conscious.

I have discussed what is projected and where the projection is to. Where is the projection from? It is either from the unconscious object representation or from the unconscious self representation. If the projection involves self and object representations in the projection, the projection is from both. This implies a further boundary disturbance between self and object representations.

Projective identifications involving projections to the experience of the real self are very important in near psychotic depressions, manias, and psychosomatic illness. They are often overlooked in early or slow-progressing work with depressed patients (see Chapters 5, 7, and 8).

98 Near Psychotic Structure

In summary, *projective identification* is a term that describes a particular mental mechanism in which what is projected, and where it is projected to, differs from neurotic projection. In projective identification, a whole self or whole object image from unconscious emotional experience is projected onto the preconscious real self or real object.

Why is the mechanism called *projective identification*? What is the identification component? Learned authors have discussed this issue for years (Kernberg, 1975; Meissner, 1980; Ogden, 1982; Porder, 1987; Sandler, 1988; Steiner, 1989). Each one has a different explanation. Klein, the originator of the term, never clarified this. I do not think she felt she had to, because she believed in an in–out/out–in process of object relations structure building. What was in went out, and what was out went in at the schizoid level of development. Some authors describe this phenomenon in Freud's term of *primary identification*, which hypothetically occurs in infants as an internalization before "self and object" are differentiated. It is unclear whether this ever happens at the conscious level (Sterm, 1985). It is usually unclear whether the psychoanalytic literature means conscious, unconscious, or both, or cognitive, affective, or both. In any case, Freud meant simultaneous and undifferentiated, whereas Klein meant sequential.

My descriptive explanation is that the projected emotion is felt also in the preconscious real self which is felt to be in response. The patient experiences his or her anger in his or her real self experience as being caused by the anger in the real object. The patient therefore experiences preconsciously a change in his or her real self related to a felt change in the object. This is identification (Sandler and Rosenblatt, 1962; Schafer, 1968b). The fact that the real object has suffered a projection is preconscious.

The same holds if the projective identification involves projection to the self experience only. Patients feel bad about themselves in response to a projection of the way they fear they really are (see Table 3.3).

The emotion can be any emotion from anger, to contempt, to eroticism. The ideational component is usually not identical in self and object.

Table 3.3 Projective Identification

Location of Projection Mechanism	Preconscious
Target of Projection	Reality experience (preconscious real object or preconscious real self)
Origination of Projected Feelings	Emotional experience; self representation or object representation, or both
Identification Component	Preconscious change in real self in response to the projection

Thus, in the adult, the phenomenon is not the same as primary identification. The adult phenomenon resembles a condensation.

Denial

Because very ill patients may seem to ignore reality, they are often said to practice denial. However, denial means not ignoring or avoiding reality, but an active intrapsychic process of denying an aspect of experienced reality. Healthier patients may deny aspects of their emotional experience, but not aspects of their real-world experience. Sicker patients actively deny aspects of their own experienced factual reality. Denial affects the experience of things in reality, the experience of the real object or the real self. The experience of reality sequence or context is also usually affected.

Denial in near psychosis refers to a mental state in which information from reality is received and stored in reality experience, and in real object and real self representations of the conscious and preconscious but is dissociated from the rest of reality experience and from conscious emotional experience. It is a type of dissociation (for a beginning discussion of this, see Freud [1925]).

Symbolic Alterations of Reality

Symbolic alterations of reality are condensations that capture and use aspects of reality experience to symbolically represent an emotional experience. The reality which is captured involves present-day experiences akin to the day residue concept in psychoanalysis and the precipitating event concept in general psychiatry. The present reality day residue is emotionally elaborated and altered, condensed with the past, experienced as real in the present, and used symbolically but not experienced symbolically. A symbolic alteration of reality is a plastic representation of reality.

In creativity, the symbolic alteration of reality is experienced emotionally or experienced in an intermediate zone (Winnicott, 1953, 1971). In creativity, the ego can use the symbolic alteration. The use is conscious and under the control of secondary processes (Arieti, 1976). In psychosis, the symbolic alteration is in conscious reality experience and not under conscious control. In near psychosis, the symbolic alteration of reality is in preconscious reality experience and is not under conscious control.

The symbolic alteration in near psychosis occurs in preconscious reality experience and not just in emotional experience or in the transitional area. This means that the symbolic processes in near psychosis not only capture reality experience, but also are not under control of conscious, creative, logical, symbolizing ego processes. The symbol processes take over an area of preconscious reality experience, dominate and control real experiences in that area, alter reality experience via primary process emotion mechanisms, and borrow reality experience qualities of perception to form a thing presentation. The resulting thing presentation symbol is not experienced as a symbol but as a concrete near reality (see Table 3.3).

Concrete means not experienced as abstract, truncated in concept, and having few referents in the immediate associations. Deeper, richer relationships and variations on the symbolic theme are repressed in the unconscious and/or dissociated in the preconscious, often in character derivatives like attitude and behavior.

The day residue has a rigidly fixed and limited position at the center of the symbolic alteration, with a fixed primary process relationship to emotional experience in the specific condensation mechanisms and defense mechanisms used. The near psychotic symbol is horizontally and vertically dissociated from processes in the ego that might translate and use the symbol. The location in the preconscious horizontally dissociates the core of the condensation from conscious reality processes. Translating mechanisms of the ego are thus cut off from the symbolic alteration of reality. In addition, conscious translating mechanisms of the ego may be flooded or broken. This varies according to illness.

The structure of all thing presentation symbols is composed of perceptual reality, but where this percept is experienced, how it is controlled, its plasticity in relationship to the emotional aspects evoked by the day residue, its relationship to the rest of emotional experience, whether it is open to secondary process use and variation, and whether it can be translated into word presentations, all determine whether the resultant thing presentation symbol is a manifestation of illness.

All thing presentations use reality experience for their formal elements of content. All thing presentation symbols have reality experience qualities. All thing presentations alter formal elements of reality experienced percept according to primary process rules. But only in mental illness does the thing presentation symbolically alter reality experience with a dissociated or rigidly fixed relationship to emotional experience and to reality experience, all taking place within reality experience.

Thing presentation experience is the experiential aspect of primary process. The term *primary process* refers to formal, organizational aspects. Symbolic alteration of reality refers to the use primary process makes of reality, focusing on the ways reality is altered. Symbolic alterations of reality are metaphorical and emotional uses of reality experience.

Are all psychoanalytic symbols thing presentations? No, thing presentation is a type of mental experience. Psychoanalytic symbols are any primary process form of emotional metaphor. Thing presentations are a specific affect–percept symbol experience of metaphor.

Much, if not most, of human mental life is symbolic. Only a minority of these symbols are consciously and preconsciously experienced as thing

Table 3.4 Symbolic Alterations of Reality in Psychosis and Near Psychosis

A Symbolic Alterations of Reality in Psychosis

1	Location (of thing presentation condensation of reality experience with emotional experience)	Conscious reality experience
2	Quality	Reality-perceptual
3	Organization	Usually primary process; because of location, may be secondary process
4	Structural location of the day residue	Symbolic alteration of day residue altered and condensed in conscious reality experience and may also be unaltered in dissociated conscious or preconscious reality experience

B Symbolic Alterations of Reality in Near Psychosis

1	Location (of thing presentation condensation)	Preconscious reality experience
2	Quality	Reality-perceptual
3	Organization	Always primary process
4	Structural location of the day residue	Symbolic representation of day residue from conscious reality experience, altered and condensed in the preconscious (and may be also unaltered and dissociated in conscious or preconscious reality experience)

C Symbolic Alterations of Reality in Neurosis

1	Location (of thing presentation condensation of reality experience with emotional experience)	Unconscious emotional experience
2	Quality	Emotional experience
3	Organization	Primary process in unconscious, much secondary elaboration in conscious
4	Day residue	From minor displaced conscious or preconscious reality experience and from major unconscious emotional experience

D Symbolic Alterations of Reality in Creativity

1	Locution (of thing presentation)	Conscious and/or preconscious and/or unconscious; if conscious or preconscious, then third space and not capturing reality experience
2	Quality	Emotional experience or intermediate experience
3	Organization	Primary process and secondary process
4	Structure	Flexible relation to day residue; flexible use of symbol; translating mechanisms intact and not dissociated or avoided

presentations. Only in psychosis or near psychosis do these symbolic thing presentations alter and dominate the conscious control of reality experience.

In psychosis and near psychosis, as a thing presentation experience emerges, the details of the symbolic alterations of reality that are involved are charged with affect. The appearance of these affect-laden details is a surprise to the patient, and their meaning is unknown to the patient because of the dissociations and because translating mechanisms are broken.

The exact and complex relationship between symbols, thing presentations, and symbolic alterations of reality will be the topic of a future work.

Understanding symbol experience and construction in near psychotic patients will enable the psychoanalyst to help the patient make the symbolic alteration of reality fully conscious and to translate the condensations of affect, ideas, and perceptual experiences into words (see Table 3.4).

Toward a Psychoanalytic Theory of Action

Enactment is dynamically meaningful behavior which analysts sometimes restrict to transference behaviors of defense resistance. I will discuss the broad use of symbolically meaningful behavioral actions.

One problem standing in the way of a psychoanalytic theory of enactment is to equate behavioral action with pathology. The therapist goes on vacation. His female patient takes her cat and kills it by putting it in the refrigerator. After years of treatment, she makes a sculpture of a dying, screaming cat at a time of separation from the therapist. In a similar example, a therapist goes away and his male patient, while hunting, "accidentally" loses his dog. At the same time, the patient, a writer, is writing a story about a lonely and abandoned dog. Of these four described actions, which is pathological? Which is sublimation? If the female sculptor had only sculpted, would that have been sublimation? If the male had only written and not hunted, would he have been free of pathology? These questions, of course, cannot be answered without an understanding of the patient's mental experience of all these actions and knowledge about the relationship of the experience of these actions to other ego functions, such as reality testing and the integrative-regulation ego function that negotiates the relationship of reality to fantasy. That there may be dynamic, even conflicted, feelings expressed in actions is true regardless of the level of ego function. Both patients felt rage and abandonment, both patients experienced emotional abandonment by one or both parents, both experienced the therapist as cold and themselves as lost and helpless victims. All four forms of behavioral enactment reversed the passive–active equation. But the actions fell along very different points of the ego pathology spectrum. Enactment occurs in normal, neurosis, near psychosis, and psychosis, although the clearest examples usually are in near psychotic behavioral borderlines where behavioral action is a wide-open channel of personality, serving defense–discharge functions in a system which is stimulated by present-day events.

The problem of action, therefore, and its relationship to pathology is a separate question from the question of action itself. Pathology and its categories can only aid a psychoanalytic theory of *pathological* enactment. It may be that psychoanalysis should confine itself to this. However, analysis also deals with behaviors that are dynamically meaningful but not particularly pathological. Every analyst, including Freud, has dealt with the psychopathology of everyday life. This includes the psychodynamics of normal behavior.

Can we as analysts say anything about action in general? Psychoanalysis has traditionally tried to do this by describing the dynamic features of behavior. Certain analysts in particular have focused on the emotional and ideational content expressed in behavior (Reich, 1925; Kernberg, 1975).

But understanding that behavior has specific meaning does not distinguish action from other mental products which also contain dynamic content expressions. The question then arises whether there are characteristic structural or organizational features of action that distinguish action from other mental products which also symbolically mediate the dynamic unconscious. Is action different? Is action a unique mental product? If so, and if this can be described, we then might re-approach the issue of why behavior seems to be a chosen modality for some patients and why behavior is pathological in some patients.

Psychoanalysis should start by describing the inner experience of action. Is the experience of symbolic behavior different from the experience of fantasy?

Action is a way of experiencing externally. Some people only consciously register something when they do something. As a patient said, "I do it; then it crosses my mind." The inside experience is made more available through an experience of outside.

Now the question psychoanalysis could profitably explore is this: what is the internal experience of the external something? The experience seems to be the experience of a particular kind of condensation in which the symbol elements of percept, affect, and concept condense with behavior. *Action* is a term used to express this type of symbol condensation.

It would be helpful if we could describe the exact relationship between percept, affect, concept, and behavior inherent in all dynamic action. Since many mental products show, in their symbolic form, a condensation of percept, affect, and concept, what is the specific arrangement of these three components when behavior is condensed with them? This may then help us understand the pleasure of behavior.

The crucial factor in the relationship of these elements is that behavior occurs in the real world and in the reality recording and reality experiencing capacities of the mind. Action takes place in reality experience, not fantasy. Action is an attempt to change the perceptual feedback of reality experience. The attempt to do this often externalizes the internal causal experience of affect and of wished-for or feared percept and ascribes them or experiences them as part of the external target of the behavioral action. But the reality experienced target of dynamic behavioral action is a day residue. It has symbolic, emotional, fantasy significance. Action is that dynamic mental product which attempts to change the day residue (see Sandler, 1990). Action does this, not just in fantasy, but in reality experience. Action attempts to change the object in reality or self in reality and the experience of the actual object (real object or real self), without conscious awareness that the actual object is symbolic.

In dynamic action, the affect tends to follow the perception of the alteration in the day residue rather than be experienced together with the concept. In dynamic action, there is an attempt by behavior to change the perceptual aspect of the day residue symbol while the inherent concept, in the patient, is maintained unchanged. This is in marked contradistinction to other dynamic mental products in which the concept is condensed with the percept–affect so the concept and affect are together. In action, the affect goes along with behavior due to the perceptual change brought about by behavior. Action is primarily a percept–affect experience rather than a concept–affect experience. Action uses behavior to experience affect together with behavior due to behavior's effect on the perceptual reality of the day residue.

Psychotic patients change the day residue by changing their own percept. Borderline patients use behavior to provoke the day residue to change. Borderline action involves a preconscious condensation between affect, day residue reality experience, and behavioral response. The condensation has perceptual thing presentation qualities in the preconscious, pushing into the conscious. This condensation transmodally changes affect experience to behavior experience. It is this affect–percept–behavior experience quality added to the reality day residue which tempts one to action.

Neurotics enact in highly disguised, indirect behaviors and avoidances. Normal action attempts mastery of the reality environment. Pathological behavior is when the behavioral response to the day residue is predetermined by emotional conflict, rigidly stereotyped in behavior, affect, and attitude, and attempts to change reality to confirm psychological conflict. The stereotypy is based on the genetic day residues and their resulting affect experiences rather than on the reality characteristics of the present day.

Motivation for Symbolic Action

The three categories of motivation for all dynamic action are the experiential motive, the defensive motive, and mastery. The experiential motive operates when symbolic action expresses a particular condensation of affect with the real object experience condensed with the object in reality. This feels different from condensations which do not involve objects in reality. Why? Some experience may not be fully translated into word presentations without risk of reduction. Translating behavior into words may cause a reduction of the complexity of the condensation by separating and changing affect contents, qualities, intensities, and domains. Behavior may therefore allow direct experience of complex combinations of primary process emotional qualities. Even fantasy discharge may be inadequate for certain types of affect experience. The complexity, intensity, and particular quality of mixture in the conflict may only be possible to experience through the perceptual and bodily experience of behavior. "I do it, then I feel it." Some people can only experience an attempt to integrate their affect in this way. Regardless of the level of ego pathology, some people can only feel, or best feel, when they see their feelings in action. This is an ego characteristic.

The experiential motive for action involves not only the resistance to the reduction of affect complexity but also the resistance to change in affect quality due to a change in affect modality. Stern (1985) describes transmodal development and the resulting symbol formation. Affect does not feel the same when the modality of the affect experience changes because affect quality partly depends on the modality of experience. Loewald (1988) alludes to this in his discussion of "stickiness of the libido" (Freud, 1937). Action is different from fantasy because action is a different mode. Affects experienced in action feel different from affect felt in fantasy. "I do it, then I feel it in the way I want to feel it."

Second, there are dynamic *defensive* motivations. Sometimes affect is placed into reality experience because the affect is frightening. Placing the affect into reality experience may enable the discharge of conflicted affect without mobilizing terrifying super-ego defenses and associated early superego affects such as shame. Behavior may enable the experience of affect through a separate physical, bodily, and perceptual channel. This may allow the affect to escape from repression without the concept escaping. The behavior is then often further dissociated from the conscious observing ego. Placing the affect in present-day reality experience while discharging it is a way of producing a defensive derivative. The present-day reality experience may mimic the genetic past closely but is not the genetic past. The affect's reappearance in the behavioral enactment, and in the reality response to the enactment, gives the patient a chance to fight and/or indulge the derivative reality instead of the genetic reality. Therefore, the behavior may bypass ego defensive and superego injunctions.

This derivative, present-day reality experience also carries with it a way of justifying. The behavioral counterreaction that is made by reality justifies the initial behavior even though the response is later in time; just as passive has become active, so, too, does the later become justification for the earlier. This is particularly true of borderline patients. Action is also used in this way to validate fantasy.

The motives for action also include various *mastery* motives for the wish to change the day residue. These motives are on a continuum of pathology from adaptation and conflict mastery to omnipotent, primary process control to delusional grandiosity. All along that axis will be found those people whose stubbornness, will, and perseverance lead them to insist on dealing with the real world. Freud discussed the pathology of these characters in "Observations on Transference-Love" (1915a) when he talked about certain stubborn women who attempt to enact the erotic transference and are therefore unanalyzable. But analysts deal with mental conflicts so that patients might be able to regain the growth element not only in their ego but also in the reality of their lives (Diamond, personal communication, 1988). This experience is pleasurable. Hartmann (1939), Jacobson (1964), and Schafer (1968b) discuss mastery pleasures of the ego.

Because of the importance of reality experience to behavior, it is no wonder that enactments often find their genetic origin in traumatic behaviors that were inflicted in reality upon the patient. Freud's first theory expressed this. It is no wonder that we also believe that the earlier such trauma is inflicted, i.e., preverbally, the more likely it will be to have only a behavioral form of expression, because that was the only form of communication at the time of the trauma. The concept of trauma ties in psychogenetics, phenomenology, psychological organization, and adaptive style. Questions of reality trauma often arise in treating psychotic or near

Table 3.5 Summary of All Near Psychotic Structure

Always

1 Real object and object representation or real self and self representation are condensed in the preconscious
2 Heavily infiltrated by primary process
3 Day residue may be displaced or may be undisplaced but in either case is also condensed in the preconscious with emotional experience. Day residue sequence and context follow the location of the day residue
4 Thing presentation quality is strong in the preconscious and passes into conscious experience
5 Preconscious defensive maneuvers condense with preconscious reality experience
6 Reality testing content is influenced by the near psychotic condensation but not reality testing processes; reality testing processes are dissociated from the near psychotic condensation
7 Observing ego is frequently captured by mediating defenses of vertical dissociation between the near psychotic condensation and the remainder of autonomous ego functions

Usually

1 Vertically dissociated from the rest of reality experience and sometimes from the rest of personality experience
2 Enabling defenses surround vertical dissociations and are part of the structure of near psychotic condensations

The form the near psychotic material takes depends on:

1 How the particular illness disrupts the ego
2 The cognitive and emotional organizational level reached before the near psychotic illness

The content depends on:

1 The content of past and present emotional and reality experiences
2 The content of psychological conflicts in and between the two areas

---

psychotic patients (Fliess, 1973). Issues of reality trauma also frequently arise in the study of group behavior and the resultant cultural product (Marcus, 1994). But trauma is not the only route to action. There is the factor of the intensity of affect, which may make it difficult to change modalities and provide a cause for "stickiness of the libido" (cf. McElroy, Hudson, Pope, Keck, and Aizley, 1992). There is the factor of how completely language function has developed and how available it is for affect containment, integration, and expression. There is also the issue of the ego barrier between affect and behavior. This barrier has an autonomous capacity that develops to various degrees in different people.

Action is different from fantasy in symbol structure, modality of experience, and affect quality. There is a different sense of mastery, i.e., of adaptation to reality. There are different defensive opportunities, i.e., of adaptation to one's own emotions. Action provides a different experience of satisfaction. Sometimes, we call it achievement!

For a summary of newer psychotic structure, see Table 3.5.

Notes

1 The issue of reality testing alterations in near psychotic states is even more complex than in the psychoses, because in some ways reality testing function seems damaged, but in some ways it seems intact. Kernberg (1977) has been articulately insistent on the existence of a specific alteration in reality testing function in borderline patients, and it is part of his definition of borderline states. Following Frosch (1964), Kernberg (1975) describes alterations in reality experience but not in reality testing. In his structural interview paper, Kernberg (1977) describes a quite different idea of reality testing being suspended but not lost, and therefore available when confronted in a psychiatric interview.

I agree that this is the striking and definitional issue. The other issue of alternations in reality experience is nut definitional, being variably true of near psychotic states and nonborderline states. (For a description of alterations in reality relations which I do not think is definitional, see Kernberg (1980, p. 15; see also chapter 1).

The issue of reality testing in near psychotic states gets further confused because of the longstanding description of "minipsychotic episodes." These are acute exacerbations of the illness in which either intense behavior or an intense idea seems to lose reality testing altogether for a period of hours to days. My own experience is that patients who truly lose reality testing even for hours or days often have a concurrent Axis I diagnosis in DSM-IV (APA, 1994), i.e., a major affective illness, schizophrenia, or organic brain syndrome. Usually, the issue in such patients is affective illness. A search for associated signs and symptoms of these illnesses is almost always fruitful. Many of these patients are, however, not delusional at all, but only intensely pseudodelusional. This can be demonstrated even at the time by a persistent and accurately targeted mental status examination during the psychiatric interview. In conclusion, my own experience has been that patients with "minipsychotic episodes" are either psychotic or not psychotic. If they are psychotic, they have some psychotic illness. If they are not psychotic, then all they have is an exacerbation of their near psychotic state. In either case, the term *minipsychotic episode* is a misnomer and may be dangerously misleading because it encourages complacency of differential diagnosis both of level and of illness type. However, even I admit that there are some patients who can be in an intense, exacerbated state, where it is impossible for a brief period of time to be sure whether they are psychotic or only near psychotic. I used to believe that, until proven otherwise, they were not. My clinical experience over the last 20 years has taught me the error of this more heuristically pure assumption. Most of the patients I was not sure about have turned out to have a psychotic illness in addition to their near psychotic illness.

2 This whole area is historically murky. Klein (1940) did distinguish reality from object relations fantasies. She used the term *actual object* for the object in reality and maybe for reality experience, although she tended to ignore this last distinction. More importantly, she felt she was writing about unconscious object relations fantasies. Kernberg and Jacobson tend to blur these distinctions. Also, they all imply that object relations fantasies determine psychic structure, its boundaries, and autonomous apparatuses, ignoring that it may also be the reverse.

But the use of object relations to define near psychotic states has other problems. Object relations theory alone deals poorly, even descriptively, with some characteristic near psychotic ego problems, such as the following: (1) nonbehavioral near psychosis; (2) reality testing alterations; (3) near psychotic symbol experience: relationship of symbol to reality experience; (4) condensations with observing ego; (5) relationship of defense to near psychotic symbol; and (6) distinguishing characteristics of near psychotic object relations structure in those who do not show marked affect splitting. All these aspects are better described in terms of mediating autonomous ego dysfunctions, especially autonomous ego function.

In addition, object relations do not deal with different illness etiologies for the near psychotic state. Object relations theory usually implies that the etiology is either inborn aggression or interpersonal experiences that shape internal object relations, or both. Yet we know that head trauma in the adult can produce a borderline patient. It is important to realize that the organization and experience of object relations is an ego function.

3 It may seem paradoxical to describe a preconscious thing presentation and percept when there is no conscious sensorial event. Why not just say that although there is no conscious perceptual event, there is a condensation of

percept *qualities* with affect qualities, including especially feelings of perceptual veracity and validity? If this seems clearer, it is fine with me. It is a bit inaccurate and a bit reductionist, however, because of the following: (1) many near psychotic patients describe more than this. They describe a perceptual experience without being able to describe an actual sensorial event. It is this psychoputhological paradox that must be described. (2) In any case, it is the capture of reality experience in the preconscious that is crucial. Patients feel that something almost really did happen! This preconscious perceptual something is constantly leaking out into illusions, pseudohallucinations, dreams, and behavioral responses. (3) Perhaps what we are talking about is a subcortical percept–sensory event. This may be why such patients *feel* they see or hear the percept. Subcortical limbic–hypothalamic areas may be capable of perceptual–sensory phenomena as well as affect phenomena (Le Doux, 1989). The cortex, especially conscious mental functioning, is better able to separate percept from affect. Remember that Freud's original concept of thing presentation was a neurological one, based on his understanding of the neurology of percept. He believed this to be different from the neurology of words (for a review of Freud's word presentation neurology, see Ojemann and Mateer [1979]; see also Damascio [1994]).

4 Winnicott (1953, 1971) was the first analyst to describe the intermediate zone of experience between reality and fantasy. His contribution to this area of play, imagination, creativity, and hence art and culture (see Kuhns, 1983) and also to development (see Grolnick, 1990) cannot be overestimated.

5 For many analysts, defenses define illness, especially in sicker patients. They disagree, however, about which defenses define which illnesses and also what definitions to use of different defenses.

Kernberg (1975), especially, uses the organization of defenses around splitting of affect as definitional. This use dates back to Klein, for whom splitting was an unconscious defense. Reich and Freud likewise felt defenses were important in sicker patients, but they used a descriptive model of dissociation which also included consciousness.

I agree with everyone, more particularly with Freud and Reich. I see sicker patients as usually having dissociation defenses which may or may not be based on affect valence. The main issue, however, is whether those defenses capture reality experiences and where they do so (in what areas of mental functioning). Autonomous ego is always involved, especially boundaries between unconscious and preconscious, conscious and preconscious, reality experience and emotional experience. The result is a particular condensation experience not previously described in the literature in which defenses of different possible types play a role, together with boundary disturbance. The etiology varies from illness to illness as does the exact relationship between defenses and autonomous ego boundaries.

6 For the history of the term *splitting* see chapter 2. The point for this chapter is that Kernberg (1975) has used the Kleinian splitting concept as a crucial aspect of his descriptive definition of borderline states. He is not always clear whether he means conscious, preconscious, or unconscious. Also, the term *splitting* does not describe the peculiar relationship of the defenses to reality experience. Finally, some near psychotic patients do not split, they dissociate. That is to say, some near psychotic patients have an *integrated* affective area which almost captures an area of conscious reality experience and is separated from the remainder of the ego's experience and functions.

Chapter 4

Mental Status Examination

General Principles

The mental status examination is an interview method psychiatrists use to gather and organize their observations about the patient's mental functioning. The mental status examination grows out of the general psychiatric tradition of noting mental signs and symptoms of psychiatric and neurological illness. Psychoanalysis adds observations about emotionally dynamic mental contents of ideas and affects. Psychoanalysis focuses especially on the process of this material as it reveals itself in sequential associations and in patients' fantasies about the interviewer. Some psychoanalysts, like general psychiatrists, also observe aspects of the mental organization of this process, called structure, that might reflect severity of illness or even illness type (Reich, 1933a; Jacobson, 1971; Bellak et al., 1973; Kernberg, 1975). Some have written about the relationship between symptoms, structure, transference, and dynamics (MacKinnon and Michels, 2016b; Kernberg, 1975). I follow this latter tradition because the structural road map is so important in the diagnosis and treatment of psychotic and near psychotic conditions. I include, therefore, as part of the mental status examination, the careful assessment of certain ego functions damaged in psychosis and near psychosis. This damage leads to the characteristic mental manifestations of these illnesses and their dynamics.

The mental status examination generates a series of evolving hypotheses. This is because the data on which the hypotheses are based are continuously evolving as new information is continuously elicited. The functional organization of the mind should not be a rigidly fixed property. Therefore, new information is regularly emerging and questions lead to constantly deepening factual and emotional information.

The examiner affects the mental status examination by having an impact on the mental experience of the patient. That the observer affects the results is both a problem and an opportunity, because it allows the observer, through the interaction of the examination, to understand more carefully with the patient the active, present functioning of mental experience. The mechanisms, contents, organizations, behaviors, and feelings elicited during the examination can also help to emotionally inform historical information. In addition, there is the opportunity to understand through the observer's own experience.

The mental status examination interview, therefore, includes information, observations, hypothetical constructs, verifications, and nonverifications about the patient and also observations of the examiner's own feelings. The content of mental life, the organization of mental life, and the interaction between content and organization are to be carefully described.

The mental status examination is designed to elicit information about signs and symptoms of illness, unconscious thoughts and feelings, and mental organization. An illness is a particular collection of signs and symptoms that together bespeak a common etiology, a common response to treatment, and a common prognosis. General psychiatrists call the signs and symptoms of these illness categories the study of *psychopathology*.

The psychoanalyst looks to the additional category of unconscious ideas and feelings. The diagnostic categories and treatment modality of analytic psychiatry are this unconscious material. Psychoanalysts call this psychological content *psychodynamics*.

A third mental category is also crucial to those analytic psychiatrists who treat very ill patients. This category is the organization of all mental functioning. It includes the organization that autonomous ego problems impose on psychological content. Autonomous ego organization should be relatively stable, relatively autonomous from breakdown due to psychological conflict, and relatively adaptive to both reality experience and emotional experience. Especially important is the ability to stably and appropriately regulate the relationship between the two areas. Autonomous ego apparatuses and functions are particularly important in very ill patients because it is these functions that are characteristically damaged in psychotic and near psychotic illness.

The mental status examination in psychosis and near psychosis involves the careful examination and exact description of ego functions. This chapter will focus especially on aspects of ego structure that define psychosis and near psychosis.

However, the mental status examination involves only one slice in time. It is a synchronic analysis making diachronic hypotheses. The phenomenon of relatively stable structure allows this deduction. Illnesses do change structure, but in characteristic, illness-specific ways and at characteristic rates. Acute illnesses abruptly change mental structure. Chronic illnesses more gradually and persistently change mental structure. Normal development and psychotherapy also change mental structure. The understanding of normal development, and of normal mental structure compared to the highly abnormal psychotic and near psychotic states, enables us to describe and categorize the general stabilities of illness structures.

112 Mental Status Examination

In addition, stable organizational rules and structured content experiences should normally vary between different levels of awareness. It may be highly pathological for one level of organization to invade another's level. Both because some aspects remain out of awareness and because of the nonverbal qualities of the experience, the patient cannot usually give a clear description of affect contents and relations. The analyst helps to elicit the full story, some aspects of which are not fully conscious. Then, the content and integrated picture will be transcribable into words and describable to the patient.

Technique of Mental Status Examination

The mental status examination is an active inquiry with patients about their mental experience. The experience of reality, the experience of emotions, conscious and unconscious, and the organizational relationship of this information over the course of development are described. The examiner's task is to facilitate the telling, to evaluate the data for diagnosis and treatment, and, in sicker patients, to help integrate experience. The techniques involve the following: (1) observation, (2) active inquiry (confrontation of the pathology, not of the patient), and (3) beginning interpretation (perhaps better described as hypothetical, interpretive descriptions).

Observation

Observation alone produces much information. The verbal stream of ideas, its organization, the emotional theme stated or implied, the affective display, interpersonal behavior, the sequence and proximity relationship of all of these to each other, and the doctor's own experience of the patient are all observable. The physician uses both secondary and primary processes in collecting, searching for, and organizing hypotheses about observations and their integration.

The observation required is a special type of observation. It is an active, empathic, integrative, observational experience. This empathic experience is in the examiner. It is both logical and emotional. It is an attempt empathetically to experience the patient's mental life. Psychotic and near psychotic patients require special capacities of their empathic interviewers.

Active Questioning

I prefer the term *active questioning* to the more standard term *confrontation*, because confrontation often implies, especially to the beginner, an aggressive stance or attitude. There is a proper but complex use of countertransference mastery and aggression in the interaction with very ill patients, but it is best to separate the issue of aggression from the technique of the interview, and I do so by changing the term to *active questioning*. The active questioning is of reality experience, emotional experience, and, especially, their relationship to each other.

Active questioning asks for more data, a different kind of data, a comparison of data, or an elaboration of data. Active questioning calls the patient's attention to a paradoxical or absent step of logic or emotion. Active questioning is focused on a particular area of interest to the examiner who sees that area as crucial to the evolving story. Active questioning often challenges defenses because dissociations of mental organization may cause absent data or paradoxical data. More importantly, integrative capacity and therefore level of illness may be unknown until challenged (see Kernberg, 1977; M. Stone, 1980).

Knowing what and when to engage and question depends on the evolving story of facts and emotions, and on the analyst's knowledge of dissociative processes, secondary processing of day residues, and primary processing of fantasies. The examiner must also be familiar with illnesses and their characteristic effects on mental organization, agency experiences and their likely conflicts, and development with its emotional phases, life task phases, and resultant important influences on day residues. Clearly, the more the analyst knows about these areas, the more effective the interview will be.

Timing in the interview is important and is a matter of clinical judgment. The more practice the examiner has, the better he or she will be able to conduct the interview rapidly, accurately, and tactfully.

Interpretive Descriptions

Emotional primary process experiences may be elicited along with or instead of secondary process. These experiences are both crucial aspects of, and defenses against, deeper layers of the evolving story. In the very ill, these defenses may maintain vertical dissociations, block observing ego, and overwhelm verbal, conceptual capacity. The analytic therapist must therefore be prepared to interpretively describe these ego problems, their resulting primary process reactions, their defensive functions, and their effect on mental organization as well as their latent psychodynamics. The analyst points out these reactions, helps the patient describe the mediated feelings, and describes the relationship to the patient's full story of reality experienced day residues. The interview may strengthen integrative, secondary processes and enable the release of new factual and emotional information and their relationship.

As one explores the relationship of reality experience to emotional experience, the patient may reorganize the relationship via secondary process and word presentations. As a result, an effective mental status interview becomes a treatment process. The patient translates thing presentation experiences with their reality quality into verbal, conceptual reports of emotional experiences. Interpretive descriptions express in words the relationship of feelings to reality in a way that describes how the patient is experiencing the relationship, the role of reality day residues, blocks to a more complete integration, and some hypotheses about the motivational conflicts and illness deficits that have produced the resultant patient experience.

Examination of Ego Functions

I will now describe the mental status examination of those aspects of ego function crucial to the organization of psychosis and near psychosis.

The ego functions I will discuss are the following:

1. Boundaries—
   a. between inside and outside,
   b. between object relations,
   c. between levels of awareness,
   d. between primary process and secondary process
   e. between affects,
   f. between affect and mood.

2. Reality testing,
3. Observing ego,
4. Day residue experiencing capacity and location,
5. Modulating capacity,
6. Integrating capacity,
7. Defenses as they intersect with reality ego,
8. Symbolizing function—
   a. thing presentation,
   b. thing presentation quality,
   c. symbolic alterations of reality.

Boundaries

The boundary between outside and inside is easily observed in the mental status examination. Patients with this difficulty will incorporate their environment into their self-reports. The environment may include the examiner. For example, an examiner reached down to scratch his leg and the patient asked, "Why are you scratching my leg?" A more subtle example, which involves emotion, is the hospitalized patient who cries when another patient is crying. The patient may not be able to say why he is crying, and the diagnosis therefore depends on the observation of the external event.

Object Relations

Object relations refers to patients' unconscious and preconscious experience of themselves in relationship to their feelings about other people in their lives. The term includes present, past, and future. The term is used to include the experience of the reality of the other person, the emotional experience (fantasies) of the other person, the characteristic phase of development in which those emotional experiences (fantasies) are first organized, the characteristic organization in specific character types, and the characteristic distortions of different illnesses (Sandler, 1991).

The main points for the mental status examination of the very ill patient are (1) whether or not the patient distinguishes between the experience of the real object and the emotional experience of the emotional object; likewise, whether the patients experience themselves in reality as distinct from the emotional experience of themselves; (2) the characteristic emotional themes that organize the experience of the patient's self and others; (3) the characteristic distortions the various illnesses impose upon the organization and themes of these relationships.

Object relations experiences are often the most difficult to describe. This is because very ill patients have great distortions in these relationships, which obfuscate coherent narrative. The object relations experiences may be intensely infiltrated with emotion that blurs the causality and sequential plot. The experience may suffer boundary problems that merge aspects of the entirety. The content may be extreme, exaggerated, or bizarre. Crucial aspects may be dissociated vertically and either not reported or reported in a paradoxical or unintegrated way. The objects may be fragmented; they may be projected or denied.

However, the same three mental status examination methods apply. Carefully observe the reports of the conscious relationship with other people and feelings about them. Inquire about those aspects that are not clear. Confront any lack of coherence, lack of integration, lack of day residue, or precipitating event reports. Descriptively interpret the distortions and resistances to questions about those experiences. Listen for emotional themes in the manifest content and associations revealing preconscious emotional themes and contents.

With these techniques, a fuller object relations story emerges, often dramatically, and usually in the first interview. The story can then be categorized according to its dominant thematic content and dynamic defensive processes. This describes character type. The distortions of organization due to autonomous ego dysfunction describe levels of illness as in neurosis, near psychosis, or psychosis.

During the mental status examination, the examiner is experienced by the patient as an object. Particularly in the sicker illness states, the reality of the examination becomes captured by the patient's emotional object world with its illness condensations. Subtle and not so subtle signals of how the patient is experiencing the physician are the most crucial and validated data about object relations themes. This transference component of the interview can be subtle in the neurotic, outrageously obvious in the borderline, and rigidly fixed and concretely encoded in the psychotic. Therefore, the examiner also gains important information about the level of ego functioning. Because the interview explores intense emotions in the patient's object world, defenses that mediate that intensity will come into play. This gives one the best opportunity to observe, describe, and interpret defenses.

Boundaries in Object Relations Experiences

The most common failures in an object relations boundary are either between the real object and the object representation or between the real self and the self representation. *Real object* refers to the inner, mental experience of the object in reality. The boundary, therefore, is a higher-level boundary than the boundary between inside and outside, because the real object experience has already been contained as an inside mental one.

The condensation of a real object with object representation may be easy to observe when the content is phantasmagoric. It is more difficult to observe when the content is either commonplace or involves projected condensations of motivation or affect. The transference can help enormously if and when the patient turns these mechanisms onto the examiner. Fortunately, because of this particular boundary problem in very ill patients, it is not long in the interview before this phenomenon does occur. Often this happens instantaneously or even before the patient walks in the door. This is especially true of near psychotic patients. When this happens, the examiner can compare what he or she did with what he or she is reported as doing, and what he or she felt with what the patient believes he or she felt. Because the examiner is the day residue, the translation of the patient's symbolic alteration of the examiner is more readily available to the examiner. This can then be described to the patient.

The examination is more difficult when real self experiences are condensed with emotional self representations, either consciously and manifestly, as in psychosis, or preconsciously and latently, as in near psychosis. The examiner must be aware of the possibility of condensation in this area and listen for the affect intensities, thing presentation qualities, primary process logic, and sense of conviction that are a part of such condensations. Active questioning from a variety of perspectives may be needed. The more logical, the more affect-muted, and the more appropriate to reported day residues such condensations are, the harder it is for the examiner to recognize them.

The boundary between self representations and object representations mediates pure emotional experience condensations, which are not unique to psychotic and near psychotic states. The phenomenon is usually examined through derivatives in latent content.

Projective identification is most reliably observed in the transference. If it is dangerous to allow this, the mechanism can be identified by active inquiry when the examiner hears an object report filled with emotion that the patient also feels or demonstrates, especially with thing presentation quality and primary process organization. Active questioning about the day residue reality experience and about secondary process causal events and sequences will highlight the emotional component of the condensation and reveal the existence of the condensation mechanism and associated status of relevant observing ego and reality testing capacities.

It is particularly in the area of object relations that skill, timing, and experience pay off. The information elicited is extremely enlightening about ego organization, mental conflict, illness category, personality category, transference, and countertransference.

Boundaries between Levels of Awareness

It is extremely important for the analytic psychiatrist to remember different organizations in different levels of awareness. The organization rules and the content experiences vary between levels. This is the normal organization. It may be highly pathological for one level's organization to invade another level.

Material of which the patient is fully aware is called *conscious material* and is given in the historical anamnesis and report of present signs, symptoms, and experiences. Preconscious levels of awareness are those levels that the patient can lead into through introspective attention focusing. Deeper layers of the preconscious are reached by letting the mind wander in an uninhibited and speculative way. This can enable a free mental stream called *free association* that leads deeper into unconscious fantasies. The organization rules at this level of mental experience change to the less logical rules of thinking and feeling called *primary process*. The easily available example is a dream.

The deepest layers of awareness are called *unconscious* and they are reached through hypothetical constructs. One gathers evidence for these hypotheses in the conscious and preconscious levels. The verification of these hypotheses is in the patient's new, affective, memory, and fantasy experiences; in evolution of the fantasy story line; and in transference and countertransference experiences. Together, these verifications enable the predictions and retrodictions of psychological, behavioral, and historical material. Some of the most important verifications of these hypotheses are found in the ongoing transference and countertransference relationship of treatment, including the initial interview and mental status examination.

Some very ill patients give a constant stream of associations instead of a logical story. This stream is called *loose associations* to distinguish it from *free associations*. Loose associations are not free; their occurrence is uncontrollable or poorly controllable; their content is rigid, repetitive, and often tangential and superficial, rather than evolving. The one advantage to the examiner is that the emotional theme is usually obvious.

Boundaries between levels of consciousness are damaged in psychotic and near psychotic patients, allowing contents, affects, qualities of experience, and organizations of lower levels to flood conscious levels of the secondary process experience. The extent to which this occurs varies, but that it occurs to some extent is universal. Sometimes it is only the quality of lower level experience that intrudes into the logic of the higher level, as when a thing presentation quality is conscious.

When this boundary rupture is subtle, it is confined to the preconscious or is very limited in extent in the conscious. It is often missed by the examiner until the problem enters the transference. This can be a shock to the examiner unprepared for incorporation into a delusion or near delusion.

Mental status clues to this boundary problem are intense affect, alterations in the quality of the experience of reality, primary process mechanisms in conscious and manifest patient reports, behavior inappropriate to the social reality of the doctor–patient relationship, or perplexity in the patient's observing ego.

Questions must be quick when these episodes are observed, and the questions must be designed to help the patient elaborate at precisely these points. Usually this leads to additional, clarifying material.

Crucial to the examination of different layers is knowing when to use direct questions, when to use open-ended inquiries, and when to remain silent. Associations are interrupted and/or derailed by closed-ended questions. However, an important associational strand may not begin unless a pointed question is asked, especially if that associational trend is dissociated and does not spontaneously enter the interview.

Primary Process Thinking

A related boundary is between logical, secondary process thinking and emotional, primary process thinking. Primary process thinking is more characteristic of the preconscious than of the conscious, and is totally characteristic of the unconscious. More important than the level of consciousness at which the processes take place is the ability of the conscious mind to distinguish and utilize the difference between secondary process and primary process thinking. Very ill patients have an inability to distinguish and to differentially use emotional and logical thinking processes.

This can usually be observed in what should be the logical stream of the patient's historical report. When observed, active questioning about illogical areas will reveal the underlying primary process condensations. The examiner's focus on these areas should also encourage unstructured free exploration. This will enable the examiner to gather logical information and emotional information, both conscious and preconscious, and to compare them. It is helpful if the examiner refuses to come to closure without thorough exploration with the patient. Interpretive descriptions are usually necessary at various blocked points, but these should be descriptions of process and not conclusions.

The primary process–secondary process boundary is listed separately from the conscious–preconscious boundary because the two boundaries are not identical. Furthermore, although the primary–secondary process boundary is always damaged in severe illness, there can be ruptures across the barrier without loss of the ability to tell the logical from the emotional. Conscious, primary process fantasy is not an illness state and is common in artistic states, upon wakening from a dream, or during a daydream. Examiners use not only their secondary process but also their own conscious capacity for primary process fantasy to follow the two patient tracks, one logical and one emotional, and to make hypotheses about their relationship.

Affect–Percept and Concept–Percept

Intense, emotionally charged percepts that are used to confirm and validate concepts require exploration through active listening and inquiry. Usually listening alone will give the examiner some knowledge about whether the patient can consciously distinguish stimuli in reality from mental percept, affect, and concept. If not, active inquiry must occur at a tactful point in the interview. This usually occurs concurrent with the examination of reality testing.

Affect–Affect

Another important boundary that is sometimes lacking or damaged in very ill patients is the boundary between affect experiences. Instead of modulated integration between love and hate, there is either (1) a wide separation or (2) a mixture without one affecting the other. Another way the affect–affect boundary may be lost is in (3) affect condensations that demonstrate a specific primary process relationship between the two.

An example of the first type of boundary loss is a patient with two intimate relationships with persons of the opposite sex, one an idealized and loved person and the other a devalued person. An example of the second type is a certain type of violent, physical attack where rage and sexual arousal are both conscious but do not dilute each other. An example of the third type is not an angry sexual attack, but the perversion form of rape in which sexual arousal is only possible during a brutal domination scene where sex is condensed with a specific type of aggression.

Careful observation of the history, questioning of the phenomena, and active eliciting of the underlying fantasies is necessary to diagnose an affect–affect boundary defect's particular category and manifestation.

There are two other common manifestations of an affect–affect boundary loss. One occurs when an affect of a particular type regularly replaces another affect or all other affects. Some common replacements are the experience of rage instead of sadness, rage instead of fear, anxiety instead of sadness, sexual arousal instead of fear, and longing instead of rage. If one of the emotions is repressed, that is a relatively healthy phenomenon. If the two are conscious and either dissociated or mixed, that is a relatively sick phenomenon. In addition, in psychosis and near psychosis, dissociative elements may be rigid, delusional, displaced to detail, primary processed, and have thing presentation perceptual qualities. It is very important to know about the stability of affect boundaries before engaging in the intense affect experience of psychotherapy.

Reality Testing

Reality testing is one of the most crucial ego functions to examine, because disturbances in this area define the difference between psychotic, near psychotic, and neurotic. It may be the sole criterion if one considers condensations between reality and fantasy as secondary to the loss of reality testing. I do not consider this to be the case, because some patients make such condensations while preserving reality testing. Although this is rare, it shows that there are two separate boundary disturbances in severe illness. Even with this view, however, reality testing is one of the most crucial ego functions in very ill patients.

Performing an adequate mental status examination in this area requires an understanding of the concepts involved in the various categories of loss of reality testing, and a knowledge of the actual technique of the examination. The technique involves helping the patient to examine reality by asking nonpsychotic aspects of the patient's ego function to engage psychotic or near psychotic areas of ego function. The examiner does this by asking the patient questions about reality experience in ways that engage the patient's capacity to consider. Nonpsychotic areas of ego functioning may first be observed in memory. They may also be observed in secondary process logic in certain aspects of mental content, especially in nonpsychotic content that contains the same or

Mental Status Examination 121

related affect content as the psychotic or near psychotic areas. Sometimes it is a nonpsychotic continuation of the same plot line. The active questioning then consists of pointing out that the patient has these paradoxical incongruities. The examination of reality testing proceeds to see if the patient is able to have an engaged and considered discussion with himself or herself from the point of view of the two sides of his or her experience. This tests the capacity to fully engage the totality of the experience and consider it from the point of view of the experience of reality as opposed to the experience of the psychotic or near psychotic condensation.

It is important to realize that one is not testing the validity of the patient's conclusions about reality for two reasons. One is that the test is of the patient's reality testing and not of the content of the reality experience or of reality itself. These are separate areas. It is possible for only reality testing to be altered, and it is only reality testing that provides the definition of illness. The second reason is the practical one that it is usually impossible to confirm reality, and some people have access to rather strange and difficult aspects of reality.

In any case, the content in reality is irrelevant to the faculty of reality testing. Someone can reach a conclusion about reality that is merely wrong. Conversely, someone may be delusional and correct. Reality testing is the ability of the mind to compare its conclusions about its experience of reality with its experience of its perception, and with its experience of fantasy. Further, it is the ability to change conclusions about reality based on new information arrived at logically. Reality testing, therefore, should be a dynamic and active process in areas about which the patient is intensely concerned. In psychotic patients, there is no active reality testing process going on. There may be an evolution of a delusional system, for instance, but there is no corresponding evolution of the process of reality testing. In this case, reality experience is only used for evidence to build the delusion.

I now turn to the categories of losses of reality testing. Reality testing can be measured along a gradient. The most severe is a loss of reality testing that is firm and fixed and without awareness that it is gone. The next most serious is the loss of reality testing that is firm and fixed with awareness that it is gone. The next is a suspension of reality testing, without losing the capacity, but without awareness of the suspension of reality testing. The first two are psychoses; the third is near psychotic.

Reality testing can be lost either globally or focally. It is very rare to have a global loss of reality testing. Even the most psychotic patient usually has some areas of response that demonstrate a reality testing ability. More common is a focal loss. The loss can be in an area of ideas or in an area of sensation; it may, instead, be in an area of affect or a domain of experience (see Table 4.1).

Table 4.1 Alterations of Reality Experience

Area of Sensation
Hallucination

- —External stimulus event negative
- —Internal sensory event positive
- —Reality testing negative
- —Emotional experience condensed with and consciously expressed in perceptual experience

Hallucinosis

- —External stimulus event negative
- —Internal sensory event positive
- —Reality testing positive
- —Emotional experience condensed with and consciously expressed in perceptual experience

Pseudohallucination

- —External stimulus event negative
- —Internal sensory event negative
- —Reality testing suspended but positive upon active questioning
- —Emotional experience condensed preconsciously with reality experience (but not in percept)

Illusion

- —External stimulus event positive but misperceived
- —Internal sensory event positive
- —Reality testing positive
- —No condensation in reality experience, consciousness or preconsciousness

Area of Ideas

Delusion
- —Idea experienced consciously as real with thing presentation form and thing presentation quality
- —Reality testing negative
- —Fantasy condensed with reality experience consciously

Pseudodelusion

- —Idea experienced preconsciously as real with thing presentation form and thing presentation quality
- —Reality testing suspended but positive upon active questioning
- —Fantasy condensed with reality experience preconsciously

Overvalued idea
- —Idea is abstract and emotional and not condensed with reality experience, conscious or preconscious, but is overdetermined
- —Reality testing never suspended
- —Fantasy condensations unconscious

If reality testing is lost in the area of ideas, the psychotic phenomenon is called a *delusion*. A delusion is an idea about which reality testing is lost. Rarely, the patient can be aware that this is the case. The near psychotic phenomenon that I call a *pseudodelusion* is an ideational area where reality testing seems to be lost, but during the psychiatric interview it can be demonstrated that reality testing has merely been suspended. An *overvalued* idea[1] is a favorite topic that is full of psychological meaning but that does not condense with reality experience and for which reality testing is never even suspended.

There is an equivalent hierarchy in the area of perception. A perceptual event about which reality testing is lost is called a *hallucination*. A hallucination has two aspects: the loss of reality testing, and the perceived mental event itself and its quality. Patients have the experience of a perceptual event occurring in a hallucination. They can describe the sensory qualities, whether auditory or visual. If it is a voice, they will be able to tell you whether it is high or low, male or female, threatening, neutral, or friendly. Hallucinating patients will be able to tell you about these qualities of the experience because they are actually experiencing these mental events. If they have not volunteered the information, they will be able to respond upon questioning. Near psychotic patients have not had such a conscious mental event. They talk as if they have, but, on close questioning, they are unable to describe the sensory qualities of the pseudohallucinatory experience. That reassures both the examiner and the patient that although a strong emotional experience has occurred, a hallucinated perception process is not occurring. A true hallucination that the patient knows is a hallucination but about which reality testing is not lost may be called *hallucinosis*. The usual example is a toxic state in which the patient, sometimes due to some externally administered substance, experiences a hallucination, almost always visual, and realizes that it is a hallucination. An *illusion* is merely a misperceived reality stimulus. Reality testing is neither lost nor suspended (Jaspers, 1923; Spitzer and Williams, 1987; Sims, 1988; Skodol, 1989; Asaad, 1990).

These are the psychotic and near psychotic phenomena. The severity will diagnostically categorize the level of illness and reveal whether it is psychotic or near psychotic. This can almost always be done in the first mental status examination. Without a facility to engage these phenomena, the therapist is left with poor diagnostic and dangerous psychotherapeutic abilities.

The examination of reality testing must be active, consistent, and methodical if these crucial issues are to be clarified. Observation alone can often be enough. The report of a hallucination with real sensorial qualities and absent reality testing needs no further elaboration to make the diagnosis of psychosis. If aspects of these criteria are absent in the patient's initial report, they can be inquired about directly. If the entire occurrence is absent in the report but seems obvious because of shifts

124 Mental Status Examination

in the patient's attention, and inquiry brings either fearful avoidance or bland denial, a descriptive interpretation of the response can be made with a question as to the underlying motivation of the covering response. This will often help the patient discuss more directly his or her conscious, but either avoided or dissociated, psychotic experience. The observation of delusional content can be more difficult, especially if the delusional idea retains secondary process logic. The rigidity of the idea, the concrete reification in the explication of the idea, and the affective intensity, often as a penumbra around the idea which charges the transference, are all clues to the psychotic condensation that is occurring in reality experience and that is taking thing presentation form and quality. Upon observing and empathically experiencing this phenomenon, the examiner can make focused inquiry so that a more complete explication of the phenomenon is forthcoming. Should this not be the case, a descriptive interpretation is often helpful, especially of the affect that has charged the transference and that guards and expresses the delusional idea.

For near psychotic phenomena, pseudohallucinations, and pseudodelusions, careful inquiries will quickly liberate the manifest content, the upper layers of latent content, and a return of more secondary process, integrated, dispassionate reality testing.

The more experience the examiner has with psychotic and near psychotic patients, the more quickly the hints of their characteristic psychotic condensations will be recognized. The benefit of experience enables recognition of the linguistic propensities for expressing, even indirectly, thing presentation experiences and qualities. Experience also helps recognize and clear the countertransference avoidances that deflect the examiner from clues in the patient's verbal production. There are also clues in the countertransference experience of the examiner.

I will now give two examples of psychotic and near psychotic spectrum phenomena.

A common defense in the very ill patient is a *compulsion*, a behavioral action that must be carried out. It is usually a required action in reality experience. Because reality experience is involved, these patients are usually sicker than neurotic patients. A compulsion, therefore, usually occurs in the psychotic or near psychotic patient. In psychotic patients, the action has to be taken to prevent a fear that is conscious and about which reality testing is lost. The patient believes that the compulsive action will forestall the feared dire event. The near psychotic patient knows that the action is based on magical thinking and is only magically related to what he or she is afraid of, but must do it anyway. Reality testing is not lost. There are a few neurotic patients with compulsive-like behavior who carry out the behavior only to ward off anxiety. The content of the fear of failing to do the action is not usually conscious. If it is conscious, they do not consciously believe that the behavior will forestall the feared event. They know that the compulsion is a psychological

Mental Status Examination 125

mechanism that temporarily relieves anxiety. Such neurotic patients can, if they wish, avoid doing the compulsive behavior, but they experience an increase in anxiety. Careful questioning and listening are required to clarify the relationship of the behavior to the necessity for action and to absent or suspended reality testing.

It may be helpful to think of a compulsion as a stereotyped, repetitive behavioral delusion or near delusion. The condensation of reality and fantasy experience is the same as in a delusional or near delusional idea (see Table 4.2).

Also common in sicker patients are *obsessions*. An obsession is a recurrent, stereotyped, repetitive, intrusive thought. The phenomenon varies from psychotic to neurotic, depending on whether the patient has reality testing, whether the patient experiences the thought as his or her own, whether the patient can control the occurrence of the thought, and whether there is a condensation of fantasy with reality intruding on conscious or preconscious reality experience (see Table 4.3).

Table 4.2 Hierarchy of Compulsive Phenomena

1 Psychotic compulsion: fear is usually conscious, reality testing always negative, action is required
2 Near psychotic compulsion: fear is often conscious, reality testing is positive but may be suspended, action is required
3 Severe neurotic compulsion: fear is conscious, preconscious, or unconscious, but reality testing is always positive; action is required only for emotional comfort
4 Neurotic compulsion: fear is unconscious, reality testing is always positive, and the action is not required for anxiety control but merely preferred for anxiety control; this phenomenon is higher-level neurotic and the name changes to a neurotic ritual

Table 4.3 Hierarchy of Obsessive Phenomena

1 Psychotic: thought is experienced as ego dystonic, occurrence is not under conscious control, reality testing is negative, form is rigid with thing presentation quality, condensation of reality and fantasy occurs in the patient's conscious reality experience
2 Near psychotic: thought is experienced as ego dystonic, not under occurrence control, reality testing is present but suspended, condensation of reality and fantasy occurs in preconscious reality experience
3 Very ill neurotic: thought is experienced as ego dystonic, some occurrence control is possible, reality testing is always positive, condensation of reality and fantasy is in deeper layers of the preconscious, and while pressing into reality experience it does not actually invade it
4 Higher-level neurotic: thought is experienced as painful but is controllable as to occurrence, reality testing is always positive, condensations are experienced in the realm of emotional experience
5 Highest level neurotic: a repetitive thought that is ego syntonic and voluntary, although painful, is called a neurotic rumination

126 Mental Status Examination

Obsessions, like compulsions and all other mental phenomena, are on a continuum of severity from neurotic to psychotic. Careful questioning in the mental status examination can clarify where on the ego continuum a mental phenomenon is placed.

Observing Ego

Observing ego is the capacity to consciously and dispassionately experience mental functioning. The observing experience should be separate from both emotional experience and reality experience. Observing ego should be more allied, however, to secondary process and reality experience. In addition, some of the sentient experience of the patient should be located in observing ego experience. For many patients, this is not true. Their sentient experience of themselves is in their behavior or is primarily in their emotional experience.

The observing ego experience is so important to treatment because the treatment alliance is best anchored through this mental faculty in the very ill patient. Reality testing may be absent and self experience may be psychotic, so these two potential anchors are not available. Like the other mental functions, observing ego is examined in three ways: by observation, by active questioning, and by descriptive interpretations.

First, patients with observing ego will often give evidence in their verbal production by describing an experience of standing back from the reported phenomenon. Such patients can engage in an impartial discussion with the examiner. Second, the examiner can ask directly for a discussion of this nature. Some patients will then be able to do so. Some patients will not be able to do so and will respond to the question in their characteristic way.

This brings us to the third method of examination. The characteristic response to active questioning can then be described back to the patient as to content and process. Such a description is called a beginning interpretation or descriptive interpretation and is based on the hypothesis that the response given is the dynamic resistance to the asked for function.

The dynamics of these resistances to the observing ego will often involve the most basic character defenses of the patient. It may be that only the most basic and resistant of character defenses could be used to block such an adaptive mental function as observing ego. Basic character defenses will organize the sickest of the illness pathology and the worst of the resistances to treatment. They form a crucial marker in a prognostic evaluation.

In very ill patients, however, observing ego may be blocked not only because of dynamic characterological defenses, but also because of autonomous inabilities of ego functioning important for this area. Observing ego involves the ability to dispassionately step back and articulate oneself. There are many subsidiary ego functions involved. One must have enough impulse control, affect modulation, anxiety tolerance, and verbalizing ability to step back and conceptualize and articulate in words. Ability to articulate oneself in words is both an inborn capacity and a trained skill that many patients lack. In addition, it is helpful if the patient's ego has a generalizing ability and an abstracting ability. This will help the patient organize a number of like experiences and discuss the general principles. In this way, generalizing and abstracting ability will help the observing ego understand thematic relationships between emotion and reality day residue experience, and this ability can be applied to symptoms. This will help therapist and patient decipher and untangle condensations of reality experience and emotional experience that form the core of psychotic and near psychotic phenomena.

It is also helpful in observing ego function to have boundary functions intact, such as the ability to separate one's own emotions, one's experience of one's own bodily functioning, one's own experience of other people's emotions, and the reality qualities of the inanimate world. Illnesses that affect ego functions, therefore, put the observing ego under strain. However, observing ego is not usually attacked directly by psychotic condensation. Many delusional or hallucinating patients, while lacking reality testing, maintain their capacity for observing ego. "I know my voices are part of my illness, but I believe what they say anyway."

Junction Point

Damage to these autonomous ego functions allows feelings to alter reality experience. The points of such intervention are junction points between psychopathology and psychodynamics. It is there that emotional psychodynamics have condensed with reality appearance to form a pathological condensation. This junction point in ego function reveals the relationship between reality experience and fantasy.

Freud used the term *nodal point*.[2] He meant the point in psychodynamics (unconscious emotional experience) where several strands of association seemed to meet in a single symbol or a part thereof. These nodal points repeat themselves in various contexts.

By *junction point*, I mean a nodal point where a symbol joins psychological themes but also condenses with an aspect of ego dysfunction. Junction points are the clearest points of disruptive emotional impact on autonomous reality ego caused by psychotic or near psychotic illness. A junction point is where illness, autonomous ego disruption, and psychodynamics clearly meet. One point, in psychosis and near psychosis, is usually at the symbolic alteration of the day residue.

128 Mental Status Examination

Day Residues

The first way to examine this function is to listen and observe. Does the patient describe what happened to him or her, and when it happened, in sequence? Note with the patient any absence of a spontaneous or sequential day residue reality report. When questioned, some patients will then be able to give some response from their area of reality experience. A second approach when this fails is to note the emotional response given instead and to conceptualize the significance of the content, process, and motivation of that emotional response. This can then be phrased as a tentative descriptive interpretation for the patient.

One of the most dramatic examples of this is the angry attack upon the examiner when a question about the missing day residue is asked of many borderline patients. Pointing out the attack and its relationship to the question and inquiring about the significance of such a phenomenon is an example of the descriptive and interpretive analytic examination of defenses against day residue experience.

The day residues are crucial because they are contact points (nodal points, switch points, or junction points) between reality and fantasy that can help decipher the emotional and reality logic of symptoms. Often, these day residues form an evolving reality story that the patient's family knows and can report, if asked. They may even be aware of the emotional significance these events have for the patient. It is then much easier to understand the symbolic alterations of psychotic condensations. Normal development in the mental life cycle also provides clues about which reality events may be day residues. Some patients know the day residue precipitating events but cannot relate them to their symptoms. In this case, a parallel history is taken of each track, one for the day residue precipitating event story and the other for the story of the evolving symptoms. This is the characteristic history needed for neurotic psychosomatic patients.

Without the day residue as a guide, symptom occurrence, subtle layers of emotional experience, sequencing of emotional layers, and dominance of one side of the conflict theme are all in doubt, ambiguous in direction, or prone to infinite regression.

Careful questioning about the capacity for conscious, observed, day residue experience is a key to deciphering the symbolic alteration of the reality. Knowing what aspects of reality were changed will give you a better chance to figure out the emotional reasons the change expresses.

Modulating Capacity

The ability of the ego to modulate its emotional responses (Krystal, 1975) can be easily observed during the verbal stream of the patient's report. There are patients who cannot contain the strength of the emotion evoked by their own telling of their story. These patients become extremely agitated as they speak. Patients at the other extreme of the spectrum cannot express emotion, despite the most emotionally evocative stories. This can likewise be observed by the examiner. Being able to appropriately express yet contain emotion as one moves from content area to content area and from reality experience to emotional experience is a hallmark of a healthy ego.

Although observation is the most important examining instrument for this faculty, active inquiry about what must be painful content areas may be necessary for a judgment to be made about this capacity.

When observation and inquiry demonstrate some problem in the modulating capacity, this fact can be told to the patient as a descriptive interpretation. A discussion will either ensue or not. If it does not, the response given in place of a dispassionate discussion can sometimes be described, the motivation postulated, and the effect of this description then observed. This descriptive interpretation may help an observing ego presence appear for dispassionate discussion of the lack of modulating capacity, may liberate affect that has been isolated, or may help the ego contain affect that has erupted. When this capacity is greatly dysfunctional in the direction of disinhibition, active and frequent comment may be necessary in order to get the full details of the story, to help make the patient aware of his or her deficit in this capacity, and, therefore, to partly control the dysfunction. Otherwise, uncontained affect explodes the interview and the treatment.

One can observe an affect appear as a patient talks; for instance, as sadness escalating to tears, then to uncontrollable sobbing. The content of ideas gets more and more despairing and associated sad ideas and memories are recruited and re-experienced and the sobbing gets worse. This experience can last beyond the interview. "Now you've spoiled my whole day!" the patient may say, and this may be an accurate description of his or her inability to control the duration as well as the intensity and spread of the affect.

Integrating Capacity

Integrating capacity of the ego is, along with reality testing, a crucial aspect of the ego to examine in the very ill patient. Very ill patients do not integrate one aspect of their mental experience with another. All the contents of a particular conscious mental experience—ideas, affects, experience of self, experience of others, and experience of reality—are separated from other areas of conscious mental experience. It is the sharp demarcation in conscious experience (or preconscious experience) that is characteristic of sicker states.

The hallmark in the mental status examination is to elicit two areas of conscious mental functioning that are paradoxically opposed in content but maintained without realization, logical or emotional, that the two states are mutually incompatible. If there is realization of incompatibility, the realization does not result in an intellectual or emotional integrative resolution. These paradoxical areas, when they are observed, can be pointed out to the patient. The patient is either able or unable to see that they are paradoxical. The patient responds either with distress or with a mental mechanism that mediates and protects him or her from that distress.[3] Thus the mental status procedures of observation, active inquiry, and beginning descriptive interpretation hold for lack of integrations just as they hold for other mental phenomena that emerge.

Vertical dissociations are maintained by autonomous integrative deficits of ego functions, ego defense mechanisms, or both. Ego deficits are often revealed by perplexity and failure to understand an active questioning by the examiner. Defensive structures that maintain vertical dissociations may be revealed by intense affective responses to the examiner's active questioning or by primary process responses. Thus, each of the major contributors to lack of integration may be recognized in the mental status examination.

It is crucial to examine the ego's secondary process, integration-building conceptualization capacity, and the associated abilities to abstract, generalize, and apply concepts. These capacities are listened for and observed in the spontaneous flow of the patient's story, and they are challenged when the interviewer asks a question about the story that requires a conceptual response.

Defenses

Defenses are mental mechanisms that change emotional experience so that painful affect is hidden from the patient's self experience and altered. In sicker patients, the experience of reality is also altered to do this. A defensive maneuver is observed when the examiner, in following the logical and affective line of the story, notes an affect absence or alteration that is not in keeping with the evolving inner logic of the narrative. Alterations are especially obvious when the patient uses these defenses in their reality experience of the interview with the analyst. Very ill patients commonly do this.

Because defenses have stability over time, these defenses are repetitive. They are also limited in number. Actually, the hallmark of a very ill patient is to have a limited number of rigid defenses.[4] These defensive maneuvers can then be observed, inquired about, and descriptively interpreted. With successful intervention, the patient will be able to observe, understand, and use autonomous ego capacities rather than defensive ego to contain the affect. These therapeutic interventions thus liberate more appropriate affect and deeper layers of story which have been repressed or dissociated because of their affect. In very ill patients, these maneuvers will often liberate relevant day residue memories. The story then begins to make more emotional sense to the patient and more logical sense to the examiner.

The examination of the defenses is undertaken not just to understand the type, organization, and level of consciousness at which they operate. It is also done to understand the rigidity with which they are maintained. Very early in the therapist's relationship with the patient, this crucial parameter can be observed if the mental status examination is active and interpretive from the beginning. Usually within the first interview, almost always by the second interview, and certainly by the third, an accurate estimate of rigidity can be made. Especially crucial to this examination with very ill patients can be the second interview when one inquires about the effect of the first interview on the patient.[5] One hopes for some effect, because it demonstrates flexibility of defenses as well as the capacity to observe, integrate, and change (see also Shapiro, 1981).

Rigidity crucially determines the prognosis, because this characteristic will contribute to the ability to change and the rate of change. Rigid defensive structures block observing ego, maintain vertical dissociations, and rigidly maintain repressions. Therefore, progress toward a more integrated state is blocked. Rigidity of defense therefore is a most serious prognostic sign. Rigid defenses occur more frequently in certain illnesses than in others and in certain phases of certain illnesses (see Chapter 5).

Rigidity of defense, more than any other ego problem, determines the prognosis. There are some psychotic and near psychotic patients who are quite plastic and adaptive to treatment. There are some neurotic patients who are so rigid that treatment is long, frustrating, and perhaps futile.

Two common defensive structures in the very ill patient are projective identification and denial of fact.

Projective identification is that form of projection in which the real object experience or real self experience is captured (see Chapter 3). It can quickly make its appearance in the mental status examination interview when the patient experiences as real a fantasy he or she has about the physician. This can be observed when a patient makes a statement to the examiner about the examiner's conscious behavior or emotion that is totally out of keeping in content or degree with the conscious experience the examiner has of himself or herself. The process of the projection, the content of the projection, and the precipitating event for the projection in the examiner's unconscious behavior, in the trigger point of the patient's narrative, or both, must all be carefully explored and described with the patient. The hypothesis that this projection occurs in all object relations that touch upon the trigger point which has been elicited in the mental status interview is usually confirmed.

132 Mental Status Examination

Many examiners try to avoid these projections in psychotic and near psychotic patients because of their own fear. They fear the patient may act on the basis of the projections. It is important to realize that avoiding these projections can only be done with sophistication. Since the exact conscious content of the trigger may not be known, and the exact latent content of the projection cannot be known early on, avoiding is difficult to do and requires experience and intuition. In any case, avoiding does not mean that the doctor should avoid recognizing the projection process. Avoiding means avoiding being a target. It is important that the physician realize that a projection process is going on in order to decide whether to try to avoid or to engage and confront the projection. The danger of avoiding is that the patient may be proceeding silently in his or her mental experience along the projective line. Not talking about the projection may not change this. It may merely allow it to continue and to build in intensity, out of control of the therapist. Therefore, if one chooses to avoid the projection, one must be certain that one is actually avoiding it. A clear statement of how the examiner experiences the reality may be necessary.

The next characteristic defense, almost definitional for very ill states, is the *denial* of factual reality (Freud, 1925). It is crucially important to remember that this is the denial of the patient's own experience of factual reality. The most dramatic and obvious examples of this occur in very ill medical patients whose mental functioning does not allow them to process the terror involved in their physical illness experience. This is commonly seen in such physically ill patients as a person with a sudden heart attack admitted to an intensive care unit. Such patients may blandly say that there is nothing wrong with them in spite of the obvious evidence available to them from their observation of their body, their physical experience of their body, or their observations of the reaction of the medical personnel around them. Mentally ill patients may also deny their own mental illness. The physician may best observe this phenomenon when the patient reports an event in which the interviewer was a participant. Observation, active inquiry, and interpretive description can all be used at this point.

Because such denial involves the experience of a reality fact, just as very young children at times will do, it is called *primitive denial*. Primitive in this case usually means both developmentally early and maladaptive. I feel it is primitive because reality experience is affected. Sometimes it is called *simple denial* because the manifest content involves only denial without symbolic alteration.

Simple denial of fact may or may not be psychotic. It depends on whether reality testing is intact or merely suspended. This requires examination by active questioning on the part of the therapist to see if the patient can question the denial. Usually such denial is not psychotic. The function of denial is to try to rid the mind of a reality day residue experience because the day residue triggers catastrophe affect and fantasy.

Thing Presentation

Because thing presentation experience dominates the very ill patient's mental life, observation and inquiry about this are important in the mental status examination. Thing presentation experience focuses on the detail of concrete things rather than feelings. Emotional causality is experienced as a property of the reality of details of things rather than of events and feelings. Thing presentation takes the form of perceived reality rather than of abstract thoughts. Thing presentation form has its own rigidities, as do reality attributes of physical objects.

This is easy to observe in the mental status examination by the attention, concentration, and obvious emotional involvement in concrete details that the patient reports. It is as if the interview gets stuck at those points. One can inquire directly about them when they do occur. A psychotic patient, in describing women who he believes are in love with him, refers to their "clear cloth coats." This phrase is repeated over and over with an intensity that indicates it is crucial.

The most common normal example from everyday life is the thing presentation content of sexual arousal. In this phenomenon, details of the sexual partner's physiognomy are arousal levers. In the description of the partner, the person will give emphasis to that detail. Depending on the intensity of the experience, the person will ascribe a greater or lesser crucialness to this detail. When asked why that detail is so crucial, the person will respond that it turns him or her on. When the reasons for that are inquired about, the person usually does not know. This is because the reasons are unconscious and condensed in the detail.

Thing presentation quality is an experience of perceptual reality quality. It is, at the same time, the experience of various affect qualities. The quality is inherent in the intensity and attitude of the patient. Sometimes an attempt, usually vague or overelaborated, is made to describe it directly. The best description is in Freud's case of Elizabeth von R (Breuer and Freud, 1893–1895). The particular condensation of perceptual and affect qualities is hard to describe in words. A picture does this automatically by encoding the experience in concrete detail, which then evokes the quality. The analyst, therefore, would do well to gather the details, try to experience the thing, and then describe back to the patient the evoked affect quality. Many times, although a patient cannot translate to word presentations, he or she can recognize the proper word presentations. This is especially true of near psychosis.

Sometimes, however, the quality is conscious but not the thing presentation content. If free-floating (unconnected to conscious, logical

134 Mental Status Examination

content), the quality may be possible to name and then the patient recognizes this if the analyst is correct. But sometimes the primary process thing presentation appears in consciousness linked to some insignificant logical content. The analyst can then point out the incongruent intensity factor and begin, in associations, to tease out the condensed thing presentation quality.

Rarely, the thing presentation quality is attached to significant logical conscious content, as in certain paranoid patients. The content and the quality reinforce and validate each other. It is still helpful to try to name the affect(s) and then to listen for subtle primary process or dissociations where one could, with available observing ego, gain entry.

Notes

1 The DSM-IV (APA, 1994, p. 402) discusses overvalued ideas. The definition there is more like my definition of pseudodelusion. The problems with their definition are as follows: (1) if the DSM-IV is accepted, then there is no category for a favorite topic of intense emotional meaning and spreading through personality and agency function, but with fully maintained reality testing. This is my definition of an overvalued idea. To merge pseudodelusion and overvalued idea as the DSM-IV seems to do blurs the distinction diagnostically and therapeutically. One is near psychotic and the other is not. The treatment of the two is quite different. (2) The DSM-IV's overvalued idea (my pseudodelusion) is not well defined. The DSM-IV uses content criteria (see earlier in this chapter for the problem with content criteria as a definition of delusion and pseudodelusion) and also does not accurately describe the reality testing function alteration (see chapter 3 for a description of the reality testing alterations in pseudodelusions).

2 Freud (1900, p. 410): "Words, since they are the nodal points of numerous ideas, may be regarded as predestined to ambiguity." Hans Sachs, quoted by Freud: "The dream work may exploit. . . [ambiguity] . . . by using the ambiguity as a switch-point: where one of the meaning of the word is present in the dream thoughts, the other one can be introduced into the manifest dream."

3 This aspect of the mental status examination is most clearly described by Kernberg (1977) but is also inherently present in Freud's (1940) discussion on the splitting of the ego and in Reich's volume (1933b).

4 This characteristic of very ill patients was first pointed out to me by Dr. Otto Kernberg.

5 This, too, was first pointed out and demonstrated to me by Dr. Otto Kernberg.

Chapter 5

Psychiatric Illnesses and Mental Structure

Introduction

This chapter describes the specific effects of certain psychiatric illnesses on ego function, and on psychotic or near psychotic ego structure. Weinshel (1990) calls for a more solid structural model of severe mental illness to support the widening scope of analytic treatment. Jacobson (1967, 1971) and Kernberg (1975) did so with object relations theory, as did Fairbairn (1952) and others. Glover (1958), Arlow and Brenner (1964), Freeman (1969), Beres (1971), and Bellak et al. (1973) began this for ego psychology.

Psychiatric illnesses have characteristic effects on the ego: delusions or hallucinations. They vary in organization, content of day residues, symbol organization, intensity of affect, and relationship to nonpsychotic ego areas. Different psychiatric illnesses have different object relations expressed in their symbolic alterations. Likewise, identification processes vary because the illnesses alter the ego's reception of the object in reality into the real object experience, the object representation, and the self representation. In addition, there are illness characteristic contents, qualities, and organizations to self and object representation. For content dynamics in psychiatric illnesses see Frosch (1990) and Gabbard (2014).

The illnesses I will discuss are schizophrenia, which fragments ego function; manic-depressive illness, which disorganizes ego function; organic brain syndromes, which destroy some ego functions and disorganize relationships between others; adult attention deficit disorder, in which certain aspects of ego function never develop completely; and severe personality disorders, whose conflict themes are condensed with reality experience by psychotic and near psychotic ego phenomena.

Schizophrenia

Introduction

There is no blood test for schizophrenia, although it is a biological condition (Tamminza, 1999; McGlashen and Hoffman, 2000). Because the disease processes are complex and vary in extent, the pathognomonic features are debated within psychiatry. This makes a psychoanalytic description of such states more difficult. The most striking aspect of those illnesses that tend to be labeled *schizophrenia* is fragmentation of mental function. Various aspects of this phenomenon have been noted since Bleuler (1950) (c.f. Iqbal, Schwartz, Cecil, Inman, and Constantin, 1993). But questions have arisen as to whether fragmentation is pathognomonic, where the fragmentation must occur within mental structure in order to be pathognomonic, and what the definition of fragmentation is. Can one reliably identify and separate a fragmented group of ego function illnesses from the broader group of disorganized ego functions characteristic of all severe mental illness (Freeman, 1969)?

In my opinion, the observation of the fragmentation of the function of idea formation, and therefore of objects, agencies, affects, symbols, processes, and condensations, is the pathognomonic feature of a schizophrenic thinking disorder (Bleuler, 1950; c.f. Andreason, 1999). See especially Kenlder (2016) and Sinott et al. (2016) for a recent review of this issue. For the latest standard diagnosis, see the DSM 5. For a critique, see Ross (2014).

The idea formation fragments along fault lines that do not obey categories of secondary process, object relations, or affect and associated content condensations. The fragmenting fault line crosses all these boundaries and therefore fragments primary process. The illness may be mild or severe, referring to the extent of mental functioning that is disrupted by these fragments. The other potentially psychotic illnesses affect thinking and the organization of ideas. But they do so by different mechanisms, so the manifest psychopathological features of their thinking are different (Freeman, Cameron, and McGhie, 1958; Vetter, 1968; Arieti, 1974; Hurt, Holtzman, and Davis, 1983; Kafka, 1984, 1989).

Fragmentation manifests itself in the mental functioning of the schizophrenic in certain ways. A crucial feature is that affect contents are disintegrated. Disintegration is different from the dissociation of thinking from feeling in which intact feeling states and their contents are kept separate either from each other or from different intact affect content areas. In schizophrenic disintegration, affect contents are fragmented and the fragments are separated. The separation therefore does not follow any known mental category. No coherent affective state can be experienced because no integrated affective state is achieved. There is no intensity with associated content that can be experienced. As a result, blandness and apathy occur.

The schizophrenic disintegration phenomenon, the characteristic way in which schizophrenic thinking is disorganized, has its impact on psychotic signs. The characteristics of schizophrenic delusions are (1) integration is fragmented, causing symbol elements to be "autistic" and "bizarre"; (2) affect is missing, apathetic, or noncongruent; and (3) cognitive dissonance of opposites is tolerated without anxiety, without recognition, and without explanation if pointed out. This disintegration phenomenon has the same effect on hallucinatory experiences, which in schizophrenia are fragmented and therefore autistically bizarre. They are bizarre because of irregular fragmentation and any meaning and validity adheres only to fragments. Pieces of all three mental agencies may appear in one mental experience and one production, within one voice or one piece of the delusional system. These structural aspects of delusions and hallucinations are often helpful in diagnosis.

Although it is said in general psychiatry that organic hallucinations are visual or somatic and schizophrenic hallucinations are auditory, in fact, schizophrenic hallucinations can be somatic and depressive hallucinations are usually auditory. Manic hallucinations can be auditory, and although it is said that they can be visual, the usual visual phenomena in mania are visual illusions and pseudohallucinations. It is therefore the organization of hallucinations and delusions that is most helpful in diagnosis.

Boundaries

The major pathognomonic boundary problem in schizophrenia is a result of a fragmentation fault line crossing all other internal boundaries. Multiple fragmentations are created, each with an unpredictable boundary, domain, and location. In the acute phase, the fragmentation boundary is not only unpredictable in shape and bizarre in the territory it traverses and dissociates, but also rapidly changing, thus adding to the bizarre experience.

In–Out Boundary[1]

The loss of the in–out boundary is often used by psychoanalysts to define schizophrenia. A fusion between inside and outside is said to be pathognomonic. Regression to a symbiotic or autistic phase of infant development is postulated. However, I have observed this boundary to be sometimes damaged in acute mania and also in organic brain syndromes. I have also seen many schizophrenics where this boundary is not severely damaged. And no one has demonstrated this in normal infants: quite the contrary (Sterm, 1985).

Can one say anything about the in–out boundary in schizophrenia? I think we can. Often in schizophrenia, the in–out boundary is damaged. Stimuli from reality fuse with mental life. This fusion tends to be restricted to acute, unmedicated patients, or some very deteriorated, chronic cases (Searles, 1964). The fragmentation of the resulting merger is pathognomonic of schizophrenia.

Conscious–Preconscious–Unconscious Boundaries

The boundaries between the unconscious, preconscious, and conscious are crossed by the schizophrenic fragmentation line, resulting in fragments with elements of all three. Fragments involve both contents and processes characteristic of the three levels. The psychological content revealed by the schizophrenic fragmentation process is difficult for either therapist or patient to use, because even the primary process is fragmented. The fragments may have layered, partial affect content conflict experiences within them, but they are difficult to assemble. Furthermore, the apathetic affect milieu together with the cognitive disruption of the patient may not permit elaborate or usable experience.

Primary Process–Secondary Process–Tertiary Process Boundaries

Secondary process is severely attacked by schizophrenic fragmentation. Logical capacities in conscious, cognitive functions are severely impaired. Secondary process becomes infiltrated with fragmented primary process. It may be as easy to observe a piece of dissociated, rigid, hypersecondary process logic in the schizophrenic patient as it is to observe a disrupted, affectless piece of primary process. The boundary between processes is unpredictable because the illness follows no stable boundary line in its disintegrative process.

Tertiary processes, integrative mixtures of the primary and secondary processes (Arieti, 1976), paradoxically may seem more intact than either the primary or secondary process, and many schizophrenic patients may seem "creative." But these seemingly tertiary constructs are the result of fragmented primary and secondary process mergers rather than of imaginative integration. They are, hence, irregular, nonrepetitive, unelaborated, and sparse in derivatives. They are reified and concrete. The observer may admire them, but the schizophrenic patient usually cannot use them. Their own experience of them may be bizarre, real, and frightening. Nonetheless, artistic schizophrenics may experience an esthetic from their creative productions even if that esthetic experience is bizarre and frightening.

Affect Boundaries

Because affect is also fragmented, the fusions of affect that occur in schizophrenia may not summate to the intensities seen in manic patients or organic brain syndrome patients. Although sometimes a schizophrenic patient can erupt with enormous force ("catatonic excitement," "paranoid schizophrenic rage"), the rare schizophrenic eruption is not coherent unless transiently directed against a tormentor in reality or against

Psychiatric Illnesses and Mental Structure 139

a delusionally perceived external tormentor, as in chronic paranoid schizophrenia.

Reality Testing

Reality testing in schizophrenia is severely impaired. Because in schizophrenia the psychotic condensations are fragmented, there can be little secondary revision or rational organization of them. In addition, nonpsychotic ego areas may also be fragmented, so that little secondary accessory ego function may exist to help the patient with reality testing. Fragments that have a condensed, fixed, delusional loss of reality testing exist alongside of nondelusional fragments. The pattern is changing in acute illness and rigidly fixed in the chronic form of the illness, but, in both cases, the resultant pattern makes neither primary, secondary, nor tertiary process make sense. Therefore, cognition makes no sense to any intact reality testing processes.

Observing Ego

Because most accessory ego functions may be badly damaged in schizophrenia, observing ego tends to be limited at best. Nonetheless, there may be observing ego of at least some aspects of routine social interaction. Because this may include the doctor–patient relationship, the little observing ego there is may be crucial. The despair of some schizophrenic patients may come from their partially intact observing ego which experiences their illness with dismay.

Integrating Capacity

Schizophrenic integration is described in the introductory section on fragmentation, the section on primary–secondary process boundary disruption, and the section on conscious–unconscious boundary problems. Emotional experience and reality experience are condensed, fused, and fragmented. Individual fragments may be further fused together, condensed, or dissociated. There is no predictable integration pattern except the fragmentation. Normal primary process, secondary process, and tertiary process integration patterns shift to schizophrenic fragmentation and fusion. This is the schizophrenic integration pattern.

Relationship of Reality Experience to Emotional Experience

Schizophrenia has profound effects on the relationship of emotional experience to reality experience. Because the relationship is characterized by fragments and fusions, because the fragmentation–fusion line crosses reality experience–emotional experience boundaries, because primary process emotional experience itself is fragmented, and because secondary process reality experience is severely affected, the relationship between reality experience and emotional experience areas is chaotic. This is especially so in acute schizophrenic illnesses because of the rapid changes in fragmentation patterns. Zones are thrown into chaotic disruption, including the transitional zone, so there is usually little or no intermediate creative play area left, although some patients can maintain a sense of humor even if it is bizarre and concretely experienced.

Day Residue

Because secondary process and reality experience are fragmented, the day residue is also. This distinguishes schizophrenia from other psychotic and near psychotic illnesses. Even a simple life history may only be obtained by talking to relatives. Some acute schizophrenic patients can at least recognize their integrative life experience if it is told to them. The lack of intact day residue makes psychoanalysis of symbols even more difficult. Observation of here-and-now day residue events can be helpful. A characteristic and classic day residue event which may precipitate an acute episode occurs when an object in reality (the patient's psychologist, for example, who is an ego integrator and support for the patient) leaves for vacation.

Thing Presentations and Qualities

Of course, thing presentations are also fragmented. Even somatosensory processing has little coherence and may lack reality qualities. No coherent validity can be achieved even in this realm. It is no wonder that patients appear perplexed. In chronic forms, stable thing presentations can be achieved, but they are conglomerates of fragments and fusions and so lack effective somatosensory understanding. Because they are not solidly in any mode or zone and have no coherent syntax, new or accessory information cannot be productively sought by the patient. The most coherent aspect achieved tends to be only analog intensities such as "electricity" or "space rays."

Thing presentation quality, because of its analog intensity, can be experienced, although not coherently and consistently. But along this mode, certain self qualities may be experienced by the patient and related to by the therapist. This is important in working with such patients (Pao, 1979). Some therapists are intuitively gifted and well experienced in understanding this mode and in making a kind of elemental but important contact with patients via this channel. They can do so either verbally through recognition/description or through the constancy of empathic and physical presence.

Symbols

One can now descriptively understand the severe disruption schizophrenia causes in the symbolizing function, in symbols, and in symbolic alterations. Symbolic elements as well as symbol construction are severely damaged. The day residue, primary process, secondary revision, and elaboration are fragmented. Some fragments are fused, others dissociated, still others are lost. Some large pieces are reified and concrete, while others are totally disorganized. Hence, symbol experience for the patient and doctor is perplexing. Symbol use is paralyzed (usually) or abrupt and impulsive (rarely).

Object Relations

Fragmentation and fusion affects object relations, of course. Because the fusion aspect may affect the relationship of real object to real self, psychoanalysts have wondered if conflicts over dependency (need fear dilemma) or over aggression (Pao, 1979) were etiologic. I feel that because conscious cognitive functioning is so disordered, because no normal developmental state is so fragmented, and because there are similarities to organic brain deterioration (boundary disruption, fusion of affect, stimulus origin confusion), the unknown biological component is paramount, probably on a neurochemical or microcellular level.

Basic to the schizophrenic object relation is not only condensation but fragmentation and the lack of boundary between inside and outside. There are fusions and then fragmentations of real object, real self, object representation, and self representation. The mechanisms may involve condensations, fusions, and then introjection and projection. The intensity of the real object may result in a fusion with the real self as easily as an intense affect state in the self representation can fuse with the real object in a projection. All object relations contents are usually from all developmental levels, chaotic and fragmented. Several levels may appear in one fragmentation (Searles, 1964).

Defenses

Personality defenses are quite disorganized in schizophrenia. Their stability, consistency, functions, and contents are usually so impaired that no coherent personality diagnosis is possible, especially in acute illness or in the middle to advanced stages of chronic schizophrenic illness. In milder forms of schizophrenia, or when it is possible to stabilize the chronic form in an early phase, there may be significant intact personality defenses with some cohesion. But because of the schizophrenic fragmentation line, such patients are very vulnerable and need an integrating, supportive treatment in which only varying degrees of uncovering occur.

Again, the issue of fragmentation as a defense is a main psychoanalytic postulate. Some say it is a defense against merger (Kernberg, 1986), some say against aggression (Arlow and Brenner, 1964; Klein, 1975; Pao, 1979; Bion, 1984), and some say it is oedipal (Brenner, 1976). Although it may seem to be used sometimes secondarily for defense, I do not believe fragmentation is caused by psychic conflict or is a phenomenon of defense. Such theorizing does violence to realities of mind–brain interactions and also to psychoanalytic ideas and observations of normal development and function. There is no such normal developmental state for regression (Stern, 1985). Interpretation of dependency and aggressive conflicts may be helpful, but postulating etiology from therapeutics is always an illogical and hazardous proposition (see Kafka [1984] for interviews). The dynamics could be the result as well as the cause of any given illness, and we know that accessory ego function can be mobilized by interpretations to help damaged ego functions even when the illness is known to be organically based, as in strokes. On special techniques of psychotherapy and psychoanalysis with schizophrenics, see Fromm-Reichman (1948, 1950, 1959), Redlich (1952), Sullivan (1953), Boyer (1961), Searles (1964), Arieti (1974), Volkan (1976), Boyer and Giovacchini (1980), Stone, Albert, Forrest, and Arieti, (1983), Letterman (1996), and Robbins (1993). For a review of modern neurobiology as it relates to schizophrenia, see Willick (1991b).

Manic-Depressive Illness

Introduction

Manic-depressive illness comes in all combinations and degrees of severities in the different forms of depressions, manias, or both, and may be single episodes, repeated episodes, sporadic, cyclical, or chronic (Goodwin and Jamison, 1990; Akiskal, 1999). The structural effect is due to the intensification of affect and the resultant changes in ego processes dealing with affect containment. Psychic boundaries are put under strain, cognitive processing shifts to primary process, defensive organization and object relations become more primitive in quality and content. Both defenses and object relations become rigid.

It is important to realize, however, that variation in severity between individuals and over time in one individual are characteristic of these illnesses. This makes it difficult to describe the structures, because the spectrum of intensity and hence the severity of structural changes is analog, i.e., infinitely varies. Any description of a point on that spectrum is therefore meant as a helpful guide and not as a necessity for the illness, for any given case or time. On the psychodynamics and special treatment considerations, see Abraham (1911), Lewin (1950), Greenacre (1953), Scott (1963), Jacobson (1971), Klein (1975), Gabbard (2014), and Frosch (1990).

Boundaries

In–Out Boundary: Introduction

Increased affect intensity spreading into mood, whether in mania or depression or both, puts boundaries under strain. The boundaries do not seem to be attacked directly, since they return to their usual functioning as the intensity of the episode subsides. But this fact does not rule out a direct but reversible attack.

In–Out Boundary: Mania

The in–out boundary is obviously and severely affected by extreme mania—stage 4 mania. External stimuli will flood mental functioning because the ego's stimulus screening and modulating barrier are lost. On a hospital unit, nurses, conversations, or even hallway noise will intrude on a patient's verbal stream and be repeated by the patient (echolalia). Affect from other people will easily evoke patient affect. Affect in the patient will seem to the patient to be in others as well. The patient will behaviorally respond as if this were true. These fusion experiences may take hallucinatory thing presentation form. There may be loss of reality testing. The more thing presentations are based on fusions, the more fleeting their content will be. But there are extreme, manic patients who can stabilize a condensation of primary process and emotional experience content with inner reality experience as a hallucination that is not only quite stable for an episode but may be repetitive with each episode. These condensations are true hallucinations of psychotic condensations rather than fusions across the in–out boundary. For example, an episodically manic woman hallucinated a cross in the sky with each episode and delusionally believed it proved that she was engaged to be married to Jesus. She dressed for her wedding and in some episodes tried to jump off a bridge to get to the combined baptism-marriage.

Lesser degrees of mania and hypomania put the in–out boundary under strain without actually breaking it. With stimulus screening and stimulus modulation-attenuation inadequate to inner intensity, stimulus augmentation occurs. This is because of failure to screen externally intense stimuli, but also because of affect augmentation with transmodal affect condensation or fusion of affect with these external stimuli. This increases the perceived intensity of the external stimulus.

Central to the description of each manic state is the degree to which the in–out boundary is strained. To what extent are fusions occurring as opposed to condensations? To what extent are inner condensations then fusing with external stimuli? The intensity of manic hallucinations and delusions is increased when a psychotic condensation fuses with a reality stimulus. This greatly increases validity and veracity, adding to conviction and therefore making behavioral enactment irresistible. Hence, manic patients may be dangerous to themselves and others.

In summary, manic hallucinations, when they occur, often involve the in–out boundary. They are composed, in large part, of external stimuli fusing with internal affect. Stimulus augmentation, stimulus overinclusion, origin confusions, and transmodal processing are all aspects of these internal–external fusions.

In–Out Boundary: Depression

In severe depression, this boundary is much more solid than in mania. Usually, only affect as an external stimulus enters the self experience and ego organization. For example, a depressed woman refused to go to sad movies because when a character cried on the screen, she cried herself. Even then, the separation of external stimulus and internal evoked response is usually maintained, even in psychotic forms of depression. The apparent in–out boundary problem is, therefore, really a form of affect coincidence and evocation with poor modulation. The difference can be seen in the condensation of content mechanism rather than fusion. The maintenance of the in–out boundary in the presence of psychosis is a strong indication of depression, although not pathognomonic.

In near psychotic depressions, the "affect leak" across boundaries may be despair, degradation, or anger in addition to or instead of sadness. The predominant affect depends, in part, on the developmental level achieved in superego integration and in ego defensive structures, hence on the characteristic dynamic character conflicts before the onset of the depression.

Some alterations of perception that may occur in depressive hallucinations (auditory, somatic) are condensations, originating in affect states and not in reality stimuli (although the day residue of a somatic hallucination may be an altered physical state). But these occur in reality experience inside an intact in–out boundary. Hence they are depressive projections rather than fusions or evocations by reality stimuli. When hallucinations or delusions involve the real object, the content is usually about the inner state of the object, which is imperceivable. The meaning of the reality stimulus qualities of the object are contaminated by projection mechanisms, but usually not the stimulus itself.

Depressive hallucinations and delusions do not, as a rule, involve fusions. If they do, and if the external stimulus barrier is damaged, the therapist should suspect a physical brain problem in addition to depression (see section on organic mental syndromes). Depressive psychotic phenomena usually involve only condensations across the internal emotional experience–reality experience boundary organized in intense thing presentation experiences, projected to the reality experience with the preserved ability to experience a separate, actual reality. Only affect may leak into the self representation from the object in reality, and then its effect is evocative of the patient's affect rather than becoming the patient's affect.

In those rare cases where percept is altered (it is usually one's self experience as in somatic delusions or hallucinations), the perceptual alteration is a transmodal processing of the patient's mood and not a fusion experience from stimuli in reality, except when there is physical illness.

Conscious–Preconscious–Unconscious Boundaries

In mania, intense affect seems to erupt from unconscious pools and primary process encoding systems. Affect and primary process push into preconscious and conscious secondary and tertiary process functions. There are the most striking shifts to primary process formation in what should be conscious secondary processes. Loose affect associations, puns, condensation of concepts and affect contents, and intense surreal symbolizations are all readily apparent. The boundary between unconscious and preconscious and conscious should normally function as an internal affect stimulus intensity barrier similar to the in–out barrier for external perceptual stimuli. In mania, this repression barrier is severely overwhelmed. The flood of intense affect brings with it primary processes that dominate preconscious and conscious functioning, sometimes obliterating the higher levels altogether. The affect eruption is usually along a broad front, affecting most areas of mental content and distorting or eliminating many ego functions.

In depression, the affect is better contained in conscious and preconscious symbolic structures, particularly in those patients who had reached neurotic levels of organization. Primary process usually does not infiltrate broadly. It is confined to a single content theme. Affect is usually also free-floating and may contaminate the quality of all content areas with depressive mood, but it does not result in massive primary processing, unlike in mania. A psychotically depressed patient may have a quite rational secondary process organization outside the delusional system, while being quite sad.

146   Psychiatric Illnesses and Mental Structure

Borderline patients who become severely depressed may show broad shifts to primary process functioning together with other evidence of poorly contained mood eruption such as angry irritability, impulsive behavior, stimulus augmentation, and intense projections. Introjection, augmentation, and projection are particularly intense in response to external criticism or anger.

Primary–Secondary–Tertiary Process Boundaries

Mania causes the most intense and widespread shift from secondary to primary process. With increasing mood disorders, one can see the progressive, increased capture of cognition by primary process.

Tertiary process is usually also disrupted, but in creative patients with extensive craft training, tertiary processes may hold together in the hypomanic phase, resulting in a creative burst of great productivity. Depression, with its less severe primary process capture of cognition, may preserve secondary and tertiary processes until the depression is so severe that it approaches stupor. Depression in trained artists may charge tertiary processes with intense affect and thing presentation qualities, resulting in a most productive creative phase. Esthetic appreciation can increase in depression because thing presentation qualities are more intense and transmodal processes are more available.

Although shifts to primary process occur in organic brain syndromes, in manic-depressive illness, the mood-congruent content, the concomitant free-floating affect, the intensity of symbolism, and the neurovegetative symptoms are all clues, as is the course of illness, which begins with affective symptoms.

Loosening of associations, i.e., jumping from one logical topic to another, in manic-depressive illness is organized by affect. The loose associations are affect congruent associations, unlike organically loose associations. In manic-depressive illness, affect intensities are no longer boundaried by ideational content, because the affect is spread past such boundaries into mood.

Remember that affective illness causes an increased shift to primary process, because primary process is an affect processing system linking ideas in an analog organization by intensity, as well as themes. For this reason, affect associated contents are incorporated into mood regardless of category or boundary. The boundary crossings to achieve recruitment depend only on intensity once the primary process system is activated in consciousness.

Affect Boundaries and Modulation Function

Affect boundaries separate different affects and also separate affect and mood (affect in all mental areas) (see Jacobson, 1971).

Psychiatric Illnesses and Mental Structure 147

In mania, there are fusions between affects and transmodal transfers of affect. The normal layering complexity, conscious to preconscious to unconscious, becomes a homogeneous conscious mass. Laughter and tears may occur together with rage. A verbal confrontation may produce an erection, a sexy picture may evoke anger. The lability and intensity may occur also in organic brain syndrome or in acute onset schizophrenia, but the affect fusions and transfers are particularly characteristic of affective illness, manic phase.

These changes may be seen in borderline patients with depression or in mixed affect states. In more integrated patients with depression, depressive affect may color or obliterate other affects, but it does not fuse with them. The exception is lustful affect in certain patients who sexualize their depressive affect.

More striking, of course, in all kinds of manic-depressive illness is the pathognomonic spread of affect across all mental areas into moods until no content area is left untouched. All ideas are colored by the same affect. The ability to prevent transient, situation-specific affect from spreading into an intensifying mood is lost. Likewise, the ability of the ego to modulate the intensity of the evoked affect or of the received affect is severely damaged, so that patients may be exquisitely vulnerable to and hence avoidant of their affective social attachments. This modulation failure of intensity, duration, and spread is the hallmark of a mood disorder. The modulation capacity is the pathognomonic ego function damage that causes the psychopathological pathognomonic features.

Mood selects, recruits, reinforces, and reintegrates many content areas and object relations. Because mood adds tone and quality to content and object relations, mood affects judgment and choice. Mood changes the intensity and hence the relative value of elements. Intensity is part of what judgment and choice use for decision. For example, a hypomanic man sees a pretty woman and says "I'm in love" and means it. If he is more intensely manic, he will think she also is in love with him. He may leave a wife of 20 years for this instant romance, even if it is unconfirmed by the target.

The relationship of content to mood is bidirectional, with content both causing and resulting from mood to differing degrees in different patients. The same is true of the day residue. If one observes evolving, intensifying depressive episodes, one can see the recruitment of content and of day residues as the mood spreads and intensifies.

Likewise, mood intensification of content make psychoanalysis difficult and are one reason for Freud's "stickiness of the libido" idea. The id does give intensity and force, but it is the ego that controls, regulates, modulates, and releases—Freud's "taming of the instincts." For example: (1) "Just thinking about it makes me uncomfortable" (i.e., content evokes affect overload). (2) In the hypomanic, overstimulation, i.e., intense external stimuli, causes lack of affect control, so turn down loud music and don't argue.

Reality Testing

Reality testing in affective illness is on a continuum from unimpaired to severely impaired (Jacobson, 1971). It may alter dramatically during the course of an illness or may be quite stable. When it varies, it usually seems to do so according to variations in mood intensity. However, there are some cases where the loss of reality testing and the delusional content are the most prominent features of the mood disorder.

Because of the potential for shifts along the severity spectrum, psychotherapeutic, milieu, and behavioral interventions are often tried and often are successful in moving reality testing back toward health. Antipsychotic medication will move psychotic reality testing across the near psychotic border but no further in both depression and mania. Antidepressant medication added to neuroleptics will dramatically shift reality testing for the better in depression, but antidepressants alone in psychotic depression either do not work well or take too long to work.

Reality testing is the most fluid in mania, with continuous shifts as affect intensity shifts from moment to moment, unless the patient is in a severe mania with a fixed delusional–hallucinatory system. Depression tends to cluster around a fixed area of content and to have only diurnal variation in intensity, and so reality testing is more stably placed along the continuum. Shifts also can be seen reflecting emotional evocation by external events and objects that actualize, or are experienced as actualizing, inner depressive content.

Observing Ego

Observing ego is most likely to be potentially preserved in the mood disorders, especially in depression. It is one of the helpful signs of a depressive psychosis that although reality testing is gone, observing ego is present, spontaneously or with active questioning. This also accounts for some of the suffering and horror of this illness. The process of self-perusal, the maintenance of dispassionate observing ego content, and the ability to use secondary process for weighing evidence and reaching conclusions about reality can all be a remarkably intact, albeit dissociated, area of complex ego function in depression. When observing ego processes are intact, but depressive content has infiltrated, this is an ominous sign and requires quick and effective intervention. The next step is capture of observing ego processes and serious suicide risk, because all sentient experience is now captured by depression and validated even by the observing ego.

In mania, observing ego is most likely to be suspended or captured, depending on the severity of the mania. This makes mania more dangerous, as a rule, than depression.

Integrative Capacity

The mood disorders are marked by primary process integrations and dissociative failures of secondary process integration. There is a failure to integrate the processing of mood with secondary process. At times, in the creatively talented and trained, tertiary process provides an intact integration pathway.

Depression preserves the integrity and authenticity of primary process integration. Mania may give the primary process a fleeting, superficial, and even disjointed form, especially if the mania is severe.

In both mania and depression, the integration task involves intense, deep, and widespread affect intensities. Moderate mood disorders, especially in the developmentally disadvantaged, make intense ambivalence hard to integrate. In children, this is normal. For example: a 3-year-old child, when denied a candy will say, "I don't love you anymore!" The same child, 6 months later in the same situation will say, "Daddy, even when you're angry at me, you still love me; that's silly!" A 4-year-old child in the same situation will say, "Daddy, even when I'm angry at you, I still love you!"

The inability to integrate oppositely valenced affect states is particularly pronounced in mania or in mixed states of simultaneous mania and depression. Patient example: "If all these feelings are mood-related, then I don't know who I am!" But of course, if the mood explanation is denied, then the patient complains of being different from moment to moment, or from phase to phase.

Splitting of affect is the adult, pathological form of intense infantile emotional storms or temper tantrums, hence its connection with mood instability in the adult. In some severely impaired, personality-disordered adults, splitting can emerge as a defense in conditions of frustration (infantile) or narcissistic confrontation (narcissistic character disorders).

Relation of Reality Experience to Emotional Experience

Because of the affect intensity and because the primary processing predominance captures the link between affect, mood and validity, especially in sentient experience, reality experience is greatly influenced by emotional experience in manic-depressive illness. Affect leaks and attachments infiltrate reality experience with emotional experience meaning. Reality experience may thus be captured to a greater or lesser extent. The interplay of these relationships along a spectrum of intensity accounts for the features of this aspect of the illness. The relationship is one of primary process and dissociation, but this does not do justice to the compelling intensity of the resultant condensations, especially when they reach a certain point of intensity and condense in reality experienced thing presentations.

150 Psychiatric Illnesses and Mental Structure

Example:

A manic-depressive, bipolar, 45-year-old man was usually chronically depressed. He was happy with his wife and three children. He found his wife supportive, calm, and effective. She shouldered many of the burdens of house and children, leaving him free to pursue his career. He liked this arrangement. But when he was manic, he felt she was a boring, unexciting, humdrum slave to hearth and home with whom he would have nothing of zest or growth. He would promptly fall in love and have an affair. He would leave his wife and chase after the other woman, usually an independent career woman who did not want to settle down. When the episode ended, he would return to his wife, blaming flaws in the mistress for his loss of interest.

This is an example of the capture of reality experience by mood-related content. It is also an example of the inability to integrate oppositely valenced object relations contents.

Day Residue

One of the most interesting intersections between reality experience and emotional experience in the mood disorders is at the day residue. Manic-depressive illness has a lower stimulus threshold for emotionally evocative events and also attaches intense affect to reality experience. These reality experiences become, in turn, even more dramatic evokers and instigators of affect. The decreased affect modulating capacity of evoked affect together with the increased intensity of the evocative stimulus due to stimulus enhancement of condensed affect is a summating cycle. In addition, bad things do happen to people, especially to some manic-depressives who enact their inner world and thus provoke their outer world to respond. Sometimes the response is a day residue trigger!

For patients with severe manic-depressive illness with autonomous cycling, the day residue may be nonexistent or irrelevant. With less autonomous cycling, the day residue may be significant but not causal, necessary but not sufficient. With still less autonomous cycling, the day residue may be causal and sufficient as a trigger. Because most manic-depressives are not at the severest end of the spectrum, understanding the day residue's power to initiate episodes is helpful for treatment. The day residue is significant because of psychological meaning, which ties in with defenses and character structure. If there is a severe character neurosis in addition to the manic-depressive illness, the neurosis must be treated to defuse the day residue. A day residue has its power not only because of what really happened, but also because of the significance it has. Because the day residue may be quite specific as an initiator, the clearest link can be seen between psychology and biology where psychology is a trigger for the biology. Nowhere, therefore, is the necessity for a psychological treatment as part of the treatment plan more clearly demonstrated in psychotic and near psychotic illness. The integration between mind and brain and between psychotherapy and pharmacotherapy is thus demonstrated. One person's trigger (loss of relationship) is not the same as another's (loss of job). The reasons for this difference have to do with the different psychological meanings of reality events for different people. In manic-depressive illness, the meaning is seen in affect and self-significance condensed with the reality evoker event. Intermediate layers linking affect to event, deeper layers of psychogenetics, and the full elaborated meaning need to be explored in analytic psychotherapy. This, together with medication, can make recovery from an episode more rapid, may result in lower doses of necessary medication, and can probably even serve to prevent episodes. There is no research yet to prove this, but it is my strong clinical impression and I believe it will be documented. In any case, even for the relief of the acute episode, if the day residue continues in reality as an irritant stress, half of depressed patients will not respond to medication (Sarwer-Foner, personal communication, 1991).

Example:

A 38-year-old woman in a stormy love relationship experiences the abrupt termination of the relationship when her boyfriend leaves her for another woman. The woman is tearful and sad, and, 24 hours later, plunges into a suicidal depression. Consciously, she feels that the relationship, although troubled, was her last chance for marriage. She also feels that being in a committed relationship proves that she is not bad, envious, domineering, controlling, and man-hating like her mother, who had divorced her father when she was young. She is not aware of exactly why a relationship with a difficult and unreliable man was seen by her as a test of her own worth. She has had two previous, less severe depressions: once when another relationship had broken up; her first depression was as a child after her father left.

In affective illness, the day residue tends to be an integrated, whole object or self experience or event. It is relatively undisplaced even in

152 Psychiatric Illnesses and Mental Structure

manifest content from childhood events and deeper object meanings. Further aspects of this day residue phenomenon will be discussed in following sections on object relations and on symbolic alterations of reality. In any case, although the undisplaced concordance with childhood events is fairly direct, the emotional significance, reverberations in the self-esteem system, reluctance to move past some traumas, intensity of the repetition compulsion, and subtleties of dynamic layers are all unknown to the patient.

The significance of the day residue and even its occurrence are often defended against, often with basic character defenses or with simple denial. The denial is often quite rigid. The defense occurs because the patient fears that full, conscious recognition will make the mood worse or trigger a severe episode because a loop will be closed. Conscious recognition will unite dissociated affect with the reality event, proving the patient's worst fears and making the mood even worse and the day residue even more evocative. Avoidance of this downward spiral is a life-and-death matter for some patients and accounts for the rigidity of their defenses against the day residue and sometimes their avoidance of social situations that may provide day residue triggers. Intensive analytical psychotherapy or psychoanalysis plus medication can disassemble the triggers without risking a serious mood episode.

Thing Presentations and Qualities

Thing presentations and their qualities are most intense in affective illness. This is a hallmark of mood disorders. Symbolic processes are intensely charged with affect and rich in transmodal processing. Percepts are charged with affect; affect and percept qualities are condensed. As intensity of mood increases, thing presentation quality increases. Symbolic details become rich with affect and their perceptual details become rich in perceptual overtones and intensity, as affect becomes transmodally processed into perceptual details and self experience.

Example:

A 30-year-old woman is in a severe, retarded depression. She sits in the hospital examining room mute, motionless, her head on her knees and her hands hanging down at her sides. Her face is in a grimace.

THERAPIST: "You look as if you are experiencing something terribly unpleasant."
PATIENT: "Shit! I'm covered with shit! Phew! It smells horrible!"

The reality experienced transmodal perceptual quality of thing presentations may spread to all areas contaminated by the severe mood. Thing presentation quality heavily skews judgment and certainty because of reality experienced thing presentation veracity and validity.

As intensity of affect–percept transmodal processing increases, the rigidity of the structure increases in an attempt to provide a perceptual thing presentation containment barrier to the spread of affect. This causes a rigid, unchanging, unyielding symbol, unavailable to word presentations and to generalization of concept. Either might spread the affect beyond the boundaries of the thing presentation. Often, however, even the rigid thing presentation cannot contain the affect. The increasing intensity of the affect then "drips over" the symbol experience into free-floating affect of the same valence, tone, and quality as in the symbol. The failure to bind affect, even in the primary process and even in perceptual thing presentation experience, leaves the ego at the mercy of the mood flooding. This is experienced as traumatic, and indeed, there is a strong resemblance to traumatic states and to traumatic symbolic processes. Like traumatic neuroses, therefore, manifest content in manic-depressive illness must be attended to because of the manifest affect charge and resulting thing presentation qualities, validities, and veracities. The affect intensity causes condensing of latent content into manifest content. This is another reason for attending to the top layers of manifest content where the leading edge of this condensation is located. One symptom of subtle affective illness is tightly condensed, rigid, manifest content material, highly charged with affect.

In manic-depressive illness, even memory may be highly charged with affect that does not fade and hence may exert a continuous traumatic effect on later ego organizations, experiences, and developmental phases. This is similar to the memory of highly traumatic episodes. Manic-depressive dreams may show the same characteristics for the same reasons. Imagination in the manic-depressive may also be so charged with validity and veracity thing presentation affect that, in memory, the fantasy seems real.

The rigid thing presentations acting as perceptual containment barriers to affect flooding resist translation along word presentation channels because generalization of concept may cause further spread of mood and hence further disruption of secondary process ego functions. "Talking about it only makes it worse!" Preliminary treatment must be done with medication containment barriers, with reinforcement of secondary processes and word presentation pathways, and also with defenses. Then with interpretive decondensing, each layer is less intense and more containable than the summation of the thing presentation. The patient gradually reintegrates along secondary process lines of conceptualization, generalization, and application.

Example of intense affect charging memory, causing a kind of eidetic memory: "My impressions of people are seared into my memory and they become a part of my life. It makes me feel they mean more to me than I do to them. I remember the color of dresses I admired in grade school!"

Symbols

Manic-depressive symbols show two related characteristic features: the intensity of affect and the dramatic alteration of reality. Because affect evokes, organizes, and leaks intra- and intersymbolically, all areas of symbol formation become colored as mood spreads. Reality experience is always affected from mild condensations of meaning to actual perceptual changes. Whether the symbol experience is in word presentations or thing presentations, conscious or preconscious, reality experience, emotional experience, or third-space experience, affect intensity is the hallmark. All aspects of symbol structure are intense: affect, perceptual qualities, detail, content, plot, day residue, and primary processing.

The intensity and easy, fluid capture of reality experience result in symbolic alterations of reality with dramatic content and rich perceptual detail. The exceptions are severe, disorganized manic states or moribund depressive states with monotonal qualities and poverty of content.

Because of the affect intensity, because primary process increases, and because the ego is not fragmented, intense symbolic alterations of reality usually involve whole, intense object relations in the manic-depressive illnesses. The contents and plots are so compelling that one can lose sight of their symbolic purposes, structures, and uses.

Object Relations

The object relations of this spectrum of illnesses are described in pioneering psychoanalytic works on mania by Lewin (1950), and on depression by Jacobson (1971). Earlier pioneering work on the object relations of depression was done by Rado (1928), Klein (1975), and Freud himself (1917a). For more recent statements about depression, see Stone (1986), Milrod (1988), and Brenner (1991). All of these texts focus mostly on psychodynamics of agency conflict and the content of object relations; Freud, Rado, and Jacobson also describe their ego structure.

I have only minor disagreements with and additions to their work on depression. My emphasis is on (1) structure, not content, (2) content as broader and more inclusive (spectrum phenomena: formes frustes), and (3) object relations as the effect, not the cause or not the only cause, of ego disruptions.

My differences about structure have to do with the ego, of course. The most characteristic are the changes in self representation. In depression, debased, criticized, failed self representations emerge in preconscious and conscious mental life, gradually capturing the real self experience. This is the defining structural feature of depressive object relations. The captures of reality testing and even observing ego are progressive changes as the illness gets worse.

The merger that occurs is a condensation, not a fusion, and it is the major and most common boundary crossing. When merger of self and object is mentioned in the psychoanalytic literature, usually self refers to the entire ego experience of self; object usually refers to a superego interject. Actually, self representation and object representation do not fuse or even condense. There may be similar affect but usually not. When object experience is contaminated, it is an object representation–real object merger, or more commonly, a self representation–real self merger. Next most common are malevolent representations of objects, especially early superego introjects that are projected onto object relations and real objects. The depressive self representation may be lying in wait in the unconscious but may not be. It may be under constant or intermittent attack by a superego object introject, may be ground down by a reality object tormentor, or may be absorbing intense, internal aggression that is not cycling through the super-ego. The aggression may be dissociated, as in certain moods or unstable, "borderline" states. What is constant along the severity axis of depression is the depressive affect of the self representation. This affect may vary from depressive despair to depressive rage. Hence, we see that there are a variety of object relations organizations of depressive affect within the general structure of the merger of depressive self representations.

The content of object relations varies according to the intensity of the depression, the level of ego function associated with the present affective episode, and the level of ego function before the episode. The content can vary from depressive loss of the positive or negative Oedipus complex, to separation/punishment fantasies of the pre-Oedipus complex, or to even earlier anaclitic loss and abandonment. The content may be rage. Depression may cast its pall over all phases of development.

The ego may be affected in all phases of illness or in some phases more than others, making the content and plot of object relations in depressive illness quite variable.

In addition, there are changes in content and plot, depending on intensity of illness. One can see manifest content, latent content, dream content, and the content of deeper unconscious layers shift in plot, structure, and motivation as affective illness intensifies. How could this be otherwise when the primary processing of affect expresses intensities with changes in symbol formation, both processes and contents? In addition, the content may express various dominant affects in depression and not just various intensities. Anxiety may be the predominant affect, with a particular depressive quality, or depressive irritability.

156   Psychiatric Illnesses and Mental Structure

There are also contentless depressions, the so-called apathetic or stuporous depressions. In milder form, they may be called *alexithymic depressions*.

We now consider the role of object relations in the etiology of affective disorders. The neoclassical psychoanalytic view is that depression has to do with oral phase ambivalence. The later neoclassical view is that depression also has to do with emotionally deprived mothering. Brenner (1976) has insisted on the oedipal aspects. I do not totally disagree with any of these etiologic statements, but ascribing etiology to psychopathology is a dangerous, circular argument, as is ascribing etiology from assumptions based on treatment. The psychopathological data on which such assumptions are based are not consistent but vary along the spectra of severity, intensity, and ego maturity. When the superego and ego have malevolent introjects, depression is a distinct possibility. But it is also true that when one is depressed, introjects get more malevolent. It is also true that then malevolent, reality day residue objects may be taken in as malevolent introjects. The oral rage at feeling not taken care of can be a reflection either of inadequate mothering or of an early childhood depression diathesis for which no mother is good enough. The interplay of nature and nurture, of cause and effect, of brain and mind is nowhere more clearly demonstrated, in all of its complexity, than in the psychiatry of affective illness. Each patient presents a different combination of etiologic factors.

In mania, the ideal self condenses with the self representation, then real self with the self in reality, depending on severity. The real object and object representation may not be affected, although they are usually influenced. The grandiosity, therefore, is of a different structural organization than in narcissism as described by Kernberg (1975). The grandiosity may be with euphoric or irritable paranoid affect. The latter can be quite dangerous. The content may be from any phase of development and often involves all phases. Lewin (1950) stressed the oral phase.

Morality may be severely affected or not much at all, depending on the level of ego maturity and superego development before the episode, if the episode is intermittent.

Example:

A responsible, middle-aged businessman suffers a manic episode, believes he can fly, and jumps from his second-story office window, breaking his leg. In the hospital, on a locked psychiatric unit, he wants discharge because he does not feel he is psychiatrically ill. When the discharge is refused by the admitting doctor, the patient

> requests a phone call to his wife. The patient phone is outside the locked ward door in the hospital corridor. The doctor wonders with the patient why the patient would return after the phone call if the patient feels he is not psychiatrically ill. The patient replies, "But you are the doctor and if you say I must stay then I must. I will be back to argue with you some more!"

Defenses

The hallmark of manic-depressive defenses is their rigidity. This rigidity has its distinctive causes and effects.

Descriptively, the "cause" of rigid defenses is the attempt to contain intense affect experience and associated object relations. The attempt is to control the intensity, the shift to primary processing of that intensity, and the spread across the range of ego functions and contents to all mental areas, a process we call *mood* (Mahler, 1966; Jacobson, 1971).

The rigid defenses can be of any type or level. They usually include vertical dissociations in an attempt to limit the spread of affect. Abstracting and generalizing are impaired by these vertical dissociations. When concept crosses a vertical dissociation, affect may spread. As intensity increases during the progressive episode, the vertical defenses may hold, resulting in an eruption of primary processing in one ego domain or content area only. An example is a somatic delusion with depressive content in a patient with an apparently minimal mood disorder.

Patients with labile affect, in hypomanic states or with hysterical characters and agitated depression (infantile borderline patients) seem to be chaotic rather than rigid. They use affect to defend against affect, and affect storm as a defense against specific and complex affect. Often overlooked is the stereotypy of response and the fixed relationship of elements: of affect type, of day residue event triggering, and of object relations organization. In these ways, such chaotic states are actually quite rigid.

Although the psychoanalytic literature talks about specific levels of defense, contents of defense, and psychogenetic origins of defense, in fact, all vary from patient to patient. It is the form the defenses take that is invariant.

The repression barrier, if it can be considered a primary defense, is both rigid and porous. Areas of repression are quite rigid and unyielding, other areas crumble and intense primary process emerges in a miniature affect storm. Dissociative defenses try to contain this eruption and exaggerate the difference between the rigid repressed areas and the erupted, flooded ego areas.

158 Psychiatric Illnesses and Mental Structure

Affective illness also seems chaotic because as intensity increases there is a shift to more intense primary process organizations and boundary crossings of defenses. Defenses are said to be "more primitive" and patients are said to be "really borderline underneath" or "really psychotic at core." What is phenomenologically occurring is a shift in defenses with affective episodes: a shift in content, organization, level of consciousness, location, domain, and processing. The shift may be temporary. This does not mean this shift is the "core." It may be and it may not be, depending on the patient. There are as many neurotics with borderline affective storms against oedipal issues as there are borderline patients with flimsy neurotic defenses.

Organic Mental Syndromes

Introduction

Organic mental syndromes involve some type of brain damage, anatomic or physiologic, diffuse or focal. The category is therefore also called *organic brain syndromes*. The diagnostic category has been under strain recently because functional biochemical and brain flow changes are being documented in affective illness (George, Nahas, Lomerov, Bohning, and Kellner, 1999; Strakowski, DelBello, Sax, Zimmerman, Shear, Hawkins, & Larson, 1999) and in schizophrenia (Sharif, Gewirtz, and Iqbal, 1993; Willick, 1993; Brown, 1999).

Traditionally, the organic mental syndrome category was composed of illnesses causing macrocellular disruptions of brain tissue, such as strokes, bleeds, tumors, and infections. In modern times, physiological disruptions such as electrolyte imbalance have been included. (Lishman [2012] is the most complete resource; in psychoanalytic psychiatry, see Freeman [1969].) Because these illnesses attack the brain, a concerted effort to find the cause must be rapidly initiated as soon as the diagnosis is made.

Learning disabilities are organic mental syndromes.[2] The many associated conditions (dyslexia, attention deficit disorder [ADD], and language disabilities) probably reflect syndromal manifestations of a group of related phenomena that vary in severity and overlap with each other (see Tupper, 1987; Rudel, Holmes, and Rudel-Pandes, 1988; Rothstein, Benjamin, Crosby, and Eisenstadt, 1988). I will use the term *learning disabilities* to refer to this whole group. Some of them represent diffuse brain problems and some of them represent focal brain problems (Galaburda, Sherman, Rosen, Aboitiz, and Geschwind, 1985; Duane and Gray, 1991; Goodglass and Wingfield, 1997). They may dramatically affect manifestations of other psychiatric illnesses when there is comorbidity (Shaywitz and Shaywitz, 1991), and they dramatically affect development and personality functioning (Denckla, 1991; Duane, 1991). They are extremely common. Because much has been written about ADD and ADHD (Bhandary, 1997; Newcorn, 2000), even their ego function (Bellak and Marsh, 1997), I will focus on the broader category of learning disabilities, especially the language disorders, including dyslexia, disorganization, and other language processing problems. This group is extremely varied in language processing, expressing, and organization problems, with or without ADD and ADHD. It has a spectrum of processing and organization problems and associated ego dysfunctions that affect psychic structure.

Boundaries

These illnesses often involve boundary problems and organization of ideas, hence the frequent confusion with schizophrenia. Confusion is especially likely when the boundary damage involves data categories and integrated secondary process cognition. But the two illnesses are very different. Schizophrenia is frequently misdiagnosed when a dyslexic with boundary problems also has an affective illness and becomes psychotic. This misdiagnosis can also occur in a nonpsychotic patient with disorganized learning disabilities causing the severe disorganization of cognition.

In–Out Boundary

The in–out boundary in organic brain syndromes may be damaged severely or mildly. The usual problem is with the stimulus barrier so that external stimuli flood.

Example:

A 6-year-old, severely retarded boy is playing in the playground. He walks under the slide just as another child, sitting high on the slide, pounds with his feet. The loud rat-a-tat-tat on the metal slide sends the retarded child underneath tumbling to the ground, his body shaking in rhythm to the sound. He appears panicked and confused.

Because the stimulus barrier is impaired, the hospital milieu treatment of these severe illnesses focuses on decreasing intense, complex, external

160 Psychiatric Illnesses and Mental Structure

stimuli and replacing them with clear, regular, predictable, and simple stimuli routines.

The in–out boundary problem can also involve transmodal thing presentation projections. Hallucinosis is the classic example.

Example:

"Doc, I'm getting DT's [delirium tremens; acute alcohol withdrawal syndrome] again."
"How do you know?"
"I'm seeing bugs crawling on the walls again!"

Example:

A 57-year-old man in a coronary care unit with myocardial infarction is being treated with intravenous lidocaine medication: "Doc! I'm going crazy!"
"What makes you think so?"
"I'm seeing people coming through the walls!"

In–out boundary problems may also exist to varying degrees. Their most common form is the stimulus barrier problem. One example is the stimulus barrier in the attention deficit disorders which has as its hallmark an uneven distribution and paradoxical density. The unevenness varies from severe to absent, from case to case or over time. Paradoxical density describes too much porosity with stimulus flooding and fusion, alternating with too much density with absent response to external stimuli. This switch sometimes depends on attention, but the deficient stimulus modulation is also present as a separate problem.

Stimulus discrimination, stimulus blocking, and stimulus flooding and fusion may be present alone or in combination. Similarly, category fusion, origin confusion, and/or causal disruptions may result. In mild cases, the occurrence, reception, and localization of stimuli will depend on attention cathexes. Depression will therefore exaggerate this problem. In mild cases, disruption is rare. In moderate cases, disruption is not rare but is compensated by intense overattention or by avoidant reaction formations (plunging ahead in behavior). In severe cases, there is an inability to function in certain cognitive domains.

Example of Stimulus Origin Confusion:

A 40-year-old obsessional man with dyslexia and attention deficit disorder reaches into his pocket just as a clock in the room clicks when the second hand rounds the twelve mark. The patient perceives his pocket as clicking and fears he is going crazy.

A paradoxical problem with the stimulus barrier is the patchy increase in density. Stimuli that should cross the in–out barrier do not until and unless their intensities increase. Sometimes it seems to require saturation intensity before the threshold is reached. In some cases, this is due to an inability to shift attention to the incoming stimulus.

Example:

Mother shouting at a child who, unknown to mother, has attention deficit disorder inattention type: "Don't you hear me unless I shout?"

Child: "Mother, why are you always shouting at me?"

The child feels reprimanded and rebuked, not for what he did, which he does not understand, but for who he is. Some parents come spontaneously to the strategy of using a variety of input channels because only some are blocked at any one time or characteristically. Tapping such a child lightly on the shoulder may be more effective than yelling. Such children and parents may come to understand that the child may need multiple, varied-angle approaches to problems, to solutions, and to learning. Saturation with varied-angle information may be needed (Samberg, personal communication 1986).

Percept–Concept–Affect Boundaries

The boundaries between concept, percept, and affect are damaged in organic brain syndromes (Deutsch, 1954; Benton, 1985). The transmodal processing among these three may be global or focal, intense or apathetic. As the ability to build abstract concepts fails and becomes more concrete, as affect controls become disinhibited, and as the boundaries between percept occurrences and organizations blur, there are confusions among these three areas. Primary process may become the dominant organizing principle, and conscious thing presentation experiences may emerge. This occurs with varying affect intensity, which distinguishes it from the manic-depressive illnesses.

Fusion of two simultaneous stimuli, fusion of associated concept with stimuli, and blurred perceptual boundaries of stimuli all predispose one to transmodal processing of concept in percept. When primary process intrudes because of emotional conflict, anxiety, mania, or depression, the transmodal shift from affect to percept, bypassing concept, starts its organizing capture of reality experience.

The dyslexias have their own characteristics. Their hallmark of the boundary problems is patchy, uneven, and varying severity from domain to domain and from time to time. Concept is particularly affected. Conceptual blurring occurs with category fusions, category reversals, category repetitions, and perseverations. Condensation of concepts may occur and be confused with primary process, which it resembles, but the specific concept junction points and secondary process overlaps that are the linkage points are not affect associations or true condensations of affect content. The verbal behavior of such patients may resemble loose associations with topic derailment and intrusions (see also Resnick and Rapin, 1991). The perseverations and repetitions may also distinguish this from primary process.

Comorbid affective illnesses (Shaywitz and Shaywitz, 1991), which are commonly seen in a psychiatrist's office, are sometimes difficult to diagnose because they produce mixed cognitive states by accentuating the dyslexic signs, which are then mixed in with the affect primary processing. In comorbidity with psychotic depression, learning disabled patients may be inappropriately concrete and abstract even outside their delusional systems.

The difficulty is in the differential diagnosis with schizophrenia, where there is early fragmentation of concept. Attention to details of concept use, pattern recognition based on experience, and neuropsychological testing all help in differential diagnosis. Because these are very different ego organizations with different treatments and prognoses, differential diagnosis is crucial. The treatment for one will not help the other.

Example:

An educated and intelligent woman sees a young, psychoanalytic friend carrying a volume of Freud's collected works. "What is Freud writing these days?" she says.

What she means is, "What book of Freud's are you reading these days?"

Psychiatric Illnesses and Mental Structure   163

This is an example of three reversals of paired categories: writing instead of reading, present instead of past, and Freud as subject instead of Freud as object. The result is a concept reversal. It may also be understood as concept fusion—Freud writing with Freud being read. The use of present for past tense may actually be a perseveration from the present-reader concept carried over into the Freud-past-writer concept. This woman on first hearing seems to have a schizophrenic thinking disorder, but on close inspection does not. There are no fragmentations only reversals.

Reversals, fusions, and primary process intrusions can, if limited in extent, with perseveration of intact secondary process ego in the highly intelligent, be very creative capacities and can be developed with discipline into great productivity. The creative capacity occurs because of leaps over categorical boundaries which provide a spontaneous transcategorical processing system. This system can be most effective if it can be disciplined, corrected, and remodeled where necessary by secondary process translation, revision, and application.

Affect–concept relationships also may be characteristic. Because secondary abstraction may lack robustness and facility, affect experience may be linked instead to either the concrete and specific or the hyperabstract and the metaphor. The language of psychoanalytic psychotherapy must be at the level of cognitive and affect veracity.

Conscious–Preconscious–Unconscious Boundaries

Particularly relevant here is the porous repression barrier. Repression is severely disinhibited in diffuse brain diseases of the organic brain syndrome category.

The learning disabilities group may show a patchy repression barrier with eruptions varying in domain, intensity, and timing. The lack of coordination with intensity helps distinguish the dyslexic repression eruptions from those of affective illness. These patients are sometimes seen as sicker than they are. The primary process eruptions may cause the interviewer to overlook the solid, neurotic defensive structure of most of the ego.

Primary Process–Secondary Process–Tertiary Process Boundaries

The failures of the repression barrier cause an eruption of primary process. It is most interesting that primary process is so much better preserved than secondary process in the organic brain syndromes. This may argue again for a nonlanguage processor. Primary process may extensively replace secondary and tertiary process in severe, diffusely degenerative brain disease. Loosening of association, unrelated to mood, is the mental status exam feature of these illnesses.

The learning disabilities may show a patchy, irregular primary process intrusion pattern, which, if not too frightening, can then be organized by secondary process and used for tertiary processes. New secondary process sequential material is difficult to learn, but analog, pattern material is easy. Such patients are sometimes said to be "intuitive."

The hallmark of diffuse brain disease is the decrease in secondary process capacities. The defect is measured by IQ decrease and especially by a decreased ability to understand higher-order abstractions. A decreased ability to assimilate new information, especially concepts, is characteristic. Patients become more concrete and less facile with analogy. Social milieu processing, often very complex, may be severely damaged early on.

The learning disabled show a patchy IQ with great variability in performance. Patients can have an outstanding verbal IQ and be almost acalculic. The reverse may be true. Social processing and judgment may be superior or severely damaged. There may be a fluent or nonfluent aphasia.

Memory defect is the hallmark symptom of all the organic brain syndromes. Retention, integration, storage, or retrieval, especially of new and complex secondary process information, is damaged. Memory is severely affected in bilateral, diffuse cortical disease of the temporal lobes.

The same may apply in learning disabilities, although not in all cases. Usually a secondary process, linear sequential occurrence memory is affected with relative preservation of process memory. Example: "I can't remember names but I never forget a story."

Sometimes recognition memory is better preserved than retrieval memory: "I know it when I see it." But recognition is tied, in part, to context, and so a learning disabled patient might remember a person in the usual context but not in a new context.

Example:

A learning disabled adult said "hello" to a fellow in the same business office when they passed in the hall once or twice a week for a year, but chatted with him at the office Christmas party for half an hour before realizing who he was.

Because process memory is better than linear sequential occurrence memory, data storage and retrieval are by complex pattern recognition rather than the usual pattern recognition via linear data recognition and recall. But, again, these analog hologram patterns are characteristic of some higher learning areas, and hypertrophy of this capacity can be quite adaptive and result in outstanding achievement.

Memory of names, phrases of speech, or categorical data may be damaged even though there may be intact concept memory. As a result, some learning disabled people seem inarticulate and perseverative. This condition is sometimes mistaken for low IQ.

The patchy memory in area and time makes continuity of experience a problem. Many such patients try to compensate by living in a timeless present. This can add to the delay in their personality growth and development. Some patients even have trouble remembering past affect states, adding to their exaggerated present moment capacity and their impulse-ridden judgment.

Affect Boundaries and Mood Boundary

Because of repression eruptions and primary processing, affect boundaries may be more unstable in all the organic brain syndromes, often including the dyslexias. There is the affect lability of the frontal lobe syndrome, the contentless affect eruption in pseudobulbar palsy, and the primary process eruptions in attention deficit disorder. In addition, affective illnesses/mood disorders are probably more frequent. With or without a manic-depressive mood disorder, affect instability is often seen in organic brain syndromes. Modulation is affected as well as affect–mood boundaries. Ease of evocation of affect is also lowered, as is the stimulus threshold in general.

In addition, fusions of affect, such as anger–sexual arousal or depression–sexual arousal, may be seen. Affect regulation problems predispose to judgment problems because judgment weighs quantity as an important factor. Affect-eruptive patients from any cause, therefore, may be impulsive because of an ego problem, not a superego problem They know it is wrong, but they can't stop themselves.

Reality Testing

Reality testing varies from severely affected with psychosis in organic brain syndromes to perfectly intact in the mild dyslexias. The spread of illness in the ego and unknown severity mediators are the covariables.

In the learning disabilities, reality experience may be altered because of dyslexic perceptual processing, while reality testing is intact. Reality testing may be hard to actualize, as when a dyslexic with poor spatial orientation is looking for something and the reality testing process is functioning. "I know I had it!" The concept of preservation of matter remains as a part of reality testing, but nonetheless it has disappeared.

Considering the problem some learning disabled children have with social and physical processing, it is amazing how intact reality testing processing is. This makes one wonder about the localization of autonomous, complex ego functions.

166 Psychiatric Illnesses and Mental Structure

These problems of reality experience predispose patients, I believe, to psychotic and near psychotic forms of comorbid illnesses such as manic-depressive disease. Learning disability patients therefore may have an increased incidence of hallucinations, pseudohallucinations, delusions, and pseudodelusions during their depressive episodes.

Observing Ego

Observing ego also varies. One of the horrors of gradual, chronic senility is the self-observation of it. Acute, severe, diffuse organic brain syndromes may be without observing ego, although there is usually some.

Because learning disabled patients are born so, there may be little observing ego or recognition of deficit. In addition, because self-esteem is often damaged secondarily, powerful character defenses, usually narcissistic, often block observing ego sentience.

Integrative Capacity

The failure to integrate complex, new information is often the earliest sign of organic brain syndromes. This is because recognition and storage functions of the brain are impaired. In addition, the integrative functions may also be directly damaged. This is especially true once higher conceptual functioning is impaired, because then rapid data sorting, already damaged, cannot be compensated by generalization. As memory failure sets in, the integration problems increase, because data important to integration patterns and strategies are missing.

Patients with learning disabilities may have characteristic integration problems. Linear occurrence sequencing is interrupted in a variable, somewhat unpredictable way, and the interruption is often unobserved by the patient. Letter reversals, word reversals, category reversals, and concept reversals are typical. Together with perseverations, repetitions, and aphasic blocks, secondary process integration is disrupted, mildly and intermittently to severely and continuously, varying from patient to patient, with phase of development, and with severity of illness. Subjunctive syntactical links may be missing either because of inattention, trouble with sequencing, or category fusion. This plays havoc with linear, cause-effect, and modifier relationships and hence with secondary process integration.

Difficulty with linear sequencing may be extensive, affecting linear memory, linear repression barrier, and linear personality development and life growth. Linear concept integration may be extensively affected (Voeller, 1991). The ego and its secondary processes may not be smoothly integrated at the cognitive level or at the emotional level.

Difficulty in distributing attention cathexis may give the whole machinery of cognition a lurching rhythm, sometimes dragging, sometimes leaping. Self-image and self-presentation are affected.

Peculiar to the learning disabilities may be the difficulty in using an appropriate level of abstraction. This may be due to a concept block, often at the level of second-order abstractions. "I can go from one to three, but I can't go from one to two to three." Very intelligent patients compensate by developing the highest levels of abstraction. However, sequential knowledge and learning remain difficult, especially of less abstract material. Such people learn best by pattern recognition and not by sequence of detail. This method is ultimately functional, because with experience, performance is pattern-based. But such patients seem stupid during the early learning phase.

With so much trouble in secondary integration, it is no wonder there are shifts to primary processing, which is surprisingly intact. When there can be a shift to tertiary processing, the rewards are so great that some "move into" this realm lock, stock, and barrel, producing one variety of the "absent-minded professor" syndrome.

It is crucial that these ego strengths and weaknesses be understood for effective treatment (Kafka, 1984; Rothstein et al., 1988).

Reality Experience/Emotional Experience

A crucial integration domain that is affected is the relationship between reality experience and emotional experience. Because secondary process, which is dependent on memory and organization of percept, has so many lapses, reality experience processing is uneven. Primary process, breaking through an uneven repression barrier, captures reality experience in an uneven way. Where the capture occurs—conscious, preconscious, or third space—will determine, in part, the level of phenomena, whether psychotic, near psychotic, or creative. The other aspect of structure is, of course, whether condensation has occurred in one of these areas. Some mergers in organic brain syndromes and learning disabilities are coincidental overlaps of primary process symbols with reality-perceptual details. There is then a lag while the sputtering secondary process sorts it out. The accompanying feeling is one of anxiety. These contents are fleeting because secondary process eventually sorts out the overlap. When a stable condensation occurs and exists over time, near psychotic or psychotic condensation processes should be suspected due to a comorbid affective illness or severe personality disorder.

Day Residue

The day residues for organic brain syndrome have overlaps and mergers which are complex reality experience percepts that are only slowly secondarily processed.

When true condensation occurs in a stable psychotic or near psychotic production, the day residue is similar to that of manic-depressive illness

168 Psychiatric Illnesses and Mental Structure

in type and location. A reality loss is a trigger for typical condensation in organic brain syndromes. The loss may be of a thing, a person, a situation, or a recognition of a loss of brain function. Change of familiar location is a common day residue as is any other increasing level of cognitive demand.

We do not know if there is also a tendency to psychotic and near psychotic processing of upsetting emotional day residues that do not involve cognitive vulnerabilities. If there is, we do not know if this is a problem of damaged repression barrier or of cognitive processing of affect or whether there is a comorbid factor. However, this level of etiological certainty is fortunately not required for successful treatment.

One pathognomonic aspect of the day residue in the organic brain syndromes, including the learning disabilities, is the disruption of the sequential ordering of the day residue event occurrence. Sequencing is disrupted at both conscious and preconscious levels. At the same time, because context is a pattern, there may be preservation of context memory of day residue occurrence. When these day residues involve intense, conflicted emotional areas, there is a high likelihood of a shift to primary process organization as affect rushes in to organize reality details that cannot be organized in a secondary process mode. It is disruption of the sequencing of the day residue that also makes the dyslexic at risk for the misdiagnosis of schizophrenia, in which the therapist mistakes disordered sequencing for fragmentation.

Example of Primary Processing of Day Residue in a Patient with Organic Brain Syndrome:

An elderly patient with multi-infarct dementia, totally dependent on an attendant for orientation, tasks of daily living, and self-esteem support, is told the attendant is planning a week's vacation in Europe. The patient does not respond even to acknowledge receipt of this information. The next day she reports a frightening dream in which she and the attendant are on a boat going to Europe. Every detail is anxiety-filled, and she experiences confusion about where she is.

The dream clearly seems to contain the day residue of the impending vacation of the attendant. It also seems to contain the wish to be with the attendant, as well as the already triggered anxiety and premonitory confusion that will occur when the attendant is gone.

Of interest is this patient's past history. When she was 4 years old, her family was abruptly driven out of Europe. She was smuggled across borders in a trunk and came to this country by boat. The patient had to leave her own culture and language and start over with few orienting cues.

Thing Presentation

Thing presentation structure in organic brain syndromes is the same as in manic-depressive illness except for affect intensity. Thing presentations are even more likely to involve transmodal processes, especially to somatic symptoms and to percepts. Boundaries of thing presentation phenomena may be affected by the boundary problems of brain disease (e.g., people coming through the walls), and thus characteristics of brain disease will appear in thing presentation organization. This feature helps diagnosis. Concrete cognitive processes, either globally, as in organic brain syndromes, or focally, as in the learning disabilities, may serve to reinforce and reify the concrete thing presentation experience. They can only be processed as a real, concrete experience. There may be difficulty going from thing presentations to word presentations because word presentation ability, secondary abstraction, generalization, and application are poorly functioning. There may be difficulty translating visceral experiences of metaphor to words, and if these are translated, the patient may not be able to shift the affect experience. Learning disability patients may resist word presentation translations, therefore, because they experience word presentations as reductionistic. Some very bright dyslexics experience affect validation at either concrete thing presentation level or at hyperabstract levels of concept, and not at intermediate, second-order abstract concepts and their word presentations. However, some dyslexics with aphasia and some organic brain syndrome patients with stroke have the concept and affect validity, but cannot put it into clear, verbal categories.

Some of the most rigidly resistant thing presentation experiences, even of a nonpsychotic nature, are in this broad category of patients. When such experiences are diagnosed, learning disability of some type should be suspected. There is a high incidence of this illness therefore in anorexia nervosa or in rigid obsessive–compulsive patients. Also typical of these thing presentation experiences is their occurrence across a range of affect intensity due to damage to the in–out boundary and to the repression boundary.

Another characteristic of these thing presentations is sexualization. Increased stimulus intensity, affect fusions, boundary fusions between self representation and object representation, transmodal processing to physical sensation, and ease of evocation by intense stimuli, all predispose to sexualized thing presentations. The cortical integration of sexuality is a developmental process that some learning disabilities interfere with and some organic brain syndromes obliterate.

Symbols and Symbolic Alterations of Reality

The keys to these symbols and their symbolic alterations of reality are (1) the variable intensities, especially of affect; (2) the particular boundary problems within the symbol structure; and (3) the uneven variability in levels of abstraction. These are due to the patchy ego function based on patchy brain function of the symbolizing and translating processes. In addition, characteristic, but not pathognomonic, is the symbol's perseverative, "sticky" occurrence quality.

Object Relations

A key to the object relations of this category is the real self/real object confusion. The characteristic boundary confusion is at this point. Distinguishing this from schizophrenia is the frequent preservation of the real self, the intact integration and organization of the object (no fragmentation), and the synchronicity and appropriateness of associated affect. In social learning disabilities, this real self/real object confusion may be minimal to mild and only present in high affect states. The high affect state may be in the real object. Some of these patients are therefore marvelously intuitive.

The real self/real object boundary problem is a type of in–out problem that may possibly predispose to the double identifications that occur in depression. Particularly with a depressed, hypercritical object in reality, the danger is an intense, unintegrated double identification triggering an affective episode.

Example of real object/real self confusion without increased affect intensity:

Patient: "You made a mistake on my bill. You need a new bookkeeper!"

Doctor: "Yeah, myself!"

Patient: "I warn you, I don't know triage!"

This sequence seems to make sense if the patient is experiencing, and complaining about being, the doctor as well as himself. "Myself" in the quotation is an ironic statement by the object-in-reality doctor referring to his own mistaken bookkeeping. That becomes an ironic statement about the real self humorously experienced by the patient, who claims he "doesn't know triage," meaning that he is not a physician. It is as if the "myself" became for the patient a statement both about the real object and about his own real self. Any intervening steps, if present, were not stated by the patient.

Problems integrating complex object relations are also a cardinal feature of severe disorganized learning disabilities.

Defenses

Personality development and functioning, like intellectual development and functioning, may not be linear in the learning disabilities personality

Psychiatric Illnesses and Mental Structure   171

defenses, but may be both chaotic and rigid. (Samberg, personal communication, 1985); For summary, see Tables 5.1, 5.2, and 5.3. Common defenses mobilized by this group of illnesses are paranoid, obsessive–compulsive, narcissistic, and masochistic. They especially relate to self-esteem issues and depend on core character. These defenses can be rigid, can block observing ego, can protect against recognition of day residue and of cognitive deficit, can guard against secondary depressions triggered by insight, and so may make psychoanalysis and psychoanalytic psychotherapy difficult. Self-esteem, any comorbid affective illness, and defenses against self-denigration must be analyzed before full day residue recognition of cognitive deficits can be achieved. But when this point is gained, further progress in psychoanalyzing core character defenses is rapidly and profoundly achieved. This is true of mild dyslexics all the way along the spectrum to severe organic degenerative brain disease. Psychoanalytic psychotherapy with these patients can be most rewarding and satisfying to both patient and doctor. Once the cognitive deficits are

Table 5.1 Summary of Autonomous Ego Characteristics of Some Types of Learning Disabilities

Boundaries:
   In–out shows increased porosity
Repression shows patchy increased porosity
Subject and object show intermittent porosity
Secondary process confusions
Horizontal, Linear Sequencing Interruptions, and Reversals
   Category reversals and gaps
   Category fusions
   Topic intrusions
   Topic incompletions
   Topic perseverations
   Concept gaps and reversals
   Memory gaps for categorical and sequential information
Vertical Cognitive Hierarchies
   Gaps in ordering of abstract concept
   Reversals of concept ordering
Resultant, patchy difficulty in translating and integrating word presentations
   from thing presentations
Affect Modulation
   Patchy loss of integrity with decreased impulse control or rigid impulse
      control

Table 5.2 Summary of Defenses in the Learning Disabilities

Primary Process
Thing Presentation Qualities
Concrete Representation
Rigid Defenses with Gaps in Repression
Chaotic Defenses

172 Psychiatric Illnesses and Mental Structure

Table 5.3 Psychiatric Illnesses and Mental Structure

	Schizophrenia	Manic-Depressive Illness	Organic Mental Syndromes
Boundaries:			
In–Out	fused	Fused in stage 4 mania only	Fused in acute states
1–2–3 Process	Fragmented	Condensed	Fused
Real Object	Fragmented	Condensed	Fused
Affect Representation	Fragmented	Condensed	Fused
Day Residue	Fragmented	Condensed	Fused
Reality Testing	Fragmented and fused	Condensed	Fused
Thing Presentation	Fragmented	Condensed	Fused

recognized and accepted by the patient, the patient is much better able to allow intact cognitive processing to compensate especially in conjunction with learning disability tutoring and rehabilitation. This can result in a most satisfying improvement in cognitive functioning! On special treatment considerations in this group, see Rosen (1967) and Kafka (1984).

Character Disorder

Introduction

Severe character disorders are also common psychiatric illnesses in psychotic and near psychotic structures. Character disorders have a level of severity, i.e., neurotic (Glover, 1926; Reich, 1933b), borderline (Kernberg, 1976a), and a type, e.g., narcissistic, paranoid, hysteric (Kernberg, 1976a). There is frequent comorbidity with manic-depressive illness, organic brain syndrome, and early trauma. The exact mix of early trauma (Hendrick, 1936) or comorbid psychiatric illness varies from case to case making differential diagnosis crucial. Comorbid psychiatric illnesses intensify and influence the organization of character and character conflicts. Therefore, the more severe the character disorder, the more likely is there to be a comorbid state (Marcus and Bradley, 1987).

I make no distinction between *character* and *personality*; general psychiatry tends to ignore any subtle academic distinction (Campbell, 1989). Character structure involves characteristic reaction propensities of temperament, characteristic concerns, and characteristic conflicts organized in characteristic ways by characteristic attitudes used as defense and as expression (see Fenichel, 1941). These emotional attitudes affect many areas of ego functioning. These emotional attitudes are conscious, preconscious, and unconscious. Major portions are unconscious. They organize and are organized by object relations scenarios that are diagnostic of character type. An inner script thus exists which imposes itself on the experience of social reality to a greater or lesser extent. The "sicker" the patient, the more this inner emotional script imposes itself on social reality experience (see Freud [1916] and reviews of the psychoanalytic concept of character in Liebert [1988] and Baudry [1954]; for general psychiatry, see Lion [1974]; for a combination of psychoanalytic and general psychiatry views, see Shapiro [1965]; MacKinnon and Michels [2016b]).

In symptom neurosis, there is a symptom organization defending and expressing unconscious emotional conflict, repressed and dissociated. There is therefore conflict but no emotional solution. In the normal, there is an unconscious primary process solution to conflict that is not dissociated in the repressed unconscious but is a dynamic part of personality, mental life, change, and growth. In symptom neurosis, there is unconscious dissociation: still anxiety and avoidance, and the rupture of primary process symptom formation into focal areas of emotional symptom experience. When this eruption is into global character attitudes, it is definitional of character disorder (see Alexander and Isaacs, 1963; Compton, 1987). Then there is no boundary between the symptom and the rest of personality functioning (Lampl-de Groot, 1963).

Boundaries

The main boundary crossing is an internal, unconscious, and preconscious one. The boundary between symptom experience and self experience never solidly develops. The more "ill" the patient, the more fluid this interchange. The result is character conflicts rather than symptom conflicts. If the character conflicts and constellations are intense or if a comorbid illness is also present, other boundaries may be affected directly or indirectly, depending on the comorbid illness.

In–Out Boundary

The in–out boundary is said to be breached in severe character disorders by behavior. This is not a true in–out boundary problem, since the mental experience of the boundary is intact. It is, rather, a condensation of reality experience–emotional experience in object relations that is then enacted behaviorally into reality across an intact in–out mental boundary. It is really an affect–behavioral ego boundary and not an in–out stimulus boundary. One key is the direction of the boundary problem, in this case, in to out, rather than also out to in.

Percept, Concept, Affect Boundaries

Percept, concept, and affect boundaries are affected variably depending on the severity. Neurotic patients show condensations in the unconscious.

174 Psychiatric Illnesses and Mental Structure

Sometimes the quality is experienced. Near psychotic patients, especially borderline behavioral types, show many of these affect–percept and affect–concept condensations through their behavior. This is especially seen in the phenomenon of enactment, in which a behavioral attempt is made in action to change the day residue in reality, to bring the percept of it into better accord with the representation of it. In addition, the behavior of such patients may display their own attempts to convey their affect and affect concepts to others, through behavioral actions influencing other persons' percepts (cf. Frenkel-Brunswik, 1974).

Affect Boundaries and Modulation

Affect boundaries and modulation are often affected because so much of the ego's dynamic content is involved with emotional conflict. The entire ego structure, defenses, and autonomous ego may act as a rigid modulator. Ego functions of affect malleability, flexibility, and adaptive capacity may be disrupted. Obsessive–compulsive characters, paranoid characters, certain narcissistic characters, and rigid hysterical characters are obvious examples.

Narcissistic–sociopathic or sociopathic characters may have a form of fluid structure in which hypermalleability and flexibility along a continuous, analog, ever-changing stance of self representations create a kind of "as if" character. Often hidden beneath is the rigid avoidance of basic aspects of human functioning and object relations (love, work, responsibility, trust, truthfulness, honest achievement, dependence, etc.) that is characteristic of this character type. Any comorbid affective illness will exaggerate modulation problems.

Reality Testing

Because of these problems, reality testing is under strain all along the severity spectrum. This is especially so with near psychosis, where reality testing is suspended. In the psychoses, it is lost. I do not include brief, apparent psychotic losses of reality testing lasting a few seconds which are not rare in all people if under great stress.

Example of Apparent Loss of Reality Testing in an Otherwise Neurotic-Level Character:

The scene is the cemetery at the burial of the adult patient's mother.

PATIENT: "Mother, mother! Don't leave me!"
ACTION: Tries to jump into the grave.

Observing Ego

Observing ego capacity in character disorders varies, but not according to severity of illness. Some "healthier" but rigid neurotics have less observing ego about their character attitudes than some "sicker" midlevel or borderline patients. Because there is no clear symptom experience line in the ego, because self representation and self-esteem are so dependent on the character attitude defenses, because superego condensations and compromise formations are part of character defenses-attitudes, and because all these functions are involved in self-sentience, the observing ego has a hard time. It may not objectively experience pathological character attitudes and it lacks an experience of validity about this pathology. Much more work early in the psychoanalysis or analytic psychotherapy must be done to achieve the goal of a relatively dispassionate observing ego. Often, life milieu and objects in reality provide the confrontation (for techniques of psychoanalysis and psychoanalytic psychotherapy that focus on and mobilize observing ego, see Reich [1933b]; Fenichel [1941]; Greenson [1967]; Masterson [1972]; Kernberg [1975]; for hospital treatment, see Kernberg [1975]; Marcus [1981]; Gray [1994]; Busch [1995]; Holmes [1996]).

Integrating Capacity

Integrating capacity varies greatly from full secondary and tertiary capacities to major interference by primary process defensive structures along the neurotic–near psychotic–psychotic continuum. The particular cognitive-defensive organization of character integration style is beautifully described by D. Shapiro (1965) according to particular character disorders. These characteristic styles may affect many areas of ego function (MacKinnon and Michels, 2016b). The most obvious arena to see this in is the relationship between reality experience and emotional experience where characteristic defensive processes of emotional experience impinge on or capture reality experience. Intense, paranoid eruptions, extremely controlling and compulsive behavior, or hysterical affect storms are all typical examples. Their capture of social reality experience varies depending on type of stress, level of ego organization, and presence of comorbidity.

Day Residue

The day residue varies in potency depending on meaning for the patient. Different character types have different vulnerabilities in this regard. This is one of the reasons psychoanalysis and psychoanalytic psychotherapy are so important in character disorder patients. This is true even, and perhaps especially, with comorbidity. The day residue becomes processed by a character style and character defense providing stimulus for character regression and character conflict. Symbolic elaboration may condense with the day residue experience and then be played out directly in behavior.

When the day residue seems to justify or confirm established character attitude defenses and/or when they strike at basic fears underlying such defenses, or when they just shift the balance of compromise formation contained in character attitudes, the behavioral reaction can be surprisingly intense. The conflict may trigger even an affective episode in those vulnerable because of comorbid mood disorders.

Thing Presentations and Qualities

The resulting intensity may condense into thing presentations and qualities which are expressed as intensely felt validations of character attitude. The thing presentation organization and content appear as a validity and veracity quality of certain attitudes and behaviors. When these concrete thing presentation qualities become very intense, they override social reality and/or inner reality testing, condense with reality experience, and become near psychotic or psychotic defenses. This is structurally why basic character defenses can be seen in the themes of many near psychotic and psychotic phenomena. The ability to translate to word presentations depends on autonomous ego assets and abilities involved in word presentation translation, concept formulation, and application. It also depends on the strength of thing presentation experience.

Symbols and Symbolic Alterations of Reality

Symbols, therefore, in character disorders are subtly intertwined in the character attitudes and are expressed as attitude themes in words or behaviors. Symbolic dramas are played out, either in behavior or on the mental stage, as part of the organization of quality and content of object relations. I call such material *character symbols*. Sometimes we can see these coalesce in the likes and dislikes of other people. The basic transmodal processing is from interpersonal reality experience, through affect, attitude, and behavior, back to perception of social reality.

Character attitudes are prone to symbolically alter reality, because these attitudes guide ego strategy of data collection, data organization, and the experience of meaning and significance. This can set up a response to social reality and a response from social reality that make the symbolic alteration of reality a self-fulfilling prophecy. When intense enough, these responses from social reality to a patient's symbolic alterations of reality enactments can become the day residue triggers for decompensation, especially with comorbid affective illness.

Object Relations

The overall outlines of these object relations dramas are typical of the various personality disorders. Their content stereotypy is their cardinal feature. The level of severity will be determined by the level of abstraction, the degree of capture of real object, of real self, of object in reality and self in reality, and condensations with other reality experiences as well as reality testing and observing ego. The relationship of the genetic past object relations to the derivative present object relations varies along the severity spectrum. Therefore, psychoanalysis is variously indicated and techniques within psychoanalysis differ. This has led to much "sturm and drang" within the psychoanalytic literature about the "correct" way to treat these various disorders. When ego function is taken into account, many of these arguments disappear because different analysts are, in fact, talking about different levels of severity.

Defenses

Defenses in character disorders are attitude organized object relations themes and contents. These character defenses manifest as resistances in treatment, especially resistances in the transference. Characteristic defenses are typical of the character disorder type. They reveal themselves as defensive attitudes and especially guard observing ego, conflict with reality day residues, self-esteem, and ego deficits. They mediate many problems with boundaries and condensations. This is why an ego-exploratory, psychoanalytically based treatment is so revealing and so helpful with these patients. Because these basic character defenses are so intermeshed with all ego functioning, they are critical to patients, and hence they tend to be rigidly unyielding. The sicker the patient, the more rigid these defenses. The sicker the patient, the more intense, aggression-filled superego tends to be part of the system, both defending and defended against (see Coen, 1988).

In comorbid affective illness, defenses intensify the rigidity even further (D. Shapiro, 1981; Marcus and Bradley, 1987) in order to cause affect rigidity, affect simplicity, affect reductionism, and affect disjunction, all to avoid deeper integrated affect states where intensities may trigger a mood cycle.

Notes

1 This in–out boundary accounts for confusion about the Schneiderian first-rank criteria for schizophrenia. Pope and Lipinsky (1978), in describing stage 4 mania, describe Schneiderian first-rank signs in mania also.
2 That these illnesses belong in the larger category of organic brain syndromes is shown phenomenologically by neurological soft signs (Tupper, 1987);

by focal hard signs like aphasias, which are common in some learning disabilities; by memory problems, which are also common in some learning disabilities; and by spatial and social processing problems, which are also common (Voeller, 1991). These then have effects on the autonomous ego functions mediated by these brain functions and, therefore, on treatment (Rothstein et al., 1988). Geschwind (see Galaburda, Sherman, Rosen, Aboitiz, and Geschwind, 1985) believed he demonstrated changes in neuronal cytogeography in the childhood dyslexias. For dynamic psychotherapy with patients who have ADD or ADHD (attention-deficit/hyperactivity disorder), see Bernstein (2015).

Chapter 6

Medication and Mental Structure

Introduction

Freud wondered if brain mechanisms were involved in psychotic illness. Now we have powerful medications that act on the brain to affect the ability of the mind to interact with reality. Psychoanalysis has, in Hartmann's ego psychology, a description of the areas of mental functioning that engage reality. Medication affects these same areas of mental structure. These are the areas affected by psychotic and near psychotic illnesses. A known intersection between neurological functioning, reality, and mental functioning is through the area of the autonomous ego apparatuses and functions.

Different medications have different specific effects on ego functioning, and therefore impact in specific ways on the structure of severe mental illness. This chapter will describe observations about the exact locus of different medication effects on different ego functions, and therefore on psychic structure in the different illness structures of psychosis and near psychosis. For early work in the area of medication and psychoanalytic treatment, see Sarwer-Foner (1960) and Ostow (1962).

Psychosis and Medication—Neuroleptics

Antipsychotic drugs are called *neuroleptics* and share the common neurological property of dopaminergic blockade. They are not medications for any specific illness. They are medications for a specific structural organization of the ego. They work in psychotic states regardless of etiology. This is because neuroleptics specifically help ego organization by acting on certain boundaries. They are extremely helpful in treating hallucinations and, to a significant extent, in treating delusions. The neuroleptics may increase the integrating ability of the ego by decreasing fusion and some condensation experiences and by increasing reality testing. The medication does this by increasing specific structural boundary integrity and stability. The neuroleptics have their most dramatic effects on the experience of reality. Because they reinforce the boundary between reality experience and fantasy experience, neuroleptic medication enables the untangling of fusions and condensations that have allowed emotional experience and primary process to capture components of secondary process and conscious perception. The reality experience–emotional experience boundary has many components: in–out, primary process–secondary process, affect–percept, concept–percept, reality testing–reality experience, unconscious–conscious, and repression–stimulus boundaries. These will affect, and are components of, the boundary between object relations. They are also part of the boundary of the day residue. They are also part of the location boundaries and use the boundary of thing presentations. When boundaries are intact, symbolic alterations of reality can remain in the conceptual domain with a separately experienced reality day residue. When these boundaries are stabilized, the relationship of reality experience to emotional experience reorganizes away from psychotic condensation experience and assumes more normal, balanced, secondary process, integrated forms.

In–Out Boundary

Neuroleptics rapidly stabilize the in–out boundary, dramatically decreasing fusion experiences within hours to days. Perceptual stimuli, their intensities and qualities, no longer flood emotional experience or logical, conceptual, secondary process thinking. Percepts can once again be relatively confined to perceptual experience. In that role, they can once again be used to make judgments about the external world of people, events, and the body. Feelings and thoughts can again be about perceptual information rather than fused with perceptual information.

Concept–Percept

Percept can be used to experience concept. When percept itself is initiated by concept, the phenomenon is usually psychotic. (When percept is triggered by reality stimuli but colored, altered, and used to express concept, the phenomenon is usually near psychotic.) Neuroleptics quickly reinforce the boundary of the sensorial ego apparatus responsible for experiencing percepts so that they are no longer triggered by concepts or affects. Sensory causality once again moves to the experience of external stimuli. Concepts can be experienced directly as abstract ideas. This means they can more easily be generalized, modified, and applied. Obviously, this makes psychoanalytic treatment easier, although it may make psychoanalytic understanding by the analyst less immediate.

Affect–Percept

The affect–percept mergers in psychosis may be either fusions resulting from in–out boundary damage or a phenomenon resulting from condensation occurring inside an intact in–out boundary. The former is dependent on external stimulus intensity, and the latter is determined by internal affect intensity and psychological meaning (the affect content). Neuroleptic medication rapidly reduces affect–percept fusions and more slowly but definitely reduces affect–percept condensations. The reduction occurs because neuroleptics repair ego containment barriers of percepts. Neuroleptics thereby reduce transmodal experience of percept as affect and affect as percept. The conscious mind can once again experience reactions to percepts rather than reactions in percepts.

Reality Testing/Emotional Experience

The content of reality testing ego experience should be potentially different from the content of emotional reality experience. This is due to the normal boundary that exists between these two domains, both of which draw on different resources and validities for their contents. In psychosis, this boundary fails, and reality testing, contents, and processes become merged in the psychotic condensation. Neuroleptics restore this boundary in days to weeks. The first aspect to return is the secondary process logic of reality testing. This helps separate reality testing processes from those processes in the psychotic condensation. Later, the content itself is restored as separate.

With reality testing once again a relatively separate mental faculty, psychoanalysis and psychoanalytic psychotherapy can proceed more rapidly to work through the upsetting concepts and affects formerly merged in the psychotic condensation.

Unconscious–Conscious

Neuroleptics reinforce the primary repression and stimulus barrier so that some aspects of perceptual intensity, evoked affect, and recruited affect content no longer flood consciousness. Together with the boundary repairs already described, external stimuli can become internal percepts. Evoked fantasies can be contained, unconscious in location. A hallucination will become a fantasy, and then an unconscious fantasy, which may appear clearly only in a dream or disguised in psychoanalytic free association.

Latent content once again is established as a relatively clear and coherent layer in the preconscious and unconscious. This has further benefit in clearing conscious mental function for secondary process logic and self-observation.

Boundaries of Object Relations

Because of the previous boundary repairs, the mental experience of people and their stories becomes more coherent. The boundary between reality experienced real object, real self, and emotionally experienced object representation and self representation can once again function in consciousness. This helps the inner object world regain coherence, causality, and proportion. Real object and real self are no longer perceptually altered in conscious reality experience, and emotional life can once again be psychoanalyzed because the affect–object domain is a separate ego experience. This enables a more classically useful treatment. Generalization and application of the emotional principles can be used by the patient for treatment, because the reality experience building blocks are now free for use by these ego functions.

Boundary of the Day Residue

The perceptual boundary of the day residue is strengthened, allowing discrimination of percept from emotional response. The result is a decrease in condensation between day residue and symbolic alteration of reality. This enables a more flexible use of the day residue by both the primary process and the secondary process. There is also a resulting decrease in vertical dissociations between the day residue and context sequence, between the day residue and concept, between the day residue and evoked affect, and between the day residue and generalization application.

Thing Presentation

The stabilizing of boundaries stabilizes thing presentation experience so that affect and concept no longer transmodally flood into conscious percept and the resultant experience of real things. Thing presentation experience can once again be contained in the unconscious. Thing presentation quality moves, therefore, out of conscious reality experience, further aiding the use of reality testing. As perceptual verification fades, thing presentation quality fades and fantasy can revert to an emotional experience.

Patient Example:

A 50-year-old man was brought to the hospital emergency room because he tried to get into the White House. He believed there was a crown waiting for him there. He was admitted to the hospital and treated with neuroleptics. After several weeks, he was no longer convinced there was a crown waiting for him in the White House, but he had a wishful fantasy that there was one. After further treatment with medication and the exploration of the emotional dynamics contained in the fantasy and crown symbol, the patient was free of this preoccupying fantasy during most of his waking hours. Periodically, he had a dream that there was a crown waiting for him in the White House.

Symbolic Alterations of Reality

Neuroleptics thus move symbolic alterations of reality out of conscious condensations with the day residue reality experience, with real object representations, and with real self representations. Symbolic alterations of reality in conscious experience become symbolic alterations in emotional experience, symbolic alterations of reality in unconscious experience, and/or symbolic alterations of reality in conscious creative experience, thereby not contaminating conscious reality experience. The ego's symbolizing function is released from perceptual and concrete experience. A true psychoanalytic process can then ensue, because a psychoanalytic, symbolic mental domain is again available. Interpretations can be given in the abstract and emotional rather than the concrete and the real.

Hallucinosis

Neuroleptic medication is dramatically and quickly effective in hallucinosis because it treats the inside–outside boundary problem that is so diagnostic of this condition. Visual hallucinosis disappears within hours. Auditory hallucinosis, when present, responds more sluggishly but within days. Because these states are so often complications of toxicities, infections, and withdrawal states, a search for etiology is mandatory and medication must be used carefully.

Delusionosis

A delusional state, with awareness that it is caused by illness but belief in the delusional idea anyway, is, strictly speaking, perhaps not psychotic. This is, however, a distinction without a difference as far as medication is concerned because hallucinosis and delusionosis are treated exactly like their full, psychotic equivalents. Neuroleptic medication is effective, although, as in all deluded states, the medication may take several weeks to be effective. Again, the boundary between real object–object representation or real self–self representation, and between primary process and secondary process cognition, is greatly strengthened and stabilized by the medication.

Both hallucinosis and delusionosis may deserve to be classified as psychotic states. It may be better to understand them as having observing ego rather than reality testing intact. However, this is probably a spectrum phenomenon. There are certainly patients who have bona fide and describable visual hallucinatory phenomena, carrying describable sensory qualities without reality stimuli, who know full well that they are mental products. Some are not quite able to test the reality of the percept as opposed to the reality of the concept. With the equivalent delusional state, these distinctions are often less clear.

Integrating Capacity

Integrating capacity refers to several subfunctions. The neuroleptics greatly help the cognitive integrative capacity of ego functioning. Neuroleptics help the ego's integrating ability because the secondary process integrates well-boundaried and categorized mental experiences. With boundaries clearly reinforced and affect–percept flooding removed from conscious reality testing and conscious reality experience, secondary process integration is again possible. Logical thinking is greatly strengthened as reality testing returns, hallucinations disappear, and the boundaries between inside and outside and between percept and concept return.

Because of these increasing stabilities, integrated ego islands begin to appear and are stabilized. An acute, constantly changing psychotic condition becomes more fixed. They then begin to slowly integrate.

The other extremely important integrative phenomena in very ill patients are the dissociations that appear between different areas of mental experience. These dissociations are helped somewhat as reality testing returns and as logical integrating capacity of cognition improves. However, there are many patients who are left with dissociated states in spite of medication, because a specific dissociated area serves defensive functions that have to do with the dynamic psychology of the dissociated material. Medication does not affect dynamic psychology. This is a crucial area for psychoanalytic psychotherapy to attend to in the patients who show these dissociated areas, and almost all very ill patients do. In fact, it is the sicker patients who do not, since they tend to have their psychotic material infiltrate the entire personality structure.

Modulating Capacity

The neuroleptic drugs do not affect the modulating capacity of the ego to a great extent. Modulation of affect requires some control of the intensity of affect. Neuroleptic changes in affect are only via sedation. Neuroleptics do so across the board of mental functioning. They swing the modulating capacity over to the extreme of frozen rigidity, so that one gets an apathetic state long before one gets a well-controlled state. This may be better than wild, uncontrolled emotional storms and dangerous behavior, but it is hardly a specific repair of affect modulating capacity. It is not an ideal result.

Boundaries between affect and affect are stabilized poorly by neuroleptic medications. To the extent that they help much at all, they do so by a sedative effect that dampens affective intensity throughout all areas of mental functioning. The affect–affect fusions become less apparent. This specific boundary is better helped by mood-stabilizing medication.

Thus, neuroleptics reduce psychotic phenomena by seeming to affect boundary phenomena of autonomous ego functioning (Karasu, 1982; Beitman and Klerman, 1984; Klerman, 1984; Bradley, 1990).

Neuroleptic Medication Effect on Defenses in Psychosis

As long as the concept of psychotic defenses was confused by equating them with the psychotic condensation itself, and as long as reality testing loss was considered caused by defenses against underlying emotional conflict, medication was viewed by psychoanalysts as either ineffective or dangerous, because medication might bury the etiologic conflicts. More recent views, my own included, hold that autonomous ego function is directly damaged. That damage, while perhaps sometimes triggered by emotional conflict, involves a biological mechanism aside from psychic conflict. The biological effect is on autonomous ego apparatuses (see Chapter 1). The emotional conflict then erupts in illness-typical ways (see Chapter 5). The result is a psychotic condensation that involves defenses in several different ways (see Chapter 2). I will now review those ways and describe medication effects.

Defenses Against Reality Experience: Reality Experience Defenses

The first situation is defenses that directly cross the reality experience–emotional experience, conscious–unconscious–preconscious, and secondary–primary process boundaries, and capture an aspect of reality experience via some condensation mechanism. Examples are delusional mechanisms such as psychotic projection, psychotic denial, psychotic compulsions, etc. Defenses that cross the reality experience boundaries become part of the psychotic condensation (see Chapter 2). Such defenses are involved in the actual boundary crossing between reality experience and emotional experience.

Neuroleptics, because they reinforce the reality experience–emotional experience boundary and also the unconscious–conscious–preconscious and secondary–primary process boundaries, resolve condensation crossings from emotional experience which capture reality experience. Defense mechanisms will then no longer be in primary process conscious reality experience. They will be confined to emotional experience and tend to move out of consciousness and into the preconscious and unconscious.

The content of the defensively altered material does not change, although once freed from a concrete, rigid reality experienced thing presentation, the underlying concepts may be more layered and flexibly experienced. Affect may then appear in more complex, varied, layered, and applicable ways. Concept flexibility and affect complexity may, however, not appear after neuroleptics have reduced the psychotic reality experience intrusion, because of other ego problems in the generalizability function and affect modulation function. However, if all the medication does is strengthen the reality experience boundary, a crucial gain, even a lifesaving one, has been achieved.

Neuroleptics do not affect the layering of affect contents within defensive structures. The following elaboration of the example just given will demonstrate this.

Patient Example:

A middle-aged homeless man is brought to the emergency room after being stopped by police as he was trying to enter the White House. He was convinced that there was a crown waiting for him there. After a short course of neuroleptics, he became quite sad because he felt his previous belief was not true, although he still felt there should be a crown waiting for him at the White House. A psychoanalytic psychotherapy ensued, revealing the following layers of affect content within the defensive wish to be crowned. At first the crown was there. Then the crown was not there, but should have been. Then the patient understood that he wished it was there and that he felt entitled to it. He felt entitled to it in order to help himself with an underlying despair that he felt about himself, based partly on a highly traumatic childhood of violence and abandonments. His sadness about the missing crown helped him understand that if it was not there he felt he was nothing and was filled with despair and hopelessness. This despair and hopelessness validated his anger, which defended against his belief that common work and hope were useless for him.

Analyzing these layered defensive experiences was crucial in untangling the complex interrelationship between traumatic deprivation and pathological character attitudes, both of which were used as defense.

A most interesting aspect of this case was that treatment for the delusion was begun by the United States Secret Service. One of their agents, after detaining the man and hearing the story, said if there was a crown waiting for him, they would be the first to know about it and since they did not know about it, there couldn't be a crown waiting for him. This statement helped the patient reinforce aspects of his secondary process logic. As a result, the patient began to feel sad, and the feeling was already conscious by the time he was in the emergency room.

Layering Defenses

This example demonstrates not only the intrusion of defenses into reality experience, but also the other way that defenses appear in psychotic phenomena, namely, in the layering that occurs in the psychotic condensation or in any complex emotional structure. Neuroleptics do not affect this substructural layering of affect content, because interlayer boundaries are in emotional experience, even though the entire macrostructure may have psychotically moved into reality experience. Therefore, psychoanalysis and psychoanalytic psychotherapy may be used. They will be vastly better applied by the patient once secondary process and testing have returned. Reality testing, reality experience, and secondary process attention cathexes can then all be used by the ego in service of the therapeutic alliance and the therapeutic situation, i.e., in being able to analyze and understand the primary process with secondary process containment.

The defensive layering of psychosis may be more accessible to analysis once the intense, dense, unyielding truncation in the psychotic thing presentation condensation is freed from entrapment in conscious perceptual reality experience. Percept and physical details inevitably truncate concept and affect complexity. Once the thing presentation is in emotional experience, layering tends to become more available, more flexible, more complex, and more integrated.

The issue of "sealing over" inevitably comes up in discussions of medication and psychosis. What is usually meant is the worry that dynamic, layered defense systems will be repressed without other changes of internal relationships, especially affect relations. The rigid, defensive layering will remain a point of vulnerability in the unconscious. This vulnerability, it is feared, will manifest itself as a trigger point for psychotic relapse when provoked by certain reality events and/or will manifest itself in the rigidity of character defenses.

This worry is not without substance. However, the situation varies from case to case and according to whether analytic psychotherapy is available along with medication. Sometimes the course described in the example occurs. However, withholding medication is not the answer. This will have the greater danger of prolonging the psychotic state, and perhaps watching it expand. Psychotic states carry a fatality rate (M. Stone, 1990). I describe the psychotherapy treatment needed to help the ego use the content in the layered psychotic symptoms rather than seal over it in Chapter 7. However, this is often impossible without medication to stabilize the boundaries of reality experience. Without medicine, psychotherapeutically uncovered layering in emotional experience will immediately condense with reality experience, leaving the patient, if anything, more psychotic. When reality testing has not established itself as a separate entity, when reality experience and emotional experience are

188 Medication and Mental Structure

merged, the patient does not experience insight for emotional change but rather an evolving psychotic experience.

Sometimes medication alone can help the ego integrate with insight, achieving a rapid resolution rather than a sealing over. This depends on the extent of the psychosis and the maturity, flexibility, and organization of the nonpsychotic ego.

Vertical Defenses

Vertical dissociations around psychotic condensations and conscious experience are often mediated by basic character defenses. They are nonpsychotic because they are preconscious emotional experiences and because they are not condensed with the psychotic thing presentation.

Neuroleptics may allow greater flexibility in these vertical enabling defenses once the psychotic thing presentation moves out of reality experience and into emotional experience. Sometimes that is all that is necessary for the rest of autonomous ego to integrate and/or repress across the dissociation and any enabling defenses. In this way, psychotic defenses integrate with character defenses as thing presentations move into emotional experience.

If the mediating defenses are rendered more flexible by neuroleptics, it is because validity has been taken from thing presentation perceptual experience in reality and moved into affect and affect content in emotional experience and into concept in secondary process experience. This interrupts intensity summation cycles between affect and percept, between character defenses and psychotic defenses, between emotional experience and psychotic defenses, between emotional experience and reality experience, and between psychotic condensation and psychotic behavior into reality that intensifies all defensive operations including mediating defenses.

Often, however, psychoanalysis and psychoanalytic psychotherapy must deal with these defenses, either the simple dissociation defense or its mediating character defenses. This is especially true for those patients with character pathology where character defenses rigidly block affect and affect content even in nonpsychotic areas and times. In fact, this situation is the most common one.

Interpretations in psychoanalysis and psychoanalytic psychotherapy can be made even more effective with medication for boundary stability. Then therapy can help the patient better understand enabling defenses, their contents, processes, and functions. Affect symbolizing processes can again use primary processing and emotional experience rather than percept and reality experience.

Reality Testing and Defenses

Reality testing is part of the psychotic condensation (see Chapter 2). Neuroleptics directly reinforce reality testing boundaries. This helps

Medication and Mental Structure 189

decondense the psychotic condensation when reality testing separates from it. Because neuroleptics reinforce the reality experience–emotional experience, secondary process–primary process, thing presentation–affect–concept boundaries, reality testing, secondary process, and a separate, reality experienced percept content can all separate from psychotic condensation. This also helps free reality testing as an autonomous ego function. If enabling defenses are blocking reality testing, exactly the same principles apply about neuroleptic and psychoanalytic psychotherapeutic effects as apply to the enabling defenses of vertical dissociations.

Observing Ego and Defenses

Observing ego is a separate ego function from reality testing and is usually not part of the psychotic condensation (see Chapter 2). Interferences with observing ego are usually nonpsychotic character defenses. Neuroleptics do not help except insofar as they shift the psychotic condensation/thing presentation experience out of reality experience and into emotional experience. When this happens, the observing ego has less sense of validity to support its misalliance. Psychoanalysis and psychoanalytic psychotherapy are very important in undermining defensive mechanisms blocking observing ego. Therapy does this by rallying secondary processes through interpretation (see Chapter 7). The psychotherapeutic interpretive process can often be so effective by itself that observing ego is separated clearly from the psychotic contents even without medication. This can help the therapeutic alliance greatly, and even reality testing to some extent. When observing ego is blocked, it is almost always by character defenses. This is the usual reason that psychotic patients stop taking their medication. Many patients complain about side effects, but they are not the most common reason for stopping. Some patients are delusional about their medication, but this is actually rare. The denial of illness and the psychologically mediated refusal to observe, accept, and deal with the illness are almost always aspects of character pathology that are readily apparent to all who know the patient well. In fact, even a beginning discussion with the patient easily reveals these psychodynamics. It is a clear indication for analytic psychotherapy in the psychotic patient. Medication alone may not help because it may leave the patient without insight into the fact of the illness, and therefore without motivation to take maintenance medications or to continue in psychotherapy. The relapse rate in such cases seems to be high.

Object Relations and Defenses

In sicker patients, defenses and object relations are one phenomenon at the same level of consciousness (see Chapter 2). The term *defenses* focuses on the mechanism and function, while the term *object relations*

190 Medication and Mental Structure

focuses on the content and affect. Neuroleptics, acting at the inside reality experience–emotional experience boundary, act on the real object–object representation and real self–self representation boundary. Also, fusions between objects in reality and self experience or vice versa are reduced because of the reinforcing effect neuroleptics have on the in–out boundary. To the extent the repression barrier between unconscious and preconscious–conscious is reinforced, the intensity of emotional experience representations flooding real object and real self is reduced. When and if vertical dissociations ease, the integration of the object world can proceed both within reality experience and within emotional experience and in the relationship between the two. Superordinate ego functions again organize the object world, in and out, real and representational. Defensive use of object relations shifts back to emotional experience, away from real object relations.

Defenses in the Day Residue

The experience of the day residue precipitating event is both altered by defenses and used defensively when altered by autonomous ego apparatus damage.

The autonomous ego boundary problems allow placement of the symbolic alteration in the same mode (reality experience) and level of consciousness as its day residue object. A symbolic alteration of reality then appears in conscious reality experience which is a condensation between the reality event and the emotional feelings that have symbolically altered the perceptual idea of the event. Neuroleptic medications reinforce boundaries and allow more flexibility in the day residue's relationship to its own symbolic alteration. Affect will become more available in direct affect experience.

Vertical and horizontal defensive dissociations may then separate sequence and context from the symbolic alteration of reality. This prevents contradicting evidential reality experience from confronting the thing presentation symbolic alteration. Such confrontation could, if successful, counter the emotional logic of the symbol and start to release the affect the thing presentation both contains and defends against (i.e., crown and sorrow), thereby freeing the reality day residue experience. In the case of the man with the crown, the day residue event was being fired from his job and losing his apartment.

The vertical and horizontal dissociations and the more elaborated enabling character defenses guarding them may become more flexible as intense thing presentations fade. Usually, if there are elaborated character defenses guarding simple dissociations, psychoanalytic psychotherapy is required. But interpretation can have a much greater effect if medication is concurrently used, because until emotional experience is separate from reality experience, interpretation will be seen as irrelevant to the reality experienced psychotic condensation.

The defenses against integration are reduced with psychotherapy after medication has established the separation in reality experience between the day residue and its symbolic alteration. The day residue no longer stands reified in perceptual-ideational reality experience. In this way, integration between a day residue object and its sequence and context is achieved. When this is not achieved, the psychotic condensation freezes affect, enabling defenses dissociate sequence and context, and the psychotic condensation ties up all available attention cathexes, priorities, and validities, thereby paralyzing remaining islands of intact autonomous ego apparatuses.

Other Defenses

Neuroleptic medication has an effect only on the defenses that involve the use of reality. Psychosis as a defense and capture of specific areas by fantasy is treated by neuroleptic medication if such capture is mainly the result of boundary problems that neuroleptic medication affects. It will not affect, in any case, the content or mechanisms of character defenses not involving the capture of reality. What this means is that a patient who is paranoid about his wife as part of a delusional system may, upon recovery, be found to have similar contents and projective mechanisms involving his wife, if not consciously then preconsciously and unconsciously. This is why the use of medication within a psychoanalytic psychotherapy does not necessarily cloud the psychological understanding of the patient, nor does it impede the progress that insight can bring to the patient. Medication can help the patient distinguish real from unreal and thus allow treatment to pay more attention to deeper layers of fantasy structures. The ability of reality to help the patient work through his or her psychological life is limited by the mostly secondary process organization of the available real world. So when emotional dynamics are trapped in paranoid projections onto reality, understanding by the patient is limited.

Thymoleptic Medication Effects on the Ego in Psychosis

Thymoleptics are drugs that affect-mood disorders. As in neuroleptics, their effects on psychotic structure (psychotic depressions and manias) are mostly on the autonomous apparatuses and functions.

Antidepressants or lithium stabilize mood (Loeb and Loeb, 1987) by stabilizing affect intensity, spread, and recruitment. They also stabilize fluctuating, autonomous, massive affect discharge propensities.

Thymoleptics stabilize and prevent the circular feedback between affect-mood and content, and hence between mood and the triggers of mood in reality via affect content evocation. They also stabilize and prevent the triggering of affect-linked regressive content. This can have a very beneficial and stabilizing effect, not only on the level of ego organization in general, but also on defensive structures. There are patients who regress to lower levels of defensive structure under the influence of intense mood disturbance.

Autonomous ego is shielded by thymoleptic medication more effectively than defenses because of the decreased intensity of affect allowing repressive barriers greater effect. The affect intensities that do escape the repression barrier now, because of their decreased intensity, may be discharged with secondary process content, with adaptive behavioral actions, with sublimations, and with contained fantasy experiences. It is this decreased intensity that seems to remove a functional block to both the autonomous ego pathways and the functional repression abilities.

Because mood stabilizers work especially on affect, they can help not only to increase the ego's reality testing, observing ego, and integrative capacity, but also decrease the intensity, frequency, and domination of primary process experiences. Thing presentation quality can decrease and the separation between perceptual and fantasy channels of experience can once again be restored. This increases the possibility for integrating and generalizing. An abstraction can then be cognitively and not just affectively experienced by the patient. This has the most dramatically beneficial effects for enabling an analytic psychotherapy to proceed. It dramatically increases secondary process use of the primary process layers of intensely affect-ridden preconscious and unconscious material. This material can then be integrated as the therapy uncovers.

Thymoleptic Medication Effects on Autonomous Ego Structures in Psychosis

I will now cover some specific ego functions, and then I will discuss specific defenses in affective illness as affected by medication. The ego functions listed will be the same as in the section on neuroleptics, because these are the ego functions that are crucial to the organization of psychotic experience. Most interestingly, they are also the ego functions that these medications affect the most.

In–Out Boundary

When the in–out boundary is affected by affective illness so that environmental stimuli arriving along perceptual channels fuse with the inside experience of bodily perceptions of affect, and of concept, and when the object in reality is fused with self and object representations, one is almost always dealing with mania. Lithium will reinforce this boundary in a week to 10 days. Neuroleptics will do so in hours to a few days. Both are usually given at first.

Neuroleptics directly reinforce the in–out boundary in all psychotic states, regardless of etiology. Lithium probably does this by decreasing affect intensities because lithium works only in affective psychosis. Lithium also works well in the mild form of manic in–out problem, where only affect is crossing the in–out boundary, both from the environmental object in reality to the inner affect experience of the patient, and from the patient to the experience of the real object, and in behavior to the object in reality.

Primary–Secondary Process Boundary

Because the primary process is an affect processing system, intense increases in affect will change the content and range of primary processing function. Increased intensity will also shift the primary process location. The intensity increase and the resulting spread of primary process and the increased intensity of its content imaging will begin to dominate preconscious and then conscious, logical, and then perceptual experience. Recruitment of memory and of present perceptual experience will be based on affect and associated affect contents. As intensity increases, this recruitment, which occurs according to primary process rules and emotional experience, will cross secondary process boundaries into logical consciousness. Primary process will then dominate in that location. This is true whether the affect is primarily depressive or euphoric-irritable. Thymoleptics will greatly reinforce this boundary indirectly, by decreasing intensity, and directly, by decreasing spread of affect into mood.

Affect–Percept Boundary

As affect intensity falls and primary processing modalities fade below the level of consciousness, affect no longer contaminates conscious percept. Affect of lesser intensity can be contained by the ego within affect experience. This dramatically reduces sensory psychotic phenomena. Again, the neuroleptics act directly and quickly on this boundary, the thymoleptics more slowly and indirectly via affect intensity, spread, and modulation.

Affect–percept relationships are crucial to thing presentation experience and therefore to psychotic condensation experience. As the affect–percept boundary strengthens, affect can be experienced directly and thing presentation experience can be repressed once again to the unconscious.

Concept–Percept Boundary

As affect separates from percept, affect-determined, affect-expressive, and affect-contaminated concept can be freed from perception. Ideas, even those associated strongly with affect, can be utilized by the ego in secondary process ways. Ideas can once again be subject to Aristotelian logic, to generalization, and to application. This step greatly helps regain reality experience. With this boundary once again functioning, a psychotic patient with a mood disorder is once again rational.

Reality Testing–Reality Experience

As affect intensity falls and affect recruitment no longer dominates reality experience categorization, reality testing can reassert its independent content and function. Thymoleptics will gradually, therefore, allow the reappearance of reality testing. Not solely determined by either reality experience or emotional experience, reality testing can again function once the contamination of its content and processes by affect-determined, reality-perceptual experiences is reduced.

Unconscious–Conscious: Repression and Affect Intensity Barrier

As intensity of affect comes under control, the repression of affect can again function as a percept–affect stimulation barrier. Primitive primary process contents expressing affect relationships and intensities can again return to unconscious mental life. Environmental evokers of affect must once again reach a certain stimulus threshold before affect breaks through into consciousness, into secondary process, and into behavior. This dramatically decreases psychotic condensations and behaviors. Therefore, thymoleptics greatly help the functional repression barrier by decreasing intensity of affect.

Object Relations

Because the ego functions just described are once again functional with thymoleptic medication, the real object world can once again be organized categorically in consciousness. Psychotic condensations can resolve/dissolve. The object in reality, the real object, can be separately experienced in consciousness from the object representation of emotional experience. The affect connections between the representational world and the perceptual reality object world return to relationships rather than to conscious condensations. The same, of course, holds true for self experience and for self–object relations. This brings secondary coherence once again to the conscious object world.[1]

Day Residue-Symbolic Alterations of Reality

An increased stability of affect intensity and mood stabilizes the ability of the ego to maintain the day residue in reality experience and its affect evocation in emotional experience. Reality evokers, emotional reactions, and resultant symbolic alterations are no longer linked by affect-intense primary process condensations in consciousness. Sequence and context, so important as precipitants of affect, can once again be tolerated in relationship to the real object or real thing event.

This separation of emotional experience from reality experience frees conscious symbolic processes for abstract concept, generalization, and application of affect. It also frees symbolic experience for third space (tertiary process; Arieti, 1976) functioning in organizing new relationships and emotional adaptations required by the changing real world and by emotional growth. The new integrations required can once again be processed because it is in this area (creative area) that such integrations are first processed (Winnicott, 1953, 1971).

Thing Presentation

As ego functions return, the intense, dominating, highly affect-charged perceptual thing presentation will decondense, ease in intensity, fade back into the unconscious, and release its grip on secondary and tertiary process functions. Percept and concept will again be available for an uncontaminated reality experience. The secondary defenses, avoidances, and floodings will disappear. A psychotic patient will become nonpsychotic. The major suffering of affective psychosis has to do with the dominating terror of this overwhelming thing presentation experience. Its rigidity, locus in consciousness, truncation of affect complexity, and content are all primary process results of affect intensity symbolization. Thymoleptics dramatically change this. Neuroleptics, by contrast, will contain the thing presentation so that reality testing returns, but in affective illness, only thymoleptics will return normal relations and flexibility to conscious symbol functioning. Thing presentation translating mechanisms of abstraction, generalization, and application, no longer flooded by affect intensity and content recruitment, and no longer rigidified and truncated, can once again function.

Thymoleptic Effects on Defenses in Psychosis

Thymoleptics affect not only autonomous ego functions but also defenses. They seem to do this indirectly by their effect on the intensity and spread of affect states. It is intense affect which plays a crucial role in the triggering and organizing of defenses.

Defenses and Reality Experience, Including Reality Testing

Defenses capture reality experience, the real object, and/or the real self in mood disorders when affect can no longer be contained, repressed, and/or dissociated. Instead, affect contaminates the perceptual experience of reality in sensations or ideas.[2] Affect and affect-recruited ideas are then usually projected. They thereby condense with reality experience. But affect can also be defended against by the denial of reality evokers of fact, sequence, or context. This is denial of factual reality. Intense affect can also be defended against through dissociation of affect from idea, or of affect from reality. When reality testing is lost as an independent process[3] and its contents condensed with emotionally captured reality experience, a psychotic condensation in conscious reality experience is formed. Thymoleptics function in mood disorders to decrease the intensity of affect and to increase the autonomous ego's capacity to modulate affect. This allows affect experience and expression along secondary process lines of organizational experience. Affect can then be contained in emotional experience. Projections onto reality experience, denials, and dissociations no longer capture, deny, or separate factual reality. Validity criteria will shift away from thing presentation experience back toward secondary process organizations, data, and abstractions.

Defenses are preconscious, primary processors of affect. They use organization by emotional association and recruitment of idea via associated affect to symbolize, express, and repress affect. They operate in a hierarchical way to spare self experience from the worst affects in a series of less to more painful. They also serve to protect reality from behavioral disruption due to impulsive affect discharge.

As mood disorders progress, one can watch the shift toward increasing intensity, primary processing, content saturation, content starkness, level of consciousness, and disruption of reality experience and reality testing. Likewise, one can watch the shifts back when treating with increasing doses of thymoleptics.

Patient Example:

A 50-year-old man with depression and without medication: "I can see my soul coming out from my stomach to be stolen by other people."

With thymoleptics: "My self-esteem leaks out."

Increasing medication: "I project my perfection fantasies and feel small by comparison."

Defenses and Observing Ego

Observing ego, the capacity to view oneself dispassionately and logically and to understand that one is ill, is often blocked by defenses. These defenses are not part of the psychotic condensation. Basic character defenses are usually involved. These defenses can intensify, spread, and rigidly block observing ego in mood disorders. Thymoleptic medication can dramatically decrease the rigidity of those defenses and shift them back toward emotional experience. When affect leaks link intense emotional experience and reality provocations, the observing ego may ally with defense experience validity rather than observational validity. This can be, and usually must be, interpreted analytically. Thymoleptic medication can also be very helpful in achieving a more plastic and less intense defensive structure which will enable interpretations to be more effective and useful.

Defenses and Vertical Dissociations

Vertical dissociations are of two types. Some separate oppositely valenced affect (splitting). Others separate affect and content (ideas) from other affect contents. Thymoleptics, by decreasing the intensity of affect, help the ego integrate splitting. Intensity reduction also helps decrease other vertical dissociations by lowering the affect component, and thereby easing primary process recruitment across vertical boundaries. Affect intensity both mediates dissociation defenses and motivates them. Affective experience can, with thymoleptic treatment, return to an emotional locus. Affect blending, complexity, layering, and neutralizing can reappear. Complex affect experiences, composed of many affect components, reappear and regain a modulated and flexible relationship to reality provokers contained in real objects, real self experience, real things, and their sequences and contexts. Affect discharge can then return to sublimatory, secondary process, and socially appropriate channels. Even more importantly, emotional discharge can return to the complex integrated emotional discharge for a change in reality that we call satisfaction.

Thymoleptic Effects on Defense Content in Psychosis

Thymoleptics may on occasion shift the content of primary process fantasies contained in defensive operations. Thymoleptics can do this because decreased intensity decreases the primary process function of containing intense affect in symbolic content (ideas). The primary process operates to express and contain affect in primary process fantasies. The content of those fantasies is in part an attempt to express intensity factors.

198 Medication and Mental Structure

Such defenses are on a continuum, e.g., narcissistic-paranoid, obsessive-paranoid. These labels attempt to convey the information that certain character types will shift defense content and mechanism depending upon the effect of stress on their emotional equilibrium. When reality confrontation interferes with grandiose fantasies, many narcissistic patients, in a last-ditch attempt to avoid contemptuous rage turned upon the self, will project this rage in a paranoid attack upon the confronting reality person or stimulus. Failures in their perfection image cannot be their fault or depressive disaster may ensue. It is, therefore, the fault of the reality intervention or intervener. The employees of such people know that they cannot be the bearers of bad news. Thymoleptics can reverse progression along such a defensive content spectrum or block the progression, greatly stabilizing both character structure and psychotic illness.

Patient Example:

A patient experiences the reality evoker of less attention from a lover (the lover does not call when expected). This triggers a fear of loss, which in turn causes hurt pride, anger, and a projected jealousy fantasy that the lover is with someone else. Thymoleptic medication can stop the progression at this point. If it is not given or if the patient does not take it, in this particular patient, the progression proceeds to feelings of being a loser, a failure, and projection of blame onto the experience of the real self. The patient, tearful, feels unworthy, is flooded by the recruitment of memories of past failures, and has an intense and validated experience of worthlessness. Self-blame intensifies in an attempt at expiation, which further intensifies depressive despair, resulting in the failure of this expiation and therefore of hope. A suicidal despair and an impulsive gesture then follow.

Other Effects of Thymoleptics

Thymoleptics have two other effects that do not have to do with the ego. The first has to do with aggression. Thymoleptics, when they work, seem especially to ameliorate the intensity of aggression, whether it is directed externally, as in mania, or internally through the superego to the ego, as in depression. This diminution of aggressive malignancy allows shifts in defenses.

The second is the effect on rhythmicity. Thymoleptics prevent the cycling of mood disorders. This is a primary effect they have on the brain, and the mental locus is presumably the id.[4]

Medication Effects on Near Psychotic Ego Structures

Near psychosis is characterized by a particular kind of condensation in the preconscious between reality experience and emotional experience (see Chapter 3). A number of autonomous ego dysfunctions and types of defense mechanisms organize the structure. I will now list them and describe medication effects for each.

Boundaries

The boundary between reality experience and emotional experience suffers the condensation crossing in the preconscious. This involves a number of subsidiary boundaries (Chapter 3).

The boundaries between inside emotional experience and inside reality experience in the preconscious, and between conscious reality experience and preconscious affect, are crucial. Condensation crossings result in a poorly boundaried preconscious experience of the affect distinction between real object and object representation, between real self and self representation, and sometimes between self representation and real object.

Neuroleptics do not reinforce preconscious boundaries except insofar as they sedate all of mental functioning and thereby sedate intensity of all affect. If the near psychotic condensation is related to a near psychotic form of schizophrenia with fragmented conscious cognition and fragmentation crossings of boundaries, neuroleptics will help the conscious, and sometimes the preconscious, aspects of that integrative problem.

The wiser choice of medication is usually a thymoleptic. By acting especially on affect and mood, thymoleptics can affect preconscious boundary function. Decreasing affect intensity results in decreasing primary process dominance. The affect capture of reality-percept experience and reality-idea experience in the preconscious fades. The distinctions between real object and object representation, real self and self representation, and self representation and real object all increase. The boundary functions resume because affect flooding, affect recruitment which crosses boundary lines, affect spread, and affect veracity all decrease as intensity falls. In addition, phantasmagoric primary process content decondenses and shifts to less dramatic content that can be more easily integrated and/or repressed.

Thymoleptics help the usual near psychotic state because the usual structure involves "affect leaks" across boundaries whenever affect is too intense and too easily triggered. This is a hallmark for certain types of affective illnesses. Affect leaks, condenses, and/or mixes without integration into other affects. This is the typical affect storm of near psychotic states. Affect contaminates concept. Affect alters percept shading, quality, evocative ability, and significance. Affect spreads quickly into mood and recruits affect associated contents. Affect shifts secondary process logic to primary process. It leaks into behavior and judgment. All these affect boundaries are affected by thymoleptic medication and improve in function. Affect and mood modulation return. The ego can then better control intensity of evocation and spread of affect. There can once again be boundaries between affect and the rest of mental experience. Reality experience can be held relatively separate from affective emotional experience, even in the preconscious.

Crucial to this separation is a decreased intensity of thing presentations. Word presentations again are able to contain and express affect. As word presentations reappear and regain validity quality, integration capacity in secondary process can reappear. Abstraction, generalization, and application processes again function along secondary process lines instead of along affect primary process lines and thing presentations.

As thing presentation experience fades, decondenses, and shifts to word presentations, the day residue can decondense from its symbolic alteration of reality. Affect and resulting validity then move away from the symbolic alteration of percepts toward words and concepts.

What happens in those near psychotic states where the boundaries themselves are weakened directly? Schizophrenia is such an illness and may take a near psychotic form. Near psychotic schizophrenia has fragmented near psychotic condensations. The near psychotic preconscious location is due to the fragmenting of the preconscious–conscious and unconscious–preconscious boundaries. Affect is usually muted. The characteristic fragmentation of secondary and primary process thinking (Bleuler, 1950) is diagnostic. Neuroleptics will help. Intraconcept cohesion and interconcept integration will improve.

A bigger pharmacologic dilemma is those patients with neurological dysfunctioning of boundaries, as in certain types of minimal brain dysfunction–dyslexias with or without attention deficit disorder. Here, concept fusion, concept reversals, and higher-order abstraction hypertrophy to (1) compensate for lower order abstraction concreteness, rigidity, and inability to shift and modulate abstraction levels that may be operative, and (2) make flexible word presentation use and containment of affect difficult. Category fusion and reversal is a kind of boundary defect that looks like primary process, and because of fusion, intense affect expressed along primary process can easily leak across a defective category boundary. Category fusion and reversal is not a true primary process, which is based on condensation rather than fusion, but the two look so much alike that it takes an experienced clinician to tell the difference.

If affective illness is present, thymoleptics will help. If attention deficit disorder is present, psychostimulants may help. If neither is present, low-dose neuroleptics may be tried. Learning disability training will

Medication and Mental Structure   201

help, depending on intelligence and intactness of higher-order abstracting ability. This can be in addition to psychoanalytic psychotherapy (see Chapters 7 and 8). These various boundary problems are the major contributors to problems with mental integration. Specific diagnoses will guide specific medication choice.

Reality Testing

Reality testing is an aspect of secondary process ego function with reality experience content. In near psychosis, it suffers a condensation alteration of content but has its process preserved, although suspended. The alterations in reality testing provide the rationale for neuroleptics: this is not a good rationale. Neuroleptics will not change reality testing in near psychosis, because the process boundary is intact in consciousness. If this boundary is particularly fragmented, as in forme fruste schizophrenia, the neuroleptics will help. But the usual near psychosis is a forme fruste of affective illness. Thymoleptics are much more effective, because they reduce the affect leaks, recruitments, and primary process shifts caused by poor affect modulation. Reality testing content can then separate from the near psychotic condensation, especially with the help of concurrent analytic psychotherapy, which challenges and reinforces the reality testing secondary processes. Further gains in reality testing are made as the preconscious near psychotic condensation decondenses, the intensity of the thing presentation experience fades, and preconscious symbolic alterations of reality separate from reality day residues. A huge shift in veracity experience then occurs and reality testing is returned to normal. (Remember that reality testing compares reality experience, logic and percept, with emotional experience. When emotional experience is so intense that percept is contaminated, reality testing will process this even if the secondary process is intact.)

However, there are some patients who are intolerant of affective doses of thymoleptics due to side effects. Then, the addition of low-dose neuroleptics to the low-dose thymoleptics may be required and effective.

Observing Ego

Observing ego is usually at least blocked and may be actually part of the near psychotic condensation. This is another rationale for neuroleptic use: it is also a poor rationale. The link between observing ego and near psychotic condensation is through emotionally experienced defensive structures. Neuroleptics do not affect this unless the sedation effect on affect intensity is sufficient, which it rarely is. If it is, there are safer sedatives than neuroleptics. Observing ego is better liberated through psychoanalytic psychotherapy (see Chapters 7 and 8). Thymoleptic use may help because it causes shifts in defensive organizations when affect modulating ability returns. This will help liberate observing ego by moving primitive projective and denial experiences away from the observing ego.

Thing Presentations and Symbolic Alterations of Reality

Neuroleptics do not dramatically change the thing presentation experience nor its condensation of day residues with symbolic alterations of reality in near psychosis, because neuroleptics do not dramatically affect the preconscious. Thymoleptics, however, will bring dramatic change because as affective intensity decreases, thing presentation intensity decreases. The ego can then more easily separate symbolic alterations of reality from reality day residues. The reality day residue can then be processed along secondary process channels.

Medication Effects on Defenses in Near Psychosis

The analyst hopes that medication in near psychosis will affect defenses by (1) shifting the defense process away from reality experience and (2) changing defense contents: neuroleptics do neither job well. Capture of reality experiences occurs in the preconscious, which neuroleptics do not specifically target. Content is unaffected even if the patient is sedated by neuroleptics.

Thymoleptics, on the other hand, may have dramatic effects on both aspects of defense. The first is the shift away from primitive processes that capture preconscious reality experience. As intensity decreases and integration shifts to secondary process, concept meanings and emotional validities are freed from condensation with percept. Projective identification can shift to higher-level projections and move away from projection onto real self or real object experience to projection onto object representations or self representations. Likewise, preconscious denials of fact can shift to denials of significance of fact, i.e., emotional experience.

Content, too, can change under the influence of thymoleptic reductions of specific affect intensities (rage, arousal, etc.) and spread. Primary processing of affect varies in content, in part according to intensity. So-called primitive contents are reflections not just of specific, condensed conflicts but also of intensities. Shifts in intensity, therefore, can have dramatic effects on preconscious defense contents (ideas). This shift toward higher-level contents is particularly dramatic after the near psychotic thing presentation experience has decondensed and near conscious perceptual qualities fade. (Remember, in near psychosis, the conscious percept itself is not captured. Only the qualities sensory percepts have in reality experience are captured in the preconscious; see Chapter 3.)

Another dramatic effect thymoleptics have on defense is on rigidity. The fixed relationship between defense mechanism, defense content, superego content, near psychotic thing presentation, and autonomous ego function eases as affect experience eases in intensity. The condensation between defenses and near psychotic thing presentation causes a rigid, preconscious reification experience filled with affect validity, which causes a preconscious certainty experience of projective identifications and denials. Without this reification and certainty quality, amelioration and integration are possible.

It is often astounding to see what this shift can do to personality function, and to availability in analytic psychotherapy. Observing ego can free up and personality organization can shift back along the spectrum of processes and contents toward the more neurotic. Rigid, paranoid, hysteric patients can shift to more flexible, predominantly hysterical processes. Rigid, obsessive–masochistic–depressed patients can shift back to primarily obsessive mechanisms. Rigid, narcissistic–paranoid–depressed patients can shift toward the narcissistic, grandiose instead of deflated, paranoid, and despairing (Marcus, 1990a). These shifts are most helpful to psychoanalysis and to psychoanalytic psychotherapy, since rigidity of structure is usually the most rate-limiting step.

Thing Presentation Quality

Neuroleptic medication has a quite variable effect on thing presentation quality in near psychosis. Neuroleptic medication may or may not be helpful, depending on whether the quality emergence is due to cognitive boundary structures that are affected by the neuroleptics. Affect intensity, integration, and generalizing incapacities are all causes of increased thing presentation thinking that will not be dramatically affected by the neuroleptics. Mood stabilizers will help the affect intensity problems, and stimulant drugs will help those patients with minimal brain dysfunction who cannot focus integrating attention. These categories of drugs are much better suited to those categories of illnesses than the neuroleptics. In addition, patients differ not just in the ability to experience thing presentation quality but in the ability to use the experience of thing presentation quality for secondary process purposes. That functioning can be greatly helped by an analytic psychiatrist who understands that the experience and the use are two totally separate mental abilities. Patients can be greatly helped by the experience of analyzing a thing presentation quality experience and understanding that it is a way of thinking that they can use. This is, after all, a hallmark of creative thinking.

Mood Stabilization

Antidepressants and lithium work by stabilizing mood in all its aspects. They stabilize cycles of fluctuating mood discharges. They stabilize and prevent the circular feedback between affect-mood and content, and hence between mood and the reality and personality triggers of mood. The affect intensities that do escape the repression barrier are now, because of their decreased intensity, able to be discharged along autonomous ego pathways with secondary process, with sublimations, and with contained fantasy experiences. Lithium alone, antidepressants alone, or the combination of both may be needed to prevent cycling.

Antidepressants seem to have a specific ameliorating effect on the discharge of aggression, whether directly from the id reservoir into the outside world behaviorally, as in borderline conditions, or into the superego and back onto ego structures, as in near psychotic depressions. Lithium will calm psychic discharges of aggression in out-of-control bipolar affective illness and will work on libidinal intensities in erotomania.

Modulating Capacity

From what has been said, it is apparent that the mood stabilizers have dramatic effects on the modulating capacity of the ego. Again, the medications seem to work on this capacity by decreasing the intensity of affect and its spread. However, they may also act directly on the modulating capacities.

Integrating Capacity

With a decrease in affective valence, the cognitive integrating capacity of the ego is strengthened indirectly because the intensity of the emotional experiences, and hence their paradoxes and contradictions are less dramatic. Therefore, they are more possible to integrate cognitively.

However, the dissociated mental experiences, while reduced in intensity, are still often unintegrated. Psychotherapy is needed to provide the integration in this area. However, the decreased intensity through medication greatly aids the analytic exploration of the defenses mediating the dissociation and the emotional reasons for these defensive structures. For a study on the efficacy of medication and psychotherapy in the treatment of depression see Weissman, Prusoff, Di-Mascio, Neu, Goklaney, and Klerman (1979). Such studies are needed for psychoanalysis and medication.

Object Relations

The threshold of the affect-triggering mechanism is raised by thymoleptics. Affect no longer so easily disrupts the distinction between real object and object representation, real object and self representation, or real self and self representation. Affect no longer clogs perceptual channels. As long as affect is incoming via percept as well as concept, and as long as there is a too-easy flow between fantasy and percept and between percept and concept, the distinction between real object and object representation will be difficult. The same is true for real self and self representation or real object and self representation.

Medication can be very useful in near psychotic states, but it must be clear for what purpose the medication is used. Medication affects certain types of near psychotic states and not others. For those that it does benefit, it is beneficial only for certain aspects of near psychotic structure. The accurate choice and dose of medication require the utmost care.

Near Psychosis/Pseudodelusional Type

The pseudodelusional patient is usually a higher-level near psychotic patient and the diagnosis of affective illness is usually relatively straightforward if a specific search is made. The usual drug of choice is one of the antidepressant drugs, which are so effective in decreasing the intensity of aggressive affect particularly, and in the case of the pseudodelusional type of near psychosis, ending the intense outpouring of aggression into superego functioning. The repression barrier is enormously stabilized, and self-esteem mechanisms, no longer flooded with recriminatory superego aggression, begin to modulate the real self experience more realistically once again.

The cyclothymic mood swinging patient almost always has behavioral borderline features, because the grandiosity and irritability are harder to contain. Lithium is the treatment of choice, and the only key to its use is to understand from the dynamic psychological material that the irritability is (1) present and (2) part of grandiosity rather than depressive agitation. Agitated depressions and irritable hypomanias may be confused in diagnosis. However, although both can be flooded with aggression and both can project this aggression, the agitated depressive tends to have a large component of that aggression directed against the real self in the form of failure and despair, while the hypomanic has almost all of the aggression directed against the object, real and representational. It is important to realize that if one does choose to use a neuroleptic rather than a mood stabilizer, one must not use as the endpoint of medication treatment the pseudodelusional idea, since it is already a nonpsychotic phenomenon. Reality testing and inside–outside boundaries are intact. The neuroleptic, therefore, will not eliminate the idea which is based on content and intensity of affect. A similar situation occurs in medicating a delusional state with a penumbra of pseudodelusion. The delusional state will be medicated and the pseudodelusional penumbra will not.

206 Medication and Mental Structure

Near Psychosis/Borderline or Behavioral Type

The main boundary problem that is so damaged in borderline behavioral states is the boundary between affect and behavior. This boundary is mildly to moderately helped by medication to the extent that the pressure of intense emotional experiences is lessened, and therefore the behavioral action is less pressured, less urgent, and less extreme. However, behavioral action as an ego style and as a defense remains, even in medicated borderline patients, although it is obviously less dangerous. Psychotherapy is crucially necessary to stuff the patient's life back into his or her mental experience and then analyze it. The dangers of medicated borderline patients with mild to moderate improvement and untreated by analytic psychotherapy are that the subtle problems remain and the life stalemates persist. Growth, development, and self-actualization remain stalemated. The dangers of activating primitive defenses remain.

Because the mediating locus of pathology is in the preconscious, reality interventions from the point of the transference relationship of the analyst can have ameliorative effects on these conditions even in the absence of medication. When the cycle of reality and psychology, each affecting, intensifying, and triggering the other, is interrupted in the transference, the psychology of the near psychotic states can be analyzed and integrated by many patients. They may then either never require medication or be able to come off the medication. Many, however, will need maintenance medication.

In summary, psychotropic medication in mental illness strengthens the ego for conflict repression, conflict integration, conflict adaptation in reality, and conflict resolution in psychoanalysis. It further widens the "widening scope" (L. Stone, 1954) of psychoanalysis. Medication with psychotherapy or psychoanalysis makes mutative treatment available to otherwise treatment resistant patients (Marcus and Bradley, 1990). The use of medication to overcome technical difficulties in psychoanalysis was first described by Ostow (1957). For overviews of combination treatment, see Sarwer-Foner (1960, 1983), Ostow (1962, 1966), Karasu (1982), Beitman and Klerman (1984), and Marcus (1990b). See Table 6.1 for summary of medication effects in psychosis and near psychosis.

Table 6.1 Effects of Medication in Psychosis and Near Psychosis

I Neuroleptics and Autonomous Ego Functions in Psychosis Reinforce Reality Experience Boundaries to Increase Distinction between:
    In–out
    Primary process–secondary process
    Percept–concept
    Percept–affect
    Reality testing–reality experience

Unconscious–conscious (repression and stimulus barriers)
Real object–object representation
real self–self representation
real object–self representation
Day residue–symbolic alteration of reality
Thing presentation–affect/concept generalization, abstraction, and application

II Neuroleptics and Defenses in Psychosis
Defenses that cross into conscious reality experience:
Reinforce reality experience boundary, unconscious–conscious boundary, secondary process–primary process boundary, real self–self representation boundary (Result: defenses shift back to emotional experience)
Layering of defenses within psychotic condensation:
Reinforces percept boundaries (Result: frees affect and affect/concept from thing presentation condensation and concrete reification)
Mediating defenses:
Reinforce emotional experience validity as thing presentations shift away from reality experience (Result: reduces rigidity of enabling character defenses)

III Thymoleptics and Autonomous Ego Functions in Psychosis
Increase ego ability to regulate and modulate affect:
Intensity
Spread
Emotional stimulation threshold; ease of evocation
Repression ability
Cycling of mood and subsequent "regression" (and thereby slowly increase functional ego boundaries; see section I)

IV Thymoleptics and Defenses in Psychosis
Increase:
Plasticity
Mobility
Repression effectiveness
Decrease:
Rigidity
Dissociations
Captures of reality experience
Shift:
Level of integration
Content spectrum

V Neuroleptics and Autonomous Ego Functions in Near Psychosis
May increase preconscious boundary function due to sedation
Decrease fragmentation in those near psychotic states caused by schizophrenia

VI Neuroleptics and Defenses in Near Psychosis
Nonspecific sedation effect only

VII Thymoleptics and Autonomous Ego in Near Psychosis
May dramatically and effectively improve preconscious boundary functions by decreasing affect: intensity, recruitment, and spread

(Continued)

208 Medication and Mental Structure

Table 6.1 (Continued)

Decrease:
    Preconscious capture of reality experience of real object and of real self
    Dominance of primary process condensation of affect qualities with percept qualities of day residue with preconscious symbolic alteration of reality
    Cycling of mood and consequent "regression"
Increase:
    Affect modulation
    Secondary process
    Thing presentation shift to word presentations
    Affect–behavior boundary
    Reality testing
    Observing ego

VIII Thymoleptics and Defenses in Near Psychosis
By increasing affect control, thymoleptics may rapidly stabilize the ego's defensive functions to:
Increase:
    Effectiveness of defense (binding of affect) (integrations of affect)
    Shift in major locus of character defenses to higher levels of contents and processes
Decrease:
    Capture of preconscious reality experience
        Of real object and real self
        Of reality testing
        Of observing ego
        Phantasmagoric content

Notes

1 Edith Jacobson (1964, 1967) was a pioneer in this area but never clearly distinguished conscious, preconscious, unconscious, or real object and real self components of psychotic object relations condensations. This is because she was writing about object relations experiences rather than focusing on ego functions of autonomous ego as it organizes the object world.

2 An idea can be a perception when concept is expressed in perceptual or sensory symbolic alterations of reality. An idea can be a perception, also, when an idea is experienced as having reality qualities and validity experiences typical of sensory perceptions.

3 Reality testing is a special, usually protected, and separate aspect of reality experience.

4 Dr. Mortimer Ostow (1966), working with medication and concepts of drive and energies, began as early as the 1950s to write about medication and its effects on psychic structure from this point of view. He remains the one who has written extensively on the problem of medication and drive.

Chapter 7

Psychoanalytic Psychotherapy and Psychoanalysis of Psychosis

Introduction

Psychoanalysis and psychoanalytic psychotherapy have been used to help neurotic patients by enlightening them about their unconscious psychology, its dynamic content and process. This same theory of treatment holds true for the psychotic states, except that attention must be paid to the ego structure of the patient which organizes these dynamics. In psychosis, that organization is severely distorted. There is a structure to psychotic psychological phenomena that must be understood by both patient and therapist for treatment to be helpful. This is because, without the analyst's attending to structural aspects of ego dysfunction, the uncovering of more unconscious material is not usable to the patient whose particular ego deficits make it impossible to use uncovering for integrated enlightenment and change.

I will leave out most modifications of technique necessitated by specific, psychotic illnesses. I will describe only the general principles and modifications of so-called classical technique applicable to all psychotic illnesses (on treatment of schizophrenia, see Fromm-Reichman [1948, 1959]; Freeman et al. [1958]; Searles [1964]; Chiland [1977]; Pao [1979]; Boyer and Giovacchini [1980]; Stone et al. [1983]; Robbins, [1993]; Letterman [1996]. On manic-depression, see Fromm-Reichman [1948]; Lewin [1950]; Greenacre [1953]; Jacobson [1971]; cf. Brenner [1976]; L. Stone [1986]; and Milrod [1988]).

This chapter is meant as a guide and not as a formula. Every patient is different: structure varies from patient to patient, and the most available aspect of the illness experience. Clinical work involves careful observation and intervention and is best done by an experienced clinician with good judgment based on that experience and on long-practiced clinical skills (Fromm-Reichman, 1955; Szalita-Pemow, 1955).

Theory of Treatment

The goal of the treatment is to empathically relate to the person suffering from the illness and then to talk to the person about the illness causing that suffering. This is the first step in liberating self-observation about the illness and engaging the patient in a therapeutic alliance. A therapeutic alliance involves two people working together on an illness problem and its suffering.

The treatment of psychotic states is different from that of neurotic states because the psychoanalytic psychotherapy and psychoanalysis of psychotic states must deal with ego dysfunction (for papers on the relationship of structure of the ego to technique, see Hartmann [1951]; Eissler [1953, 1958]; Lowenstein [1958, 1972]; Blanck [1966]). There are two aspects of this ego dysfunction: (1) the autonomous ego deficits and (2) the psychotic structure (psychological content and experience of psychosis) as organized by those ego deficits.

Integration of dissociations, increases in observing ego, increases in reality testing, shifts from thing presentation to word presentation, decondensation of psychotic symbol experience, and reinstitution of effective boundaries must all be achieved for real insight and change to be possible. Then, the narrative story of the patient's life can emerge in an integrated and coherent form. Then, the patient's life story, emotional story, and psychotic story will be related rather than dissociated. See also Macnaughten and Sheps et al. (2015).

Analysis does not mean only uncovering the unconscious or discovery of the psychogenetic origins of symptoms in childhood. It also means describing very carefully and specifically how the mind is organizing its experiences so that the conscious ego can gain mastery of those processes. It is this aspect of the theory of psychoanalytic treatment that is so important in working with psychotic patients. The description of ego dysfunction so that it becomes conscious can be as helpful to psychotic patients as the description of unconscious emotional conflict is to the neurotic patient.

I realize that the description of unconscious conflict in the psychotic is also important. As in any mental state, the analytic treatment involves engaging the psychology of the patient and progressively unfolding the unconscious conflicts. However, the ego dysfunction of the psychotic and near psychotic imposes an additional task on the therapist—a task of integrating psychodynamic material with ego function. (For other cognition problems and other techniques, see Rosen [1967]; Renick [1972]; Kafka [1984]; Rothstein et al. [1988].)

Integrating the new material has two aspects. The first is integrating the mental experience within the mind. The second is the integrative application to life, growth, and change. Both are a problem in very ill patients because there are psychotic links between reality, psychopathology, and psychological structure. These links are in the ego, and all psychoanalytic psychotherapy works mainly with the ego. In neurotic patients, these relationships are neurotic and the ego's flexibility to use analysis of them is assumed. With very ill patients, there are linkages which are part of the psychotic structure and therefore interpretation is important. But it needs to be used together with techniques of bridging, strengthening, and integrating the relationship between the three areas: reality, psychopathology, and psychodynamics in the psychotic structure. This is called "working through" by psychoanalysts treating neurotic patients. It has the same meaning for those of us who work with psychotic and near psychotic patients, except that it means applying psychodynamic information not only to different life areas and to different aspects of the neurotic symptom, but also to the ego experience areas within and between psychotic and nonpsychotic ego structure. Doing this in psychotherapy depends on the structure and function of nonpsychotic ego areas.

The goal of technique in the psychoanalytic psychotherapy of psychotic states is to enlighten nonpsychotic areas of ego function so that they can intervene and resolve the areas of psychotic process (see also Basch, 1981). One does this technically by confronting intact but dissociated autonomous ego functions and by analyzing defenses against intact ego function, especially dissociations. Intact secondary process ego areas can, when mobilized, take over the function of damaged ego areas which mediate psychotic processes.

Crucial to this goal of psychotherapy is the use of medication which directly strengthens secondary process ego function (see Chapter 6; Ostow, 1957, 1966; Sarwer-Foner, 1983; Marcus, 1990b).

Because of the complexities of the theory and technique of treatment, I will summarize this chapter now, before going into detail, rather than at the end. I will then return and cover specific points in detail. The basic theory could be restated briefly as follows: analyze what needs to be uncovered, support what needs to be supported, and integrate what needs to be integrated. Pay attention at all times to reality testing, observing ego, and integration. Stay in technical neutrality unless forced out and then return as soon as possible. In order to do this:

1 Specifically diagnose ego dysfunction;
2 Specifically analyze the psychodynamics of psychotic and near psychotic systems;
3 Put together the ego dysfunction and psychodynamics of psychotic and near psychotic systems.

This treatment chapter, thus, focuses on those aspects of treatment determined by psychotic ego deficits rather than only content dynamics (for excellent reviews of content dynamics in psychotic illnesses, see Freeman [1988]; Yorke, Weissberg, and Freeman [1989]; Frosch [1990]; Gabbard [1994]; Marcus [1996]).

212 Psychotherapy of Psychosis

A summary (see Table 7.1) of purely interpretive technique, in the usual order of importance, would be (1) empathize with the thing presentation quality of psychotic experience; (2) locate and clear observing ego; (3) marshal intact secondary processes; (4) interpret dynamics of the

Table 7.1 Summary of Psychoanalytic Psychotherapy of Psychotic States

I. Diagnose Ego Dysfunction by Accurately Observing:

  A Autonomous ego, especially:

    1 Boundaries
    2 Reality testing
    3 Observing ego
    4 Integration

  B Observe changing contours of these ego apparatuses:

    1 Acute psychosis by definition means rapidly changing contours of ego islands
    2 Chronic psychosis by definition means stable ego island boundaries, hence, stable psychotic material, even if fragmented

II Treatment Interventions Based on These Diagnostic Observations:

  A Support autonomous ego with medication; use specific medications for specific ego problems:

    1 To stabilize boundary between inside experience and outside experience, thereby decreasing fusion
    2 To increase reality testing
    3 To increase stability and secondary process integration of ego islands
    4 To stabilize the relationship between reality experience and emotional experience in the direction of conscious secondary process dominance
    5 To decrease the intensity of affect and the spread of affect into mood, thereby easing rigidity of defense

  B Support autonomous ego psychologically:

    1 With structure of hospital routine and rules
    2 With object constancy of therapist in reality
    3 By recruiting and engaging unimpaired ego (i.e., memory, secondary process logic, reality testing in nonpsychotic areas)
    4 Use this recruited unimpaired ego to engage psychotic areas so that conscious, cognitive dissonance about the psychotic areas is experienced, acknowledged, and actively used by the patient
    5 Interpret resistances to this therapeutic process (interpret mediating character defenses against observing ego and of vertical dissociations)
    6 Support and encourage nonmediating defenses, integrations, and sublimations of dynamic affect content conflict as it is released from psychotic condensations
    7 Support and engage observing ego
    8 Support self-esteem by interpreting superego attacks of shame and failure

C Interpret, analyze, uncover:

1 Mediating defenses and resistances to treatment
2 Mediating defenses against observing ego and against vertical dissociations
3 Then analyze delusional and hallucinatory psychotic condensation systems by interpreting:

  a Character defenses and resistances within the psychotic system (repeats the psychoanalysis of mediating defenses)
  b Affect content of psychotic dynamics, making sure to translate thing presentation contents and qualities into word presentations and affects
  c Day residue and reality objects; derivatives in the present linked with the psychogenetic day residue and reality objects of the past
  d Character conflicts of nonpsychotic areas; origins in the past

III Summary of Psychoanalytic Therapy of Ego Deficit Itself:

A Empathize, especially with the quality of thing presentation experience (in the beginning, sometimes this is all that can be done, but it is crucial)
B Observe ego deficit
C Describe ego deficit
D Allow intact autonomous ego functions to take over functions of damaged areas; crucial to this is to:

  1 Analyze any mediating defenses of the ego deficit
  2 Analyze any defensive functioning and use of the ego deficit itself, as part of conflict analysis
  3 If secondary process systems are damaged, such as second-order abstractions, remedial help with this function may be required
  4 Challenge intact but dissociated secondary processes

---

symbolic alterations of day residue reality, thus revealing the primary process pattern linking the psychotic content, the dissociated character conflict content, the dissociated day residue, and the newly freed real object or real self. This will result in a decondensing of the psychotic experience into layered affect contents, reality day residues, and the psychogenetic past.

I will now give a patient example, but first I would like to say something about such examples. Clinical examples can be crucial to understanding mechanisms, but they have a problem in illustrating treatment with this group of patients. A long and detailed treatment report is best equipped to show the complexity, depth, psychogenetics, and progress of a treatment. But I would have to annotate a lengthy case to describe the intervention rationale at each step, making the case report quite long. I have used short reports of verbatim therapeutic dialogue to illustrate particular points of technique. This can sometimes seem facile, superficial, and reductionist. This is especially so because the initial descriptive interpretations of thing presentation condensations may appear to use metaphor (Reider, 1972; Arlow, 1989) or be a clever pun or play on

214   Psychotherapy of Psychosis

words. Actually, word presentation channels and translating ego mechanisms are so blocked or damaged that the patient cannot conceptually experience even these superficial layers. This is why these interventions "work." The release of affect and of greater complexity of content is proof that the validity and veracity of certainty are correctly captured at the proper beginning level by the interpretation. The emotional effect on the patient is easily observed if the interaction is accurate. It is difficult or impossible to convey this in print, especially if for the reader, seeing is believing. Nonetheless, I will proceed with such brief examples in the hope that they will suffice to illustrate certain technical points (for descriptions of standard psychoanalytic and psychotherapy technique, see Greenson [1967]; Langs [1973]).

Example:

A woman in her mid-80s suffered several cerebral infarctions (strokes) and several heart attacks, leaving her in chronic heart failure, confused, mildly disoriented, and with memory defects. She complained that the people in the neighborhood were talking about her. They say she didn't pay taxes after World War II. Why would they say that? She doesn't steal. Once she was accused of stealing money when she first started working, but it wasn't true. Now they say she's a shoplifter. She feels that her maids and her sister are stealing from her. She then said to the analyst, "You work in this neighborhood. You must have heard them saying this."

The first session was spent taking the history, including the details of her delusional system. Because of her medical illnesses, psychotropic medication was dangerous. At the end of the session, when the patient reiterated to the analyst that he must have heard this, the analyst said, "I have not heard this. It may not be true that they are talking about you. It may not be true that they are accusing you. I have not heard it." In addition, her husband, who brought her to the session, was instructed not to support the delusion anymore with reassuring and calming statements about paying no mind to what other people say. On the contrary, he was to reiterate that he had not heard such things and feels they are not true.

SESSION 2: The patient says she is feeling better. Now her worries bother her only at night, when she awakens at 1:00 A.M. with a low fueling. They accuse her of stealing.
ANALYST: "You have a low feeling about yourself."

PATIENT: "I always had a high feeling about myself, maybe too high. I was always a leader at work. Then I retired four years ago and they began talking about me." (The day residue precipitating event has just appeared! It is not the strokes, as the analyst first thought, but the retirement! Why has retirement affected her so?)

ANALYST: "You had a high feeling about yourself, but underneath you felt your feeling about yourself was too high. Then you stopped work, which had helped maintain your high feeling about yourself, and now you feel low, as if your former high feeling about yourself was undeserved—stolen! (This integrative interpretation ties together manifest content statements that she has made and the delusional content.)

PATIENT: "I used to be a leader in the neighborhood association. I urged my husband to go to the meetings. He would have no part of it. Now he's president of the association. I don't go anymore. They might say something bad about me. But I'm not sad. My memory's no good anymore. This makes me feel bad. I used to keep my work in my head."

ANALYST: "Did you keep all the business in your head?"

PATIENT: "No, I had index cards."

ANALYST: "So, you didn't keep the business in your head. You had index cards."

PATIENT: "Why are they saying bad things about me?"

ANALYST: "It's your feelings about yourself. Your mind is looking in the past for your bad feelings about yourself. The problem is now."

PATIENT: "What is the problem now?"

ANALYST: "After your strokes, your memory went bad. You feel you relied on it. Now at association meetings, you're not a leader anymore."

PATIENT: "My job! I kept it all in my head."

ANALYST: "No, you had index cards."

PATIENT: "So what?"

ANALYST: "So your memory was never perfect. The memory loss now is also a symbolic loss attaching itself to a newly revealed low feeling about yourself which really began when you stopped working."

PATIENT: "Not being able to do! I feel guilty about not being able to do! As a little girl, I made all my own clothes for myself and my brothers and sisters."

ANALYST: "Almost as if you were the mother, an honor which you felt you stole and made up for your guilt by working hard. Now you can't work."

That was the end of the second session. In follow-up by phone a few days later, the patient and her husband said she was greatly improved. She was sleeping again. She said she was troubled in her mind but now she was over it.

216 Psychotherapy of Psychosis

In this two-session supportive and uncovering treatment, I supported observing ego, reality testing, memory, logical secondary process, and self-esteem via interpretations geared to increase understanding of the patient's problems with self-esteem. I did this by integrating manifest elements: delusion, history, current events, behavior, associations, affect, all put in an integrated secondary process statement by the analyst—an integration indicated by the primary process and the structure of the psychotic symbol. This treatment process rapidly resulted in insight—an understanding of the relationship of feelings to reality to psychotic symptom.

I will now describe the techniques of treating specific ego deficits.

Boundaries

The most distressing boundary that is frequently lost in acute psychotic states is the boundary between inside experience and outside experience. Loss of this boundary is a conscious, cognitive dysfunction. There is much confusion in the literature which ascribes this cognitive deficit to an unconscious fantasy. It is much more than a fantasy, however. Some authors go so far as to say that there is difficulty telling this fantasy from reality. In fact, the deficit is far worse even than that. It is a true inability of the mind to contain its own experience separate from percepts of outside stimuli. Percepts that would ordinarily be contained in outside experience seem to be part of the inside experience. With the mind a totally open system, no treatment can take place, because there is no coherent, stable experience of oneself or of the therapist. An example is shown when the therapist scratches his leg and the patient says, "why are you scratching my leg?"

The treatment for loss of the inside–outside boundary is medication. However, before medication was available, and even nowadays while the medication is taking effect and in those for whom medication is ineffective, an attempt to connect with and enlighten the patient about this experience can be made. (The pioneers in this area were Fromm-Reichman [1950, 1959]; Sullivan [1953]; Searles [1964]; Pao [1979]; Boyer and Giovacchini [1980]; Stone et al. [1983].)

The late Dr. Harry Albert (Stone et al., 1983), an extraordinarily gifted therapist with psychotic and near psychotic patients, used to offer the following example: he is sitting in his office with a new patient who is talking word salad. There is no coherent sentence structure. Dr. Albert lifts his two hands and clasps them together intertwining the fingers. "See?" he says to the patient. "There are really two but they seem as though they're one." He opens and reclasps his hands, several times. "It seems as though they're one, but they're really two." He demonstrates this again

Psychotherapy of Psychosis   217

several times. Patient response: "This is the only sensible thing a psychiatrist ever said to me." (It was also the first time that she used a syntactically intact sentence!)

Another Example:

While sitting for my psychiatry specialty board examination, I was asked to interview a young man in the presence of an examiner. The patient entered the room agitated, excited, and fearful. His thinking was obviously fragmented, but he managed to convey his great anger that he was being tested and that he might fail the test and lose all possibility of a weekend pass. To make matters even worse, he said, I was trying to confuse him by not making sense. His rage was close to physical assaultiveness. Attempts at reassurance and denial did nothing, and so I told him that if I was trying to confuse him, it was too bad for me, not him, because the examiner was examining me, not him, and if I was confusing him I would fail, not him. He calmed considerably, sat down in his chair, and asked if I was sure the examiner was examining me, not him. I said I was sure and asked the examiner to verify this. He did so. The patient then asked the reason for the examination. I said it was for my certification as a psychiatrist. He said I was in a lot of trouble because I was confusing him and therefore I would probably fail the exam, and could he help me out in any way so that I might pass the exam! I thanked him and asked my next question: had he ever thought he was confused? He got angry and said I was again trying to confuse him because he had just said I was confused, not he. I said I wasn't trying to confuse him and asked him if other people had said to him that he was confused. He said yes, and I empathized with him about how difficult this must be for him, since he felt he wasn't confused, but they were saying that he was. In this way, we both got through the 30-minute interview.

Even more common than the totally open boundary of acute psychotic states are lesser degrees of this same dysfunction. Emotions which can enter from experience outside directly into experience inside disrupt self experience, even when the boundary to reality is intact and factual event stimuli is maintained. Similarly, ideas that other people (objects in reality) have may be immediately incorporated into the self experience and verbalized as if those ideas had originated in the person himself or herself. Both affect and ideational boundary porosity are easier to work with than a total loss of inside–outside boundary in which all perceptual stimuli are blended in a fused inside–outside state.

In all these patients, there is some degree of fusion, with inability to tell the therapist object in reality from the real object from the object representation from the real self or the self representation. Technique involves immediate and active intervention at the boundary of in–out to delineate a difference, at least in the object in reality.

Example:

PATIENT: "The voices are threatening me again. I'm fed up. They sound somewhat like your voice, doctor!"
ANALYST: "I have nothing to do with those voices!"

For a discussion of psychotic transference, see Reider (1957); Searles (1963); Little (1981).

In–out boundary problems, whether or not they capture the therapist in reality, are often highly distressing to the therapist. Countertransference confusion and panic can result. Sometimes active interventions are needed to help the therapist as much as to help the patient. Each of us has his or her own tolerance limits. With experience, those limits grow more secure. Hospitalization during acute episodes helps both patient and therapist in this regard. A physical boundary is drawn between patient and therapist. A schedule boundary is drawn between the patient's disorganization and social reality. That schedule boundary is both sequential and multidimensional (space, time, logic, behavioral). Multiplicity of staff provides instant relief and support to the solitary therapist and to the in–out boundary.

Reality Testing

Reality testing, lost in both acute and chronic psychotic states, is usually lost around condensations of real object and object representation or of real self experience and self representations. It is along this boundary that therapy can be so helpful. The submerging of day residue in emotional material, which is organized along primary process lines due to the capture of reality by fantasy, further impairs reality testing. Therapy can also, therefore, help reality testing along the boundary of the day residue–symbolic alteration of reality.

Reality testing is also helped by liberating observing ego. The description of day residues and reality niduses contained in events and in real

Psychotherapy of Psychosis   219

objects, as revealed in the primary process organization of the psychotic phenomena, enables the observing ego to understand that condensations are occurring as a mental process. This mobilizes intact logical processes and therefore buttresses reality testing.

It is relatively easy to do this, particularly in the acute phase, because all real objects, including the psychotherapist, are day residues that become immediately incorporated into the psychotic experience. If one observes and is aware of this happening, it forces an intervention by the therapist that validates real object distinction. This is extremely helpful to the patient.

Because the delusional patient has reality testing outside of the delusional content area, the therapist need not necessarily tell the patient what reality is. The therapist has to get the patient to tell himself or herself from the vantage point of his or her own secondary process ego. Although this is easier said than done, it enables the therapist to maintain technical neutrality and therefore to allow the patient to observe, thus building more effective ego. The advantage in technical neutrality is that it maximally mobilizes the patient's intact reality ego.

Example:

A 75-year-old man who lives with and is taken care of by his 50-year-old son presents with a 2-month history of feeling infested with worms in his intestines. He feels them "thrashing" around. He feels that he passes a lot of flatus, is swollen, and smells bad. His flatus, the worm flatus: he can feel them and smell them. Others can smell them too, and think he's repulsive. The worms keep him up at night and bring him to tears. He looks in his stool for them but never sees them. Once he found a white kernel, but it was only undigested corn.

THERAPIST: "What do you make of the fact that you feel them but you don't see them?"
PATIENT: "Oh, no! It's not in my mind! They are really there!"
THERAPIST: "What do you make of the fact that you feel them but you don't ever see them?"
PATIENT: "Could it be in my mind? I don't believe it. Maybe a doctor could see them."
THERAPIST: "Have the doctors seen them?"
PATIENT: "My son says I should go to a doctor."
THERAPIST: "Your son?"
PATIENT: "Yes."
THERAPIST: "Tell me about him."

220 Psychotherapy of Psychosis

PATIENT: "He's sick, too. He had a heart attack two months ago. He's only 50 years old."

THERAPIST: "That has been very upsetting to you."

PATIENT: "I am very agitated."

THERAPIST: "You feel like you're thrashing around."

PATIENT: "He's my last child and only son. I didn't really want another child but we became very close."

THERAPIST: "He wormed his way into your affections."

PATIENT (LAUGHING): "He was a very cute baby. Very active."

THERAPIST: "Like a wiggly, thrashing worm."

PATIENT: "And eager to please!"

THERAPIST: "Although you didn't want him around at first, the thought of losing him now is eating away at you."

PATIENT: "I feel terrible."

THERAPIST: "You feel repulsive."

PATIENT: "I do (tears)."

THERAPIST: "You feel your initial rejection of him was a repulsive thing and now you feel you deserve to be treated like a worm."

PATIENT: "I don't know what I'd do without him."

THERAPIST: "Is he very sick?"

PATIENT: "Yes, he's going downhill right in front of my eyes (tears)."

THERAPIST: "And your health?"

PATIENT: "I had cancer of the bowel two years ago, but I'm fine now."

THERAPIST: "When was your operation?"

PATIENT: "About this time of year."

THERAPIST: "Any new symptoms?"

PATIENT: "Yes I haven't felt well and I've intermittent diarrhea."

The therapist called the patient's internist and sent the patient to the internist. A stool culture for worms was done that day. Haloperidol (neuroleptic) was given, 0.5 mg once at night. The stool culture came back the next day—negative. The patient asked the internist if he had ever seen patients who thought they had worms but it was all in their minds. The internist said yes. Two days after that the patient returned to the therapist and said it had all been in his mind. He never knew such a thing could happen. He discussed his feelings about his son again and stopped the medication, saying he was feeling better. A week later, blood tests came back, and cancer of the bowel metastasized to the liver was diagnosed by the internist. The patient has not been psychotic again, now one year later.

In this example, there were multiple condensed day residues: the son's being ill, the recurrence of diarrhea, etc., all were eating away at him at an unconscious level. These day residues were eating away at him literally in reality (the metastatic cancer, the son's heart attack) and also emotionally. The treatment sessions challenged observing ego and used that observing ego to challenge reality testing. This was done by using the fact that he never saw the worms to challenge intact logical processes. This was also done by elucidating relevant psychodynamics and by relating those dynamics to the uncovering day residues, thus decondensing the psychotic symbol. The worm symbol seemed to be a condensation of his experience of his real self, of his self representation, and of the object representation of his son. It symbolized how he felt about himself in his depressive guilt and how he felt about his son in his aggression and fondness for that son. The condensation of self representation and object representation was at an unconscious level. The condensation of real self experience and self representation in the repulsive feelings about himself in the worm symbol was conscious. At no time was there conscious fusion between real self and real object.

Observing Ego

The fact that patients can have an observing ego about their psychosis leads to the distinction between observing ego and reality testing and the hypothesis that observing ego and reality testing are two separate ego functions. Because analytic therapists are used to having patients with the ability to distinguish the treating physician from their conscious ideas about the physician, who have some understanding that they are ill and even some understanding of the problem they would like to begin to focus their attention on, the fact that observing ego is obliterated in sicker patients is often overlooked or its implications are not fully appreciated. A true treatment alliance in which a patient and a physician are working together in order to help the patient with the patient's problems is possible only when an observing ego exists so that there can be some beginning agreement about what those problems are. The true therapeutic alliance is attached through the receiving locus of the observing ego (Sterba, 1934). Therefore, evaluation and treatment of this mental faculty are crucial in psychosis and near psychosis. To help a delusional patient to the point where he or she says, "I understand that what I believe is part of my illness, but I believe it anyway" is a monumental step forward, because true mutual work on the illness delusion can now occur. When observing ego is able to view illness, it is a hair's breadth away from being able to observe day residue and real objects. This is a step on the road to being able to experience self and object representations in emotional experience rather than in reality experience.

The dispassionate discussion of the patient's illness, and therefore the examination of observing ego, take place from the very first contact with

222 Psychotherapy of Psychosis

the patient when the analyst is able, one way or another, to say to the patient, "What's wrong?"

A differential diagnosis of absent observing ego must be explored immediately upon observing it. The differential diagnosis is made by the verbal observation and engagement of the psychology of this issue with the patient. The differential diagnosis includes psychosis with severe boundary disturbance obliterating observing ego, or delusional inclusion of observing ego. These two are actually not common. More commonly, a third problem exists. This is the barrier to observing ego due to character defenses that are intensely mobilized, either by the psychotic phenomenon itself or as part of the character defense environment of the illness. It is these basic character defenses that must be engaged and interpreted early so that observing ego may then be possible. The therapeutic query, "I notice you don't tell me about your illness," is followed, in those patients with defenses against observing ego, by a patient response that expresses the defense. These defenses include simple denial, projective paranoid rage, omnipotent control, negative evaluation of the therapist, narcissistic self-aggrandizement, and hysterical emotionality. The defenses chosen as resistances are often characteristic of the basic character organization in specific mechanism and thematic character type. These basic core defense resistances are testimony to the emergency experience that psychosis is. The emergency defense reaction hides the discomfort that could help the illness be removed from (or alien to) the ego, but also extremely painful. In addition, because exploration of observing ego leads to rapid diagnosis of character problems and their interdigitation with psychotic illness, the work can focus early on central issues that in a healthier patient might take years. As with much of the analytic treatment of very ill patients, there is opportunity in crisis.

One problem is that these character defenses are along an axis of neurotic to borderline to psychotic. The technique of dealing with them will vary depending on their location along this health-sickness axis. However, it is amazing how often in psychotic patients the character resistances to observing ego are at a neurotic level of organization.

Example of Separating Observing Ego from Reality Testing:

THERAPIST: "Hello. I am Dr. X. How may I help you?"
PATIENT: "The rays are entering my body and destroying my brain. I must get out of here. Please open the door."
THERAPIST: "I am a doctor. I help people who have illnesses."

Psychotherapy of Psychosis   223

> PATIENT: "Can you help me?"
> THERAPIST: "Could it be that you have an illness?"
> PATIENT: "Perhaps I do. But the rays are entering my body and ruining my brain."

This early intervention has begun to separate a bit of observing ego away from its merger with the psychotic process. It easily separates, as we can see, with a simple noninterpretive statement of fact by the therapist. This is because observing ego function may not be condensed in a primary process attachment to the psychotic process. In this patient, no basic character defenses were mobilized that prevented observing ego from separating, and therefore no interpretive statements about character defense are necessary. If the intervention by the doctor had elicited character defenses, those would have been interpreted.

Example:

PATIENT: "X-rays are destroying my brain!"
THERAPIST: "I am a doctor. How can I help?"
PATIENT: "A doctor can't help me, you idiot!"
THERAPIST: "When I talk to you about being ill, you get very angry. Your anger may be because were you to acknowledge that I am a doctor, you would logically have to realize that you are ill. This could be very devastating to you. Perhaps you fear you would then feel humiliated, helpless, and totally vulnerable, like an idiot."

There may, however, be neurocognitive deficits mediating failure in self-observation (Gharmi, 1997; McGlynn and Schafer, 1997).

Integrating Capacity

Most important in working with psychotic and near psychotic patients are the vertical dissociations of one mental experience from another. Again, basic character resistances may be involved in the separation. These are engaged and interpreted when the dissociation is pointed out. This can be done by simply asking, "And what is the relationship between experience

224 Psychotherapy of Psychosis

A and experience B?" The response may be an early attempt at integration or it may be a dispassionate observing ego discussion. Either of these is good. Even "I don't know" is a step forward, since it is a statement by a nonpsychotic observing ego. More commonly, one gets the same basic character resistances that got in the way of an exploration of the observing ego function. These must then be interpreted, even if it is very early in the treatment and even if the patient is still psychotic. It is particularly helpful to interpret these dissociations that occur between psychotic and nonpsychotic content and any character resistances between the two. The worry that this will incorporate nonpsychotic areas into the psychosis is balanced by the opportunity that psychotic areas may become more reality-oriented and integrated with nonpsychotic areas. The key is to take the risk of doing it and to observe very carefully the immediate results of the intervention: whether it leads more toward the loss of secondary process integration and reality testing or more toward the gain. If it leads more toward the loss, point this out. Reinterpret any character defenses that appear. If this leads still further into loss of secondary process, then back off, readjust medication, and start again at some later time. Almost always, however, interpretation in this manner improves things considerably, even if only for the period of time of the analytic interview with the therapist. Once again, this is because the integrating capacity of the ego is not entirely lost in all areas of a psychotic patient's ego functioning; the intact areas have been dissociated from the delusional areas.

Modulating Capacity

The modulating capacity of the ego is severely damaged in acute psychotic states and may be somewhat damaged in chronic psychotic states. This means that evoked affect easily and explosively increases in intensity and/or affect is rigidly frozen and unavailable to self and object representation experience. The first is the most frightening and the second is the most trying for the therapist. Comments about explosive affect and its evocation must be made immediately, before the eruption spills over into behavior. Great care must be taken in the interview not to free affect or affect-triggering experiences into the damaged ego. Anything can be said by the therapist if it is said calmly and with great concern, respect, and empathy for the patient's ego dysfunction. Preparation of nonpsychotic areas of ego function can be made so that the exploratory engagement of psychotic material is with the patient's permission, cooperation, and planning. In those patients with rigidly frozen and unavailable affects, this too can be noted with the patient, and the appropriate affect supplied by the patient's secondary process logic. This is not an experience of the affect. It is an intellectualizing defense. But it is a higher-order defense than denial and extreme affect isolation. The intellectualizing step may

Psychotherapy of Psychosis 225

allow the understanding before insight that permits less anxiety and more available affect experience. The defenses against affect in rigidly frozen patients, including paranoid patients, are best engaged early, since they will lead to emotional experiences that can integrate with, and dilute the power of, the aggression that these patients may be experiencing. Once again, it is important to realize that even the more tender emotions may carry, for paranoid patients and others, humiliation experiences that are even more painful than the frightening retaliation fantasies they suffer because of their aggression.

The bottom line of defense analysis in psychosis is that defenses are interpreted that serve as resistances to treatment and provide barriers to higher-level ego integrations by blocking observing ego and permitting vertical dissociations. These are interpreted because they must be. Higher-level neurotic defenses that help contain affect and organize experiences, such as intellectualization, may be encouraged early in treatment. They are not interpreted early unless they are used as resistances to treatment. One is, therefore, working with a graduated series of defensive structures from psychotic to borderline to neurotic, even in many psychotic patients. The psychotic defenses are layered in the delusional system, the borderline defenses usually surround the delusional material in the gap of vertical dissociations, and the neurotic defensive structures are farther away in stable, nonpsychotic character areas. The diagnosis is made by the sickest areas. Although it is confusing, it is the very spectrum of ego defenses in most psychotic patients that makes analytic treatment possible and useful.

Object Relations

Remember that the usual, crucial problem in object relations, pathognomonic for psychosis, is the condensation of real object with object representations or the real self experience with self representations, or real object with self representation, in conscious, cognitive experience. There are often other boundary problems as well, such as the inside–outside boundary problem. But all stable psychotic states show this problem in object relations. Exact configurations will vary from illness to illness and also from patient to patient, depending on the psychotic structure.

Psychoanalytic psychotherapy and psychoanalysis attempts to help the patient separate the real object from the object representation and the real self from the self representation. An attempt is first made to liberate enough observing ego to engage concern about this condensed experience. The patient must be helped toward the separation. This takes place in the observing ego at first, from the transference and from outside the transference. The therapist remains in technical neutrality unless reality-based interventions are required. Sometimes all this is to no avail, and the

226 Psychotherapy of Psychosis

analysis of thematic content must proceed even though the condensation of the object world is occurring and perhaps becomes transiently worse with the analysis of thematic content. It is helpful to have such patients in a hospital. The point is that although defenses against observing ego and integration may be rigid, very often defenses against deeper layers of object relations material are not so rigid. The analyst should proceed cautiously, but deeper analysis will uncover recurrent object relations themes, recurrent coincidences with objects in reality, recurrent content of the patient's past, and crucial present-day residue events with their sequences and contexts. This will help the potentially available secondary processing of object relations, because the psychological organization of the psychotic object relations structure becomes clearer and clearer in contrast to objects in reality. This makes it harder and harder for observing ego to ignore the difference and for defensive structures to prevent the recognition of psychotic objects by nondelusional secondary process areas of mental functioning. This statement describes a crucial aspect of the theory and tactics of analytic, that is to say uncovering, treatment of psychosis. It is the reason the analytically trained therapist has so much to offer the psychotic patient. However, attention to ego synthesis is required and this means constant vigilance by the therapist. Analytic treatments that uncover but do not use this material to help the patient with nonpsychotic integrative capacities may make the patient worse and lead to the chronic psychotization of more and more ego areas that, prior to treatment, had been nonpsychotic areas. It is for this reason that psychoanalytic treatment of psychotic states in the past got such a bad name (Wallerstein, 1986). This was especially true when medication was not used. However, awareness of vertical dissociations, of observing ego lack, and of reality testing loss will enable the analytic therapist to avoid the pitfall of ignoring integration and synthesis.

At what point should unraveled layers of deeper emotions and repressed factual experiences be used for the integration of partially separated psychotic experience is a constant question. Clinical judgment is most difficult because it involves a constant measure of the plasticity of the psychotic condensation and the integrative capacity of the autonomous ego. The guideline is, however, really quite simple. Every time new object relations dynamic material emerges that makes sense to the therapist and that is not utilized for synthetic integration by the patient, this must be inquired about and the resistances to this process interpreted. This is especially true when a glaring coincidence of thematic material emerges or when a factual detail emerges that was previously unknown or disputed, but that is now seen clearly by the patient and that throws secondary process doubt on the primary process psychotic story. A simple question by the therapist "What do you make of that?" is usually enough to start the integrative process. One is asking the patient, therefore, not to lead into more dynamic material, but to consider the significance of the material exposed. In this way, intact areas of secondary process can be mobilized for integration along with any mediating defenses, which can then be interpreted (for other approaches, see Jacobson [1964, 1967]; Rosenfeld [1965]).

Thing Presentation

It is important to comment on the thing presentation experience in psychosis and its treatment. If one remembers that thing presentation experience is the experience of feelings condensed with the experience of perceptual things, with the quality of reality binding the emotional experience of affect, one can understand that the treatment of the thing presentation experience is to translate it into word presentation experiences, including descriptions of the affects. The therapist must describe thing presentation experiences in words. The patient is helped to describe that experience in his or her own words. The affect experience can be deduced from free associations of the patient, empathic resonance in the therapist of the psychotic symbol, more available similar affect in derivative symbols, and free-floating affect in the patient when it occurs. The affect can then be experienced in the patient's self experience of affect.

The ego functions involved in word presentation processing for affect are impaired in psychotic patients. Which ones are impaired depends on the psychiatric illness. The translation of emotionally contaminated percept experiences into higher-level, verbally organized conceptual and affect experiences allows for greater separation of complex condensations involved in the thing presentation experience. The translation function is a higher ego function. It may be damaged by acute illness or it may be an ongoing problem for patients, especially some of those with learning disabilities.

Patients understand the power of the therapeutic translation process and express their understanding in their resistances. A nonpsychotic example is sexualized thing presentations, because the quality of erotic affect experience is condensed in the perception of the reality thing. "Telling it in words ruins it." But although the statement is not totally false, it is not totally true. The statement represents despair about the capacity of higher-level ego functioning to (1) contain, (2) express, and (3) experience real self and real object integrated with ambivalent, complex, layered affect. In fact, word presentation mental experience evolved presumably because of the power it gives to organize reality in ways that are beneficial not just for dealing with reality but for satisfying one's own emotional desires and reassuring one's own fears.

Changing thing presentations to word presentations involves some level of interpretation, because the thing presentation condenses present and past, concept and affect. As the interpretive word presentation statement

228   Psychotherapy of Psychosis

is made, the patient will experience and provide confirmation: often a startle reaction, often an affect reaction, always a process of elaboration that reveals new material (Langs, 1973). This is because the thing presentation experience is decondensing as word presentation processes provide discharge and conceptual pathways (Sarnoff, 1976, 1987). Therapeutic facility and accuracy in catalyzing this process comes with practice and with the intuitive familiarity that experience with very sick patients gives.

It is crucially important to diagnose the reason for the predominance of thing presentation experience. It may be due to the disorganization of thinking permitting the emergence of primary process material. It may also be due to the overwhelming affect that condenses in thing presentation experiences to provide a containment barrier to intensity and spread. Word centers in the brain may be damaged, as in neurological illness (remember that learning disabilities may be a neurological illness). A treatment plan based on the proper diagnosis can then be planned.

Thing Presentation Quality

One crucial aspect of the thing presentation experience is the peculiar quality of the experience. It is a condensed affect–percept experience and has the qualities of both affect and percept. Therapeutic empathy with this quality is important in early treatment. Such empathy helps patients feel their psychotic experience is understood by the therapist and therefore that they can get help from the therapist. An empathic statement about this quality should be part of the first intervention. Tone, gesture, and attitude of the therapist can all convey this empathic concern. But the beginning attempt to decondense and psychoanalyze involves expressing this quality in words.

Example:

A young woman who lives in her own apartment in the same building as her father, and who left her mother, grandmother, and stepfather one year ago, presents to the emergency room with a 2-week history of acute psychosis. The world is coming to an end. God is killing all the people by burning them because of their sins. She believes she is Judas, who betrayed Christ. God's voice says she can fly. If she opens the window and jumps, she can save the world and get forgiveness for sins. God told her to jump and she smelled the burning building.

THERAPIST: "You must have been terrified!"
PATIENT: "I was!"

THERAPIST: "And sin?"

PATIENT: "The sin of lying."

THERAPIST: "How so?"

PATIENT: "I didn't speak up."

THERAPIST: "How so?"

PATIENT: "A boy recently kissed me and I couldn't tell him I didn't want him to do that."

THERAPIST: "But sin is Judas, and God burning the world?"

PATIENT: "Well, sex."

THERAPIST: "How so?"

PATIENT: "My stepfather molested me from age 8 until age 12. He fondled my breasts and vagina. I kept a knife and wanted to murder him. I told my family but my grandmother and mother didn't believe me."

THERAPIST: "You felt betrayed by your mother and grandmother who didn't believe you and didn't stop your stepfather from sexually molesting you. They allowed it to continue. You feel frightened and guilty because you are so angry about it and because the sexual activity was frightening to you then. You suffer from this now. It interferes with your sexual relations with men now. The guy trying to kiss you stirred all this up again. You badly need treatment."

PATIENT: "But I shouldn't have allowed him to kiss me . . ."

THERAPIST: "But maybe you were sexually aroused."

PATIENT: "I hate sex!"

THERAPIST: "You hate your sexual desire because it reawakens all the anger and fear of what happened back then. But it isn't back then now. You couldn't say no then, but you can say no now. The problem is will you ever be able to say yes! Now when you sort of say yes, you feel terrible."

PATIENT: "I do!"

Notice the progressive affect decondensation into emotional experience and expressed in words as the exploratory interchange progresses. Affects of anger, sadness, and guilt are moving out of the perceptual, otherworldly experience of percept into words and into the direct experience of affect. Psychogenetic day residues of the past are separating from present-day residue reality precipitating events.

Analysis of Psychotic Structure

Now we are at last ready to proceed to discuss analysis of delusional content. Analytic therapists should be quite comfortable with this aspect

230 Psychotherapy of Psychosis

since it involves the same uncovering work with much the same technique as with neurotic patients. It requires only a greater observational attention as the unraveling of the dynamic system of the delusion occurs so that attention can be paid to the liberated day residues, real objects, and recurrent dynamics which intact ego areas must integrate and work through. Working through is left to the intact neurotic ego of neurotic patients, by and large, and requires little effort on the part of the analyst other than to point out the recurrence of the dynamic themes. The analyst of neurotic patients may consider the working through aspect as part of the patient's job and therapist abstinence in this area as part of technical neutrality. However, even in neurotic patients, working through requires attention to the same dynamics in other areas at other levels, and some neurotic patients require a good deal of this therapeutic attention. Psychotic and near psychotic patients, in particular, need help in this area. They need help not just in uncovering similar themes in different areas but in integrating and applying this knowledge.

Remember that around every delusion is an area of pseudodelusion: an area of the same dynamics with slightly different application in which reality testing seems to be gone but is in fact present. Technique in this content area can be freer and more engaging than in the delusional area itself, because reality testing processes are potentially intact in these areas. The goal is to free the delusion from associated psychological areas of pseudodelusion and, in that way, reduce the delusion to its essential core.

In order to do this analysis, one must maintain technical neutrality unless forced out of it by the pressure of behavior or of imminent behavior. This is because in the area of pseudodelusion, reality testing is possible and the patient's own reality testing must be challenged rather than replaced by the therapist's. In psychotic patients, the therapist may actually have to provide reality testing. But do not expect this supplied reality testing to immediately change the reality testing of psychotic structure. Psychotic condensation and its capture of reality testing is usually quite rigid. The technical intervention should, however, increase observing ego and increase secondary process logic, and these two newly freed and recruited autonomous ego areas can begin to help reality testing and to decondense the psychotic symbol. The movement out of technical neutrality that is required is usually a statement about reality or about the real object. It is important to return to technical neutrality as soon as possible so that potentially available aspects of the patient's own ego functioning can be engaged.

Technical neutrality in psychotic and near psychotic states, however, does not mean passivity or failure to interact, or to question, sometimes relentlessly. On the contrary, the therapist must be very active in tactfully but clearly challenging intact ego areas by pointing to the primary process logical inconsistences of delusional and pseudodelusional material.

It is only in this way that intact ego islands can be recruited for therapeutic benefit.

The next important issue is to use free association. Consider as free association all of the communication stream of words, of affect display or lack of display, of other behavior, and of psychotic symptomatology. Many psychotic patients can, in fact, truly free associate and do so more than many neurotic patients. These psychotic patients are those who are only somewhat unintegrated and in whom primary processing has not dominated all of cognition. The diagnostic question with psychotic and near psychotic patients is whether there are true free associations or whether you are really dealing with loose associations, which are primary process intrusions, unwanted, into secondary process communication. Loose associations, like free associations, will enable the therapist to follow affect content themes to guide interpretation. But patients with loose associations have an ego deficit and the therapist must be clear if patients can use such information. If not, some diagnosis of why not must be made and some treatment plan within the analytic therapy provided.

There are many frozen delusional patients who do not truly free associate. Nor do they have loose associations. However, their verbal streams, which go from content of delusion to content of character dynamics to statements about the condensed real object–object representation, are a type of dynamic information. This involves a verbal stream in which latent and manifest contents are condensed with each other and in which the relationships between vertically dissociated aspects of mental experience are demonstrated to the therapist by their contiguity in the verbal stream. That they are related is hypothesized, and their exact relationship requires analysis. Sometimes the relationship is quite clear to the therapist because a dissociated or displaced affect experience is observed which links them. This does not mean that the patient is aware of this link or able to use the link. That requires some analytic help. Once again, basic character resistances may need to be analyzed. Again, ego deficits of secondary process integration need to be diagnosed.

In unraveling delusional systems, all analytic therapists have struggled with the rigid loss of reality testing and rigid denials of fact that many psychotic patients suffer. The delusion, therefore, does not unravel. Often, however, delusional systems unravel, but the analyst does not recognize the unraveling because the elements are dissociated from each other or are in the transference. Alternatively, the analyst may recognize the unraveling but does not know how to help the patient use this unraveling. However, in some patients the delusional system truly does not unravel in a behavioral–affect–verbal stream, despite engaging the material and analyzing basic resistances. This may be because of the rigidity of cognitive deficits, or because of the rigidity of defenses within the delusion, or because of rigid character defenses blocking observing

232 Psychotherapy of Psychosis

ego and secondary processes. Proper diagnosis and analysis of blocks may be necessary. Hospitalization for these rigid patients is extremely helpful because then some of the reality day residue triggers of increased psychotic symptomatology can be observed by the staff and used by the analytic therapist to understand the structure and linkage points of the psychotic symbol. Presenting this information to the patient may result in a reaction and subsequent verbal productions that elaborate the delusional story and progress the treatment toward unraveling the delusion.

If all of this fails, then the technique is to deal with the same dynamics in character pathology, both manifest and latent, and with their associated reality triggers. Once the unraveling of this related material is clear, a new attempt can be made to deal with the same dynamics in the delusional system. This enables the progressive unraveling and understanding of the dynamic material in areas not blocked, as it is in the delusion. It allows the patient and the therapist to gain access to unconscious areas inaccessible in the delusional area. This information can then be used in integrative interpretations to help the patient understand and unpack his or her delusion by showing the similarity of dynamic content.

Example of Analyzing a Delusion:

A young woman is convinced that her two children have tuberculosis, in spite of the fact that the doctors have reassured her that this is not so.

PATIENT: "They are coughing."

THERAPIST: "But the x rays are negative."

PATIENT: The doctor says they don't have it but I know they do. Because I am their mother and I see them every day."

THERAPIST: "But the tests are negative. The x rays are negative and the doctor says no. Most mothers would be relieved."

PATIENT: "I am relieved. But I still know they have tuberculosis and the doctor hasn't realized it yet. I don't let the kids visit. Other children might get the tuberculosis. I do let them go to school and parties because I don't want to jail them."

As therapy progressed, more of the reality history was revealed by focusing on the reality sequence of her illness, a so-called parallel history. Her boyfriend had tuberculosis, and now she has a positive skin test for tuberculosis. The children have negative skin tests. The children were both born out of wedlock with different fathers. The woman now does not date. She has no sexual life. She has never told the pediatrician that the boyfriend lived in the house. He had not only a positive skin test but also a positive x ray. She saw him coughing and losing weight. She broke up with that boyfriend because he had tuberculosis. He got angry, broke into the apartment, and raped her. She then started feeling sad. She cries all the time and has trouble sleeping.

Antidepressant medication was begun and therapy sessions continued. With the therapist empathizing with her difficulties with men and with sex, she said that she had lied about the boyfriend raping her. She was out drinking and found herself in bed, naked, with her boyfriend touching her vagina. She was furious and wanted to kill him. She expressed her anger, but he just laughed and said she better not do anything. She was afraid. She also said that she had sex after this episode with a male friend whom she doesn't love. He came into the house and saw the tuberculosis pills and asked what they were. She said it was asthma medicine. She wants the therapist to call the pediatrician and tell him about her boy-friend who had tuberculosis. The therapist commented on the guilt she felt about not telling the pediatrician about the boyfriend with tubercu-losis, maybe because she felt embarrassed about their sexual relationship. She responded that she first got pregnant when she was 14. Her father said, "Disgusting." Her boyfriend at the time contracted gonorrhea and passed it along to her when she was two months pregnant. Her older brother said, "You are a woman now. You can't stay in this house." So she left and lived with the boyfriend who had contracted gonorrhea. She moved in with her grandmother just before the baby came. Her grand-mother taught her how to take care of the baby. This daughter is now the patient's father's favorite. Both of her children do have asthma, with many hospital emergency room visits. The younger child has a chronic cough. The elder daughter is 11 and starting to develop physically.

As this information came out over the next few sessions and her guilt and shame were interpreted, the patient began sleeping, stopped crying, and began dating. Her worry now became reversed. She was afraid that the children would give the man some disease.

Therapist: "Your children, two girls, now approaching adolescence, have, like you yourself, what you believe to be an illness—female sexual-ity. It infects men and then it comes back to infect the woman."

After the session in which this interpretation was given, the patient felt very much better. She felt so much better that she stopped her medication and had sex for the first time in quite a while. Unfortunately, she promptly came down with trichomonas vaginitis and became depressed again and worried that the children would get vaginitis from her. The antidepres-sant was restarted and the therapy continued with a rapid resolution of her worries that the children would either be infected or would infect.

At a conscious level, the real object boyfriend with tuberculosis was merged with object representations of her children. Both had sexuality as the common denominator. More latently, there was a condensation of real self with self representation: The tuberculous illness that she was positive for in reality condensed with her own feelings about her sexuality as being dirty and infectious. This latent self representation infecting her real self experience was displaced to the children's infection in the delusional system. More unconscious was her guilt over the tuberculosis infection coming from the man and her sexual relationship with the man and her anger that her daughter had become her own father's favorite. Tuberculosis in the children was punishment of both her and her attractive child rival whom she feared would soon be more attractive than she to her boyfriend. She felt very guilty about this worry (for an example of early work in this area, see Sechehaye [1951]).

Symbolic Transformations of Reality

In both neurosis and psychosis, analytic therapy analyzes symbolic transformations, but in the case of psychosis, these symbolic transformations are of reality. The symbolic alteration of reality is the manifest, conscious, and easily recognizable manifestation of psychotic structure and its primary processes. As the many examples in this chapter show, analysis of these symbolic alterations of reality, if done with the technical recommendations illustrated here, may lead to the decondensation of the day residue from its primary process symbolic alteration.

The question always arises of when to analyze the delusional symbolic transformation, and when to avoid it and analyze the same dynamics in the character structure. This is the same question as when to support and when to analyze an aspect of ego function. The answer to these questions has to do with the structure of the patient's ego. In fact, with most psychotic patients, one does different things at different times, depending on the content areas and associated autonomous ego functions that have been captured or not captured. The question is whether or not the patient's ego requires this or that and whether or not the appropriate technique is used to further the progressively unfolding description of the unconscious for the purpose of integrated growth and change.

Day Residues

In the acute and disorganized psychotic state, real objects—but also real events, their sequencing and context—are lost in the chaos of object representations and self representations. Therefore, the day residues of emotional experiences, the instigators and organizers, are lost to the mental experience of the patient and to the purview of the physician. Logical sequence of events is lost. One crucial advantage of treating such patients in hospitals is the ability of the milieu to maintain, organize, and record

Psychotherapy of Psychosis   235

those sequences. The observations of these sequences will become crucially important as the patient begins to organize and make a recovery. Linking these sequences with emotional states and the interplay between reality and psychotic symptoms is one of the overall tasks of the therapist in the beginning phase of treatment.

As the dynamics of the delusional system unravel, it is the common experience for day residues of the present to pop into view. Interestingly enough, in adult psychosis, the triggering reality genesis or aggravator is discoverable because that genesis is so recent, reportable, and in a hospitalized patient, observable. These triggering events may be surprisingly parallel to reality day residue genetic events of the past. Sometimes, these genetic past events pop into view before the reality triggering events of the present. Therefore, the analytic therapist uses this to confront reality testing and observing ego. Improved observing ego and reality testing helps liberate the present reality nidus from the psychosis where it is trapped by unraveling the psychological dynamics of the symbolic transformations of that disguise. Unconscious layers of delusional content and affect are uncovered. These layers can then be related to conscious and unconscious here and now day residues and to conscious and unconscious there and then day residues. This uncovering technique is ego supportive, provided that the therapist carefully attends to reality testing, observing ego, and ego integration. The analyst must use unimpaired autonomous ego in nonpsychotic areas. The analyst must leave nonmediating defenses alone or support them, but must interpret mediating defenses as needed.

As the analytic therapist unravels delusional material, he or she must make sure the day residue is not captured by primary process and reified, but rather integrated in secondary process. This is done by observing the capture of primary process, pointing it out to the patient, inquiring about the reasons for this, listening to the associations to the engaging of this issue. One must see whether one is getting resistance to the analytic process or more information about the difficulty that the patient is having in moving day residue material into secondary process. This difficulty may be caused by character resistances, intensity of liberated affect, unrecognized transference intensification, or undiagnosed and condensed attachment points to reality triggers at the core of the genetics of psychotic phenomena. Alternatively, it may be caused by severely damaged secondary process cognition which has been unrecognizably present in all areas of ego function, psychotic and nonpsychotic. This is only a partial, differential diagnostic list, no doubt, but it serves to provide examples.

Sometimes, just as the day residue/precipitating event emerges in the unraveling of the delusional system, great resistance seems to be engaged because of the uncanny resemblance between psychology and reality, between the present and the past. These attachment points of the delusional system are very difficult for observing ego and reality testing to

236 Psychotherapy of Psychosis

work with because there is this uncanny overlap. This becomes especially problematic when thing presentation quality is present in these focal experiences and in psychosis. Thing presentation quality provides the percept verification of the condensed experience and may be present in the elements of that experience even after the decondensations.

Many therapists make the mistake of breaking with therapeutic neutrality and distinguishing the object representation from the real object and from the day residue object in reality. This rarely works, because the therapist is leading to reality testing, which is damaged, rather than to observing ego, which is intact. There is less of a problem if the therapist empathically understands that the patient cannot experience the difference between the delusion at that point and the day residue in reality. Instead, there is a delusional attempt to organize elements of experience that have perceptual thing presentation quality. When a patient says that the physician doesn't understand, that the delusional thought is real, the only answer the therapist can make is that it is more real than the patient can understand and admit at this point! The analyst thereby comments on the use of psychotic reality to defend against day residue reality and affect reality. The day residue reality coincidence is crucial because its recognition and acknowledgment would be the first decondensation from the psychotic structure. Needless to say, patients are extremely resistant to acknowledging these present-day realities. Most delusions have a kernel of reality to them. The problem is that there is also a condensed, symbolic transformation of that reality. A delusion is a symbolic transformation along primary process lines. The patient cannot translate this primary process but the analytic therapist can. In that way, the therapist ought to be discovering the day residue and affect reality of the delusion before the patient. It is the descriptive explanation of this to the patient that is so helpful. Ironically, the greatest resistances may engage at the point where the therapist finally understands all aspects of the reality of the delusion and attempts to help the patient understand it. This ought to be expected in advance, since the rigidity of the delusional system speaks not just to the illness attacking autonomous ego functioning, but also to the intense pressure of the psychological material involved. This is the reason that the paradox expressed in the epigraph to this book is used. The question was this: "Are you real or are you part of my imagination?" The answer was as follows: "Your imagination is real and since I am part of your imagination, I am real!" I would go even further. Because the real experience is captured by the delusional system, the delusional system contains the real experience as well as the imagined experience (Freud, 1907). The problem with recognizing the real experience is the affects generated, the conflicts evoked, and their conscious condensation with reality experience. Hence, defenses of all types, character and psychotic, within and approaching the delusional system are intensified at the point this present reality starts to separate. Interpretation of those resistances can be extremely beneficial, resulting in the final decondensation of this present material and the liberation of affect experience. The patient's intact secondary processes are then much better able to see the difference between the reality day residue of the present, the primary processing of that day residue of the present, and the reality day residue of the genetic past. When these separate, they will be seen to be uncannily similar and at the same time remarkably different in crucial ways.

In summary, if psychodynamic material is exposed, help integrate it; if hidden, uncover it; if defended against, interpret the defense; if the defense is unyielding, undermine the delusional systems by seeking the same themes in nonpsychotic character derivatives.

It is important to realize that, for the psychotic patient, clarification of reality is a neutral confrontation, because the patient is condensing that reality with fantasy. In this way, the condensation might separate and the conflict contained in the two aspects can be clarified. The evocative similarity of affect fantasy and of fact becomes apparent.

This process does not lead just to supporting intellectualization as a defense, but rather to secondary process integration. Psychotic and near psychotic patients have a primary process that is dominating. Primary process is an integrating mode, and in patients where secondary process is too severely damaged, this is all the therapy has at first. The goal and the usual accomplishment of treatment are to restore secondary process integration capacity.

Timing and Sequencing of Interpretation

Patients vary as to when and how much affect, content, and transference they can tolerate. This varies with illness, patient, phase of treatment, particular transference content, particular affect, and associated particular captured autonomous ego aspects. Clinical judgment is empathically sensing this balance. Very ill patients are as unpredictable a priori as are neurotic patients. This is because the specific autonomous ego functions captured by specific affect and content are quite variable and quite unpredictable from patient to patient and from layer to layer within one patient. Hence the need for analytic technique, empathy, intuition, and clinical experience, the combination of which is called *clinical judgment.* Timing and sequencing of treatment make the most demands on this clinical judgment.

The variability of patients according to level of illness, type of illness, and individuality is given much lip service in psychoanalysis but poorly appreciated at times. Much psychological argument about metapsychology and treatment is based on experiences with different patient populations who have a very different ego structure.

In any case, much working through must be done from the ego areas which can tolerate the dynamic material. This will help those ego islands

238   Psychotherapy of Psychosis

grow, and they may be then used as integrated areas from which the patient can consider the more difficult areas.

Self-Esteem and Technique

As therapy progresses, the relationship of the ego to superego as it affects self-esteem is often a crucial issue. It often triggers the most resistant character defenses to treatment and to observing ego.

This leads to a brief discussion of sealing over versus integration as psychosis remits. Of course, this theory of treatment would hold that it is important for patients to integrate psychotic phenomena rather than to seal over and repress them. A practical reason for this is that psychotic patients often do not take their medication, and a revolving door process of repeated hospitalization ensues. It is very important not just for psychological growth but for maintenance of remission that patients understand that they were psychotic. As a patient seals over, if that is happening, and denials of fact enter along with repression of dynamic content, vigorous attempts at interpreting those defenses must be made, even though they are nonmediating defenses. Almost always, these defenses have to do with the self-esteem system and the defenses against the superego experience of psychosis. When the defenses are successfully analyzed so that the sealing over process stops, the patient almost always feels depressive affect. This is the confirming evidence that the self-esteem system was involved and this depressive affect can then be analyzed.

It is important, however, to realize that sealing over is a complex phenomenon that requires an accurate differential diagnosis. Some patients are, in fact, still psychotic with delusional denial or denial of delusion. Other patients are intellectually slow and have not cognitively grasped what has happened. Only some patients are using neurotic and borderline defenses of denial, both of which buttress the self-esteem system in patients who have had an acute psychotic episode.

Empathy with psychotic qualities is the crucial first self-esteem supporter. Then one can, perhaps, be able to empathize with the observing ego of psychotic experience. Next, it may be possible to empathize and analyze the superego's reaction to psychosis as well as the superego condensations in psychotic symptoms. This superego material is often found in character defenses that have been lifelong in the patient.

Regression with Treatment

Analytic reconstructive treatment with psychotic patients always raises the specter of making the patient worse. Making the patient worse involves one of two common structural problems or both. The first is increased integration problems. The second is a sinking into more and more primitive psychological material in content and affect. From my point of view, the real problem is the first complication rather than the second. If the patient is integrating or intermittently integrating the unraveling of more primitive content and intensities, then the therapy is useful, at first to the therapist and then to the patient. Particularly in chronic psychotic states or in chronic severe character disorders of near psychotic proportions, the regression breaks a longstanding stalemate and is therefore a potentially progressive regression. The problem is to make sure the regression is a useful one rather than merely another stalemate. The decision about whether or not regression, if it occurs, is a necessary evil is not made by the content and structure of the regression but rather by the functioning of intact observing ego and integration faculties of the ego. There are patients who are so chronically ill, and some dangerously so, that the risk of a regressive experience is worth it. A quick example of this is the patient who is riddled by psychotic phobias and secondary suicidal elaboration, who goes to the hospital, becomes even more regressed, but finally breaks free of a symbiotic reality relationship, has observing ego about his or her illness, finally accepts medication, and moves on in analytic treatment to understand the dynamics of his or her psychosis and associated character defenses (on psychoanalytically based hospital treatment, see Chiland [1977]; Marcus [1987b]).

Some patients are already in a very regressed state when seen. These patients can be analyzed if attention is paid to integration and to nonpsychotic derivatives in character structure. In sicker patients, much psychological material is repressed in derivatives and much primitive material is used to block existing higher-level ego functioning. In any case, the reparative psychoanalytic technique is often greatly aided, and in some cases only possible, in a hospital setting.

Regression is true of all psychoanalytic experience. The question is not whether regression occurs and not whether the regression is theoretically good or bad. The problem is in the control of the regression. All psychoanalysis involves controlled regression, and all psychoanalysis thus involves interventions to allow regression or to defuse or contain it. The analytic therapist does this with silences and with interpretation at appropriate times in the neurotic patient. The analytic therapist must be more vigilant and active with psychotic and near psychotic patients. The analyst must be particularly vigilant about transference phenomena and be prepared to interpret early and/or defuse them. In any case, the technique of controlling regression is determined by the structure of the ego, as are all other therapeutic interventions in very ill patients.

Psychotherapy versus Psychoanalysis

The debate over psychoanalysis versus psychotherapy, what is which and if there are two or if there is one, is extensive, ongoing, and a little futile. Semantics looms large in such discussions, much to the detriment of the progression of knowledge. These distinctions should depend on

240 Psychotherapy of Psychosis

the ego structure of the patient. In fact, there are varying degrees and varying intensities of analytic therapies, along an infinite analog spectrum depending on patient, therapist, and illness. The more fruitful issue is how one can help a particular patient unravel and integrate his or her own psychology for the purpose of symptom relief and personality growth in present-day real life. Different degrees of reality interventions, integrative interpretations, transference intensities, and setting and frequency will be required, depending on particular ego structure and phase of treatment. Such questions are better answered in the specific than in the general (Hoch, 1992; Morris, 1992; McNutt, 1992).

Psychotherapy may be used in preparation for psychoanalysis (see Rapaport, 1960; Namnum, 1968; Weil, 1973; Bernstein, 1983). Important for the success of this technique is the specific diagnosis of ego problems (Bellak and Meyers, 1979) and an active engagement of those problems in the treatment (Bieber, 1980).

Use of the Couch

The subject of regression and of psychotherapy versus psychoanalysis usually brings up the issue of the couch. Psychoanalysts by and large have moved away from the use of the couch with near psychotic and psychotic patients, for good reason. Lack of visual feedback makes it more difficult for the patient to separate real object and object representation in the transference. It also encourages a passivity in the therapist that is inappropriate, considering the ego dysfunction of the very ill patient. A silent therapist and a rambling psychotic patient only lead to further psychotization. However, the couch can be used for integration as well as for regression (see Khan, 1960), and there are certain advantages in the use of the couch over the chair for the task of integration with certain patients.

The following are some possible indications for the use of the couch in psychotic states. Criterion 1 is a stable, chronic, organized delusional system. Criterion 2 is that observing ego has already separated from reality testing, and beginning interpretations increase reality testing. Criterion 3 is that an increased understanding of the dynamics causes an increase of observing ego and a decrease in the psychotic symptom. Criterion 4 is autonomous ego strengths of (a) intelligence, crucial aspects of which are abstracting and generalizing abilities; (b) the ability to free associate without severe regression of autonomous secondary processes; (c) a firm behavioral control; (d) boundaries between in and out; and (e) boundaries between real and fantasy experience in the transference. Intact, albeit dissociated, secondary processes is Criterion 5. Criterion 6 is an accessible overlap of dynamics in the delusion and in character, and that the character is neurotically organized, rigid, and needs psychoanalysis. Criterion 7 is that the delusional system needs greater intensity to be analyzed, free association provides this intensity, and free association in this particular patient needs a decrease of visual feedback. Criterion 8 is that regression can be controlled because of the boundary between the delusional system, the character structure, and stable, higher-level autonomous ego areas. Criterion 9 is that the transference has a lack of engagement and intensity, so that the couch can be used successfully to increase intensity of the transference, but without causing psychotic condensation of the transference. Criterion 10 is that the autonomous ego is healthy enough to make use of this transference material.

The question is this: are there any patients who meet these criteria? Very few. Most are those whose active psychosis is in remission. But these criteria can help choose the few who need to use the couch as well as guide treatment for those who can't use the couch.

The couch works best with patients who are rigid, neurotic characters who suffer an acute, time-limited psychotic episode. It is especially helpful if the psychosis is rapidly brought under control by medication and by psychoanalytic psychotherapy. Because the underlying dynamics of rigid character are often clearly seen in psychotic eruptions, because psychoanalytic psychotherapy often quickly localizes attachment points between the two, and because this then opens derivative dynamic structures in the character, the analyst is sometimes tempted to an early reconstructive treatment in these patients. I have found this temptation well warranted because such patients usually respond rapidly and well.

But great efforts must be made to avoid psychotic transference. Near psychotic transference can usually be engaged and analyzed if done so vigorously and consistently from the beginning. Transference elements are also important because they may involve similar dynamics as the psychotic material and mediating defenses.

Example:

A 28-year-old woman was seen in consultation because of increasing anxiety over 3 months. She was afraid to be alone with her 2-year-old son. Would she be able to take proper care of him? Suppose she felt like killing him? A psychiatric history revealed many depressive symptoms including insomnia, tearful feelings, anhedonia, decreased appetite, and passive suicidality. There were three previous episodes, two mild but one severe, which included a serious and nearly successful suicide attempt. Mental status examination revealed that desperation and panicky ruminations about her son had not yet reached delusional condensation. However, thing presentation quality, rigidity, and beginning confusion and despair were evident.

Nonpsychotic ruminations, they completely dominated her mental content and affect experience. Her involvement had a conviction and certainty, especially about fears of killing her child, that seemed to have strong thing presentation quality, and hence may have been an impending psychotic episode if the intensity of the depression worsened, as it seemed to be in the process of doing. Reality testing processes were fragile, but intact. Observing ego was excellent and impulse control strongly present. Defense mechanisms were higher-level obsessive with good integration and consisted of intellectualization, affect repression and isolation, partial day residue repression with rationalization and denial of significance, some displacement of affect, but no projection except perhaps to the child. Reality experience was being flooded with depressive anxiety and condensation capture of conscious self representation; reality experience of failure was beginning to occur. Further history revealed longstanding family, employment, and marital problems, all resulting from and leading to chronic conflicts over assertion and aggression. Crippling and frustrating moral scruple against assertion and aggression was organized in a masochistic way with castration and abandonment fears. Longstanding psychic conflict played out into the environment and created repetitive, complex day residues from employment and the family. Both summated in the patient's part-time work in the family-owned business.

This, then, was a patient with a neurotically organized ego who was being overwhelmed with a depressive episode approaching, but not yet, psychotic. The depressive illness was erupting through character defenses. Antidepressant medication was begun, resulting in a decrease in flooding intensity of depressive anxiety. The patient was seen four times a week sitting up in an active, exploratory psychotherapy.

After 2 weeks, the patient felt ready to move to the couch, and psychoanalysis and medication were conjointly used. The depression rapidly eased over the next 2 months. By 6 months, the patient refused further medication saying she no longer required it. Dynamic issues quickly evolved and deepened in the psychoanalysts in the context of a benevolent transference interrupted periodically by paranoid depressive anxieties that were immediately interpreted before they were either of intolerable intensity or began to capture reality experience of the therapist. Intense depressive affect was seen to have primary process content that both made clear and was made clear by the day residue triggers. These triggers, past and present, became more and more clear. This permitted a shift to secondary processing of those day residues and several bursts of ego growth and life change. Psychoanalysis became more and more classical as the intensity of the affective illness eased and the repression barrier assumed its usual functioning. The psychogenetics had preoedipal loss issues, but these were reorganized at the oedipal competition level where guilt, fear, and loss were the main issues.

Psychotherapy of Psychosis 243

In summary, in almost all cases, the couch is not used nowadays in the psychoanalytic treatment of very ill patients. I support this. There are, however, some patients who not only can use the couch, but require it. I have listed some criteria and have shown a case example to help the analytic therapist understand who those patients are (see also Waelder, 1924; Federn, 1934; Namnum, 1968; Bellak and Meyers, 1979).

Chapter 8

Psychoanalytic Psychotherapy and Psychoanalysis of Near Psychosis

Introduction

Near psychotic structure involves a specific alteration of reality testing (see Chapter 3). I divide near psychosis into two categories: those who are near psychotic in ideas and attitudes only, and those who are also near psychotic in behavior. Illness etiology of near psychosis varies from formes frustes of schizophrenia, manic-depressive illness, organic brain syndromes, severe trauma, severe character pathology and its various subtypes, and combinations of these etiologies.

Because of this variation of illness phenomena, the literature on psychoanalytic psychotherapy technique with near psychotic patients varies a great deal as to relevant psychodynamics, tactics of intervention, and types of treatment. The psychodynamic issues range from a focus on narcissism, aggression, and splitting defenses (Kernberg, 1975), to a focus on separation anxiety (Adler, 1983), to a focus on infantile abandonment/depression (Masterson, 1972). The tactics range from consistent confrontation (Kernberg, 1975), to empathic support (Adler, 1983), to limit setting (Masterson, 1972), to supportive psychoanalytic treatment (Kohut, 1971), to so-called unmodified (neo)classical psychoanalysis (Porder, Abend, and Willick, 1983) (for a review of dynamics, see Gunderson [1984]; Frosch [1990]; Gabbard [2014]).

I have used each approach at various times, to varying degrees, with different patients. This is because with different etiologies, the intensity of a given dynamic system and the exact arrangement of ego problems varies.

But if there are commonalities of structure (see Chapter 3), then there ought to be some commonalities of ego treatment. A summary of psychoanalytic psychotherapy with this broad group would be as follows:

1 Empathize with near psychotic thing presentation qualities of perceptual affect in the near psychotic idea or behavior.
2 Separate observing ego from the near psychotic condensation.

Psychotherapy of Near Psychosis 245

3 Make near psychotic condensations fully conscious: contents and affects, especially of object relations, especially of real self or real object.
4 Make reality-testing processes fully operative by confrontation of near psychotic condensations with the patient's secondary processes and memory.
5 Demonstrate how these contents and affects have condensed with and influenced behavior, attitudes, and conscious ideas.
6 Deal with behavior early: feeling versus impulse versus action of near psychotic condensation.
7 Deal early with negative transference, reality experience–altering defenses, and dissociations.
8 Deal with here and now before ontogenesis, especially with behavior.
9 Look for, recover, and describe complexities of affect revealed in associations, behavior and attitude, especially as manifested by transference and countertransference.
10 Look for day residue event and help reassemble sequence and context. Integrate day residue, object relations content, and affect themes, showing the relationship among all three that expresses itself in near psychotic attitudes, behaviors, and relevant dissociations.

Because many autonomous functions are intact, the analytic treatment of such patients can proceed provided the analytic therapist understands that, in the focal area of near psychosis, the patient will soon, if uncovering proceeds, appear to be delusional. However, if reality testing is intact, and as the material is uncovered and as the therapist makes active attempts to help the patient separate real object from object representation or real self from self representation, or real self affect from real object affect, the analysis can often progress quite well. There is a momentary affect explosiveness as the condensed material is entered and a momentary inability to integrate at the point of the dissociation. The most primitive character defenses are now often engaged. This has several dangers. One is that the therapist will be captured by an intense affect fantasy in a pseudodelusional transference. This always begins to happen. Active interpretive efforts are necessary at that point to forestall a breach of the therapeutic alliance or, worse, the treatment alliance itself. However, one can usually remain in the technically neutral position because there are significant areas of reality testing, observing, and integrating ego available. If forced out of technical neutrality temporarily, it is usually into clarification and affirmation of reality, usually the reality of therapist affect in his professional role. Clarification, along with engaging intact secondary process, is usually swiftly efficacious and permits the movement back into technical neutrality. It is combined with immediate analysis of what happened and the underlying fears and wishes that caused the capture.

The other danger is that mobilized affect will trigger an affective episode in those patients so predisposed due to an underlying mood disorder, especially unstable, rapid cycling manic-depressive illness. Again, quick, interpretive intervention about the fact, organization, and content of such experiences is crucial to treatment. Medication mood stabilizers, usually, are also crucial.

Descriptive work can be most rewarding, as it often leads back to the psychogenetic past. This may go a long way toward disassembling these affect-triggering vulnerabilities and toward integrating ego function. Medication is often necessary, especially during crisis points of the early and midphase of treatment. One can anticipate and preemptively treat those crises because of the predictability of their day residues and content dynamics due to the stereotypy of their structure.

A premonitory sign of difficulty in analysis is the rigidity of defense. There are some patients in whom the rigidity is so great, the affect contained in the pseudodelusion or behavior is so intense, and the pressure to capture the therapist so relentless that the therapist decides, either after a trial of directly analyzing the material or, through empathic intuition alone, to avoid the matter. This is much like stepping around a fixed delusion. Just because it is a pseudodelusion does not mean that one can always take it head on, directly and early. Almost always one can, but not in every case. If the material must be stepped around, the same rules apply as in psychosis. The dynamics are explored in areas other than the pseudodelusion in more neurotically integrated and repressed character derivatives. After months to years of working through this material, the pseudodelusional area, including the transference manifestations and mechanisms, can often be reapproached. Medication often is very helpful at this point. Again, it is not the content or structure of the pseudodelusional states that decides this indirect approach, but rather the intensity and rigidity. Remember that rigidity is the best measure of severity of illness and of prognosis. Extremely rigid defensive structures, whether psychotic, near psychotic, borderline, or neurotic, should be considered serious, and great care should be taken by the therapist to diagnose the reasons for that rigidity. Many patients with subtle affective illness have very rigid defenses because they are attempting to defend against overwhelming intensities of affect that are easily evoked. The question then arises whether a trial of medication might help make those defenses more pliable (see Chapter 6). It is worth such a trial. In some cases, the results are so beneficial that an impossibly stalemated treatment is converted into an evolving and ameliorative analytic process.

Although the experience of treating near psychotic patients is intense and the sense of danger is never far, the sense of accomplishment at helping them is large, and the relief the patient experiences is gratifying.

Psychotherapy of Near Psychosis 247

I will now elaborate this summary in a detailed description of ego functions and the implications for technique.

Near Psychotic Patients

Near psychotic patients are those whose near psychotic condensation does not emerge mainly in behavior. Their affect–behavioral boundary is good. They tend to have higher-level ego function in general than the behavioral type. Many have ego function organized along neurotic lines, with only one breach through neurotic defenses of an intense, near psychotic area of concern that condenses with and captures an area of reality experience in the preconscious. The result is a near psychotic idea or relationship. The same can be true of near psychotic attitudes, although those tend to express themselves more broadly throughout the ego and in behavior, classifying the patient, usually, as borderline. The context of near psychotic ideas is, however, often a condensation of attitude defense. The level of pathology within that defense varies from case to case and from time to time. Treatment of the attitude may precipitate a near psychotic transference. The near psychotic potential of the transference can be seen in other intense relationships the patient has or has had.

Boundaries In–Out

The in–out boundary is, in my view, intact. There are no conscious fusion experiences, except in some near psychotic severe disorganized learning disability or other organic brain syndrome patients, and then not as a consequence of their near psychotic condensations. The reason it seems as though the in–out boundary is damaged universally in near psychotic patients is twofold. First, there is the capture of reality experience—the real object or the real self—by emotional experience. Then, in behavioral borderlines, the resultant condensation is acted out into behavior which then has an effect on the object in reality or the self in reality. The treatment for the behavior problem is covered later in this chapter. The point for now is that this is a condensation acted out into reality, rather than a fusion state of stimuli from reality entering, unmodified, into the self experience.

The treatment for the near psychotic capture of reality experience by emotional experience is to make that capture conscious. The transference is often an especially useful vehicle, because the therapist has knowledge of the fact of condensation, the reality event coinciding with that merger, the affect display by the patient, and the therapist's own affect. Therefore, the therapist has information about all the elements of the near psychotic condensation, at least as it is focused at that moment. This gives

248 Psychotherapy of Near Psychosis

the therapist the ability to engage, describe, interpret, challenge, refute, and empathize accurately. This informational accuracy will help the therapist to help the patient make the near psychotic condensation fully conscious and then analyze its elements. Where one begins depends on what aspect touches the transference with what degree of available intensity yet potential flexibility. Technique also depends on which defense mechanism is used to condense reality experience with emotional experience.

Defenses

There are many different defenses possible, including projective identification, denial, affect storm, and rigid dissociations. The classic ones are projective identification and denial.

The treatment of projective identification involves making the condensation clear, especially in the transference. The therapist says, in one way or another, that the patient acts as if the therapist has an attitude toward the patient. Actually, the patient's attitude toward the therapist comes from the patient's feelings about himself or herself (see Chapter 3). The correct labeling of the attitude in the patient, pointing out the concomitant feared attitude in the therapist, the primary process organization of the content of the attitude, and the affect expressed and defended against in the attitude: all are used to challenge observing ego and reality testing. Sometimes it is necessary or simpler to use refutation. It is crucial to pick up the projective identification and its attitude-determined condensation of content when it happens, to note with the patient what seemed to have triggered it, and to locate the relevant affect states properly in the self representation, the real self, the object representation, and the real object. The actual mechanism involved, projection onto the real object or the real self, must be part of the descriptive interpretation.

Likewise, denial, when it occurs in treatment, can be focused on for the dissociation it is. One can point out to the patient what he or she said or did, that he or she did mean it, that it has meaning, and it has meaning even in the present. This bridges dissociative denial of fact, of meaning, of time, and of validity. A general statement of the use of this defense by the patient can also be made. The affects and object relations scenarios thus defended against on each side of the dissociative denial must be part of the interpretive work. The relevant psychogenetics of content and of defense organization can then often be recovered.

Defense resistances to the interpretation of the defenses are crucial and often, fortunately, involve the same defense mechanisms. Therefore, the two often coincide in the transference, making this an opportune interpretive time.

The main difference from neurotic patients in near psychotic defense mechanisms is the near perceptual veracity of conviction and the resultant intensity of near psychotic reality experience captures. Again, the transference helps because the countertransference is known and, if discordant to the patient's experience or accusation, can help the therapist with therapeutic conviction which can help with therapeutic courage. The tricky thing is when the countertransference is concordant (Racker, 1968). Then one must remember that behavior or attitude in the patient provoked this concordant countertransference (Kernberg, 1976b). One can then describe the evolution and evocation of this experience. One can point to the sequence beginning with patient projection, affirmed in patient attitude or behavior, which then provoked the therapist's feeling or behavior.

Because defenses usually operate in the preconscious, they are usually part of the near psychotic condensation. This means that defenses will be "primitive," i.e., capture reality experience in the preconscious. They often will also be basic character defenses. These are the problems of, and opportunities for, defense analysis in near psychosis.

Projective identification, denial, and dissociations are all readily available as part of the near psychotic symptom, the resistances, and the transference. They come quickly and often. This gives the opportunity to interpret methodically, consistently, and from a variety of therapeutic and empathic contexts.

As defenses are interpreted, near psychotic transference clears, observing ego increases, near psychotic condensation emerges into consciousness and decondenses, reality testing strengthens, and a complex affect experience emerges, which can then be integrated as dissociative defenses are interpreted. The psychogenetics, often all too apparent but without influence except for justification of the near psychotic content, can now be more truly, realistically, and usefully integrated with present-day affect evokers and symptoms.

The irony is that in just some of the illnesses where classical defense analysis is seen as difficult or impossible, it is so helpful. But the therapist must understand the peculiar nature of these defenses consequent to their involvement with near psychotic structure—their near perceptual quality and seeming capture of real object or real self experiences. The stormy defensive transference eruptions, if faced head-on with consistency and bravery by both patient and therapist, can ease into a dramatic therapeutic progress.

Crucial to the analysis of defense in these states, therefore, is an understanding of the near psychotic experience and the near psychotic ego structure. This understanding will guide necessary adaptations of technique toward ego deficits and "primitive" ego experiences. This is crucial if the classical defense analysis goal is to be achieved. Too much silence, ignoring of structural problems, or failure to attend to observing ego, or reality testing, or integrative processes can result not in a therapeutic process but in disaster. Such disaster often manifests itself as a transference explosion and/or a serious suicide attempt.

250 Psychotherapy of Near Psychosis

Medication is also helpful in easing the rigidity, intensity, and chaotic manifestations of near psychotic defenses (see Chapter 6).

Preconscious, Conscious Primary Process, Secondary Process

Analysis is greatly aided by the subtle intrusion of primary process into the near psychotic story line as a consequence of the preconscious location of the near psychotic condensation. This makes martialing and use of secondary process obvious and effective. It is especially effective when the day residue sequence and context are known or deducible. The primary processing of near psychotic symbolic alterations of day residues then stands out clearly. Its depressive significance is often obvious.

Affect Boundaries and Modulation

Because of the intensity, stereotypy, overlap, and rigidity of affect responses that drown or mix affect with affect, considerable attention must be given to describing affect states in words. Affect recognition by the analyst can accomplish many goals. It addresses the translation problem, the veracity problem, the chaos problem, the action problem, the dissociation problem, and the contamination of the real object or the real self. All of these structural problems due to intense affect boundary crossings must be described when appropriate. Doing so has the potential of greatly strengthening the ego functions of containment, control, and verbal–conceptual expression of affect. Observing ego and reality testing both dramatically improve when affect control improves and the real object or real self is freed from affect-determined near psychotic condensations. Medication may be crucial to treatment of modulation problems (see Chapter 6).

Reality Testing

Reality testing is suspended but potentially present in the pseudodelusional area of the near psychotic idea, in the behavioral enactment of the borderline, or in both in patients with mixed features. Most patients do have mixed features.

Consequent to the structural fact that reality testing contents are condensed in the near psychotic symbolic alteration of reality, but reality testing processes are not, is the technical recommendation of confronting reality testing in the pseudodelusional or behavioral areas that betray the near psychotic condensation (Kernberg, 1977). Consistent reality testing confrontation can aid in the decondensing of the near psychotic symbol.

The key to the technique, as with all psychotherapeutic technique, is clinical judgment about when, where, with what degree of neutrality, and with what degree of affect. Remember that *confrontation* is a technical term meaning to engage the patient's attention to and interest in the issues. It does not necessarily imply countertransference aggression.

The interplay between reality testing confrontation and exploration of psychodynamics is mutually reinforcing. As reality testing is challenged, more of the near psychotic story emerges to buttress the near psychotic argument, only to reveal primary processing which helps the therapist reinforce reality testing and other secondary processes. Reality testing, which was flooded preconsciously by the intense demands of the near psychotic condensation, can now function once again independently.

Example:

PATIENT: "And then I heard music, somber funeral music, as if someone bad left the tape recorder playing."

THERAPIST: "That must have felt very spooky."

PATIENT: "It was! Do you think my wife could have purposely done that?"

THERAPIST: "It must have been very distressing to think so."

PATIENT: "Yes! (tears) To think she hates me so; to torture me like this!"

THERAPIST: "Did you look for the recorder?"

PATIENT: "I didn't."

THERAPIST: "How come?"

PATIENT: "I was afraid I wouldn't find it."

THERAPIST: "And then?"

PATIENT: "And then either I'd be crazy or. . ."

THERAPIST: "Or your wife is a witch!"

PATIENT: (laughs) "She is a witch!"

THERAPIST: "Her anger stops at nothing! She's capable of anything!"

PATIENT: "Oh, she is a mean woman; and very angry with me."

    One can also explore the percept condensation:

THERAPIST: "What comes to you about funeral music?"

PATIENT: "Like a funeral dirge; slow, low."

THERAPIST: "Somber, foreboding, sad."

PATIENT: (tears) "Yes, as if I were dying. I feel that way!"

THERAPIST: "Your feelings for her may be dying. You may feel that her feelings for you are dying; the relationship is dying. To you, this may feel like you are dying" (preconscious capture of real self experience).

Notice the progressive affect decondensation into emotional experience and expressed in words as the exploratory interchange progresses. Affects of fear, sadness, and despair are moving out of the near perceptual, otherworldly experience into words and into the direct experience of complex affect. In addition, this example indicates the avoidance of reality testing that near psychotic patients characteristically demonstrate. The patient would rather worry that it was true that his wife has supernatural powers or purposely hid the tape recorder to play music to torture him than face his feelings about his wife: that he feels she's a witch in the emotional sense. As treatment progresses, he learns he is afraid to face this because of the implications he feels it would have for the relationship, for his ability to maintain any relationship, and for his self-worth.

The use of the word *witch* by the therapist is an attempt to summarize the affect content using a primary process concept "witch," an affect-rich symbol. The therapist uses an object representation to clarify the real object. Sometimes this primary process approach will work, if accurate or close to accurate, when secondary process is blocked (Glover, 1931).

The psychogenetics in this patient involved intense attachment ambivalences, traumatic attachments and abandonments, and depressive superego reactions to loss and aggression. In repetition compulsion, it did seem as though he had married an angry woman whom he then provoked.

Observing Ego

Observing ego may be free or flooded. In near psychosis, it tends to be flooded and guarded by character defenses. Stubborn negation, haughty grandiosity, and intense rage are all common character attitudes used as defense against observing ego. These must be descriptively interpreted.

Observing ego is the aspect of ego function that recognizes the illness state of the patient and the helper state of the therapist. This recognition should hold in spite of patient apprehensions about helpers. Observing ego absence usually makes itself known immediately in attitude or in the way the patient treats the near psychotic condensation phenomena. It is also usually immediately apparent in behavior and attitude toward the patient's own illness and the helper. When observing ego is missing, the patient's total experience of the illness and of the helper is captured preconsciously by his or her fears or wishes. The psychotherapeutic approach to observing ego in near psychosis is to confront it together with reality testing, at the same time trying to make near psychotic condensations conscious. This approach is taken because observing ego and reality testing are part of the near psychotic condensation.

Integrative Capacity

The major integrative scheme in near psychosis is primary process in the preconscious. This is aided by dissociative processes in the preconscious and conscious. The major treatment strategy is to fully elicit the preconscious primary process near psychotic story with its affect, so that integration can shift into secondary process channels of concept which only operate in conscious ego function, and into conscious affect experience linked to and validating those conscious concepts. The techniques for doing this are observations of associational verbal, behavioral, attitude, and affect material, when spontaneous or in response to open-ended inquiries. The patient can be invited to associate when associations do not occur spontaneously or when they are too tangential.

Defenses that interfere with this process are interpreted, just as in neurotic cases. In near psychotic cases, those defenses tend to be intense and almost to capture reality experience, especially in the transference. But they must be interpreted nonetheless.

Early, consistent attention to integration is a prerequisite for a useful, unfolding psychotherapy. It is as much a requirement as increasing observing ego and increasing reality testing. Integrative capacity must increase concomitantly with near psychotic decondensation, or an immediate defense interpretive investigation of the reasons for failure to integrate must ensue. Do defenses need interpreting? Is affect too strong? Are there undiagnosed cognitive problems, especially of abstraction and generalization?

Relationship of Reality Experience to Emotional Experience

In shifting the near psychotic ego integration strategy toward secondary process, one alters the near psychotic relationship of reality experience to emotional experience where primary process dominates. Because the organization of the relationship is primary processed and because the location is in the preconscious, the infiltration into reality experience of emotional experience has an almost real, uncanny quality that triggers conscious anxiety even as it triggers conscious, partial conviction.

It is this anxiety and partial conviction that can be empathically engaged with such benefit. The technique is to get the patient's conscious, secondary process reality to do the engaging by labeling and empathizing with both sides of the conflict, both the anxiety and the partial conviction.

Questions like "What do you make of it? or "So what do you think of that?" or "Does that logically follow?" can begin the dialogue between conscious, secondary process and preconscious, near psychotic condensations.

Patients often respond by saying, "It may not make sense, but . . ." and then repeating the near psychotic concern. The therapist then says, "But you just said that it doesn't make sense." The patient agrees, says, "Yes, but," and begins to reveal the elaborate details of his or her near psychotic condensation which cause his or her near psychotic conviction.

"And what do you think about that?" says the therapist, to which the patient often responds, "It doesn't make logical sense." The therapist can then say, "But you feel it so strongly. This takes priority." The patient responds, "Right!"

"That's too bad," says the therapist, sympathetically, "because although it feels satisfying to let those feelings dominate, that very domination causes you anxiety because part of you still realizes the illogic, and hence the danger to you and the injustice to the other. And your feelings remain unresolved." This points out the dissociation of the price paid for the near psychotic symptom from the symptom itself. This technique alternates with open-ended questions which help open up new material. "What comes to you about that?"

The alternating psychotherapy pattern of uncovering and integrating has its own special rhythm with each patient. Following the patient's needs in this regard involves the mastery of technique in timing, accuracy, and empathy that experience teaches. This therapeutic skill is a crucial aspect of the "analytic instrument" in work with very ill psychiatric patients.

Dissociation

The vertical dissociations are usually apparent in near psychotic states. They are so apparent because near psychotic states involve eruptions of primary process content and affect that are not integrated with other areas of conscious mental functioning. Pointing to these different areas can begin the process of integration by engaging autonomous ego and also by interpreting mediating defenses and that which is defended against in the dissociation. Although analytic uncovering of latent condensations and bringing them fully to consciousness may result in easy integration, many near psychotic patients need considerable help in working through this integration process. This is because translation of exposed or uncovered primary process material into an understanding of its secondary process derivatives is an ego capacity. This translation capacity may be blocked by character defenses and will improve when those defenses are interpreted. But it is also a cognitive function which people have to varying degrees. The diagnosis of innate capacity in this area is crucial to treatment. Cognitive incapacity shows up on a mental status examination, with careful observation of the patient's spontaneous generalizing and abstracting abilities, or in neuropsychological testing. Observing a patient's abstracting and generalizing abilities can greatly aid the therapist in understanding how active to be at points of the treatment process when these ego functions are especially required. If a cognitive disability in this area is present, it can be identified and spoken about directly. Teaching higher cognitive functions to be brought to bear at these points can be extremely helpful. These ego functions may improve with practice. What we are

Psychotherapy of Near Psychosis 255

talking about essentially is a subtle type of learning disability which is more common than has been recognized in the near psychotic patient. These cognitive disabilities can be one of the mechanisms mediating the vertical dissociation. The other is when defense mechanisms block ego functions or when the ego functions are used for defense.

The summary of technical recommendations for treatment of the dissociations in these states follows:

1   Through observation and free association, evoke the full latent story with the hidden real object and object representation condensations or the hidden real self and the self representation condensations on each side of the dissociation.
2   Elicit the day residue in the present.
3   Elicit day residues of past genetic experiences that are thematically stirred by present-day residues and dissociated.
4   Integrate all vertical dissociations when fully conscious.
5   Integrate horizontally with the repressed affect as that affect becomes conscious.
6   Consistently interpret defenses that mediate dissociations.

The matter is simpler when the major dissociation is of affect valence, as in splitting. The matter is somewhat more complicated when the dissociations involve mixtures and layers of affect, as in higher-level near psychotic patients.

Day Residue

The reality of the day residue in near psychosis is usually heavily primary processed. Therefore, it is very helpful when the therapist observes the day residue, e.g., by incidentally walking into the ward common room at just the right moment when two hospitalized patients get into an argument or when the day residue is a therapist action or inaction. The symbolic alteration of reality in the transference and the sequence are clear to the therapist, who can, with conviction and accuracy, interpretively describe this to the patient.

Fortunately, most near psychotic patients soon enact in the transference. For those high-level near psychotic patients who do not, progress toward unraveling the day residue must await partial decondensation of the near psychotic symbol and therefore report of the day residue by the patient. The therapist must be alert to its emergence. Secondary process by the therapist must be brought to bear, if even only silently, so as to make a hypothesis that might allow technically neutral interventions designed to mobilize the patient's secondary processing and conscious reality experience of the day residue.

256 Psychotherapy of Near Psychosis

What happened can then be separated by the patient from the reaction to what happened. Then one can get to why the particular patient reaction occurred, and to why this type of reaction constantly occurs.

Thing Presentation and Thing Presentation Quality

Near psychotic thing presentations emerge with conscious thing presentation qualities. Ideas, behavior, or both have the conviction of perceptual quality, validity, and veracity. Such patients almost actually "see" their affect content (see Chapter 3; Frenkel-Brunswik, 1974). Therapeutic empathy with this perceptual quality is crucial. Help the patient have empathy with this quality yet maintain his or her observing ego about it. Only if the thing presentation quality is viewed as its own affect justification, but not logical justification, will there be a chance that it will no longer so intensely be both fought for, dissociated from, and partially repressed to protect it from conscious secondary process reality function. Empathy about this aspect of near psychosis is, therefore, crucial. The techniques used can be technically neutral by merely descriptively pointing out the quality, the significance of the quality for the patient, the use the patient makes of the quality, and the conscious fear of this quality. This usually allows a more complete emergence into consciousness of the preconscious thing presentation content. Once fully conscious, it tends to disappear, sometimes quite abruptly.

Example:

An army captain is being driven in a jeep, part of a convoy of vehicles in a motorized infantry division. The line stretches for miles and travels relentlessly through heat and dust for hours. Gradually, he becomes aware of funeral music playing over the armed forces radio band. Panic ensues as he realizes that music doesn't play over the armed forces radio band, only weather reports and encoded troop movements. Furthermore, he doesn't remember turning the radio on. Before turning himself in to the division psychiatrist as "crazy," he decides to check and see if the radio is on or off. He puts his fingers on the dial and finds that the radio is off. The music instantly disappears as reality testing reasserts itself with the reality feedback of finding that the radio is off.

Empathy with both the reality quality conviction and the secondary process anxiety reassures patients that full elaboration in consciousness will neither prove their worst fears literally true, nor prove their emotional experience invalid (see "witch" example from earlier in this chapter). The army captain, of course, was afraid of being killed. As the story unfolded, because he eventually did talk to the psychiatrist, there was good reason for him to fear this. There was also good reason for him to want to deny and partially repress that fear. It was a fear of being killed by his own troops.

Thing presentation's emergence into consciousness at a junction point of ego dysfunction when, for a moment, the near psychotic structure is in view, but undiluted by secondary process, is a therapeutic moment of great excitement and satisfaction for therapists who like working with very ill psychiatric patients. The dexterity required to "carry water on both shoulders," to maintain both primary and secondary process tracks until they meet at the transference or the day residue, is a gratifying act of mastery. The relief of the patient seconds later is so great and the progress solidified so helpful, the risks involved seem suddenly worthwhile to both patient and therapist.

Agencies

Dynamic conflict of the agencies id, ego, and superego is organized and experienced as part of intense object relations condensations by the near psychotic patient. Psychoanalyzing into agency elements without recognition in early treatment phases of their object relations experiences with their thing presentation qualities and without addressing ego problems of reality testing, observing ego, and dissociations is experienced by the patient as irrelevant, inaccurate, or reductionistic. This is because thing presentation conviction quality is not attached to the abstract elements of the conflict. It is not even attached to the affect elements. Elements of agency are not in concept form and are not even fully in affect form, especially in the preconscious near psychotic condensations. If they are, then one is dealing with much higher-level ego organizations, not near psychotic or borderline as I and other hospital psychiatrists define it.

But agency conflict is at issue. Especially relevant are superego introjects and condensations with attacks against real self experience. Likewise, ego ideal condensations with the real self exist in narcissistic or hypomanic conditions.

As these object relations and thing presentation experiences become conscious and decondense, the agency conflict elements are seen more clearly. They are more linked to affect veracity and are then more describable in concepts and word presentations and can be analyzed with classical technique.

Psychoanalytic Psychotherapy of Near Psychosis: Behavioral Borderline Type

The treatment of the behavioral borderline near psychotic is exactly the same as the treatment of the pseudodelusional type, but with one prior step and one complication. The prior step is to convert behavior into a report of the pseudodelusional idea and attitude which was in the premise for the action taken. The pseudodelusional explanation, which is preconscious, contains the reality condensations with fantasy that are latent in the behavioral actions. The complication is that behavioral defense structures may be based on splitting mechanisms which separate positively valenced from negatively valenced self and object relations. This separation may not be limited to a focal area of pseudodelusional content. These defenses are across the board in those patients that I define as borderline. These are very ill patients who do not function well in the world, who have never functioned well, and who always end up for shorter or longer periods of time in the hospital because their behavior is so impulse-ridden.

Affect splitting is a defensive organization that maintains condensations of reality with fantasy in multiple vertical dissociations of affect states that defend against integrated reality and feelings about that reality. The unintegrated affect state is then projected onto reality experience. This is the mechanism of multiple projective identifications and involves the projection of loving, positively valenced affect just as it does aggression. Aggression is usually spoken about more in the technical literature because it is deemed etiologic by some (Kernberg, 1975; Klein, 1975; Bion, 1984). Splitting defends against reality percept and integration of percept. Without splitting, reality percept would confront the affective day residue experience of the patient.

Splitting defenses may also be contributed to by an integrative defect in the ego that is not based only on affect integration. These difficulties in cognitive integration show up in the mental status examination, neuropsychological tests, and cognitive histories of such patients. Sometimes, these ego defects exist as developmental delays due to the intensity of affect in unstable affective illness. Thus, a concerted diagnostic attempt must be made to diagnose the cause of the splitting and find whether there are defects of autonomous cognitive functioning, as in covert minimal brain damage, unstable affective illness, or mild schizophrenic fragmentation of cognition. Another common etiology for affect splitting is extreme traumas of upbringing that have made integrative character structure impossible due to intense traumatic affect states. Combinations of these possibilities are not rare.

The technique for eliciting ideational content of behavioral material in borderline patients is as follows:

1 Observe behavior and understand that it is the enactment of fantasy material. It is, therefore, a type of free association (Kernberg, 1975).

Psychotherapy of Near Psychosis 259

2 Some limit setting, particularly with more out-of-control patients and those who are hospitalized, must be taken in order to provide motivation and attention to the word processing channels (Masterson, 1972; Kernberg, 1975).

3 The day residue instigating event must be observed and identified with the patient. Observation of behavioral sequence and context, together with a basic knowledge of human motivation, will enable hypotheses about the instigating day residues if not observed. Separating these day residue experiences from the ensuing emotional storms will clarify the mechanisms and contents of symbolic transformations that are expressed by behavior.

4 Careful observation of interactions in the transference will verify hypothesized reality triggers and the mental capture mechanisms.

5 Loose associations and free associations are both used by the therapist in the therapeutic setting to uncover the fantasy underpinnings of behavior.

This method will quickly yield the elaborated fantasy, which includes the object relations and the condensations with reality that mediate disordered behavior in the present. It is material that is the beginning of reconstructive work with these patients.

Example:

A young, suicidal, borderline, female patient is voluntarily admitted to a psychiatric unit. She arrives on the unit, and as soon as the locked door closes she turns over a chair and yells, "You better let me out of here! I'm not crazy! If you don't let me out of here I'll tear up the place! I'm not crazy!"

Psychiatric aide: "If you don't want us to think you are crazy, why are you acting crazy?"

The patient calms down and is able to talk about her fears of being mistreated on the unit. She then presents a list of demands if she is to stay. It seems as though her fear of being mistreated is her fear of not getting her own way.

The immediate day residue for the affect storm in this case was hospital admission. Her behavior was an angry temper tantrum. The implied effect on the real object seemed to be intimidation. The intervention was a confrontation of the paradoxical dissociation of content between her words and her behavior. Although her stated fear seemed to be domination and control by real objects, her latent wish seemed to be to domineer

260   Psychotherapy of Near Psychosis

and control those objects. The mechanism was projective identification acted out in behavior onto objects in reality.

If this behavior is not confronted immediately, this patient will stay, but with a whole list of demands, from passes to visitors to diet to television shows. If she does not get her way, a suicide threat or gesture may ensue. This is one reason hospital units have come to the idea that these patients should be medicated and quickly discharged. This is too bad, since it overlooks an opportune time to diagnose and interpret what goes on outside the hospital anyway. (On hospital treatment, see Kernberg [1976b, Chapter 6]; Marcus [1981, 1987a,b]; Chapter 6 of this volume).

Sometimes one gets past genetic day residue precipitants rather than present ones. These past evokers are thematically related, superficially, to present-day residues and will give the therapist strong clues about what has happened in the present. Particularly if it is transference material, the therapist ought to have access to information about those events. The therapeutic focus must be placed on the present and the full rush of affect and elaborated fantasy material will ensue. This is because there is displacement back and forth through time of affect and object relations. One can then go back to the past evocators and delineate the more unconscious aspects of affect experience there that are truly encased, displaced, and triggering present-day pathology. It is difficult to get at those deeper layers of the past directly through the genetic material because of (1) the rigidity with which those layers are defended against, (2) the rigidity with which they defend against complex affect in the present, (3) the conscious use of the fact of the past to defend against full emotional significance of both the past and present, and (4) the displacement of some of their past complex affect to present-day evocators. Major aspects of past validity and veracity are therefore in the present. The use of the present to defend against the past is true for all patients. The use of the past to defend against the present is true of sicker patients. One ego reason for this phenomenon is that more complex layers of psychological material, involving triangular situations and reality complexities, require higher-level ego function to articulate and mediate. These ego functions are damaged in very ill patients.

Splitting Mechanisms

The treatment recommendation for affect-splitting mechanisms (Kernberg, 1975; Klein, 1975) is not to permit the maintenance of what is essentially a vertical dissociation. Efforts must be made to help the patient experience objects and self as not separated by affect states and as continuous over time. This is particularly true in the transference. Simply pointing to the discrepancy from the vantage points of technical neutrality will often suffice.

Psychotherapy of Near Psychosis   261

The point is that technical neutrality has to concern itself with ego dysfunction when that dysfunction is compelling. It does not violate technical neutrality to focus on one agency or another. Analysts have considered themselves technically neutral for years while focusing on repressed drive or conscious material in the neurotic. Why not focus on the ego when necessary? Crucial to the ego focus necessary for the treatment of splitting is to describe both sides of the conflict and to engage the patient in a discussion that might prove synthetic.

An example is the borderline patient who tells the therapist that he is wonderful in response to some administrative action concerning the patient taken by the therapist in the hospital. After the provoking day residue is pointed out, the therapist may wish to point out that the patient said that he was terrible and thought he was mean only a moment before when she thought the request would be refused. The patient will usually respond with a simple denial. The therapist may wish to respond with a confrontation of that denial. The patient may then respond with a recognition that indeed she did say a moment before that she hated the therapist and did curse at him but didn't mean it. The therapist may wish to point out that the patient said it and appeared to mean it at the time. The patient may then respond that although she did say it, and she did mean it, that was before and now is now. The therapist may wish to point out that the therapist has been the same all along. It was, in fact, the patient who felt differently about the therapist and all because the patient was not getting what she wanted at the moment. This is the repetitive experience of treating borderline, infantile patients.

The experience of yesterday as yesterday but today as today points to the lack of integrated continuity over time that borderline patients experience partly because of the extremes of their affect states. It is difficult for the beginning therapist to realize that integrated states of positive and negative valence are more painful to the patient than the rage attacks that they experience. This is because the very angry patient who has been traumatized in life by inconsistent objects and/or by his or her own inconsistent affective stability, worries that the experience of the integrated object will only be more bad than good (Kernberg, 1975; Klein, 1975): this can cycle into a despair that is truly dangerous in patients with associated affective illness and poor impulse controls. It is the reason that the integrative interpretation of such patients is sometimes a hospital procedure.

The handling of behavior is the most vexing aspect of treating borderline patients (Masterson, 1972). It is important to realize that some limit setting must be done. In the hospital, the limit setting must be early, consistent, and directed at all out-of-control behavior. In outpatient treatment, the limit setting focuses particularly on the transference. Very often, in healthier borderline outpatients, engagement of the issue of dissociation of behavior from other differently valenced and split-off affect behaviors is enough to bring behavior in the transference under control. At other times, the therapist must move out of technical neutrality and into the ego function of behavioral control through the technical intervention of limit setting.

It is important to realize that being silent or passive in the face of extremely disordered behavior, especially in the transference, is not a maintenance of technical neutrality (Zeligs, 1960; Calogeras, 1967). This is because the condensation between reality and the fantasy in the ego continues unabated in the face of silence on the part of the therapist. The technical neutrality of treatment has been violated by the ego condensation which does not allow any technically neutral space between the fantasy object world and the reality object world at that point. Therefore, there can be no midway between ego, superego, id, and reality because ego boundary has failed in relationship to affect reality relationships.

Limit setting, whether achieved by verbal engagement of the conflict or by overt limit setting commands on the part of the ward staff or the therapist, should be loose enough to let the patient get involved with the therapeutic environment, but tight enough to contain dangerous behavior and to engage word presentation channels. The milieu must be relaxed enough to let behavior, within limits, proceed along a path of unfolding psychological life, especially as the uncovering of the psychological life may only be possible with some behavioral manifestations.

The difficulties of doing this are many. One must recognize the illness-relevant behaviors. One must then hypothesize the near psychotic content. One must also hypothesize the complex affect. The affect will be expressed poorly in the impulse discharge of the behavioral action. This is not only because behavior is ambiguous, but also because deeper layers of complex, integrated affect are prevented by the immediate behavioral discharge of one side of the conflict. At first, the other side of the intense affect and the complex integrations of affect will appear in the therapist's experience long before they appear in the patient's experience. It permits the next step of interpretation to take place in which a tactful way is found, in the patient's own experience and language, to talk about what is essentially a countertransference-based hypothesis (see Racker, 1968; Kernberg, 1976b, Chapter 6). One must be especially careful not to impose one's own countertransference-based hypotheses on patients but, rather, to listen carefully for associations and to observe behavior carefully and to invite associations about that behavior so that countertransference hypotheses, which have focused the therapist's inner attention, can be validated or invalidated by the patients themselves.

One important warning: if analysis of content proceeds without analysis of behavioral dysfunction and before repair of the ego boundary between affect, fantasy, and action, then deeper layers of repressed material will emerge and, if affectively charged, erupt immediately into behavior. The patient and the therapist will be worse off!

Psychotherapy of Near Psychosis   263

It is important to focus immediately on behavior not only because that is where the relevant dynamics are, but also because it is where the true resistances to the treatment lie with their basic character defenses (cf. Reich, 1925; Sterba, 1953; Boesky, 1983). In the borderline patients, there is no resistance to transference, but there is great resistance to the treatment alliance. The situation is different in the neurotic, where there is often a treatment alliance but great resistance to the transference. It must be understood, however, that, for the borderline patient, transference does not mean fantasy, but behavior and attempted satisfaction in the real world. There is an overwhelming distinction between real object and object representation based on intense object representations. The same is true of self representation, real self, and self in reality, especially for depressed, borderline patients. Although the behavior is with the real object as manifested by the object in reality, or the real self as manifested by the self in reality, the motivation for this behavior is a condensation between reality and fantasy in the preconscious. This is why one must move in quickly to identify content when affect erupts in the transference and the transference threatens to become actualized. Identifying the relevant day residue, the particular wish to change the day residue, and the stubborn, unyielding, mediating defenses is helpful.

It is important to realize the extent of behavior and its approach to the psychotic boundary. The best example of this is the anorexic who will starve himself or herself to death, all the time proclaiming he or she is too fat. Some of these patients are actually psychotic, but often they are not. If they are not psychotic, they do respond to engagement of the denial of factual reality. Although with tears and anger, it will emerge that they consciously do know they are too skinny. At that point, they say they feel too fat and they will go with the feeling rather than their secondary process view. This is of great help in advancing the analysis of their psychological state.

This example is true of all borderline behavior because of the following:

1   The ego deficit is between mental experience and behavior.
2   The ego boundary problem between reality experience and emotional experience permits condensations of reality and fantasy in the preconscious.
3   Character defenses make the emotion more important than the fact.
4   Thing presentation quality of reality contaminates perception with affect rather than linking affect with the conceptual mental life of ideas.

Because of all this, there is a push toward enactment; action process becomes caught up with and part of affect content. The therapist must describe the elements of this enactment: the relationship of elements to each other and to the attempt at integrating, but also defending against the underlying conflicts. It is important to realize that the conflict takes two different forms in this kind of behavioral pathology. The first is the dissociation of parts of the conflict into different behaviors, or one side in the behavior, and the other side in a partly repressed fantasy. The second way the conflict is expressed is in the stereotyped repetition of the behavioral paradigm which moves back and forth from the expression of the intense negative side to the expression of the intense positive side. The intense negative and positive aspects form the superficial level of a conflicted story that never progresses. It is a "lock" that is expressed in behavior, just as, in neurotic patients, the "lock" is expressed in their symptom. In psychotic patients, the "lock" is the delusion. In all three levels of ego organization, growth in real life is blocked at these specific points.

Borderline patients have an action style that is an extreme example of milder forms of behavioral ego styles. A variety of patients have this behavioral style, including some normal people who are not involved in extremes of behavior or neurotic "locks" in their life. Some people need to experience their behavior in order to experience their feelings and thoughts. All people need to work out their psychology of motivation within the reality of their lives. The question is not only the degree of integration or of sublimation, but the degree of progress and growth. A better name for this kind of healthy action might be acting through rather that acting out. A focus on behavior with the goal of analyzing blocks to the progressive acting through conflicts into growth is a potential technique that can be very helpful in that minority of borderline patients where the action style is fixed.

The last recommendation on technique that is usually made by theoreticians in the field has to do with negative transference. The recommendations fall into two groups. There are those who say deal immediately with negative transference, even and especially if it is latent (Kernberg, 1975). Others say to avoid the negative transference at all costs (Adler, 1983). Again, the quarrel has to do with different groups of borderline patients. If one takes neither approach but waits to see which approach is forced by the patient's psychopathology, almost always in sicker, hospitalized, borderline patients, the negative transference is brought to bear immediately in an open attack on the therapist, directly as a person, indirectly as a physician, or more indirectly as a member of the hospital unit. Alternatively, the patient may idealize the therapist or the treatment in exaggerated descriptions and expectations. It is important to interpret these idealizations. With interpretation, there is a flip into the oppositely valenced aspect of the conflict. It is important to keep interpreting; otherwise, you will always be stuck in one half of the conflict and will have made no integrative progress. Once you have gone back and forth a few times, the fact of the oscillation can be described and the relationship of the two sides can be analyzed with the patient. Therefore, even positive transference should be analyzed early in the borderline patient when it is part of the dissociation of conflict.

Because the therapist is often the focus of intense transference fantasy and behavior, the treatment of these patients is very difficult. The reason is that latent transference is in the preconscious, is primary processed, and is separated from conscious secondary processes. The open affect–behavioral boundary means that this material is often enacted. Interceptive interpretations are therefore often required to prevent dangerous behavior. One must translate, with instant speed and timing, the presentations of behavior into words describing the patient's affect and integrative conflicts.

Rigid Character Neurosis with Near Psychotic States

When near psychosis is comorbid with rigid, neurotic character disorders, there is opportunity and leverage for change. This is because intercurrent near psychotic illness causes a different degree of repression and integration than is usual in the rigidly fixed neurotic character. As a result, the psychology of character may be clearer and experienced with greater veracity by the patient. Therefore, insight is potentially rapid. The understanding of neurotic character can be used by the observing ego in understanding the near delusion, but the near delusion can also be used by the observing ego in understanding character conflicts (on the treatment of rigid character disorders, see Shapiro [1981]; Schafer [1991]; Winnicott [1991]).

In analyzing the relationship between character and psychosis or near psychosis, one observes the recapitulation of theme in the psychotic or near psychotic material and also in reality, behavior, fantasy, the past and the present, and character derivatives. Psychotic and near psychotic decompensation provides an opportunity for character analysis. It is not an opportunity to be sought, but it is an opportunity to be used if decompensation occurs. In rigid character, the dynamic material and its themes are more apparent during psychotic or near psychotic decompensation. Character defenses are often increasingly plastic during such times. Further, thing presentation quality is suddenly available as affect veracity linked to the psychodynamics of character conflicts and themes. This is because the breakdown of ego function results in less rigid repression.

In severely ill patients, drive material must not be interpreted before ego dysfunction is engaged and on the way to being repaired. Behavior will grow increasingly disruptive and near delusional material will spread if this rule is violated. But the potential, if character analysis and analysis of psychotic and near psychotic material are carried out in tandem, is for rapid and mutative change in both. Points of character resistances in mediating defenses that maintain vertical dissociations are particularly accessible points. These mediating defenses not only protect the vertical dissociations and observing ego, but often protect the delusion or pseudodelusion from a reality engagement. Reality is the most powerful antidote to fantasy. These character defenses manifest themselves as resistance to treatment because the treatment will focus on the real self and the real object. We thus have a phenomenon that overlaps the defenses against reality, integration, and treatment and coincides with basic, organizing content, themes, and processes of character. The phenomenon is expressed in numerous nodal points of condensation and overlap. It is at these points that character treatment can be unlocked. It requires quick identification of the nodal points and analytic unraveling of dynamic psychological life. It requires experience, patience, and time.

The benefit to be hoped for is twofold. First, analysis of character defenses along with psychosis and near psychosis can lead to a more rapid amelioration of both than supportive treatment can alone, if attention is paid to integrating vertical dissociations, liberating observing ego, and separating reality from fantasy. The second great benefit is the hope that the reality triggers will be incapacitated by unraveling the psychological resonance between character and psychotic or near psychotic theme both in the present and in the genetic past. The hope is that one will then have a patient less vulnerable to near psychotic recurrences. And lastly, it can unlock a rigid, stalemated, or neurotic character organization with a resultant surge in growth and in life gratification.

A simple way the character dynamics of repeated hospitalization express themselves is in patients who continually stop prophylactic medication for their psychotic or near psychotic illness. Many patients stop their medication not because they are delusional about the medication, and not because of side effects, which are numerous and often unpleasant, but because of psychological reasons that express their most basic character defenses. This is another way in which analysis of selected character defenses and of character functioning more broadly can prevent recurrent hospitalizations.

A word, before closing this section, about rigid character problems in the absence of psychosis or near psychosis. These patients often seem to be purely neurotic, but, because of the rigidity of their defenses, they do not change either with or without treatment. Some of them are so rigid that they do not really form accessible transference that can be analyzed. It is important, before giving up on such patients, to realize that the rigidity of their defenses characterizes them in the very ill group.

A differential diagnosis must be done. Sometimes the greatest areas of rigidity have the structure of near psychotic phenomena. In fact, some of them are quickly discovered to be suffering from this organization. There are, however, other points in the differential diagnosis of rigid character structures. There is the rigidity of defense against psychosis or near psychosis, either as acute decompensation or as in a chronic delusional or near delusional introject. The other is rigidity of defense against ego deficits. An example is the adult attention deficit disorder patient with rigid, obsessional, paranoid, or narcissistic defenses. A further example is rigid defenses against intensity of affect. Examples are chronic, mild, hypomanic patients and chronic depressives.

The point that I wish to stress, however, is that with rigid, neurotic characters with a failing psychoanalytic treatment, it is important to diagnose the cause and look especially for covert ego problems. Do a careful, symptomatic review looking for formes frustes of known psychiatric illnesses. A trial of medication may be indicated and most helpful.

The rigidity, however, may be a higher-level, superego-infused guilt over change and progress at a purely neurotic level (see Coen, 1988). This guilt must be engaged early and consistently if treatment is to move forward.

In all rigid characters who are locked out of life growth and treatment possibilities, there are certain nodal points in real life that provide opportunity for change. New socialization experiences, present-day traumas, physical illnesses, life disappointments, and life opportunities are all examples of stresses that challenge character organization. At such times, therapy which has been previously unfruitful can be very helpful and change a potential life crisis leading to worse and more entrenched character pathology into a life crisis leading to character change and positive ego growth.

A shift in psychoanalytic technique to take into account the ego problems of rigidity is also helpful. The techniques involve labeling, confrontation, and manifest warmth and concern with interpretations about anxieties that this then evokes. The technique of psychoanalyzing rigid character defenses is a combination of patience, confrontation, elaboration of latent attitude, and exploration of dynamic affect expressed in attitude. At times, one can only deal with the psychodynamics in less rigidly fixed derivatives. When to do what varies with the patient and with time, that is, with the variations in the rigidity. Careful observation is necessary to see which technique or sequence of techniques is most helpful. Interpretations that liberate affect may make defenses more rigid, even though affect exploration is necessary to ease rigid defenses. Therefore, in technique, how much and when is as important as how. Each patient has his or her own ego pattern of attitude defenses and his or her own affect tolerance limits within those defenses. The rigidity of the pattern, however, has one advantage: the pattern is rigidly fixed and the therapist can therefore come to know this pattern. One can find the tolerable and useful sequence, type, and degree of intervention that usually helps the patient. The key is a flexible, trial-and-error attitude in the therapist, so that the type and dose of intervention can be discovered.

Use of the Couch in Near Psychosis

The use of the couch in pseudodelusional near psychotics does not depend on the near psychotic condensation but on the intensity and rigidity of character defenses and whether that intensity and rigidity are directed into the transference or whether they need to be. It also depends on whether the dynamics are available in reports of interactions outside the transference. If the transference is a necessary vehicle, and if the couch is helpful in bringing the dynamic transference life to clarity, it should be used. Some near psychotic patients find relief from transference intensity on the couch, where without the observing gaze of the therapist, transference intensity actually decreases. This is especially true where the transference affect is shame.

Other pseudodelusional patients find their projective identifications increase to unmanageable intensity on the couch. Often, the therapist can see this in the first consultation and properly avoids a couch analysis (cf. Greenspan and Cullander, 1973).

Some seem to need the couch and then cannot handle it. It is helpful if the analyst is alert to the possibility of near psychotic transference intensities and condensations projected onto the therapist so that immediate interventions can be made (see Kernberg, 1976b; also Little, 1981). Alertness to countertransference is crucial. Flexibility, tolerance, patience, tact, sensitive empathy, insistence, and timing are all required. An ability to articulate object relations and affect content scenarios at the affective level of abstraction is also important. With these technical suggestions, many near psychotic patients do well in couch analysis (see Reich, 1933b; Fenichel, 1941; Giovacchini, 1975; Kernberg, 1991).

The worst problem is with near psychotics who are the behavioral borderline type. Their affect–behavior condensations and lack of control make a couch psychoanalysis often impossible or counterproductive. It usually encourages too much passivity in the therapist and too much intensity in the patient. Many of them have instant, intense transference and constant free associations, so the couch is superfluous anyway. The treatment can, however, proceed through early and early midphases to a point in the middle phase where the couch is helpful. On the other hand, patients often do well at this point, coming to treatment three or four times a week in the sitting-up format, so that a therapist may properly hesitate to change a beneficial treatment situation (on psychoanalytic psychotherapy with such patients, see Langs [1973]; Kernberg [1975]; Kernberg, Selzer, Koenigsberg, Carr, and Appelbaum [1989]; Searles [1986]; D. Shapiro [1989]).

In my opinion, these are the relevant issues in the sometimes-heated debate about psychotherapy versus psychoanalysis, sitting up or lying down. It is at this ego level of conceptualization and at the specific ego function level of specific patients that the discussion is most productively engaged.

Chapter 9

Hospital Treatment

Introduction

Hospital treatments are for the sickest patients, those who cannot exist outside without danger to themselves or others. Self-care is disorganized, fragmented, unmotivated, or attacked, depending on the illness and its specific effects on ego functions. The need for hospitalization therefore reflects failures of ego function.

The hospital takes care of the patient by providing for the physical needs of existence—shelter, warmth, food, hygiene, and the sleep/wake cycle. It goes further by organizing the delivery of these functions in a scheduled pattern that is regular, predictable, clear, unvarying in its routine: temporal, geographic, and personal. These predictable environmental factors place an external ego splint on the damaged ego functions of patients who need this organized and predictable environmental structure to help organize their ego functions for organizing mental experience and tasks of daily living (see Cumming and Cumming, 1963).

These aspects of external ego splinting are present de facto as part of the necessity of organizing and routinizing care for any group of people. We can use this by making sure we regularize the hospital environments. But we can also tailor the milieu for specific individuals with specific illnesses and specific patterns of ego dysfunction.

The organization of this specificity requires careful observations of ego dysfunctions, a staff trained to intervene in them, a stability of such staff over time so they gain the needed training and experience, and a daily routine of rounding where patients can be discussed and the treatment plan adjusted. Many psychiatric hospital units already have rounds on a daily basis, but mostly for the purpose of medication adjustment and the correlation of medicine therapeutics with changes in the mental status exam. The mental status exam in such pharmacological rounds usually focuses primarily on behavior signs. A more sophisticated approach also focuses on ego functions and emotions that mediate illness experiences and behaviors. The ego-centered psychodynamic rounds provide a venue to focus on the pertinent psychodynamics involved in the patient's illness, ego dysfunctions, life distress, and their longstanding patterns of emotional maladaptation.

Such rounds should involve all staff who have contact with the patients: doctors, nurses, mental health aids, rehabilitation specialists, recreational therapists, and even housekeeping and orderlies. This is because all staff have important observations to make about patients; their reality and emotional functioning on the unit. Because no individual, but the staff as a whole, is there for 24 hours, the complete observation of the patient may emerge from the group and not from any single individual. This will capture important variations over the 24-hour cycle, such as diurnal variation, emotional splitting of staff, effect of medication, sleep/wake cycles, and even delayed effect of interpretations aimed at the patient's ego dysfunctions and psychodynamics.

Doing rounds in this more comprehensive way makes rounds longer, but makes the hospitalization vastly more effective. Specific, descriptive interpretations of ego dysfunction can emerge from staff observations and can then be given to the patient by all staff. If hospitalization's goal is to make a definitive intervention that changes the course of the patient's illness, this approach is useful. Even if the goal of hospitalization is a short one, meant to stabilize only the worst aspects of ego dysfunction that caused the patient's admission to the hospital, such rounds are still crucial because they reveal the specific ego dysfunctions and the effect of medication and verbal interventions on the ego dysfunction and thereby point the way towards a more effective outpatient treatment.

The problems of achieving a sophisticated hospital milieu as just described are not the problems of a lack of knowledge. They are the problems of lack of dedicated financing and of societal socio-economic failures of devotion to the care of very ill psychiatric patients.

Organic Brain Syndromes

A regular, predictable, and highly organized milieu can be successful remarkably quickly for patients with organic brain syndrome ego dysfunction. Organic mental syndromes disorganize mental contents, disrupt the in–out and therefore the me–not me boundary, may fluidly effect the reality testing function, may confuse and disorganize the observing ego function, and shift ego synthetic data and processes away from reality experience and towards emotional and sensory experience. The hospital milieu's precisely demarcated spatial and sequential divisions and their boundaries are space and time organizations. The physical organization of rooms with walls and doors set the spatial environment boundaries which reinforce the in–out and me–not me boundary.

A similar function of organization is played by the scheduled time sequences of hospital routine. The organization of time is another type of sequence organization. Categorical thinking is greatly aided by the order and sequence precision of these reality parameters.

Clear staff identities and demarcations in role function help organize the me–not me because the physical environment has its reflection in the mental representation inside the patient's mind. It is an old observation that very psychotic patients when moved to the medical or surgical intensive care unit reorganize in a nonpsychotic way when they are in that highly regulated and structured environment. Ego function is reinforced by differentiated staff uniforms, staff name tags, and social role title use in addressing patients and staff. Trained staff notice self–other and other–other confusion in the patient and correct it immediately.

The structured and controlled environment is also helpful in reinforcing the ego function of stimulus modulation. The stimulus environment may appear chaotic and frightening to the patient with an organic brain syndrome who does not have an established self–not self-boundary. This boundary normally functions together with a modulation capacity that screens and regulates the intensity of incoming stimuli. For extremely disorganized patients, removal to a quiet room which is stimulus poor can immediately help organize them.

The stimulus modulation function problem is reflected in the affect modulation problem that such patients often show. Emotions are internal stimuli and their modulation and appropriate social expression are ego functions. The hospital can be quickly effective there too when trained staff help the patient observe their poor emotional modulation and encourage them to make an extra and focused effort at self-control. Anxiety goes down when boundary function, stimulus modulation, and affect control are re-established or reinforced because the feeling of being disorganized and out of control is very frightening. In organic brain syndromes, affect is easily triggered and intensely recruited, therefore the proper, psychiatric unit is not only highly organized but affectively modulated and calm. Staff speak quietly and calmly and try never to be provoked into emotional display. This is because it will trigger emotional overreaction in emotionally sensitive and modulation-challenged patients.

Because of poor in–out boundaries, and because of poor stimulus modulation and affect intensity control functions, primary process emotional thinking intrudes on the experience of reality organizing processes. Resulting primary process mechanisms of condensation may be primary experiences of emotional intensity or secondary attempts at emotionally organizing stimulus fusions. They can be observed by the trained staff and articulated in words as a description of what staff observes when patients are in this mental state.

Describing the patient's mental states will aid patients in separating their reality experience from their emotional experience, others from themselves, their emotions from their logic, and their feelings from their behavior. These are the ego boundary functions that mediate inner experiences and the ego functions that allow one to organize and navigate through the day's events and tasks of daily living.

When staff are observing and describing these issues to patients, it reinforces the patient's observing ego capacity, which is a helpful step in the patients gaining more organized control of their ego functions and inner experiences. The observation comes first and most easily through the patient's observation of the clarity of the physical environment and the others in the environment. It is this which the hospital milieu and staff do so well.

With observing ego more stabilized, and with boundary function returning, an attempt is made to help the patient with reality testing. When the entire staff understands the reality testing problem, they can help with any psychotic condensations.

> ### Example:
>
> A paranoid patient hears his "private business" being discussed by voices in the streets outside the hospital. A nurse comments: "You are important, Mr. Jones but you're not that important!" Mr. Jones smiles.

Because the in–out boundary is disrupted, because emotional experience and reality experience are fusing, and because the boundaries between concept, affect, and percept are disrupted as emotion invades not only conscious logic but also sensory experience, patients with organic brain syndromes often have intense, hallucinatory thing presentation experiences and nocturnal dreams that seem real. Again, trained staff on an inpatient unit can help the patient set boundaries and untangle this information so that reality processing and emotional processing—percept, concept, and affect—are once again separate tracks. Medication rapidly helps with these boundaries, and lowers stimulus intensity, which helps the patients' observing ego understand what their mind is doing. Expressing emotions and sensory information in words can also quickly help the patient reestablish reality-organized, conscious mental function. Together with medication, a more complete result is achieved.

It is helpful if the staff understands the acute terror that such patients are in as they experience chaos in their conscious mental experience. Depending on previous personality organization, some patients experience this

274 Hospital Treatment

state with great paranoid rage and attempt to establish their ego boundaries by attacking the environment. Such patients do need restraint, medication, stimulus-poor quiet rooms, but also one-to-one nursing care so that their language processing can be used and strengthened in the verbal interchange between them and the staff member, and so that their paranoid fears can be calmed. Helping a patient put his or her emotions into words helps with concept formation, affect modulation, self-observation, self–other discrimination, and social appropriateness. Some are paranoid only, but not agitated. Their silence and a hyper vigilant stare may be the only markers of their experience. Great caution should be exercised with these patients because the inhibited aggression is tenuous and may be triggered at any moment and unexpectedly. They need to have clear, calm, concerned, articulate staff explain to them what is going on and ask what their fears may be.

Mania

Acute mania is frightening to observe. It can present with extreme disorganization looking like a revved up organic brain syndrome. Some organic brain syndromes do have a hypomanic associated state. The treatment of acute manic states, therefore, often involve the differential diagnosis possibility of an organic etiology.

Similar ego dysfunctions may involve the boundary between in and out, the boundary between emotional experience and reality experience, and the boundary between affect and behavior. The conscious distinction between self and other physically is usually maintained, although the distinction between self and other affect states is usually absent. Here, staff intervention if consistent and targeted can be extremely helpful in pointing out that the affect (and not the staff) is what the patient feels.

The affect localization problem is severe in mania because the affect is intense and involves all aspects of object relations. Self, object, material reality, and the ego ideal in superego structures of self may all be involved in the affect leaks and contaminations of a severe mood state. The mood state may be euphoric, irritable/angry, euphoric/sad, or mixtures. All the staff intervening with the patient help the patient localize the affect state to their own minds, and help them disentangle their emotional reactions from the causality of reality objects in the present.

Staff may say "You are angry, Mr. Jones, but I haven't done anything that should make you angry." Or, "You seem to be responding to me angrily, Mr. Jones, as if I'm angry at you. I am not angry at you. You are angry at me but I don't know why." Or if the patient is euphoric, the conversation may go like this, "You seem very happy, Mr. Jones, but your hospitalization is a serious matter and we are all very serious about helping you."

The most severe forms of mania, called Stage 4 mania, involve hallucinations and delusions. These psychotic phenomena are hallmarks of a State 4 mania. They mark a severity of mania that is associated with a suicide rate as well as death from sleeplessness and inanition. Hospitalization is mandatory. The grandiosity, anger, impulsiveness, and psychosis make the patients a danger to themselves and to others.

The hospital milieu can be helpful when staff inform the patient that they don't see what the patient sees, they don't hear what the patient hears, and that what they do see and hear is that the patient is very illogical, filled with emotion and irritability and that behavior based on these emotions goes against everyday logic. This gets at the manic's personal sense of grandiosity when he or she tries to validate his or her experience as based on the special or higher powers that he or she discovered or feels has been granted, seemingly in reality. Repeated discussions then involve why the patient needs to be so special and why he or she can't wait on line with the rest of us!

Depression

Severe depression carries with it a suicide rate and also tremendous suffering. In the severe forms, the patient may be delusional, hallucinatory, and intensely suicidal.

Hospitalization is mandatory in these severe depressive states. The patient may not be eating, not sleeping, in a state of hopelessness and despair, or, if delusional, the patient may feel worthless, or fear attack on his or her life. Command hallucinations may tell the patient to kill himself or herself.

Hospitalization provides an environment of safety, especially when staffing is adequate to provide one-to-one suicide observation help for the period of time when needed. The determined and despairingly suicidal patient needs careful watching 24/7. "Contracting for safety" in which the patient agrees to tell a staff member if his or her suicidal impulses become impossible to control, are paradoxical agreements because the patient who can make such an agreement doesn't need it and the patient who can't make such an agreement will disobey it. Therefore, such contracts only give staff a false sense of security and may end disastrously.

If the patient is hallucinating or delusional, staff may function in the same way as with organic brain syndromes or mania to disconfirm the phenomena, to understand its dynamic content and psychological meaning, and to validate the patient's reality experience, not the hallucinatory experience.

The hallucinations and delusions can be a rich source of psychological information about the patient because the content and organization reflect the emotional experience of the severe, depressive state. In the

276 Hospital Treatment

hallucination and delusion are the emotional problems that are bothering the patient. Often, the inciting event is incorporated. Therefore, both the inciting event and the emotional reaction to it can be understood by the staff and discussed with the patient.

The pathognomonic feature of psychotic depressive symptoms is the attack on the self as bad, evil, a failure, inferior, worthless. The suffering of the depression is seen as deserved and there is often the covert wish that the suffering will expiate their moral failure or sin. This depressive content attacks the self representation with intense, aggressive intent. This aggression and its guilt-ridden motivation and justification form the substance of the psychological discussions that are required to help patients gain observing ego and better reality testing about their psychological issues. Insight into those psychological issues can, together with biological interventions, help patients recover from the depression, understand some of what got them to that state, and help prevent the next depression.

In both mania and depression, continuity of care is crucial. It is helpful if a longer hospitalization can be maintained so that the recovery is more apparent and consolidated before the patient's discharge. There then must be a coordinated handoff to the outpatient psychiatrist and to the milieu to which the patient is returning. Any precipitants that were active in the patient's milieu must be dealt with before the patient is discharged. It is an old observation that if there is an inciting event, and if that inciting event is still active in the patient's milieu, medication is much less effective.

Personality Disorders

Personality disorders are common in hospitalized patients because their severity may make the patient's behavior dangerous to himself or herself or others, or their behavior may have triggered a potential life-altering environmental reaction. They are often also implicated in an acute or subacute mood episode.

Patients with personality disorders, also called character disorders, are in the hospital because their behavior has resulted in a reality response that has exploded part of their real-life situation (see Marcus, E. R., 1981; Marcus, and Bradley, 1987). Their resulting psychological collapse, perhaps triggered or complicated by a severe depression, has rendered them either suicidal or temporarily incapable of conducting some major aspect of their normal life. It is therefore, broadly speaking, ego dysfunction which has landed them in the hospital. The attacks on ego functioning are either due to the mood disorders, or to their character defense structures now under stress.

One way of understanding character disorders is to understand that such patients have a rigid, preformed inner conscious and unconscious attitude that organizes and scripts their experience of interpersonal relationships and unconscious object relations. This script has a theme or group of related themes that turn real people and real human interactions into actors in the patient's emotional object relations dramas.

The more severe the character disorder, the more the script imposes itself on their experience of interpersonal interactions, on their anticipations of reactions, and on their behavior that induces the reactions. When they are severely decompensated, enactments are predominating.

It is this observation about enactments that gives the psychodynamic hospital unit its power. In the 24-hour custodial environment, the staff is instantly incorporated by the patient into the drama of his or her inner world. Diagnosis of the script and its effect on behavior and therefore on the reactions of the human environment to the patient, are all played out within the hospital milieu. The daily rounds setting allows each of the staff members, who may have a different piece of the drama, to report on interactions with the patient so that the story may be understood. Then, the staff may focus on pointing out to the patient the presence of this drama, how the patient enacts it, and how the patient then triggers responses that are detrimental to the patient. The patient can thus be helped to realize that the reality interaction they thought was other initiated was in fact responsive to their initiation.

The staff can in this way not only identify the drama but also the underlying ego dysfunction. Particular attention is paid to the enactments and the suspension of observing ego of the enactment and its sequencing. Attention is also paid to the faulty affect–behavioral boundary, the conscious unconscious boundary, the affect modulation boundary, and the affect stimulus self–other boundary.

The types of personality disorders that end up in the hospital are limited in number. Perhaps the narcissistic personality disorder, often with a concurrent mood disorder, is the most frequent. Because their narcissistic grandiosity may have collapsed, the diagnosis may be overlooked at first. It could however be diagnosed even at that time by the grandiosity of the collapse experience. But soon after admission, the patient usually tries to re-inflate the grandiose structure by attempts to be treated specially, and dividing the staff into the worthy and the contemptible depending on whether or not they gratify the specialness. The manipulations surrounding this division and its orchestration, and the vulnerability to rage, tears, or suicidality when this scenario is not gratified is typical. This gives the staff the opportunity to diagnose the specialness drama and begin to talk to the patient about how this attitude makes him or her vulnerable because it depends on reinforcement from reality and is easily

278 Hospital Treatment

damaged by failures of reality to pay attention to this need. This may get to the grandiose self and its function to repair damage to self-esteem that comes from longstanding emotional trauma and its internalization into self-esteem systems. There is often an underlying continuous denigration. When the environment fails to confirm the grandiose specialness and need for attention and confirmation, the patient may feel rage at the real object or despair about the real self or both. If it is despair, especially if despair is the result of a real-life support collapse due to the patient's rage or entitlement, a depression may be triggered in those vulnerable to depression. All this can emerge in the clarifications and discussions staff have with the patient as they point out the behavior and attitudes underlying the behavior.

The severely masochistic–sadistic patient comes in two varieties. The more sadistic is by far the more dangerous because the enactments are so aggressive and ultimately so alienating to others, hence, self-destructive to the patient. Suicide is a real threat, particularly when complicated by depression and when the aggression abruptly turns back on the patient.

Their typical behavior is easily identified in its self-righteous, angry infliction of emotional punishment on the staff for infractions both slight and imaginary. Limit setting and feedback about the dynamic is crucial. The attempt is to always place the behavioral enactments back into the mind of the patient. The defenses against enlightenment are rage, righteous justification, particularly of the patient's view of staff actions and the punishment that the patient then inflicts.

The masochistic patient experiences the staff as causing them suffering. They also experience this in a self-righteous and punishing way and also blame the staff for infractions both slight and imaginary. But they punish themselves, not the staff. They respond to interpretations with sadness, denial, and anger, but with less overt, uncontrollable rage than the sadistic patient. Because their tolerance for suffering is greater, they are less likely to become abruptly suicidal.

In both the more sadistic and the more masochistic patient, the beginning understanding of how he or she plays out his or her inner script and how this determines, through induction, the suffering he or she complains about, is the crucial turning point in the treatment of these illnesses. This can be done so much more effectively in the hospital where staff is trained to recognize and to provide constant and consistent feedback with empathy for the suffering.

A common character disorder seen in the hospital is the infantile, histrionic, or so-called borderline personality disorder. They also usually end up in the hospital because of concurrent depression or manic-depression, with a concomitant erosion in ego functions and perhaps a suicide gesture. These patients are characterized by dramatic displays of anger, splitting of staff into good and bad groups, and extensive, manipulative behavior between the two groups, all in the service of equating their wants with needs. Need gratification of the moment is their motivator and organizer.

Staff setting limits on their behavior and interpreting the want/need equation fallacy is the power of the hospital environment. When effectively done, those patients with depression will momentarily get more depressed. The way out can be pointed to when the patient comes to understand through staff help that their way of experiencing the world is setting up their disappointment, which triggers their depression. The turning point comes when they realize that they do have the power to control their behavior and their emotions and to think through what behavior might be more effective for them and that their wants are not vital needs.

The key to doing this kind of work with all character types is the ability of the staff to observe, contain, and respond in an empathic, calm and thoughtful way. The ability to do this depends on the ability to absorb, digest, and thoughtfully re-deliver in words the patient's inner world, especially their aggression. The trick is to be able to do this without contaminating the self experience of the staff.

It is very helpful to have a setting in which staff can share observations and responses. Daily rounds is a setting where the group may consolidate through sharing so that they can voice, empathize, and help each other with the inevitable countertransference of treating very ill patients with severe character disorders.

Psychotic Transference and Countertransference

Psychotic transference often announces itself soon after its condensation. The patient talks about it because it is conscious and involves reality experience. The psychotic condensation influences all of the patient's reactions to the therapist and the patient feels these reactions are justified by reality. Whether it is erotomania or paranoid hatred and fear, the content is irrelevant to the fact of the psychotic transference's capture of the reality aspects of the therapist and of the treatment. Sometimes the more frightened paranoid patient may not talk about psychotic transference and the therapist must pick up the early clues in behavioral traces and avoidances or suggestive references. Therefore, therapists of very ill psychiatric patients are attuned to any personal reference to the therapist, overt or covert.

Psychotic transference has certain characteristics. It may be abrupt in onset with few prodromal signs. It may be intense. It is usually distressing to the patient. It may be expressed, at least partially, in action.

Psychotic transference is organized by the characteristic ego problems of the patient's illness. Schizophrenic transference is fragmented even in its emotional content. Manic-depressive transference is intense. The

280 Hospital Treatment

transference in organic mental syndromes is confused as to time, place, and sequence, and may merge real self and real object. All of these illness transferences are usually heavily primary processed.

Often the first inkling of psychotic transference is in the therapist's countertransference feelings about the patient. Fear or anxiety, strong rescue fantasies; conscious confusion; frightening, intense, or bizarre countertransference fantasies; and intense countertransference dreams all are countertransference warnings of intense, possibly psychotic transference. Because psychotic transference captures reality experience, countertransference with psychotic patients feels unsettling because certainty about reality experience may blur in the analyst who may then feel "crazy."

There are also specific transference and countertransference issues related to the elements of psychotic structure. The first is the in–out boundary. When a patient incorporates the therapist's thoughts and words into his or her own, confusion about who is who may ensue. The signal of conscious confusion is therefore an important marker for the therapist. Once recognized, it can be traced back to its source in the patient, the structural abnormality of in–out boundary disturbance can be diagnosed, and the illness etiology differentially diagnosed. When confusion appears overwhelmingly in the countertransference or transference, look to see if a major in–out boundary is missing in the patient (see the example in Chapter 7 about the psychiatry board examination).

When the boundary between reality experience and emotional experience is lost in the patient, the countertransference is more likely to be uncanny feelings rather than confusion. Uncanny feelings relate to anxiety about the real and the unreal. This can occur in countertransference feelings when a patient speaks of emotional experience as reality experience in such a logical manner that there is a delay in the therapist's realization. The first marker may be the uncanny countertransference feeling. It gets better when the therapist recognizes the uncanny feeling, realizes it has to do with reality experience/emotional experience blurring, and remembers that the blurring is a problem in the patient. It isn't the therapist's job to straighten this out, but to diagnose it and help the patient straighten it out. Exploration will diagnose the reality testing, observing ego, and structural boundaries involved in reality experience/emotional experience mergers of psychosis and will calm the countertransference because the therapist will recognize the patient as instigator. The specific structural diagnosis will help the therapist with a therapeutic treatment plan, further calming the countertransference.

Losses of reality testing tend to provoke delusional transference and the same countertransference as boundary loss between emotional experience and reality experience. The two structural abnormalities are involved together in all psychotic condensations. Dysfunctional countertransferences to loss of reality testing may take many forms. Either the therapist doesn't quickly see the negative reality testing, causing countertransference denial or confusion; or suspects it but isn't sure, causing countertransference uncanny feelings; or is sure but too relentless in confronting it, causing countertransference certainty, which is one form of countertransference aggression that Freud called *terror therapeuticus.*

The boundary between object relations in psychotic patients arouses strong countertransference when such boundary losses involve the therapist as a real object, causing delusional patient comments or behavior aimed at the therapist. When the content of such delusional projective identifications is aggression, the evoked countertransference is hostile, frightened, or both. Therapists should remember that fight or flight responses to aggression are normal. Such countertransference is a normal indicator of delusional aggression and is a useful motivator to treatment planning which may need a quick rethinking.

When the delusional content is idealizing or romantic/erotic, the countertransference danger is that of unconscious emotional seduction and tolerating such transference because it is emotionally gratifying. Tolerating delusional or hallucinatory transference is always dangerous, regardless of content, because it overlooks the loss of reality testing and the danger of enactment. Such delusional systems are rarely stable. Such delusional transference tends to stalemate treatment because the patient is seeking delusional gratification of transference, not ego building work. The same issues are involved in hallucinations with transference content.

Hallucinations and delusions are usually separate ego experiences, dissociated from any nonpsychotic ego. For some psychotic patients, the gap between rational and psychotic ego areas is especially wide. A common countertransference reaction to these dissociations is to treat the patient as sane because he partly is, but to forget he is partly insane and that the sane part is not in control of the insane part. Such therapists are constantly surprised by the strange, even dangerous enactments of such patients. Alternatively, a therapist may be overwhelmed with recognition of the psychotic ego and give up psychotherapy, forgetting that there is some intact, healthy ego also. It is that healthy ego island which must be located, therapeutically allied, and used in dealing with the psychotic part of the ego. The opposite countertransference reaction may be evoked when the therapist tries to heal the dissociation through relentless confrontation of the psychotic material without being able, through medication, to increase reality testing and to decrease psychotic condensation processes. The treatment becomes a harangue and the patient ends up feeling bad, a failure, and controlled. Patients may then either attack or quit or remain stalemated.

Near Psychotic Transference and Countertransference

The boundary problems, especially between the condensation and the rest of personality functioning, are the hallmark of near psychotic states. Aspects of the near psychotic condensation are conscious and the associated ego dysfunctions of blurred reality testing, projective identification, the capturing of observing ego experience, and the pressure to enactment across the affect–behavioral boundary all seriously strain the therapeutic relationship.

In the more usual form of near psychotic state, the etiology is related at least in part to affect illness. Therefore, intensity of affect and affect–mood dysregulations are the major features in the boundary crossings. Affect boundary crossings crucially effect the boundaries between object relations experiences. The characteristic but most therapeutically disconcerting affect boundary crossing is to the real object or the real self, from either the object representation or the self representation (see Chapter 3, Table 3.5). When the real object is involved, patient behavior usually indicates it through enactment on the part of the patient against the therapist in reality. The usual enactment is a reaction to a projective identification, first in patient behavior and then in the therapist counterbehavior. Each may discover their behavior only by knowing the reaction in the other.

Cycles of enactment that are only partly conscious can lead to stalemated treatments or to crises in treatments. However, they can also be diagnostic and used to great therapeutic gain. Dynamic content, specific near psychotic structure, specific boundary problems, and specific day residue triggers with affect contents and organizations can all be seen in these enactments. The problems in making use of them are the problems of intense, only partially conscious countertransference reactions. The key to their use, therefore, is the conscious recognition of countertransference and the tolerance of the associated, intense countertransference affects and fantasies. Racker (1968) first defined, and Kernberg (1976a) has most extensively described and elaborated, these characteristic near psychotic transferences and countertransferences. Because of their importance and ubiquity, again, it could be said that the treatment of near psychotic states is first the treatment of the countertransference.

Because intensity of affect is a particular trigger and accelerator of dynamic content, analysts of near psychotic patients quickly learn to avoid intense or provocative behaviors and statements. Therapeutic tone is calm, soothing, and reasonable (Adler, 1983). This is because once the patient's emotional intensity increases to the point where recruitment of object relations begins, primary process elaborations, projective identifications, and resulting condensations with the real object therapist start to occur. Boundaries between object relations, between levels of consciousness, between primary process and secondary process, and between

Hospital Treatment   283

emotion and behavior all start to blur. This freezes psychoanalytic and psychotherapeutic work and may trigger a mood episode.

These transference and countertransference reactions, seemingly chaotic, have a stereotype that is strikingly seen by any psychotherapist over a length of time. For each patient, and to some extent in each illness, the themes, affects, triggers and reality object targets are the same over and over. This gives the therapist the opportunity to treat longstanding dysfunctional dynamic patterns. The stereotype and durability of these reactions also give the therapist encouragement that if in any one instance the reaction goes unrecognized, or if the therapist is overwhelmed and paralyzed, there will be another opportunity coming along soon enough. The key to treatment is to have enough of these projections in the transference for the therapist to be able to understand and describe them. This will help the patient see, analyze, and understand them. The patient can then gradually gain observing ego and reality testing about them. The patient begins to see that it is then his or her own emotional reaction that is the issue, not the usually more minor day residue reality triggers. It will particularly help when the patient sees that even the reality triggers may have been a reaction to the patient's unconscious attitude and preconscious projective identification behavior.

Remember that projective identification is a projection onto the real object or real self and is usually enacted with the object in reality or self in reality, if only via attitude. This results in a counterreaction on the part of the object in reality either in behavior or in attitude.

Specific boundary problems involved in projective identifications are the rigid boundary between reality and the preconscious of the patient, the porous boundary between the preconscious affect attitude and reality experience, and the resulting porous affect boundary between self representation and real self or object representation and real object. The therapist must respond clearly, succinctly, repetitively, and precisely in describing these cycles and their boundary problems so that the patient begins to improve his or her boundary function, his or her reality testing, and his or her observing ego (Kernberg, 1976b). Then the psychogenetic episodes which encode much of this affect content can be explored in a now more technically neutral psychoanalytic or psychotherapeutic setting, the calm and orderliness of which can help promote exploration, interpretation, and understanding.

Example:

A young therapist treating a suicidal borderline patient in the hospital has an upsetting dream early in treatment with this patient. The dream is repeating throughout the night, disturbing the continuity of sleep for the therapist. In the dream, the therapist is wearing a tall black hat and incising the axillary fossa (armpit) of the patient. The therapist in the dream is preparing to insert tubes for embalming fluid and the therapist realizes with horror that the patient is dead and that he is embalming her.

The next two days of treatment with the patient were frozen and uneventful, as had been true for the previous two weeks. But on the third day, the patient reported a highly disturbing repetitive dream that had repeatedly awakened her. In her dream, she was lying in her hospital room when she noticed a coffin beside the bed. She looked up to the door and saw the therapist coming in with a tall black hat and a bag of instruments and realized that he was going to embalm her.

The interceptive countertransference dream, disturbing in its own right, caused great feelings of uncanny anxiety in the young therapist when he heard the patient's transference dream. Had the countertransference dream come after the patient's transference dream, the uncanny feeling would have been less. However, it is not rare for countertransference reactions which are unconscious to manifest themselves as conscious fantasies or dreams in the therapist first because the therapist's ego is better able to handle it.

The supervisor of the young therapist pointed out that the embalming process in which the therapist was involved might refer to the process of the therapeutic work, which had become frozen and stalemated before the dreams. That the therapist in both dreams played a role in this stalemate raised the possibility that repression and suppression of the therapist's feelings about the patient were involved in this stalemate. In the supervisory discussion that followed, it seemed clear that the therapist had intense empathic feelings for this patient's suffering, greatly wished to help her with an intensity that while romantically idealistic was also somewhat unrealistic, and that the anger that the therapist might feel at the patient for stultifying the treatment was warded off by the fear of the patient's suicidality and the therapist's fascination with her frozen state. The patient did not discuss her feelings for the therapist any more than she discussed her feelings for the boyfriend whose break-up with her had precipitated her serious suicide attempt preceding her hospital admission. Therefore, not only was the treatment stalemated, dead, but it ran the risk of becoming the day residue of a suicide attempt as had the break-up of the stalemated relationship with her boyfriend.

Interpretation of her dream with knowledge of the countertransference allowed these issues to be opened up to the treatment process, revealing painful feelings of anger that the patient had and which were being enacted by withholding and with suicidality both against her boyfriend and against her therapist.

A most helpful aspect is the discovery that the countertransference is not only relevant to the self experience of the helper, but often specifically induced by the behavior of the patient. The countertransference is therefore an inner radar that can help see below the surface into the patient's warded off, projected, and enacted experience of the object. Then the object-in-reality experience of the staff becomes clearly understood as the patient's emotional object and not the staff member's self representation. Then, by logical sequence, the patient's self representation can be understood as either concomitant or concordant to the projected and enacted object representation (see Racker, 1968).

The staff can also understand better, through their own reactions, the reactions of the patients' environment that has led to their life collapse that has led to their hospitalization. They therefore, will be in a much better position to describe and explain this to their patients at the affect-rich moment of its occurrence in the hospital milieu. This transference–counter transference-dreams patient consistently blocked staff efforts to help her. She did not attend therapy groups. She did not seek support services. She isolated herself from other patients. These two dreams provided the psychology of the vicious, cyclical repetition compulsion expressed in her avoidant behavior. Discussing the two dreams motivated the staff to more consistently approach and encourage her, to point out how her avoidance interfered with her treatment, and to show her that she herself suffers from the isolation that her own behavior induced.

Transference and countertransference can thus be useful tools in understanding and using our experiences with hospitalized patients.

This covers the major psychiatric illnesses seen in hospital. A united staff, trained in the articulation of ego dysfunction, can make the hospital experience a turning point for the better. We need more of such units.

This book has been an attempt to help the treatment of very ill psychiatric patients.

References

Abraham, K. (1911), Notes on the psychoanalytical investigation and treatment of manic-depressive insanity and allied conditions. In: *Selected Papers of Karl Abraham*. London: Hogarth Press, 1927, pp. 137–156.

Adler, G. (1983), *Borderline Psychopathology and Its Treatment*. New York: Jason Aronson.

Akiskal, H. S., Ed. (1999), Bipolar spectrum disorders. *Psychiatr. Clin. N. Amer.*, 22(4): 517–34.

Alexander, J., & Isaacs, K. S. (1963), Seriousness and preconscious affective attitudes. *Internat. J. Psycho-Anal.*, 44: 23–30.

American Psychiatric Association. (1980), *Diagnostic and Statistical Manual of Mental Disorders*, 3rd ed. (DSM-III). Washington, DC: American Psychiatric Press.

———. (1987), *Diagnostic and Statistical Manual of Mental Disorders*, 3rd ed. rev. (DSM-III-R). Washington, DC: American Psychiatric Press.

———. (1994), *Diagnostic and Statistical Manual of Mental Disorders*, 4th ed. (DSM-IV). Washington, DC: American Psychiatric Press.

Andreason, N. (1999), A unitary model of schizophrenia: Bleuler's "fragmented phrene" as schizoencephaly. *Arch. Gen. Psychiat.*, 56: 781–787.

Aragno, A. (1997), *Symbolization: Proposing a Developmental Paradigm for a New Psychoanaltic Theory of Mind*. Madison, CT: International Universities Press.

Arieti, S. (1974), *Interpretation of Schizophrenia*. New York: Basic Books.

———. (1976), *Creativity: The Magic Synthesis*. New York: Basic Books.

Arlow, J. (1985), The concept of psychic reality and related problems. *J. Amer. Psychoanal. Assn.*, 33: 521–536.

———. (1989), Delusion and metaphor. In: *Psychoanalysis and Psychosis*, ed. A. L. Silver. Madison, CT: International Universities Press, 173–182.

Arlow, J., & Brenner, C. (1964), *Psychoanalytic Concepts and the Structural Theory*. New York: International Universities Press.

Asaad, G. (1990), *Hallucination in Clinical Psychiatry*. New York: Brunner/ Mazel.

Auchincloss, E. L. & Samberg, E. (2012) *Psychoanalytic Terms and Concepts*. New Haven, CT: Yale University Press.

Banglow, P., & Sadow, L. (1971), Visual perception: Development, maturation, birth to adult. *J. Amer. Psychoanal Assn.*, 19: 433–450.

References 287

Basch, M. F. (1981), Psychoanalytic interpretation and cognitive transformation. *Internat. J. Psycho-Anal.*, 62: 151.

Baudry, P. (1954), Character: A concept in search of identity. *JAAA*, 32: 455–477.

Beitman, B. D., & Klerman, G. L., Eds. (1984), *Combining Psychotherapy and Drug Therapy in Clinical Practice*. New York: Spectrum.

Bellak, L., & Goldsmith, L. (1984), *The Broad Scope of Ego Assessment*. New York: John Wiley.

Bellak, L., Hurvich, M., & Gediman, H. (1973), *Ego Function in Schizophrenics, Neurotics, and Normals*. New York: John Wiley.

Bellak, L., & Marsh, H. (1997), The use of ego function assessment for the study of ADHD in adults. *Psychiatr. Ann.*, 27: 563–571.

Bellak, L., & Meyers, B. (1979), Ego function assessment and analyzability. *Internat. Rev. Psycho-Anal.*, 2: 413–428.

Benton, A. L. (1985), Visuoperceptive, visuospatial and visuoconstructive disorders. In: *Clinical Neuropsychology*, ed. K. M. Heilman & E. Valenstein. New York: Oxford University Press, 151–186.

Beres, D. (1960), Perception, imagination and reality. *Internat. J. Psycho-Anal.*, 41: 327–334.

———. (1971), Ego autonomy and ego pathology. *Psychoanal. Stud. Chil.*, 26: 3–24. Chicago: Quadrangle.

Beres, D., & Joseph, E. (1970), The concept of mental representation in psychoanalysis. *Internat. J. Psycho-Anal.*, 51: 1–9.

Bernstein, S. B. (1983), Treatment prepatory to psychoanalysis. *J. Amer. Psychoanal. Assn.*, 31: 363–390.

Bernstein, S. B. (2015), When the analytic patient has attention deficit hyperactivity disorder. *J. Amer. Psychoanal. Assn.*, 63(2): 213–245.

Bhandary, A. N., Ed. (1997), Attention deficit hyperactivity disorder in adulthood. *Psychiatr. Ann.*, 27(8): 543–544.

Bieber, I. (1980), Psychoanalysis—A cognitive process. *J. Amer. Acad. Psychoanal.*, 8: 25–38.

Bion, W. R. (1984), *Attention and Interpretation*. London: Tavistock/Karnac.

Blanck, G. (1966), Some technical implications of ego psychology. *Internat. J. Psycho-Anal.*, 47: 6–13.

Blanck, R., & Blanck, G. (1979), *Ego Psychology*, Vols. 1–2. New York: Columbia University Press.

———. (1986), *Beyond Ego Psychology*. New York: Columbia University Press.

Bleuler, E. (1950), *Dementia Praecox or the Group of Schizophrenias*. New York: International Universities Press.

Blum, H. P. (1978), Symbolic processes and symbol formation. *Internat. J. Psycho-Anal.*, 59: 455–472.

Boesky, D. (1983), Resistance and character theory: A reconsideration of the concept of character resistance. *J. Amer. Psychoanal. Assn. (Suppl.)*, 31: 227–246.

Boyer, L. B. (1961), Evaluation psychoanalysis with few parameters with schizophrenics. *Internat. J. Psycho-Anal.*, 42: 389–403.

Boyer, L. B., & Giovacchini, P. L. (1980), *Psychoanalytic Treatment of Schizophrenia, Borderline and Characterological Disorders*, 2nd ed. New York: Jason Aronson.

Bradley, S. (1990), Nonphysician psychotherapist-physician pharmacotherapist: A new model for concurrent treatment. *Psychiatr. Clin. N. Amer.*, 13: 307–322.

288 References

Brenner, C. (1976), *Psychoanalytic Technique and Psychic Conflict*. New York: International Universities Press.

———. (1991), A psychoanalytic perspective on depression. *J. Amer. Psychoanal. Assn.*, 39: 25–44.

Breuer, J., & Freud, S. (1893–1895), Studies on hysteria. *Standard Edition*, 2. London: Hogarth Press, 1955, pp. 183–251.

Brockman, R. (1998), *A Map of the Mind: Toward a Science of Psychotherapy*. Madison, CT: Psychosocial Press.

Brown, A. S., Ed. (1999), The neurodevelopmental hypothesis of schizophrenia. *Psychiatr. Ann.*, 29: 128–130.

Bucci, W. (1997), *Psychoanalysis and Cognitive Science: A Multiple Code Theory*. New York: Guilford Press.

Busch, F. (1995), *The Ego at the Center of Clinical Technique*. Northvale, NJ: Jason Aronson.

Calogeras, R. C. (1967), Silence as a technical parameter in psychoanalysis. *Internat. J. Psycho-Anal.*, 48: 536–558.

Campbell, R. (1989), *Psychiatric Dictionary*, 6th ed. Oxford: Oxford University Press.

Cassirer, E. (1955), *The Philosophy of Symbolic Forms*. New Haven, CT: Yale University Press.

———. (1979), *Symbol, Myth and Culture*. New Haven, CT: Yale University Press.

Checkhov, A. (1932), The black monk. In: *The Stories of Anton Checkhov*, ed. R. N. Linscott. New York: Modern Library, pp. 23–51.

Chiland, C., Ed. (1977), *Long Term Treatment of Psychotic States*. New York: Human Sciences Press.

Coen, S. J. (1988), Superego aspects of entitlement in rigid characters. *J. Amer. Psychoanal. Assn.*, 36: 409–427.

Colibazzi, T., Yang, Z., Horga, G., Yan, C.-G., Corcoran, C. M., Klahr, K., Brucato, G., Girgis, R. R., Abi-Dargham, A., Milham, M. P., Peterson, B. S. (2017), Aberrant Temporal Connectivity in Persons at Clinical High Risk for Psychosis. *Bio. Psych.*, 21 January.

———. (2015, November 7), Psychoanalysis revealed through the connectome: A neuro psychoanalytic perspective on psychosis. Talk given at Arnold Pfeffer Center for Neuropsychanalysis of the New York Psychoanalytic Society and Institute.

Compton, A. (1987), Objects and attitudes. *J. Amer. Psychoanal. Assn.*, 35: 609–628.

Cumming, J., & Cumming, E. (1963), *Ego and Milieu*. Chicago: Aldine.

Damascio, A. R. (1994), *Descartes' Error: Emotion, Reason and the Human Brain*. New York: Avon Books.

David, A. S. (1999), Auditory hallucinations: Phenomenology, neurophysiology, and neuroimaging update. *Acta Psychiatr. Scand. (Suppl.)*, 395: 95–104.

Denckla, M. (1991), Academic and extracurricular aspects of nonverbal learning disabilities. *Psychiatr. Ann.*, 21: 717–724.

Deutsch, F. (1954), Analytic synesthesiology and intersensory perception. *Internat. J. Psycho-Anal.*, 35: 293–301.

References   289

DSM-5 (2012) Washington DC, APPI, for latest dx of psychosis see DSM5, for critique see Ross, C. A., (2014)

Duane, D. D. (1991), Dyslexia: Neurobioiogical and behavioral correlates. *Psychiatr. Ann.*, 21: 703–708.

Duane, D. D., & Gray, D. B., Eds. (1991), *The Reading Brain: The Biological Basis of Dyslexia*. Parkton, MD: York Press.

Eissler, K. R. (1953), Effect of the structure of the ego on psychoanalytic technique. *J. Amer. Psychoanal. Assn.*, 1: 104–143.

———. (1958), Remarks on some variation in psychoanalytic technique. *Internat. J. Psycho-Anal.*, 39: 222–229.

———. (1962), On the metapsychology of the preconscious. *Psychoanal. Stud. Chil.*, 17: 9–41. New York: International Universities Press.

Fairbairn, R. (1952), *Psychoanalytic Studies of the Personality*. London: Routledge & Kegan Paul.

Federn, P. (1934), The analysis of psychotics: On technique. *Internat. J. Psycho-Anal.*, 15: 209–214.

———. (1952), *Ego Psychology and the Psychoses*. New York: Basic Books.

Fenichel, O. (1941), Psychoanalysis of character. In: *Collected Papers, Second Series*. New York: W. W. Norton, pp. 198–214.

Ferenczi, S. (1952), *First Contributions to Psychoanalysis*. New York: Brunner/Mazel.

Fliess, R. (1973), *Symbol, Dream and Psychosis*. New York: International Universities Press.

Freeman, T. (1969), *Psychopathology of the Psychoses*. New York: International Universities Press.

———. (1973), *A Psychoanalytic Study of the Psychoses*. New York: International Universities Press.

———. (1988), *The Psychoanalyst in Psychiatry*. New Haven, CT: Yale University Press.

Freeman, T., Cameron, J., & McGhie, A. (1958), *Chronic Schizophrenia*. New York: International Universities Press.

Frenkel-Brunswik, E. (1974), Personality theory and perception. *Psychoanal. Inq.*, 31: 92–160.

Freud, A. (1936), *The Ego and the Mechanisms of Defense*. New York: International Universities Press, 1966.

Freud, S. (1895/1950), Project for a scientific psychology. *Standard Edition*, 1: 281–391. London: Hogarth Press, 1966.

———. (1900), The interpretation of dreams. *Standard Edition*, 5. London: Hogarth Press, 1953.

———. (1907), Delusions and dreams in Jensen's Gravida. *Standard Edition*, 9: 1–93. London: Hogarth Press, 1959.

———. (1915a), Observations on transference-love (Further recommendations on the technique of psycho-analysis, III). *Standard Edition*, 12: 157–171. London: Hogarth Press, 1958.

———. (1915b), The unconscious. *Standard Edition*, 14: 159–215. London: Hogarth Press, 1957.

———. (1915–1916), Introductory lectures on psycho-analysis. *Standard Edition*, 16 & 17. London: Hogarth Press, 1961.

———. (1916), Some character-types met with in psycho-analytic work. *Standard Edition*, 14: 309–333. London: Hogarth Press, 1957.

———. (1917a), Mourning and melancholia. *Standard Edition*, 14: 237–258. London: Hogarth Press, 1957.

———. (1917b), A metapsychological supplement to the theory of dreams. *Standard Edition*, 14: 217–235. London: Hogarth Press, 1957.

———. (1919), The "uncanny." *Standard Edition*, 17: 217–252. London: Hogarth Press, 1955.

———. (1923), The ego and the id. *Standard Edition*, 19: 1–59. London: Hogarth Press, 1961.

———. (1924a), Neurosis and psychosis. *Standard Edition*, 19: 147–153. London: Hogarth Press, 1961.

———. (1924b), The loss of reality in neurosis and psychosis. *Standard Edition*, 19: 181–187. London: Hogarth Press, 1961.

———. (1925), Negation. *Standard Edition*, 19: 233–239. London: Hogarth Press, 1961.

———. (1937), Analysis, terminable and uniterminable. *Lat. J. Psa.*, 18: 395.

———. (1940), Splitting of the ego in the process of defence. *Standard Edition*, 23: 271–278. London: Hogarth Press, 1964.

———. (1958), *On Aphasia*, tr. E. Stengel. New York: International Universities Press.

Friedman, L. (1989), Hartman's "Ego psychology and the problem of adaptation." *Psychoanal Inq.*, 58: 526–550.

Friedman, S., & Fisher, C. (1960), Further observations on primary modes of perception. *J. Amer. Psychoanal. Assn.*, 8: 100–129.

Fromm-Reichman, F. (1948), Notes on the treatment of schizophrenia by psychoanalytic psychotherapy. *J. Psychiatr.*, 2: 263–270.

———. (1950), *Principles of Intensive Psychotherapy*. Chicago: University of Chicago Press.

———. (1955), Intuitive processes in the psychotherapy of schizophrenia. *J. Amer. Psychoanal. Assn.*, 3: 5–6.

———. (1959), *Psychoanalysis and Psychotherapy: Selected Papers*. Chicago: University of Chicago Press.

Frosch, J. (1964), The psychotic character. *Psychoanal. Quart.*, 38: 81–96.

———. (1983), *The Psychotic Process*. New York: International Universities Press.

———. (1988), Psychotic character versus borderline. Parts I and II. *Internat. J. Psycho-Anal.*, 69: 347–357.

———. (1990), *Psychodynamics of Psychiatry: Theory and Practice*, Vols. 1–2. Madison, CT: International Universities Press.

Gabbard, G. (1994), *Psychodynamic Psychiatry in Clinical Practice*. Washington, DC: American Psychiatric Press.

Gabbard G, ed. (2014), *Gabbard's Treatment of Psychiatric Disorders*. Arlington, VA: American Psychiatric Publishing.

Galaburda, A. M., Sherman, G. F., Rosen, G. D., Aboitiz, F., & Geschwind, N. (1985), Developmental dyslexia: Four consecutive patients with cortical anomalies. *Ann. Neurol.*, 18: 222–233.

George, W. S., Nahas, Z., Lomerov, M., Bohning, D. E., & Kellner, C. (1999), How knowledge of regional brain dysfunction in depression will enable new somatic treatments in the next millenium. *CNS Spectr.*, 4: 53–61.

Gharmi, S. N., Ed. (1997), Insight and psychiatric disorders. *Psychiatr. Ann.*, 27: 782–790.

Giovacchini, P. (1975), *Psychoanalysis of Character Disorders*. New York: Jason Aronson.

Glover, E. (1926), The neurotic character. *Internat. J. Psycho-Anal.*, 7: 11–30.

———. (1931), The therapeutic effect of inexact interpretation: Suggestion. *Internat. J. Psycho-Anal.*, 12: 397–411.

———. (1958), Ego distortions. *Internat. J. Psycho-Anal.*, 39: 260–264.

Goodglass, H., & Wingfield, A., Eds. (1997), *Anomia: Neuroanatomical and Cognitive Correlates*. San Diego, CA: Academic Press.

Goodwin, F. K., & Jamison, K. R. (1990), *Manic Depressive Illness*. New York: Oxford University Press.

Gray, P. (1994), *The Ego and Analysis of Defense*. Northvale, NJ: Jason Aronson.

Greenacre, P., Ed. (1953), *Affective Disorders: Psychoanalytic Contributions to Their Study*. New York: International Universities Press.

Greenson, R. (1967), *The Technique and Practice of Psychoanalysis*. New York: International Universities Press.

Greenspan, S. I. (1988), Ego development: Insights from clinical work with infants and children. *J. Amer. Psychoanal. Assn. (Suppl.)*, 36: S3–S55.

———. (1989), Ego development: Biological, environmental specificity defenses. *J. Amer. Psychoanal. Assn.*, 37: 605–638.

Greenspan, S. I., & Cullander, C. H. (1973), A systematic metapsychological assessment of the personality: Its application to the problem of analyzability. *J. Amer. Psychoanal. Assn.*, 21: 303–327.

Grolnick, S. (1990), *The Work and Play of Winnicott*. New York: Jason Aronson.

Grossman, W. (1992), Hierarchies, boundaries, and representation in the Freudian model of mental organization. *J. Amer. Psychoanal. Assn.*, 40: 27–62.

Gunderson, J. (1984), *Borderline Personality Disorder*. Washington, DC: American Psychiatric Press.

Hartmann, E. (1991), *Boundaries of the Mind*. New York: Basic Books.

Hartmann, H. (1939), *Ego Psychology and the Problem of Adaptation*. New York: International Universities Press, 1958.

———. (1951), Technical implications of ego psychology. *Psychoanal. Quart.*, 20: 31–43.

———. (1964), *Essays on Ego Psychology*. New York: International Universities Press.

Hendrick, I. (1936), Ego development and certain character problems. *Psychoanal. Quart.*, 5: 320–346.

Hinsie, L., & Campbell, R. (1963), *Psychiatric Dictionary*, 4th ed. Oxford: Oxford University Press.

Hoch, S. (1992), Psychoanalysis and psychoanalytic psychotherapy—Similarities and differences: Conceptual overview. *J. Amer. Psychoanal. Assn.*, 40: 233–238.

Holmes, D. W. (1996), Emerging indications of ego growth and associated resistances. *J. Amer. Psychoanal. Assn.*, 44: 1109–1119.

Holt, R. (1965), Ego autonomy re-evaluated. *Internat. J. Psycho-Anal.*, 46: 151–167.

Hurt, S., Holtzman, P., & Davis, J. (1983), Thought disorder: The measurement of its changes. *Arch. Gen. Psychiatr.*, 40: 1281–1285.

Hurvich, M. (1970), On the concept of reality testing. *Internat. J. Psycho-Anal.*, 51: 299–312.

Iqbal, N., Schwartz, B. J., Cecil, A., Inman, Z., & Constantin, C. (1993), Schizophrenic diagnosis. *Psychiatr. Ann.*, 23: 105–110.

Izard, C. (1978), On the ontogenesis of emotions and emotion-cognition in infancy. In: *The Development of Affect*, ed. M. Lewis & L. Rosenblum. New York: Penguin Press, pp. 389–413.

Jacobson, E. (1964), *The Self and the Object World*. New York: International Universities Press.

———. (1967), *Psychotic Conflict and Reality*. New York: International Universities Press.

———. (1971), *Depression: Comparative Studies of Normal, Neurotic and Psychotic Conditions*. New York: International Universities Press.

Jaspers, K. (1923), *General Psychopathology*. Manchester, UK: Manchester University Press, 1963.

Jones, E. (1912), *Papers on Psychoanalysis*. Boston: Beacon Press, 1961.

———. (1948), The theory of symbolism. In: *Papers on Psychoanalysis*, 5th ed., ed. E. Jones. Baltimore: Williams & Wilkins, pp. 129–186.

Kafka, E. (1984), Cognitive difficulties in psychoanalysis. *Psychoanal. Quart.*, 53: 533–555.

———. (1989), *Multiple Realities in Clinical Practice*. New Haven, CT: Yale University Press.

Karasu, T. B. (1982), Psychotherapy and pharmacotherapy: Toward an integrative model. *Amer. J. Psychiatr.*, 139: 1102–1113.

Karush, A. (1966), An adaptational approach to psychic representation, perception and the psychic apparatus. In: *New Developments in Psychoanalysis*, ed. D. Shapiro. New York: Columbia University Press, pp. 3–31.

Kendler, K. (2016), Phenomenology of schizophrenia and the representativeness of modern diagnostic criteria. *JAMA Psychiatry.*, 73(10): 1082–1103 (to page 174p, last graph).

Kernberg, O. (1975), *Borderline Conditions and Pathological Narcissism*. New York: Jason Aronson.

———. (1976a), A psychoanalytic classification of character pathology. In: *Object Relations Theory and Clinical Psychoanalysis*. New York: Jason Aronson, pp. 139–160.

———. (1976b), *Object Relations Theory and Clinical Psychoanalysis*. New York: Jason Aronson.

———. (1977), The structural interview. In: *Borderline Personality Disorders*, ed. P. Harticollis. New York: International Universities Press, pp. 87–122.

———. (1980), *Internal World and Outer Reality*. New York: Jason Aronson.

———. (1986), Identification and its vicissitudes as observed in psychosis. *Internat. J. Psycho-Anal.*, 67: 147–160.

References   293

Kernberg, O., Selzer, M. A., Koenigsberg, H. W., Carr, A. C., & Appelbaum, A. C. (1989), *Psychodynamic Psychotherapy of Borderline Patients*. New York: Basic Books.

———. (1991), Transference regression and psychoanalytic technique with infantile personalities. *Internat. J. Psycho-Anal.*, 72: 189–200.

Khan, M. M. R. (1960), Regression and integration in the analytic setting. *Internat. J. Psycho-Anal.*, 41: 130–146.

Klein, M. (1940), Mourning and its relation to manic depressive states. *Internat. J. Psycho-Anal.*, 21: 125–153.

———. (1975), *The Writings of Melanie Klein*, Vols. 1–4. New York: Free Press.

Klerman, G. L. (1984), Ideological conflicts in combined treatment. In: *Combining Psychotherapy and Drug Therapy in Clinical Practice*, ed. B. D. Beitman & G. L. Klerman. New York: Spectrum, 17–34.

Knight, R. P. (1953), Borderline states. *Bull. Menn. Clin.*, 17: 1–12.

Kohut, H. (1971), *The Analysis of the Self*. New York: International Universities Press.

Kosslyn, S. M. (2003), Understanding the mind's eye and nose. *Nat. Neurosci.* 6(11), 1124–1125.

Kraepelin, E. (1915), *Clinical Psychiatry*, ed. A. Drittersdorf. Abstr. & adapt. from 7th German ed. New York: Macmillan.

Kris, E. (1950), On preconscious mental processes. *Psychoanal. Quart.*, 19: 540–556.

Krystal, H. (1975), Affect tolerance. *Ann. Psychoanal.*, 3: 179–183.

Kubie, L. S. (1953), The distortion of the symbolic process in neurosis and psychosis. *J. Amer. Psychoanal. Assn.*, 1: 59–86.

———. (1978), Distortion of the symbolic process in neurosis and psychosis. *Psychoanal. Inq.*, 44: 87–96.

Kuhns, R. (1983), *Psychoanalytic Theory of Art: A Philosophy of Art on Developmental Principles*. New York: Columbia University Press.

Lampl-de Groot, J. (1963), Symptom formation and character formation. *Internat. J. Psycho-Anal.*, 44: 1–12.

Langer, S. (1942), *Philosophy in a New Key*. Cambridge, MA: Harvard University Press.

Langs, R. (1973), *The Technique of Psychoanalytic Psychotherapy*, Vols. 1–2. New York: Jason Aronson.

Laplanche, J., & Pontalis, J. (1967), *The Language of Psychoanalysis*, tr. D. Nicolson-Smith. New York: W. W. Norton, 1973.

Le Doux, J. (1989), Cognitive-emotional interactions in the brain. *Cognit. & Emot.*, 3: 267–289.

———. (1996), *The Emotional Brain*. New York: Simon & Schuster/Touchstone.

Le Doux, J., Iwata, J., Cicchetti, P., & Reis, D. J. (1998), Different projections of the central amygdaloid nucleus mediate autonomic and behavioral correlates of conditioned fear. *J. Neurosci.*, 8: 2517–2529.

Letterman, A. (1996), *Specific Techniques for the Psychotherapy of Schizophrenic Patients*. Madison, CT: International Universities Press.

Lewin, B. (1950), *The Psychoanalysis of Elation*. New York: W. W. Norton.

Liebert, R. (1988), The concept of character: A historical review. In: *Masochism: Current Psychoanalytic Perspectives*, ed. R. Glick & D. Meyers. Hillside, NJ: Analytic Press, pp. 27–42.

294 References

Lion, J. (1974), *Personality Disorders*. Baltimore: Williams & Wilkins.

Lishman, W. (2012), *Organic Psychiatry*, 4th ed. Oxford: Basil Blackwell, 1987.

Little, M. (1981), *Transference Neurosis, Transference Psychosis*. New York: Jason Aronson.

Loeb, F. F., & Loeb, L. R. (1987), Psychoanalytic observations on the effect of lithium on manic attacks. *J. Amer. Psychoanal. Assn.*, 35: 877–902.

Loewald, H. (1988), *Sublimation*. New Haven, CT: Yale University Press.

Lotterman, A. (2015), *Psychotherapy for People Diagnosed with Schizophrenia*. New York: Routledge.

Lowenstein, P. (1958), Remarks on some variations in psychoanalytic technique. *Internat. J. Psycho-Anal.*, 39: 202–210.

———. (1972), Ego autonomy and psychoanalytic techniques. *Psychoanal. Quart.*, 41: 1–22.

MacKinnon, R. A., Michels, R., & Buckley, P. J. (2016a), *The Clinical Interview in Psychiatric Practice*, 3rd ed. Washington, DC: APPI.

———. (2016b), *The Psychiatric Interview in Clinical Practice*. Washington, DC: APA Press.

Macnaughten, E., Sheps, S., Frankish, J., & Irwin, D. (2015), Understanding the development of narrative insight in early psychosis: A qualitative approach. *Psychosis.*, 7(4): 291–301.

Mahler, M. (1966), Notes on the development of basic moods. In: *Psychoanalysis— A General Psychology: Essays in Honor of Heinz Hartmann*, ed. R. M. Loewenstein. New York: Basic Books, pp. 152–168.

———. (1968), *On Human Symbiosis and the Vicissitudes of Individuation*, Vol. 1. New York: International Universities Press.

Mahler, M., Pine, F., & Bergman, A. (1975), *The Psychological Birth of the Human Infant*. New York: Basic Books.

Maquet, P., Peters, J. M., Aerts, J., Delfione, J. T., Degueldre, C., Luxen, A., & French, J. G. (1996), Functional neuro-anatomy of human rapid-eye movement sleep and dreaming. *Nature*, 383: 163–165.

Marcus, E. R. (1981), Use of the acute hospital unit in the long term treatment of borderline states. *Psychiatr. Clin. N. Amer.*, 4: 133–144.

———. (1987a), Relationship of illness and intensive hospital treatment to length of stay. *Psychiatr. Clin. N. Amer.*, 10: 247–256.

———. Ed. (1987b), Intensive hospital treatment of psychotic and borderline patients. *Psychiatr. Clin. N. Amer.* (Spec. Issue), 10.

———. (1990a), Integrating psychopharmacotherapy, psychotherapy and mental structure in the treatment of patients with personality disorder and depression. *Psychiatr. Clin. N. Amer.* (Spec. Issue), 13: 255–264.

———. Ed. (1990b), Combined treatment: Psychotherapy and medication. *Psychiatr. Clin. N. Amer.* (Spec. Issue), 13.

———. (1994), Paranoid symbol formation in social organizations. In: *Paranoia*, ed. J. Oldham & S. Bone. New Haven, CT: Yale University Press, pp. 81–94.

———. (1996), Psychic reality in psychotic states. *Internat. J. Psycho-Anal.*, 77: 565–574.

———. (1999), Modern ego psychology. *JAPA*, 47(3): 843–871.

References 295

Marcus, E. R., & Bradley, S. (1987), Concurrence of Axis I and Axis II illness in treatment resistant hospitalized patients. *Psychiatr. Clin. N Amer.* (Spec. Issue), 2: 177–184.

————. (1990), Combination psychotherapy and psychopharmacotherapy with treatment resistant patients with dual diagnosis. *Psychiatr. Clin. N. Amer.* (Spec. Issue), 13: 209–214.

Masterson, J. (1972), *Treatment of the Borderline Adolescent*. New York: John Wiley.

Matte-Blanco, I. (1959), Expression in symbolic logic of the system unconscious. *Internat. J. Psycho-Anal.*, 40: 1–5.

McElroy, S., Hudson, J. I., Pope, H. G., Jr., Keck, P. E., Jr., & Aizley, H. G. (1992), The DSM-III-R impulse control disorders not elsewhere classified: Clinical characteristics and relationship to other psychiatric disorder. *Amer. J. Psychiatr.*, 149: 318–327.

McGlashen, T. H., & Hoffman, R. F. (2000), Schizophrenia as a disorder of developmentally reduced synaptic connectivity. *Arch. Gen. Psychiatr.*, 57: 637–638.

McGlynn, S. M., & Schafer, D. L. (1997), The neuropsychology of insight: Hysterical awareness of deficits in a psychiatric context. *Psychiatr. Ann.*, 27: 806–811.

McNutt, J. E. (1992), Psychoanalysis and psychoanalytic psychotherapy— Similarities and differences: Indications, contraindications, and initiation. *J. Amer. Psychoanal. Assn.*, 40: 223–231.

Meissner, W. W. (1980), A note on projective identification. *J. Amer. Psychoanal. Assn.*, 28: 43–68.

Milrod, D. (1988), The psychoanalytic theory of depression: Identification, orality, anxiety. *Psychoanal. Stud. Chil.*, 43: 83–99. New Haven, CT: Yale University Press.

Modell, A. (1968), *Object Love and Reality*. New York: International Universities Press.

Morris, J. (1992), Psychoanalysis and psychoanalytic psychotherapy: Similarities and differences: Therapeutic technique. *J. Amer. Psychoanal. Assn.*, 40: 211–222.

Morris, J., Frith, C. D., Perrett, D. I., Rowland, D., Young, A. W., Calder, A. J., & Dolan, R. J. (1996), A differential neural response in the amygdala to fearful and happy facial expressions. *Nature*, 383: 812–815.

Namnum, A. (1968), The problem of analyzability and the autonomous ego. *Internat. J. Psycho-Anal.*, 49: 271–275.

Nersession, E. (1989), Review of the interpretation of dreams in clinical work. *Internat. J. Psycho-Anal.*, 70: 736–738.

Newcorn, J. H., Ed. (2000, July), Toward a fresh understanding of ADHD. *CNS Spectr.*, V(6).

Nunberg, H. (1931), The synthetic function of the ego. *Internat. J. Psycho-Anal.*, 12: 123–140.

Obeyeskere, G. (1990), *The Work of Culture: Symbolic Transformation in Psychoanalysis and Anthropology*. Chicago: University of Chicago Press.

Ogden, T. (1982), *Projective Identification and Psychotherapeutic Techniques*. New York: Jason Aronson.

296 References

Ojemann, G., & Mateer, C. (1979), Human language cortex: Localization of memory, syntax and sequential motor-phenome identification system. *Science*, 205: 1401–1403.

Ostow, M. (1957), The use of drugs to overcome technical difficulties in psychoanalysis. In: *The Dynamics of Psychiatric Drug Therapy*, ed. G. J. Sarwer-Foner. Springfield, IL: Charles C Thomas, pp. 443–464.

———. (1962), *Drugs in Psychoanalysis and Psychotherapy*. New York: Basic Books.

———. (1966), *The Complementary Role of Psychoanalysis and Drug Therapy in Psychiatric Drugs*. New York: Grune & Stratton.

Panel. (1961), The psychoanalytic theory of the symbolic process. *Reporter: N. Segal. J. Amer. Psychoanal. Assn.*, 9: 146–157.

Pao, P. N. (1979), *Schizophrenia Disorders*. New York: International Universities Press.

Piaget, J. (1953), *Intelligence and Affectivity*, tr. T. A. Brown & C. E. Kaegi. Palo Alto, CA: Annual Reviews Monographs, 1981.

———. (1954), *The Construction of Reality in the Child*. New York: Basic Books.

———. (1977), *The Development of Thought: Equilibration of Cognitive Structures*, tr. A. Rosin. New York: Viking Press.

———. (1981), *Intelligence and Affectivity*, trans. T. A. Brown & S. C. E. Kaegi. Palo Alto, CA: Annual Reviews Monographs.

Piaget, J., & Inhelder, B. (1958), *The Growth of Logical Thinking from Childhood to Adolescence*, tr. A. Parson & S. Milgram. New York: Basic Books.

———. (1979), *Mental Imagery in the Child: A Study of the Development of Imaginal Representation*, tr. P. A. Chilton. New York: Basic Books.

Pine, F. (1990), *Drive, Ego, Object and Self*. New York: Basic Books.

Plutchik, R., & Kellerman, H. Eds. (1980), *Emotion, Theory, Research, and Experience: Vol. 1. Theories of Emotion*. New York: Academic Press.

Pope, H. G., Jr., & Lipinsky, T. (1978), Diagnosis in schizophrenia and manic-depressive illness: A reassessment of the specificity of schizophrenic symptoms in the light of current research. *Arch. Gen. Psychiatr.*, 35: 811–828.

Porder, M. (1987), Projective identification: An alternative hypothesis. *Psychoanal. Quart.*, 56: 431–451.

Porder, M., Abend, S., & Willick, M. (1983), *Borderline Patients: Psychoanalytic Perspectives*. New York: International Universities Press.

Raballo, A., & Laroi, F. (2011), Murmurs of thought: Phenomenology of hallucinatory consciousness in impending psychosis. *Psychosis.*, 3(2): 163–168.

Racker, H. (1968), *Transference and Countertransference*. New York: International Universities Press.

Rado, S. (1928), The problem of melancholia. *Internat. J. Psycho-Anal.*, 9: 420–438.

Rapaport, D. (1951a), The autonomy of the ego. In: *Collected Papers of D. Rapaport*, ed. M. Gill. New York: Basic Books, pp. 357–367.

———, Ed. (1951b), *Organization and Pathology of Thought*. New York: Columbia University Press.

———. (1959), A historical survey of psychoanalytic ego psychology. *Psychiatr. Issues.*, 1: 5–17.

Rapaport, E. (1960), Preparation for psychoanalysis. *Internat. J. Psycho-Anal.*, 41: 626–632.

Redlich, F. (1952), *Psychotherapy with Schizophrenia*. New York: International Universities Press.

Reich, W. (1925), *The Impulsive Character*. New York: New American Library, 1974.

———. (1933a), The characterological resolution of the infantile sexual conflict. In: *Character Analysis*, ed. W. Reik. New York: Simon & Schuster, 1975, pp. 153–168.

———. (1933b), *Character Analysis*. New York: Simon & Schuster, 1975.

Reider, N. (1957), Transference psychosis. *J. Hillside Hosp.*, 6: 131–140.

———. (1972), Metaphor as interpretation. *Internat. J. Psycho-Anal.*, 53: 463–469.

Renick, O. (1972), Cognitive ego functions in the phobic symptom. *Psychoanal. Quart.*, 41: 537–555.

Resnick, T., & Rapin, I. (1991), Language disorders in childhood. *Psychiatr. Ann.*, 21: 709–716.

Rizzuto, A. M. (1989), A hypothesis about Freud's motive for writing: On Aphasia. *Internat. Rev. Psycho-Anal.*, 16: 111–118.

———. (1990), Origin of Freud's concept of object representation: On Aphasia. *Internat. J. Psycho-Anal.*, 71: 241–248.

Robbins, M. (1993), *Experiences of Schizophrenia*. New York: Guilford Press.

Rosen, V. (1967), Disorders of communication in psychoanalysis. *J. Amer. Psychoanal. Assn.*, 15: 467–490.

Rosenblatt, A., & Thickstun, J. (1977), *Modern Psychoanalytic Concepts in a General Psychology*. Psychological Issues, Monograph 42/43. New York: International Universities Press.

Rosenfeld, H. (1965), *Psychotic States: A Psychoanalytical Approach*. New York: International Universities Press.

Ross, C. A. (2014), Problems with the psychosis section of DSM five. *Psychosis.*, 6(3): 235–241.

Rothstein, Arden, Benjamin, L., Crosby, M., & Eisenstadt, K. (1988), *Learning Disorders: An Integration of Neuropsychological and Psychoanalytic Considerations*. Madison, CT: International Universities Press.

Rudel, R., Holmes, J., & Rudel-Pandes, J. (1988), *Assessment of Developmental Learning Disorders: A Neuropsychological Approach*. New York: Basic Books.

Sacco, T. and Sacchetti, B. (2010), Role of secondary sensory cortices in emotional memory storage and retrieval in rats. *Science*, 6: 649–56.

Sandler, J., Ed. (1988), *Projection, Identification, Projective Identification*. London: Karnac Books.

———. (1990), On internal object relations. *J. Amer. Psychoanal. Assn.*, 38: 859–880.

———. (1991), Character traits and object relations. In: *Handbook of Character Studies*, ed. M. Kets de Vries & S. Penzow. Madison, CT: International Universities Press, pp. 191–203.

298 References

Sandler, J., & Holder, A. (1973), Frames of reference in psychoanalytic psychology, VII. The topographical frame of reference: The preconscious and conscious. *Brit. J. Med. Psychiatr.*, 46: 143–153.

Sandler, J., & Rosenblatt, B. (1962), The concept of the representational world. *Psychoanal. Stud. Chil.*, 17: 128–145. New York: International Universities Press.

Sandler, J., & Sandler, A.-M. (1978), On the development of object relationship and affects. *Internat. J. Psycho-Anal.*, 59: 285–302.

Sarnoff, C. (1976), *On Latency*. New York: Jason Aronson.

———. (1987), *Psychotherapeutic Strategies in Latency Through Early Adolescence*. New York: Jason Aronson.

Sarwer-Foner, G. J., Ed. (1960), *The Dynamics of Psychiatric Drug Therapy*. Springfield, IL: Charles C. Thomas.

———. (1983), An overview of combined psychopharmacology and psychotherapy. In: *Psychopharmacology and Psychotherapy*, ed. M. H. Greenhill & A. Grolnick. New York: Macmillan, 165–180.

Schafer, R. (1968a), The mechanisms of defence. *Internat. J. Psycho-Anal.*, 49: 49–62.

———. (1968b), *Aspects of Internalization*. New York: International Universities Press.

———. (1991), Character: Ego syntonicity and character change. In: *Handbook of Character Studies*, ed. M. Kets de Vries & S. Penzow. Madison, CT: International Universities Press, 169–189.

Schur, M. (1966), *The Id and the Regulatory Principles of Mental Functioning*. New York: International Universities Press.

Scott, W. C. (1963), The psychoanalytic treatment of mania. *Psychiatr. Res. Rep.*, 17: 84–90.

Searles, H. (1960), *The Nonhuman Environment in Normal Development and Schizophrenia*. New York: International Universities Press.

———. (1963), Transference psychosis in the psychotherapy of chronic schizophrenia. *Internat. J. Psycho-Anal.*, 44: 249–281.

———. (1964), *Collected Papers*. New York: International Universities Press.

———. (1986), *My Work with Borderline Patients*. New York: Jason Aronson.

Sechehaye, M. A. (1951), *Symbolic Realization*. New York: International Universities Press.

Segal, H. (1978), On symbolism. *Internat. J. Psycho-Anal.*, 59: 325–319.

Shapiro, D. (1965), *Neurotic Styles*. New York: Basic Books.

———. (1981), *Autonomy and Rigid Character*. New York: Basic Books.

———. (1989), *Psychotherapy of Neurotic Character*. New York: Basic Books.

Shapiro, T., Ed. (1988), The concept of structure in psychoanalysis. *J. Amer. Psychoanal. Assn. (Suppl.)*, 36: iii–iv.

Sharif, Z., Gewirtz, G., & Iqbal, N. (1993), Brain imaging in schizophrenia: A review. *Psychiatric Anns.*, 23: 123–134.

Shaywitz, B. A., & Shaywitz, S. E. (1991), Comorbidity: A critical issue in attention deficit disorder. *J. Child Neurol. (Suppl.)*, 6: 13–20.

Silbersweig, D. A., Stern, E., Frith, C., Cahill, C., Holmes, J. A., Grotoonk, S., Seaword, J., McKenzie, P., Chua, S. E., Schnoor, Z., Jones, T., & Frachowlak,

R. S. J. (1995), A functional neuroanatomy of hallucinations in schizophrenia. *Nature*, 378: 176–179.

Sims, A. (1988), *Symptoms in the Mind: An Introduction to Descriptive Psychopathology*. Philadelphia: W. B. Saunders.

Skodol, A. (1989), *Problems in Differential Diagnosis: From DSM-III to DSM-III-R in Clinical Practice*. Washington, DC: American Psychiatric Press.

Slap, J., & Slap-Shelton, S. (1991), *The Schema in Psychoanalysis*. London: Karnac Books.

Sinott, R., Franco, A. L., Schimidt, P., Higushi, C., DeArrugo, G., & Bressain, R.(2016), What do bizarre delusions mean in schizophrenia? *Psychosis.*, 8(3): 270–276.

Spitzer, R., & Williams, J. (1987), *Diagnostic and Statistical Manual III Revised*. Washington, DC: American Psychiatric Association.

Steiner, R. (1989), Projection, identification, projective identification, ed. J. Sandler (Review). *Internat. J. Psycho-Anal.*, 70: 127–208.

Stern, D. (1985), *The Interpersonal World of the Infant*. New York: Basic Books.

Sterba, R. (1934), The fate of the ego in analytic therapy. *Internat. J. Psycho-Anal.*, 15: 117–126.

———. (1953), Clinical and theoretical aspects of character resistance. *Psychoanal. Quart.*, 22: 1–20.

Stone, L. (1954), The widening scope of indications for psychoanalysis. *J. Amer. Psychoanal. Assn.*, 2: 567–594.

———. (1986), Psychoanalytic observations on the pathology of depressive illness: Selected spheres of ambiguity or disagreement. *J. Amer. Psychoanal. Assn.*, 34: 329–362.

Stone, M. (1980), *The Borderline Syndromes*. New York: McGraw-Hill.

———. (1990), *The Fate of Borderline Patients*. New York: Guilford Press.

Stone, M., Albert, H., Forrest, P., & Arieti, S. (1983), *Treating Schizophrenic Patients*. New York: McGraw-Hill.

Strakowski, S. M., DelBello, M. P., Sax, K. W., Zimmerman, M. E., Shear, P., Hawkins, J., & Larson, E. R. (1999), Brain magnetic resonance imaging of structural abnormalities in bipolar disorder. *Arch. Gen. Psychiatry.*, 56: 254–260.

Sullivan, H. S. (1953), *The Interpersonal Theory of Psychiatry*. New York: W. W. Norton.

Symons, N. J. (1925), Note on the formation of symbols. *Internat. J. Psycho-Anal.*, 6: 440–443.

Szalita-Pemow, A. B. (1955), The "intuitive" process and its relation to work with schizophrenics. *J. Amer. Psychoanal. Assn.*, 3: 7–18.

Tamminza, C. A. (1999), *Schizophrenia in a Molecular Age*. Washington, DC: American Psychiatric Press.

Thoma, H., & Kachele, H. (1985), *Psychoanalytic Practice*, Vols. 1–2. New York: Jason Aronson.

Tupper, D., Ed. (1987), *Soft Neurological Signs*. Orlando, FL: Grune & Stratton.

Varese, F., Tai, S. J., Pearson, L., & Mansell, W. (2016), Thematic associations between personal goals and clinical and nonclinical voices (auditory verbal hallucinations). *Psychosis.*, 8(1): 12–22.

Vetter, H., Ed. (1968), *Language Behavior in Schizophrenia*. Springfield, IL: Charles C. Thomas.

Voeller, K. (1991), The social and emotional learning disabilities. *Psychiatr. Ann.*, 21: 735–741.

Volkan, V. (1976), *Primitive Internalized Object Relations: A Clinical Study of Schizophrenic, Borderline, and Narcissistic Patients*. New York: International Universities Press.

Waelder, R. (1924), The psychoses: Their mechanisms and accessibility to treatment. *Internat. J. Psycho-Anal.*, 6: 259–281.

———. (1936), Principle of multiple function. *Psychoanal. Quart.*, 5: 45–62.

Waldheim, R. (1984), *The Thread of Life*. Cambridge, MA: Harvard University Press.

Wallerstein, R. (1986), *Forty-Two Lives in Treatment: A Study of Psychoanalysis and Psychotherapy*. New York: Guilford Press.

Weil, A. P. (1970), The basic core. *Psychoanal. Stud. Chil.*, 25: 442–460. New York: International Universities Press.

———. (1973), Ego strengthening prior to psychoanalysis. *Psychoanal. Stud. Chil.*, 28: 287–301. New Haven, CT: Yale University Press.

———. (1978), Maturational differences and genetic-dynamic issues. *J. Amer. Psychoanal. Assn.*, 26: 461–491.

Weinshel, E. (1990), How wide is the widening scope of psychoanalysis and how solid is its structural model? Some concerns and observations. *J. Amer. Psychoanal. Assn.*, 38: 275–296.

Weissman, M. M., Prusoff, B. A., DiMascio, A., Neu, C., Goklaney, M., & Klerman, G. L. (1979), The efficacy of drugs and psychotherapy in the treatment of acute depressive episodes. *Amer. J. Psychiatry.*, 136: 555–558.

Werner, H., & Kaplan, B. (1963), *Symbol Formation*. New York: John Wiley.

Westlundh, B., & Smith, G. (1983), Perceptogenesis and the psychodynamics of perception. *Psychoanal. & Contemp. Thought*, 6: 597–640.

Weston, D. (1990), Towards a revised theory of borderline object relations: Contributions of empirical research. *Internat. J. Psycho-Anal.*, 71: 662–693.

White, R. (1963), *Ego and Reality*. New York: International Universities Press.

Willick, M. (1983), On the concept of primitive defenses. *J. Amer. Psychoanal. Assn. (Suppl.)*, 31: 175–200.

———. (1991a), The psychoanalytic concepts of the etiology of severe mental illness. *J. Amer. Psychoanal. Assn.*, 38: 1049–1081.

———. (1991b), *From Freud's Schreber to Modern Neurobiology: Evolving Concepts of Schizophrenia*. H. A. Brill Lecture. New York: New York Psychoanalytic Society.

———. (1993), The deficit syndrome in schizophrenia: Psychoanalysis and neuroscience perspectives. *J. Amer. Psychoanal. Assn.*, 41: 1135–1157.

Winnicott, D. W. (1953), Transitional objects and transitional phenomena. *Internat. J. Psycho-Anal.*, 34: 89–97.

———. (1971), *Playing and Reality*. London: Tavistock.

———. (1991), Psychotherapy of character disorders. In: *Handbook of Character Studies*, ed. M. Kets de Vries & S. Perzow. Madison, CT: International Universities Press, pp. 461–476.

Yaholom, I. (1967), Sense, affect and image in development of the symbolic process. *Internat. J. Psycho-Anal.*, 48: 373–383.

Yorke, C., Weissberg, S., & Freeman, T. (1989), *Development and Psychopathology*. New Haven, CT: Yale University Press.

Zatorre, R. J. and Halpern, A. R. (2005), Mental concerts: Musical imagery and auditory cortex. *Neuron*, 47: 9–12.

Zeligs, W. A. (1960), The role of silence in transference, countertransference, and the psychoanalytic process. *Internat. J. Psycho-Anal.*, 41: 407–412.

Name Index

Abend, S. 244
Aboitiz, F. 158, 178n2
Abraham, K. xix, 143
Adler, G. 244, 264, 282
Aerts, J. 21
Aizley, H. G. 107
Akiskal, H. S. 142
Albert, H. 142, 209, 216
Alexander, J. 173
Andreason, N. 136
Appelbaum, A. C. 268
Aragno, A. 36
Arieti, S. xxi, 16, 99, 136, 138, 142, 195, 209, 216
Arlow, J. xviii, 19, 48, 65, 135, 142, 213
Asaad, G. 123
Auchincloss, E.L. xx

Banglow, P. 12
Basch, M. F. 211
Baudry, F. 173
Beitman, B. D. 185, 206
Bellak, L. xx, xxi, 9, 40n2, 83, 86, 110, 135, 159, 240, 243
Benjamin, L. 158, 167, 178n2
Benton, A. L. 161
Beres, D. 12, 35, 135
Bergman, A. xviii
Bernstein, S. B. 240
Bhandary, A. N. 159
Bieber, I. 240
Bion, W. R. 142, 258
Blanck, G. xviii, 1, 40n2, 83, 210
Blanck, R. xviii, 1, 40n2, 83
Bleuler, E. 74, 136, 200
Blum, H. P. 36
Boesky, D. 263
Bohning, D. E. 158
Boyer, L. B. 142, 209, 216

Bradley, S. xi, xx, 172, 177, 185, 206, 276
Brenner, C. xviii, 19, 29, 41n7–8, 42n8, 65, 135, 142, 154, 156, 209
Breuer, J. 18, 73n1, 133
Brockman, R. 21
Brown, A. S. 158
Bucci, W. 36
Busch, F. 175

Cahill, C. 21
Calder, A. J. 20
Calogeras, R. C. 262
Cameron, J. xviii, 136, 209
Campbell, R. 1, 9, 172
Carr, A. C. 268
Cassirer, E. 36
Cecil, A. 136
Chiland, C. 209, 239
Chua, S. E. 21
Cicchetti, P. 20
Coen, S. J. 95, 177, 267
Compton, A. 97, 173
Constantin, C. 136
Crosby, M. 158, 158, 167, 178n2, 210
Cullander, C. H. 268

Damascio, A. R. 109n3
David, A. S. 21
Davis, J. 136
Degueldre, C. 21
DelBello, M. P. 158
Delfione, J. T. 21
Denckla, M. 159
Deutsch, F. 161
Diamond 106
Di-Mascio, A. 204
Dolan, K. J. 20
Duane, D. D. 158, 159

Name Index

Eisenstadt, K. 158, 167, 178n2, 210
Eissler, K. R. 77, 210

Fairbairn, R. 30, 75, 135
Federn, P. 9, 13, 243
Fenichel, O. 172, 175, 268
Ferenczi, S. 36, 43n10
Frith, C. 21
Fisher, C. 11
Fliess, R. 56, 73n1, 107
Forrest, P. 142, 209, 216
Freeman, T. xi, xviii, xx, xxi, 135,
    136, 158, 209, 211
French, J. G. 21
Frenkel-Brunswik, E. 174, 256
Freud, A. xviii, 41n7
Freud, S. xvii, xviii, xix, xxi, 1, 13, 17,
    18, 19, 20, 24, 30, 39n1, 40n4–5,
    41n6, 42n9–10, 47, 48, 49, 50, 51,
    52, 70, 73n1, 77, 81, 98, 99, 105,
    132, 133, 134, 154, 173, 236
Friedman, L. 2
Friedman, S. 11
Frith, C. D. 20
Fromm-Reichman, F. 142, 209, 216
Frosch, J. xvii, xviii, xxi, 40n4, 50,
    65, 70, 75, 80, 107n1, 135, 143,
    211, 244
Fruchowlak, R. S. J. 21

Gabbard, G. 50, 135, 143, 211, 244
Galaburda, A. M. 158, 178n2
Gediman, H. xx, xxi, 9, 40n2, 83, 86,
    110, 135
George, W. S. 158
Geschwind, N. 158, 178n2
Gewirtz, G. 158
Gharmi, S. N. 223
Giovacchini, P. L. 142, 209, 216, 268
Glover, E. 40n2, 135, 172, 252
Goklaney, M. 204
Goldsmith, L. xx
Goodglass, R. 158
Goodwin, F. K. 142
Gray, D. B. 158
Gray, P. 175
Greenacre, P. 143, 209
Greenson, R. 175, 214
Greenspan, S. I. 3, 268
Grolnick, S. 109n4
Grossman, W. 19
Grotoonk, S. 21
Gunderson, J. 75, 244

Hartmann, E. 9
Hartmann, H. i, xix, xx, xxi, 1, 2,
    40n2, 75, 83, 106, 179, 210
Hawkins, J. 158
Heimarck, G. 40n3
Hendrick, I. 172
Hinsie, L. 1, 9
Hoch, S. 240
Hoffman, R. F. xix, 135
Holder, A. 77
Holmes, D. W. 66, 175
Holmes, J. 21, 158
Holt, R. 2
Holtzman, P. 136
Hudson, J. I. 107
Hurt. S. 136
Hurvich, M. xx, 9, 40n4, 83, 86, 110,
    135

Inhelder, B. 5, 36
Inman, Z. 136
Iqbal, N. 136, 158
Isaacs, K. S. 173
Iwata, J. 20
Izard, C. 40n3

Jacobson, E. 30, 55, 65, 75, 106,
    108n2, 110, 135, 143, 146, 148,
    154, 157, 208n1, 209, 227
Jamison, K. R. 142
Jaspers, K. 123
Jones, E. 36, 42n10
Jones, T. 21
Joseph, E. 35

Kachele, H. 40n4
Kafka, E. 136, 142, 167, 172, 210
Kaplan, B. 36
Karasu, T. B. 185, 206
Karush, A. xx, 12
Keck, P. E., Jr. 107
Kellerman, H. 40n3
Kellner, C. 158
Kernberg, O. xi, xviii, 14, 30, 55,
    67, 73n1, 75, 80, 83, 89, 98, 103,
    107n1, 108n1–2, 109n5, 110, 113,
    134n3, 135, 142, 156, 172, 175,
    244, 249, 250, 258, 259, 260, 261,
    262, 264, 268, 282, 283
Khan, M. M. R. 240
Klein, M. xviii, 30, 40n3, 42n9, 73n1,
    75, 98, 108n2, 109n5, 142, 143,
    154, 258, 260, 261

304 Name Index

Klerman, G. L. 185, 204, 206
Knight, R. P. 75
Koenigsberg, H. W. 268
Kohut, H. 56, 57, 244
Kraepelin, E. 3
Kris, E. 77
Krystal, H. 128
Kubie, L. S. 39, 70
Kuhns, R. 36, 109n4

Lampl-de Groot, J. 173
Langer, S. 36
Langs, R. 214, 228, 268
Lipinsky, T. 177n1
Laplanche, J. 1, 40n4–5, 41n7
Larson, E. R. 158
Le Doux, J. 20, 109n3
Lewin, B. 143, 154, 156, 209
Liebert, R. 173
Lion, J. 173
Lishman, W. 158
Little, M. 218, 268
Loeb, F. F. 191
Loeb, L. R. 191
Loewald, H. 1, 36, 105
Lomerov, M. 158
Lotterman, A. 142, 209
Lowenstein, P. 210
Luxen, A. 21

MacKinnon, J. R. 110, 173, 175
Mahler, M. xviii, 157
Maquet, P. 21
Marcus, E. R. xx, xxi, 107, 172,
    175, 177, 203, 206, 211, 239,
    260, 276
Marsh, H. 159
Masterson, J. 175, 244, 259, 261
Mateer, C. 19, 109n3
Matte-Bianco, I. 36
McElroy, S. 107
McGhie, A. xviii, 136, 209
McGlashen, T. H. xix, 135
McGlynn, S. M. 223
McKenzie P. 21
McNutt, J. E. 240
Meissner, W. W. 98
Meyers, B. 240, 243
Michels, R. 110, 173, 175
Milrod, D. 154, 209
Modell, A. 30
Morris, J. 20, 21, 240

Nahas, Z. 158
Namnum, A. 240, 243
Nersession, E. 42n8
Neu, C. 204
Newcorn, J. H. 159
Nunberg, H. 40n2, 83

Obeyeskere, G. 36
Ogden, T. 98
Ojemann, G. 19, 109n3
Ostow, M. 179, 206, 208n4, 211

Pao, P. N. xviii, 140, 141, 142, 209,
    216
Perrett, D. I. 20
Peters, J. M. 21
Piaget, J. 3, 5, 11, 20, 36
Pine, F. xviii, xxii, 30
Plutchik, R. 40n3
Pontalis, J. 1, 40n4–5, 41n7
pope, H. G., Jr. 107, 177n1
Porder, M. 98, 244
Prusoff, B. A. 204

Racker, H. 249, 262, 282, 285
Rado, S. 154
Rapaport, D. xxi, 2
Rapaport, E. 240
Rapin, I. 162
Redlich, F. 142
Reich, W. 84, 103, 109n5, 134n3,
    141, 172, 221, 224, 338, 345
Reider, N. 213, 219
Reis, D. J. 20
Renick, O. 210
Resnick, T. 162
Rizzuto, A. M. 19
Robbins, M. xxii, 142, 209
Rosen, G. D. 158, 178n2
Rosen, V. 172, 210
Rosenblatt, A. 40n3
Rosenblatt, B. 98
Rosenfeld, H. 73n1, 227
Rothstein, A. 158, 167, 178, 210
Rowland, D. 20
Rudel, R. 158
Rudel-Pandes, J. 158

Sachs, H. 134n2
Sadow, L. 12
Samberg, E. xx
Samberg R. 161, 171

Name Index

Sandler, A.-M. 30
Sandler, J. 30, 77, 98, 104, 115
Sarnoff, C. 36, 70, 228
Sarwer-Foner, G. J. 151, 179, 206, 211
Sax. K. W. 158
Schafer, D. L. 223
Schafer, R. xxi, 1, 2, 16, 30, 42n9, 85, 98, 106, 223, 265
Schnoor, Z. 21
Schur, M. 24
Schwartz, B. J. 136
Scott, W. C. 143
Searles, H. 19, 83, 137, 141, 142, 209, 216, 218, 268
Seaword, J. 21
Sechehaye, M. A. 234
Segal, H. 36
Selzer, M. A. 268
Shapiro, D. 16, 131, 173, 175, 177, 265, 268
Shapiro, T. x, xv
Sharif, Z. 158
Shaywitz, B. A. 158, 162
Shaywitz, S. E. 158, 162
Shear, P. 158
Sherman, G. F. 158, 178n2
Silbersweig, D. A. 21
Sims, A. 123
Skodol, A. 123
Slap, J. xv
Slap-Shelton, S. xv
Smith, G. 11
Spitzer, R. 123
Steiner, R. 98
Sterba, R. 221, 263
Stern, D. xx, 20
Stern, E. 21
Stone, L. 206, 209

Stone, M. 75, 83, 113, 142, 154, 187, 209, 216
Strachey 40n2, 42n10
Strakowski, S. M. 158
Sullivan, H. S. 142, 216
Symons, N. J. 36
Szalita-Pemow, A. B. 209

Tamminza, C. A. 135
Thickstun, J. 40n3
Thoma, H. 40n4
Tupper, D. 158

Vetter, H. 136
Voeller, K. 166, 178n2
Volkan, V. 142

Waelder, R. 42n8, 243
Waldheim, R. 36
Wallerstein, R. xix, 226
Weil, A. P. 3, 27, 240
Weinshel, E. 135
Weissberg, S. 211
Weissman, M. M. 204
Werner, H. 36
Westlundh, B. 11
White, R. 3
Williams, J. 123
Willick, M. xix, 67, 96, 142, 158, 244
Wingfield. A. 158
Winnicott, D. W. xxi, 16, 59, 70, 99, 109n4, 195, 265

Yaholom, I. 36
Yorke, C. 211
Young, A. W. 20

Zeligs, W. A. 262
Zimmerman, M. E. 158

Subject Index

abandonment, emotional 102
"absent-minded professor" syndrome 167
abstraction-application discoordinations 57
abstraction capacity: in character disorder 172–173; disruption of 46; in learning disabled 200; observing ego and 148; in translating thing presentation 195; uneven variable levels of 200
acting out 264
acting through 264
action; dynamic 103–105; pathology and 102–103; psychoanalytic theory of 102–103; structural or organizational features of 103; symbolic 104–106
active questioning: about day residue reality experience 117; in mental status examination 144–145, 153; of modulating capacity 166; of observing ego function 162; of reality testing function 155
actual object 42n9, 104, 108n2
acute illness 111
adult attention deficit disorder 135, 267
affect 5; ability to modulate 146–147; all-encompassing 43n10; blending, complexity and layering of 197; blurring of in transference and countertransference reactions 280; complexity of with neuroleptic therapy 185–186; condensations of 133; control of intensity, generalization, and spread of 12; encoding of 19; environmental evokers of 194; free-floating 43n10,

146, 153; fusion and 13–14, 165, 169; layering of contents of 186–187; modulation of 85, 127, 165, 171, 174, 184, 186; in organic brain syndromes 172; progressive decondensation of into emotional experience 229–230; replacement of 120; rigidly frozen 224–225; splitting of 57, 62, 108n2, 109n5, 149, 258–260; in thing presentation experience 57–58
affect-affect boundaries 45, 46–47; disruption of 47; in mental status examination 119–120; neuroleptic effects on 184
affect-behavior boundary: in character disorder 172–173; in near psychosis 75, 96–97
affect boundaries 12–13; in character disorder 173–174; functions of 78–9; in near psychosis 78–107; in organic brain syndromes 146–147; in schizophrenia 78, 138–139; treatment of 250
affect-concept boundaries: condensations of 173–174; in organic brain syndromes 161–163; perceptual symbolic representation of 23
affect experience: complexity of 105; organization and stability of 78–79
affect intensity 13, 58, 77, 78, 85, 116, 272; barrier of 194; in manic-depressive illness 74, 78, 95, 135, 142–143, 146, 149, 169; neuroleptic effects on 181; quality and 6; reduced 204; uncontrolled 13

Subject Index

affect lability: of frontal lobe syndrome 165; in manic-depressive illness 157

affect leaks 144, 149; thymoleptics and 197, 199

affect-modulating capacity 79; in character disorder 184; observing ego 148; in organic brain syndromes 146–147

affect-percept boundaries 193; condensations in 173–174; intensity of transmodal processing of 153; in mental status examination 119–120; neuroleptics and 180–181; thymoleptic effects on 193–194

affect-reality fusion 79

affect storm 248; day residue of 259

affective illness: comorbid with character disorder 167; comorbid with learning disabilities 162, 166; comorbid with organic brain syndromes 158; precooscious in 77–78; *see also* depression; manic-depressive illness; mood disorders

agencies 24; boundaries between 24–25; contents of 24; dynamic conflict of 257

aggression: antidepressant effects on 204; in behavioral borderline near psychosis 250–251; defense against 177; delusional 280–281; thymoleptics and 198–199

alexithymic depression 156

all-encompassing affect 43n10

amygdala fear circuit 20–21

amygdala-hippocampal affect encoding areas 20

analog intensity 140

antidepressants xix, 148, 191, 204, 205, 233, 242; effects of 245–246; in mood stabilization 262; in pseudodelusional near psychosis 263–264

antipsychotic drugs *see* neuroleptics; thymoleptics

anxiety tolerance 127

apathetic depressions 156

aphasia 19

application: disruption of 55; in translating thing presentation 250–251

associational material, open-ended questions about 254

associations 41n8; loosening of 188, 209; observations of 324; *see also* free associations; loose associations to delusional material 75–76

attachment ambivalences 252

attention deficit disorder (add) 158; stimulus barrier in 159–160

attention deficit hyperactivity disorder (adhd) 159

attitude neurosis 97

auditory hallucinosis 183

autonomous cycling 150

autonomous ego: characteristics of with learning disabilities 171; defenses and dysfunction of 75; deficits of 28; medication in support of 211; neuroleptics and 185; organization of 111; psychological support of 211; strengths of 240; thymoleptic effects on 192–194; thymoleptics and structures of 174; transformations of in psychosis 72

autonomous ego apparatuses 2, 34, 44, 75–76, 111; in mental status 111; in near psychosis 75; neuroleptic effects on 185; in object relations condensations 85–86; primary 2, 34; in secondary process thinking 4

autonomous ego boundaries 87, 109n5; defenses erupting through 26–27, 67; in differential object relations experiences 87; disruption of 16–17; neuroleptic effects on 190

autonomous ego functioning 2, 4; affect boundary phenomena of 185; confronting 237; in delusions 65; disturbances in 30; impaired integrating capacity of 83–85; in near psychosis 80, 82–83, 86; reality experience mediated by 4

autonomous secondary process reality 67

awareness levels, boundaries between 117–118

behavior: boundaries of in near psychosis 82–83; dyscontrol of 75; justifying 105–106; in reality 31, 49

behavior neurosis 97

behavioral action 102–104

308 Subject Index

behavioral borderline near psychosis 82, 95; action style of 264; affect-percept and affect-concept condensations in 174; analysis of 261–262; handling of 261; in-out boundaries in 247–249; medication effects on 184; treatment of 281–283, 285
bizarre delusions 137
borderline action 104
borderline personality 75, 278; defensive material in 65; delusional material in 62; reality testing in 79–80; rigidity in 66
borderline states: behavior boundaries in 82–83; definition of 74–75; ego criteria for 75; primary process functioning shifts in 146; types of 75
The Borderline Syndromes (Stone) 75
boundaries 12–17, 54–56, 146; conscious-preconscious-unconscious 13–14; between levels of awareness 117–118; mental 9–10; primary process-secondary process 45; between psychic agencies 24–25; psychotic alterations in 56; *see also specific boundaries*
boundary problems: in character disorder 173–174; in learning disabilities 170; in manic-depressive illness 143–147; medication effects on in near psychosis 199–201; in mental status examination 114; in near psychosis 76–77; neuroleptic effects on 179–180; in object relations experiences 32–34, 155; observing ego and 127; in organic mental syndromes 159–165; in projective identification 258, 260; psychoanalysis for 216–218; in schizophrenia 137–139; transference and countertransference issues of 280–281
brain: in affect encoding 20; in dreaming 21; impaired recognition and storage functions of 166–167; pathology of xviii

categories 5–6; medication and fusion of 200; reversal of 200; synthesizing of 29

cause-effect relationships 7
character: near psychosis and 265–268; psychosis and 265–268; severe pathology of 267; structure of 172
character attitudes 173
character defenses: analysis of in near psychosis 266–267; analysis of in psychosis 242; in borderline behavior 263; in character disorder 175–176; interpretation of 54; nonpsychotic 54; observing ego and 175; plastic 265; primitive 245; in psychosis 54, 66; reinterpreting 224; rigid 225, 231, 267; rigidity and intensity of 267; treatment technique for 276; in vertical dissociations 254
character disorder: boundary problems in 173–174; day residues in 175–176; defenses in 177; integrating capacity in 175; levels of severity of 172–173; object relations in 177; observing ego in 175; reality testing in 174; symbols and symbolic alterations of reality in 176; themes of 97; thing presentations and qualities in 176
character symbols 176
character symptoms 57
chronic illness 111
clarification 237, 245
cognitive deficits: in organic brain syndromes 171, 216; in vertical dissociations 254
competitive loss, reaction formations against 68–69
compromise formation 20, 24; in character disorder 175, 176
compulsion: examination for 124–125; hierarchy of phenomena of 125
concept: affect and 86; condensations of in dyslexia 162; flexibility of 174; fragmentation of in schizophrenia 145; fusion of 162; reversal of 162–163, 166
concept-affect experience 104
concept boundaries 12
concept-percept experience: in mental status examination 119; neuroleptics and 180; thymoleptic effects on 194

Subject Index

conceptualization 12; disruption of 46; in secondary process integration 16
concrete near reality 100
condensation 7–8, 10, 11–13; affect 81; in affect-percept and affect-concept boundaries 174; within and between agencies 24; altered reality in 70; in character defenses 68; of concepts 162; of conflict 20; conscious 250; content of 80; in day residues 17–18, 53, 69, 150, 177, 255; between day residues and emotional experience 91; detection of 139; fusion of 144; of in-out boundaries 272–273; medication effects on 179–181; merger of 33; merger points in 11; near psychotic 75–76, 90–91; neuroleptic effects on 179–180; of object relations 155; of object relations in manic-depression 143–144; in organic brain syndromes 162; percept-concept-affect 47; of percepts, affects, and concepts 37; preconscious 85–90, 100; of primary and secondary processes 162; primary process 22–23, 116; psychotic 46–47, 75–76; of real object 54; real object-object representation 55, 116; real self-self representation 190; of reality and fantasy 18, 25, 38, 81; of reality experience, emotional experience, and reality testing 81–82; reality experience defenses and 185; reality experience-emotional experience 93; of reality testing content 95–96, 201; of self and object representations 46; symbol 103; symbolic alteration of reality and 182; symbolic mileus of 8; symbolic representations in 18; of unconscious, preconscious, and conscious experience 138; of unconscious conflict 23; unconscious in neurosis 266; vertical dissociations around 188; *see also* psychotic condensations
conflict formation 25
conflicts; defenses against 25; in dreams, delusions and hallucinations 50; primary process and 25–26; triggering psychotic symptoms 68

confrontation: of pathology 112; of reality testing problems 250
confusion: in countertransference reaction 280; with organic mental syndromes 161
conscious condensation 38
conscious material 61, 67, 111, 117
conscious objects 30
conscious-preconscious-unconscious boundaries 13–14, 138, 145, 163; in organic brain syndromes 163; in schizophrenia 138
conscious psychotic experiences xvi
conscious thinking 13–14
conscious-unconscious boundaries, disruption of 45
consciousness, levels of 6, 36; boundaries between 77, 131; dissociation across 56–57
consciousness, screening impressions and emotional reactions from 13
content, recruitment of 12
continuous emotional reactions, screening of 13
continuous sensory impressions, screening of 13
cortex, in affect encoding 20
couch, use of 240–243; in near psychosis 268–269
countertransference: alertness to 268; awareness level boundaries in 117; confusion in 218; definition of 279–280; effective use of 281–282; ego function organization in 273; in psychosis 268–269; self analysis of 270; structural issues of 272; treatment of 279–281
countertransference aggression 281
countertransference avoidances, recognizing 124
countertransference dreams, intense 280–281
countertransference fantasies 280, 282
countertransference hypotheses 262
creativity: intermediate zone of experience in 109n4; medication effects on thing presentation quality and 203; in organic brain syndromes 167; in schizophrenia 138, 140; symbolic alteration of reality in 70; thing presentation in 59
cyclothymic mood swings 205

310   Subject Index

data categories: boundary damage in 159; in condensations 7

day residue 17–18, 48, 52–53; active questioning about 113; of affect storm 259; in analysis of behavioral borderline near psychosis 258; analysis of in near psychosis 255; analysis of in psychosis 234–237; in character disorder 175–176; condensed 220; defenses in with neuroleptic therapy 180, 182; disrupted sequencing in 190; in dream structure 52; location of 91; in manic-depressive illness 150–152; medication effects on 195; in mental status examination 150–152; in near psychosis 90–92, 128; neuroleptics and boundaries of 182; in organic mental syndromes 167–169; past evokers of 260; in pathological structures 53; precipitating event of 48–49; present reality 91; in psychotic structure 52–53; in schizophrenia 140; sequence and context of 190–191, 195, 245; symbolic, emotional, and fantasy significance of 104; symbolic alteration in 17, 19; triggering psychotic transference 282

day residue object 48, 53, 90–91, 156

defense mechanisms, preconscious 84–85

defense resistance: transference 102; treatment of 276

defenses: analysis of 249; character 54, 68–69; in character disorder 177; content of 96, 157, 197–198; in day residue 113; against day residue experience 128; definition of 25–26; in ego functioning 61; interfering with integrative process 249; layered experiences of 185–188; in learning disabilities 158; in manic-depressive illness 157–158; mediating 65–66; medication effects on in near psychosis 202–203; in mental status examination 130–133; near psychotic 75, 95–97, 248–250; neuroleptic effects on 185–191; object relations and 189–190; observing ego and 189; in organic mental syndromes 170–172;

preconscious, primitive 249; primitive 75; psychoanalytic concept of 63; in psychosis 25–29, 207; purposes of 28; against reality experience 25–27; reality testing and 188–189; repetitive 130; rigid 130–131, 157, 171, 246, 267; in schizophrenia 141–142; splitting 244, 258; surrounding psychotic phenomena 66; thymoleptic effects on 192, 195–199, 202–203; thymoleptic effects on rigidity of 203; vertical 157, 188; vertical dissociations and 197

defensive derivative 105

defensive ego 24

defensive functioning 86

defensive motive 104–105

defensive object relations 86

defensive structures 63–65

déjà vu experience 81

delusion 14; analysis of content of 262–264; character defenses in 54; characteristics of 124; classification of psychotic structure of 59–63; as condensation of conflict 26; content of 231; in day residues 17; defenses against reality and 65; defenses around 65–66; definition of 122–123; ego and 135; emotions in 26; latent content of 60; in learning disabled 162; manic 162; manifest content of 67; neuroleptic effects on 179, 183; observing ego in 53–54; perceptual reality experience in 22; protecting from reality engagement 266; reality-fantasy condensation in 48–50; reality testing with 245; schizophrenic 136–137; stereotyped, repetitive behavioral 125–126; structure of 48–49, 60; thing presentation and structure of 57–59; wishes and conflicts in 50

delusional symbolic transformation 234

delusional systems: conscious and unconscious layers of 235; day residues in 234–237; evolution of 121; examination of 123; in organic brain syndromes 225; real experience in 236; stable, chronic, organized 240; thing presentation quality in 236

Subject Index 311

delusional transference 245, 280–281
delusionosis 183
denial 87, 96, 99, 189, 196, 202;
    engagement of 261–262; in near
    psychosis 99, 261; primitive 62, 132;
    reality experience and 196; in refusal
    to take medication 189; simple 152,
    222; treatment of 278, 281
depression: atypical 74; contentless
    156; day residues in 150–151;
    delusional 60–61, 88; in-out
    boundary disturbances in 144–145;
    integrative capacity in 149; object
    relations experience in 154–156;
    observing ego in 148; preconscious-
    conscious-unconscious boundary
    in 145; primary-secondary-tertiary
    processes in 146; reality testing in
    148; treatment of 275–276
depressive hallucinations 137, 144–145
descriptive analysis: of modulating
    capacity 128–129; in near psychosis
    248; of observing ego function 126
descriptive clinical theory xvii
descriptive theory xix–xx
diffuse brain disease 163
discoordinations 57
discrimination function 40n4
disintegration, schizophrenic 136–137
displacement 7; in day residues
    17–18; in thing presentation 22
dissociated preconscious condensation
    experience 84
dissociation: of affect 196;
    analysis of 210–211; analysis
    of in near psychosis 254–255;
    countertransference and 280; of
    day residues 91; definition of 56;
    of delusional content 60; versus
    disintegration 136–137; horizontal
    56–57, 84; integration of 210;
    medication effects on 204; in near
    psychosis 250; of preconscious
    experience 84; reality experience
    and 184; of reality testing processes
    80; vertical 56–57, 65–66, 95–96,
    106–107, 130–131, 157, 188–189,
    197, 212–213, 223, 254–255, 258
distortions, descriptive interpretation
    of 115–116
dopaminergic blockade 179
dreams: ambiguity in 134n2; brain
    circuitry in 21; day residue

in 17–18, 52–53; intense
    countertransference 280; location
    of day residue in 91; reality-fantasy
    condensation in 48–50; structure of
    49; wishes and conflicts in 50
DSM-II criteria xx
DSM-II-R criteria xx
DSM-III-R borderline criteria xx, 75
DSM-IV criteria 75; borderline 75;
    reality testing loss categories of
    134n1
DSM-V criteria xx
dynamic action 103–104
dyslexia: boundary problems in
    200–201; conceptual blurring in
    161–162; reality testing in 165

ego 24; affect modulating capacity
    of 184–185; in compromise
    formation 42n8; definition of 1,
    8; description of dysfunction of
    210; dynamic conflict of 257;
    fragmentation of 140; integrating
    capacity of 129–130, 184; levels
    of organization of in psychosis 61;
    modulating capacity of 128–129,
    224–225; near psychotic structure
    of 257; in object relations 30;
    organization and stability of 79;
    organization of 54; reality and 2,
    4–7; splitting of 73n1; symbolic
    forms in 37; thymoleptic effects on
    191–194; *see also* observing ego
ego apparatuses 1–2
ego boundary functions 10–14;
    disrupted 13, 37–39; modulating
    and screening functions of 13;
    object relations and 87–90
ego deficit 249
ego dysfunction 27; diagnosis
    of 240; transference and
    countertransference reactions to
    282, 285
ego dystonic dissociations 57
ego function 1–2, 1–43; affected by
    affect-affect boundary disruptions
    46–47; affected by psychosis 47;
    aspects of 75; autonomous 2–3;
    in borderline illness 75; changes
    in, xvi; in countertransference
    279; damage to 3; defensive 3,
    65; examination of 114–134;
    integrative-regulation 102;

312 Subject Index

medications and 174; neuroleptic effects on 185; in observing ego 126; preservation of 46; primary and secondary 2–3; psychiatric illness effects in 135–178; in reality experience 5; reality quality and 22; superordinate 4; thymoleptic effects on 192–194; in use of symbols 37; variable levels of 61
ego psychologists 86
ego psychology 2–3; tripartite divisions of 60
ego structures; defining psychosis and near psychosis 111; medication effects on in near psychosis 199–208
ego synthesis 226
eidetic experience 59, 94
eidetic fantasy 40n4
emotional attitudes 172
emotional causality 133
emotional conflict xvii, xviii, 1, 3, 5
emotional displacement 41n6
emotional experience xvi, 50; affect decondensation into 252; condensed with reality experience and reality testing 68; day residues and 91; defenses against 24; defensive functioning in 86; inability to integrate 83, 149; neuroleptics and 180–181; primary process and 5–6; reality experience and 10–11, 85–86; reality experience and in psychotic structure 47–59; regulation of relationship to reality experience 16–25; in thing presentations 18–19, 38–39
emotional information 110, 113
emotional metaphor 100
emotional process thinking 13
emotional representations 28, 36, 42n9; symbolic 30, 34
emotional revelation 29
emotionally contaminated percept experience 227
emotions; conflicted 13; experience of 5–8
empathy: in analysis of thing presentations 256–257; in psychoanalysis of near psychosis 254; as self-esteem supporter 238
enabling defenses 66, 96
enactment:in borderline behavior 250; in character disorder 176; cycles of

282–283; definition of 102; genetic origin of 106–107; psychoanalytic theory of 102–107
endocrine abnormalities xix
erotic affect condensation 227
erotic transference 106
etiology xvii–xviii; biological-neuromental, xviii; emotional, xviii
experiential motive 104
external stimuli 3

fantasy: condensation of with reality 48–50; discharge of 105; neuroleptics and containment of 200; versus reality objects 30; validation of 106
flashbacks 94
flooding 13–14; defenses against 25; of external stimuli in organic brain syndromes 159–160
foreboding, delusional 60
fragmentation 57, 162–163; in awareness levels boundaries 163; of concept 162; as defense 142; of in-out boundary fusion 170; neuroleptic effects on 200; of object relations 136; schizophrenic 136; of thing presentations 140
free associations 117–118; in analysis of behavioral borderline near psychosis 205; in analysis of delusional content 231; in analysis of vertical dissociations 255
free-floating affect 6, 43n10
frontal lobe syndrome 165
fusion 10–11; of affect 141, 144; of affects 45; of concepts 162–163; in depressive hallucinations 144; neuroleptic effects on 179–180; of object and self experience 54–55; of object relations 141; of outer and inner experiences 45; schizophrenic 163; self and object 33; structure of 10

generalization: disruption of 47; in observing ego 148; in translating thing presentation 169
grandeur, delusions of 60
grandiose fantasies 198
grandiosity: delusional 106; in mania 156
guilt, delusional 60–61

Subject Index   313

hallucinations 14; auditory 14, 21, 144, 183; characteristics of 123; classification of psychotic structure of 59–63; defense against emotional experience in 26; definition of 123–124; depressive 144–145; ego and 144; emotions in 41nn5–6; in learning disabled 166; manic 137, 144; neuroleptic effects on 181; reality-fantasy condensation in 48–50; somatic 144–145, 157; visual 183; wishes and conflicts in 50

hallucinatory structure 72

hallucinatory transference 281

hallucinosis 14, 40n4, 123, 160; characteristics of 123; neuroleptic effects on 183; in organic brain syndromes 166

Haloperidol 220

historical anamnesis 117

horizontal defenses 95

hospitalization: for borderline patients 261–265; repeated 238, 266

hysterical characters, rigid 174

id 24; dynamic conflict of 257

ideal self, condensation of with self representation 156

ideas: fragmentation of 142; as perception 208; separation of from affect 205

ideational content, eliciting 258–259

illness, defining levels of 66–67

illusion 123, 137; characteristics of 123; visual 137

imagination 94

impulse control 127

impulsive behavior 146, 260

in-out boundary 45; in character disorder 173; in depression 170–171; disruption of 25; fusion of 160; loss of in schizophrenia 137; in mania 143–144; in manic-depressive illness 172; in near psychosis 87–88, 98, 137, 247–248; neuroleptic effects on 180–181, 190; in organic brain syndromes 159–160; psychotherapy for loss of 247; thymoleptic effects on 192–193; transference and countertransference issues of 280

inheritance patterns xix

instincts, taming of 147

integrated secondary process problems 159

integration processes 23

integrative capacity 15–16; of affects 129–130; analysis of problems of 253; autonomous ego in 252–253; in character disorder 175; defenses against 252–253; failure of in near psychosis 83; lack of 261; in manic-depressive illness 149; medication effects on 184; in mental status examination 129–130; in near psychosis 83–85; neuroleptic effects on 184; in organic mental syndromes 149; psychotherapy for 252–253; in schizophrenia 139; versus sealing over 238

integrative ego function, lack of 57

integrative-regulation ego function 102

intermediate zone experience 109n4

internal fusion 10

interpretation: in mood disorders 278; with negative transference 264; timing and sequencing of 237–238

interpretive descriptions 113–114

interpretive technique 212, 223

introjections; *see also* projective introjection; real object 87, 88–90, 98–99; real self 88–89

junction point 127

language function 107

learning disabilities 158–159, 165; abstraction problems in 163–164; autonomous ego characteristics in 171; awareness level boundaries in 183; damaged word centers in 228; defenses in 170–172; linear memory deficits in 166; personality development and functioning in 170–172; primary process intrusion in 163–165; primary-secondary process mergers in 155; reality testing in 165–166; thing presentation in 169; translating emotionally contaminated percept experience in 227–228

libido, stickiness of 105, 107, 147

limit setting: in analysis of behavioral borderline near psychosis 259; for borderline behavior 261

314 Subject Index

linear concept integration 166
linear sequencing problems 166
listening, active 119
lithium: in cyclothymic mood swings 205; effects of 191–192; in-out boundary effects of 193; in mood stabilization 204
logical information 118–119
logical thinking 184
loose associations 118; in analysis of behavioral borderline near psychosis 259; in analysis of delusional content 231; in manic-depressive illness 146; in organic brain syndromes 146

malevolent introjects 156
mania 146–147
manic-depressive illness 74, 142, 246; affective triggers in 246; boundary problems in 143–147; day residue in 150–152; defenses in 157–158; ego function in 147; integrative capacity in 149; mental structure and 135; object relations in 154–157; observing ego in 148; reality-emotional experience relationship in 149–150; reality testing in 148; symbols in 154; thing presentations and qualities in 152–154
manic-depressive transference 279
manic hallucinations 137, 144
mastery motives 106
mediating defenses 95; interpreting 238; resistances in 248
medication: mental structure and 179–208; for near psychosis 266–267; for near psychotic defenses 250; in psychotherapy 211; for rigid defenses 246; in support of autonomous ego 211
memory defect: linear 164; in organic brain syndromes 163–164
memory recruitment 193, 198
mental categories 111, 136
mental conflict, screening of 25
mental experience xv–xvii; behavior and 82–83; integration of 210; stable structures of xv–xvi
mental functioning: aspects of 1; organization of 111–112
mental life, integrative and compartmentalized 2

mental processes: primitive 67; reality-mediating 3
mental representation: encoding of 18–19; versus perception 40n4
mental status examination: ego function in 114–134; evolving hypotheses in 110; general principles of 110–112; interview in 110–111; technique of 112–114
mental structure xv, xvii; changes in with acute and chronic illness 111; development of xvi; medications and 179–208; psychiatric illnesses and 135–178
merger 33, 34; defense against 142; of inside-outside boundary 137, 248; in loss of reality testing 51; of object and self experience 54; of object relations in manic-depression 155; in organic brain syndromes 167; in psychotic condensations 77
metaphor 100
minimal brain dysfunction 200, 203
minipsychotic episodes 108n1
modulating capacity 79; in manic-depressive illness 147, 150; medication effects on 204; in mental status examination 128–129; neuroleptic effects on 184–185; psychotherapy for 224–225; treatment of problems in 277
mood boundaries 165
mood disorders: affective triggers in 277; comorbid with character disorder. 176; cycling of 198; drugs for 191–192
mood intensification 147
mood stabilization 204
mood stabilizers 192, 203–205, 246; in cyclothymic mood swings 205; day residue-symbolic alterations of reality and 195; defenses and 245–246; ego functions and 191–192; in modulating capacity 204; object relations and 205; thing presentation and 203
motivation, symbolic action 104–106
multi-infarct dementia 168
multiple function principle 42n8

narcissism: affect boundaries and modulation in 174; reality confrontation and 198

Subject Index   315

near psychosis 17–18; affect boundaries in 78–93, 250; agencies in 257; day residues in 52–53, 99–104, 263; defenses in 95–99, 211–213, 222–227; definition of 86, 209; dissociations in 254–255; etiology of 108n2; hierarchy of real object organization in 32–33; in-out boundary problems in 247–248; integrative capacity in 252–253; level of pathology of 247; medication effects on ego structures of 192–194; modulation in 250; observing ego in 252; preconscious and 81–82; preconscious-conscious primary process-secondary process boundaries in 250; psychoanalysis of 244–269; psychoanalytic psychotherapy of 258–265; psychoanalytic techniques for 211–214; psychological structure of 81; reality experience-emotional experience relationship in 82–83; reality testing in 250–252; rigid character neurosis with 265–268; structures of 249; symbolic alterations of 99–102; thing presentation in 92–93, 256–257; thing presentation quality in 93–94, 256–257; types of 75; use of couch in 240–243; without near psychotic structure 94; *see also* borderline personality; borderline states

near psychotic structure 74–109

neuroimaging technology 20–21

neuroleptics xix; in autonomous ego functions in near psychosis 207; in autonomous ego functions in psychosis 206; boundary effects of 179–181; day residue-symbolic alterations of reality and 182; defenses and 187–191; effects of on near psychotic ego structures 199–208; effects of on psychosis 179–185, 191–194; effects on defenses in near psychosis 185; ego and in psychosis 191–194; in psychoanalysis 205; thing presentation and 195; thing presentation quality and 203

neurological dysfunctioning 200

neuromental functioning xix

neuropsychology xix

neurosis xvi; analysis of symbolic transformations in 234; attitude 97; behavior 97; behavior action in 102; day residue in 53; defense against reality experience in 65; defenses in 24; defensive structures in 64; delusional material in 62; ego organization in 62; hierarchy of real object organization in 32–34; integrating capacity in 16; integration and disguise in 67; loss of reality testing in 174; observing ego capacity in 175; reality-fantasy condensation in 50; rigid, with near psychotic states 265–268; rigidity in 58; symbolic alterations of 101; symbols in 43n10; symptom 173

neurotic locks 264

neurotic projection 87

neurotic symptoms 24, 26, 28

neutrality, technical 211; advantage of 219–221; in analysis of delusional content 230; disordered behavior and 259, 262; with splitting mechanisms 260–262

nodal point 127–128

"not-me" experience 57

object 30; presentation of 18, 30; in reality 30, 31

object experience-self experience fusion 54

object relations 30–39; boundaries in 32–34; in character disorder 172–174; concrete thing presentation form of 93; definitions in 39; distortions of 32; ego boundary functions and 83, 85–87; emotional experience of 274; hierarchy of organization in 34–35; intensity of in near psychosis 257–258; in manic-depressive illness 142, 144–145, 147; medication effects on in near psychosis 204–205; in mental status examination 115–116; in near psychosis 85–90; neuroleptics and 204–205; in organic mental syndromes 172; psychotherapy for 225–227; psychotic 54–56; reality versus fantasies of 104; in schizophrenia 136; in severe

316 Subject Index

mental illnesses 55; theory of 30, 104

object relations boundary: neuroleptics and 181–182; transference and countertransference issues of 279

object relations experience: boundaries in 116–117; inability to integrate 83–85

object representation 30, 31–34, 42n9; condensation of with real object 54; definition of 30; in near psychosis 116–117; real object introjections from 89–90; real object projected to 89; real self introjections from 88; real self projected to 88; symbolic 36

object representation-self representation merger 54–55

object world 42n9

observation: in analysis of behavioral borderline near psychosis 259; in analysis of vertical dissociations 254; in mental status examination 112; of modulating capacity 129; of observing ego function 126

observational hypotheses xvii

observing ego 15–16, 53–54, 80–81, 148; analysis of problems of 253; blocking of 189; in character disorder 239; defenses and 197; in delusions 53–54; in depressive patient 252; differential diagnosis of absence of 222; dynamic resistances to 126; level of illness and 66; liberation of 201–202; in manic-depressive illness 148; medication effects on 201–202; in mental status examination 126–127; in near psychosis 80–81, 94; neuroleptics and 189; in organic mental syndromes 271; psychotherapy for 221–223; in schizophrenia 139; separated from reality testing 230, 235

obsession, hierarchy of phenomena of 125–126

organic brain syndromes 74, 271–274; ego function in 142; preconscious in 78; primary process shifts in 146; psychotherapy for 244, 247; see also organic mental syndromes

organic mental syndromes 158–159; boundary problems in 159–165; day residue in 167–169; defenses in 170–172; integrative capacity in 166–167; mental structure and 158; object relations in 170; observing ego in 166; reality experience/emotional experience in 167; reality testing in 165; symbols and symbolic alterations of reality in 170; thing presentation in 169

overvalued ideas 123; characteristics of 123–125

paradoxical density 160

paranoid eruptions 175

paranoid projections 191

pathological enactment 103

pathology: behavioral action and 102–103; confrontation of 112

perceived reality 49

percept-affect-concept boundaries 47; in character disorder 173–174; disruptions of 47; in organic brain syndromes 161–163

percept-affect experience 104

percept boundaries 11–12

percept qualities, condensation of 108–109n3

perceptions: ideas as 208n2; versus mental representation 40n4

percepts: affect and 75; in thing presentation phenomena 92–93

perceptual containment barriers 153

perceptual experience: mental experience and 12; neuroleptics and 180, 188

personality: character and 172; dynamic themes in 68

personality conflicts, triggering psychotic event 65

personality defenses 141–142

personality disorders: borderline 65; ego function in 142

phobic avoidance 68

pictorial symbolic thinking 23

plastic representation 42–43n10

preconscious affect, intense, condensed 82

preconscious condensations 10–11; in near psychosis 81–84

preconscious-conscious boundary 277

preconscious defenses 202

Subject Index   317

preconscious experience: horizontally dissociated 84; near psychosis and 78; symbolic alteration in 99; vertically dissociated 84, 92–93
preconscious thing presentation 93, 108n3
preconscious thinking 13
primary identification 98–99
primary process defenses 185–186
primary process organization: in reality-emotional experience condensation 81–82; in thing presentation phenomena 92–93
primary process-secondary process boundary 13; disruption of 45; in near psychosis 78; thymoleptic effects on 193; treatment of in near psychosis 248
primary process-secondary process-tertiary process boundaries: in organic brain syndromes 163–165; in schizophrenia 138
primary process thinking 118–119
primary processes 6–8, 67; in condensation 12–13; condensed symbolic transformation and 236; conflict and 25–27; day residue captured by 250; in day residues in organic brain syndromes 167–169; definition of 70; in emotional experience 6–8; eruptions of in organic brain syndromes 157; felt reality in 22–23; integration in 16, 21; intense affect with 153–154; interpretive descriptions of 113–114; intrusions of 162–163; in learning disabilities 171; primitive 67; rupture of in character disorders 173; thing presentation experience in 76; thymoleptic effects on 200–201
primitive defenses 81, 86
primitive material, degree of 67, 239
process structure xvi
projection mechanisms 145
projections 196
projective identification 87, 97–99, 117, 131, 202–203; delusional 268; medication effects on in near psychosis 202; in near psychosis 258; with pseudodelusions 268; rapidly shifting 281; in transference 268–269; treatment of 258–259

projective introjection 141
pseudodelusion 14, 122–123; behavior boundaries in 83; characteristics of 123; examination for 123–124; in learning disabled 166; medication effects on 205; protections of from reality engagement 266; reality testing and 79, 230–231; use of couch in treating 268–269
pseudodelusional condensation 75
pseudodelusional near psychosis 75, 79–80, 82–83
pseudodelusional transference 245
pseudohallucination 14; characteristics of 122; examination for 123–124; in learning disabled 166; reality testing in 80; visual 137
psychiatric illnesses: categories of, xv–xvi; mental structure and 135–178
psychic agency boundary 24–25
psychic reality 48
psychoanalysts: defenses in 24; medication with 185; of near psychosis 244–269; of psychosis 209–243; versus psychotherapy 244–269; of psychotic structure 244, 249, 257; regression with 240–241; self-esteem and technique in 238; technique in 175; timing and sequencing of interpretation in 237; treatment theory of in psychosis 177; unmodified neoclassical 156
psychoanalytic illness categories xvi
psychoanalytic psychotherapy: goal of 211; medication in 241; of near psychosis 244–269; of psychosis 209–243; technique in 209; treatment theory of in psychosis 209–216
psychoanalytic symbols, signals to 38
psychodynamics 111
psychogeneticists xix
psychological conflict: in psychosis and near psychosis 26–27; triggering psychotic symptoms 68–69
psychological structure 44, 52
psychological trigger points xix
psychopathology 127; classification of xv–xvi

318 Subject Index

psychosis: analysis of symbolic transformations in 259; biological factors in xix; boundary alterations in 56; character and 68–69; day residue in 17–18, 52–53; defensive layering of 187–188; defensive structures in 63–65; defining levels of 77–78; delusional material in 60–61; ego functions affected by 35–36; etiology of xvii–xviii; experience of 50; hierarchy of real object organization in 33; neuroleptics and 179–185; object relations in 54–56; open inside-outside boundary in 205; psychoanalytic psychotherapy and psychoanalysis of 244–269; reality-fantasy condensation in 48–50; sequence and context of 52–53; stable mental experience structures in xv–xvi; symbolic alterations of 127–128; transference and countertransference reactions in 279–281; treatment theory in 209–216

psychotherapy: medication with 206; versus psychoanalysis 240–243

psychotic condensations: conscious 250; detection of 121; reality experience defenses and 185–186; resolution/dissolution of 188; vertical dissociations around 188

psychotic ego phenomena 63

psychotic experience 71; in reality experience zone 10–11

psychotic merger 33

psychotic processes, mechanisms of 44–45

psychotic structure 44–73; analysis of 244–247; classification of 60–63; day residue in 52–53; elements of 73; relationship of reality and emotional experiences in 44–63; symbolic representation and symbolic alteration in 71

psychotic symbol 72

psychotic transference 268–269; therapeutic reality day residue triggers of 270

psychotropic medication 87

rage: paranoid schizophrenic 138; replacing fear or sadness 120

reaction formation 69

real object 32; condensation of with object representation 71; condensations of 52; definition of 31; hierarchy of organization of 34–35; in near psychosis 106; real self introjections from 89; real self projected to 88; symbolic transformations of 34

real object experience 33; in day residue 52

real object introjections 89–90

real object-object representation boundary 116–117, 183; neuroleptic effects on 181–183

real object-object representation condensations 231

real object projections 89

real self 32; definition of 32–34; introjections of 88–89; in near psychosis 104; projections of 87–88; real object introjections from 90; real object projected to 89

real self-real object confusion 170

real self-self representation boundaries 190; neuroleptic effects on 181, 183

real self-self representation condensations 207

real thing 31

reality: behavior in 92–93; condensation of with fantasy 48–50; defenses against 63–65; definition of 48–49; denial of 152; dramatic alteration of in manic-depression 154; ego and 3–5; perception of versus feelings about 49; symbolic alteration of 35–39, 69–73, 99–102; symbolic representation of 69–73; symbolic transformations of 234

reality day residue 69–70

reality-emotional experience integration 150

reality experience 3–4, 76; alterations of 35–39, 91; defenses against 25–28, 65–66, 202–203; emotional conflict and defenses in 26; emotional experience and 8–9, 81–82; emotional experience and in psychotic structure 47–59; feelings evoked by 49; momentary uncertainty about 81; neuroleptic

Subject Index 319

effects on 179–181; observing ego reinforcing 94; percept boundaries and 12; regulation of relationship to emotional experience 16–29; symbolic alterations of 17; validation of 149–150

reality experience-emotional experience boundary: analysis of in near psychosis 253–254; in manic-depressive illness 149–150; neuroleptic effects on 180; in organic mental syndromes 162; in schizophrenia 140; transference and countertransference issues of 279

reality objects 30; themes of in thing presentation 69

reality quality: from conscious experience 93–94; in thing presentation 22

reality representation, symbolic 36–37

reality revelation 29

reality stimulus barrier, damaged 28

reality testing 14–15, 50; altered 76; blurred 280, 282; categories of loss of 148; in character disorder 174; in compulsion 124–125; content of 102–103, 201; defenses and 75, 80–81; definition of 14, 50; fragile 242; loss of 44, 49, 51, 57, 62, 66, 68, 72, 120–121, 123, 139, 143; in manic-depressive illness 148; medication effects on 201; in mental statue examination 120–126; in near psychosis 79–80, 86; neuroleptic effects on 179, 180, 181, 182–183; in neurosis 44; observing ego separated from 252; in obsession 125; in organic mental syndromes 165; process of 79–80; in pseudodelusion 204; in psychosis 50–51; psychotherapy for 226, 230–231, 235; in schizophrenia 139; separating from observing ego 242; transference and countertransference issues of 280–281; treatment of problems in 280–281

reality testing-reality experience boundary 194

recognition memory 164

refutation 248

regression: to symbiotic or autistic phase 137; with treatment 240–241

relationships, secondary process 5

repetition compulsion 58, 152, 252

representability 40n5

repression 9, 25–26, 45, 57, 95; affect intensity and 199; eruptions of in organic brain syndromes 163; rigidity of 67

repression barrier 157, 163; between unconscious and preconscious-conscious 190

repression boundary 9, 169

resistance: in borderline behavior 263; interpreting 212

rigid character defenses: in delusions 231–234; differential diagnosis of 267; ego problems of 267

rigid character neurosis 265–268

rigid defenses 157; in character disorder 177; thymoleptic effects on 200; in treatment of near psychosis 267

rigid dissociations 248

rigidity 57, 67

schizophrenia 78, 244; boundary problems in 137–139; concept fragmentation in 208; day residue in 140; defenses in 141–142; ego fragmentation in 139–140; ego function in 139; integrating capacity in 149; mental structure and 220; object relations in 136; observing ego in 139; versus organic brain syndromes 158; preconscious in 78–79; reality-emotional experience relationship in 139–140; reality testing in 139; schneiderian first rank criteria of 177n1; symbols in 201; thing presentations and qualities in 200

schizophrenic disintegration phenomenon 136

schizophrenic transference 279

screening function 10, 13

sealing over 187; versus integration 238

secondary process boundaries 193

secondary process hyperlogic 138

secondary process thinking 4, 14

320 Subject Index

secondary processes 4–5; blocking of 231–232; confusion of in learning disabilities 159; of ego 130; integration in 16, 23; interpretive descriptions of 113–114; primary process fusion with 78

self: and object fusion 33; in reality 31, 32–33; versus self representations 33; see also real self; self representation

self-esteem: in learning disabled 166; psychoanalytic technique and 239

self experience object experience fusion 54

self-object merger 54–55

self-object representation condensation 255

self representation 20, 30, 33; definition of 31; in near psychosis 97; projection of unconscious affect from 85; real object introjections from 90; real object projected to 89; real self introjections from 88; real self projected to 87; symbolic 34; see also real self; self

self representation-object representation boundary 116

self representation-object representation merger 54–55

sensory cortex, neuroimaging of 20–21

sensory emotional experience 23

sexual arousal, thing presentation content of 120

sexual fantasy, unconscious 69

sexualization 169

signals 35

social milieu processing 164

social reality, symbolic alteration of 176

sociopathic character 174

splitting 56, 96; affect 57, 108n2, 258, 260; definition of 56; hospitalization for 278; longitudinal and transverse 73n1; in manic-depressive illness 149; mechanisms of in borderline behavior 260; thymoleptics and 197

stereotyped behavioral delusion 125

stereotyped repetition 264

stereotypy 104, 157, 177; in character disorder 177

stimulus augmentation 143

stimulus discrimination 160

stimulus flooding 159–160

stimulus fusion 160

stimulus origin confusion 160

stimulus screening 143

stress 22, 27

stroke, psychotherapy after 214–215

structure xv–xvii, 44–73; definition of 44; near psychotic 74–109; psychotic 72

subcortical limbic-hypothalamic areas 109n3

subcortical percept-sensory event 109n3

sublimation 102

superego 24; condensations of in character disorder 175; delusions of 60; depressive delusions and 61; dynamic conflict of 257; organization and stability of 79; reaction of to psychosis 238

superordinate ego functions 4

superordinate reality experience 70

symbol experience: affect-percept 100; in near psychosis 102; in thing presentations 20

symbolic action, motivation for 104–107

symbolic dramas 176

symbolic merger points 10

symbolic milieus 8

symbolic process 46, 51; definitions of 70

symbolic representation 35–39; in day residues 18; psychotic 72; structure of in psychosis 69–73

symbolic thinking, pictorial 23

symbolic transformations 30, 34, 48; along primary process lines 234; analysis of 221; in character disorder 176; condensation of day residue with 221; of day residue 90–91, 132–133; in dreams or delusions 49; medication effects on 202; near psychotic processing of 250; neuroleptics and 180; in organic mental syndromes 170; in psychiatric illnesses 141; of reality 99–102; in transference 255

symbolism 35–36

Subject Index 321

symbols: in character disorder 176; definition of 42n10, 70; in manic-depressive illness 154; at nodal points 127; in organic mental syndromes 170; primary process 25; psychoanalytic 100; in schizophrenia 141; thing presentation 19–20, 100; transmodal development and 105

symptom neurosis 173

temper tantrums 149

temperament 27

tertiary processes 138; disruption of in manic-depressive illness 146

thalamus, affect-encoding areas of 20

therapeutic alliance, observing ego in 68

thing in reality 31

thing presentation 18–24, 70; analysis of in near psychosis 256–257; changing to word presentations 227–228; in character disorder 176; decreased intensity of 192; definition of 31, 69; emergence of into consciousness 256–257; eruption of into reality experience 58; experience of 57–59; in manic-depressive illness 152–154; medication effects on 202; in mental status examination 133–134; in near psychosis 92–93, 105; neuroanatomy of 21; neuroleptics and 182; in organic mental syndromes 169; psychotherapy for 256–257; psychotic condensations in 38–39; quality of 22–24, 57–59; rigid 152; rigidly resistant 169; in schizophrenia 140–141; sexualized 169

thing presentation quality 140; analysis of in near psychosis 256–257; in character disorder 176; in delusional system 265; in manic-depressive illness 152–154; medication effects on 203; in near psychosis 93–94; psychotherapy for 256–257; in schizophrenia 140–141

thing presentation symbols 38–39; structure of 100

third space functioning 195

thymoleptics: in autonomous ego functions in psychosis 192; in autonomous ego in near psychosis 195; boundary effects of 192–194; effects of on near psychosis 199; in defenses in psychosis 195; effects of on defenses 195–198; effects of on near psychosis 199, 201–203, 205–206; effects of on psychosis 195; ego and in psychosis 192–194

transcategorical crossing 12

transcategorical syntheses 29

transference: awareness level boundaries in 124; definition of 279–281; hallucinatory or delusional 281; lacking engagement and intensity 241; manic-depressive 279; in mental status examination 116–117; near psychotic 241; negative 264; preconscious, primary processed 265; pseudodelusional 245; psychotic 241, 247, 249; resistance to 235; schizophrenic 279; structural issues of 280, 282; symbolic alteration of reality in 255

transference behaviors 102

transference enactment 106

trans modal processing 47

trauma 94; concept of 106; severe 244

traumatic behaviors 106–107

treatment interventions, diagnosis-based 212–213

treatment resistances 266

uncanny experience 58, 81–82, 94, 235; countertransference 280

unconscious: conscious and xv; defenses against 66; dreams or delusions in understanding 49; dynamically 36

unconscious conflict: among psychic agencies 25; description of 210; transmodal condensation of 23

unconscious-conscious boundaries: neuroleptics and 180–181; thymoleptic effects on 194

unconscious fantasy 11

322   Subject Index

unconscious mental experience, dusters of xvi
unconscious object 30
unconscious object representation 97
unconscious-preconscious boundary 138–139
unconscious thinking 13

validity experiences 71; thing presentation experience and 93
veracity experiences 71
verbalizing ability 127
vertical cognitive hierarchies 171
vertical defenses 188
vertical dissociations 56–57, 130; analysis of in near psychosis 254–255; defenses and 197; hospitalization for 258; interpreting 212–213; mediating defenses of 95–96; transference and countertransference reactions to 266
visual hallucinosis 183

wishes, in dreams, delusions and hallucinations 50
word presentation 18; blocking of 214; changing thing presentations to 210; ego functions in 227; linked to thing presentations 46; medication effects on 200; resistant 153; translation of in character disorder 176
word salad 216
working through 211